Praise for
Immeasurable Outcomes: Teaching Shakespeare in the Age of the Algorithm

"Gayle Greene gives her readers a clear picture of what education should be and how it has been distorted by entrepreneurs, grifters, and phonies. What every parent, teacher, and student should focus on is Greene's clear understanding of what real education is. The measures we use are killing it. Dig deep and find the treasure of a great education."
—**Diane Ravitch**, Founder and President of the Network
   for Public Education

"Gayle Greene captures the fun of teaching and learning while offering profound insights into the transformative power of liberal education. In the process, she makes a compelling case for reclaiming colleges and universities as catalysts for human development and society's betterment."
—**Lynn Pasquerella**, President, American Association of Colleges
   and Universities

"Gayle Greene gives her readers a great gift—she invites us into her seminar on Shakespeare. We become one of her lucky students, as we learn how 'to think qualitatively about human need and value.' She shows liberal education in action, a transformative form of learning with immeasurable outcomes."
—**Michael S. Roth**, President, Wesleyan University

"Gayle Greene takes us inside her Shakespeare class to give a remarkably vivid and moving account of the ways in which 'relationship-rich' liberal arts teaching changes students' lives. As her students learn to understand Bottom, Kate and Petruchio, Hamlet, and Lear, they grow to understand themselves and the world they inhabit more profoundly, with a lasting impact on who they become."
—**Carol Christ**, Chancellor, University of California at Berkeley

"Turn away from click-bait headlines crowing about the demise of the academy and death of the humanities and take a seat in the classroom of a world-class liberal arts professor. With passion, erudition, and wit, Gayle Greene champions a human-scale pedagogy that inspires students to discover their own worth and sense of purpose. As Greene makes abundantly clear, the value of an educated citizenry is enduring and profound. If you are considering college, know someone who is, or if you seek to defend higher education against its numerous detractors, this book is required reading."
—**Audrey Bilger**, President, Reed College

"I loved this book. *Immeasurable Outcomes* not only makes the case that a liberal arts education is 'immeasurable' in our era of student learning outcomes but also describes, better than I have ever seen it described, what actually happens in a classroom. This is a knowledgeable account from a master practitioner. The descriptions of teaching moved me to tears. *Immeasurable Outcomes* will provide a powerful how-to guide for teachers whose life mission is to lead humane classes that can help students transform their lives."
—**George Justice**, author of *How to Be a Dean*

"Gayle Greene has the mind of a brilliant scholar and the heart of a superb teacher: both are dramatically on display in this remarkable book."
—**Mark Edmundson**, author of *Why Teach?* and *Why Write?*

"In our age of numeracy, literacy is more important than ever before—not as an ornament or résumé-enhancing credential, but on account of its power to change the way we live and what we value. Gayle Greene takes us inside her classroom and helps us feel the promise of the humanities firsthand. *Immeasurable Outcomes* is a personal and vivid defense of the aims of liberal education."
—**Anthony Kronman**, author of *Education's End: Why Our Colleges and Universities Have Given Up on the Meaning of Life*

"The value of the humanities is difficult to describe; rather, it must be experienced. Gayle Greene takes us inside a classroom and, in allowing us to sit among the students, brings the humanities to life."
—**Brian Rosenberg**, President in Residence, Harvard Graduate School of Education, President Emeritus, Macalester College

"Brushing aside the dry abstractions of academic prose, *Immeasurable Outcomes* is a beautiful, full-throated revelation of what actually happens in liberal arts classrooms and colleges. By turns impassioned, insightful, angry, and delighted, professor and author Gayle Greene is entranced by the actual students she teaches, furious with the destructive stupidity of educational 'reform' (NCLB, Common Core, 'assessment'), and at once despairing but hopeful of what higher education does and might mean for students and teachers alike. She pulls no punches and spares no tears in this wonderful, challenging, and inspiring book."
—**Daniel F. Chambliss**, coauthor of *How College Works*

Immeasurable
Outcomes

Immeasurable Outcomes

Teaching Shakespeare in the
Age of the Algorithm

Gayle Greene

Johns Hopkins University Press

BALTIMORE

© 2023 Gayle Greene
All rights reserved. Published 2023
Printed in the United States of America on acid-free paper
2   4   6   8   9   7   5   3   1

Johns Hopkins University Press
2715 North Charles Street
Baltimore, Maryland 21218-4363
www.press.jhu.edu

Library of Congress Cataloging-in-Publication Data

Names: Greene, Gayle, 1943– author.
Title: Immeasurable outcomes : teaching Shakespeare in the age of the
algorithm / Gayle Greene.
Description: Baltimore : Johns Hopkins University Press, 2022. |
Includes bibliographical references and index.
Identifiers: LCCN 2021056375 | ISBN 9781421444604 (hardcover ; acid-free
paper) | ISBN 9781421444611 (ebook)
Subjects: LCSH: Education, Humanistic—United States—History—
21st century. | Education, Higher—United States—History—21st century. |
Humanities—Study and teaching (Higher)—United States. | Shakespeare,
William, 1564–1616—Study and teaching (Higher)—United States. |
Greene, Gayle, 1943– | Literature teachers—United States—Biography.
Classification: LCC LC1023 .G738 2022 | DDC 370.11/20973—dc23/eng/20220622
LC record available at https://lccn.loc.gov/2021056375

A catalog record for this book is available from the British Library.

*Special discounts are available for bulk purchases of this book. For more information,
please contact Special Sales at specialsales@jh.edu.*

To the teachers and students who've endured so much,
in hopes of reclaiming education from educrats and ideologues

We . . . need to hear the voices of those whose lives are touched by these humanities majors after college. . . . It's by listening, as humanists do best, to stories, and seeing what the narratives can teach us. Open your ears and . . . you'll hear stories that don't resemble what you read in the media.

Counting won't get us where we have to go. We need to talk, and even more, we need to listen.

—ANTHONY GRAFTON AND JAMES GROSSMAN, "The Humanities in Dubious Battle: What a New Harvard Report Doesn't Tell Us"

The human sciences must explain in better ways what human development is, why it must be available to everyone. . . . They will need to explain again the power of the imagination. . . . The humanities have a long history of revolts on behalf of human development. These fields are particularly close to the ancient forms of human creativity . . . to the unquantifiable forces that comprise experience and history.

—CHRISTOPHER NEWFIELD, *Unmaking the Public University: The Forty-Year Assault on the Middle Class*

CONTENTS

Immeasurable Outcomes

Introduction

I'm not sure public schools understand that we're their customer—that we, the business community, are your customer. . . . What they don't understand is they are producing a product. . . . Now is that product in a form that we, the customer, can *use it*? Or is it defective, and we're not interested?
—REX TILLERSON, former ExxonMobil CEO and US secretary of state

Could it be that there is a form of education that increases a student's chances of being an excellent human being?
—ANTHONY KRONMAN, *The Assault on American Excellence*

The impetus for this book was anger, but that turned to something sadder as I saw how much ground the liberal arts have lost, what a beating we've taken. When I first heard the term "war on education,"[1] I thought it was hyperbole, but when I read more, I realized *war* is exactly the word. But why would anybody want to destroy the educational system that's served us so well? Higher education in the United States has been unique in requiring general education courses based in the liberal arts, insisting that those who study science and engineering be exposed to a wide range of courses aimed at human development. It's been this cultivation of the individual, idiosyncratic, nonstandardized that's fed the stream of originality and creativity that's generated more scientific breakthroughs, technological and industrial innovation, than any other country's.[2]

Why are we killing the goose that laid the golden egg?

So I set forth to find out what hit us, and, in the process, do some soul-searching—what has it been worth, my teaching at a small liberal arts college, these many decades? What is the *value* of the liberal arts, when my sense of value and the world's seem to have drifted far apart? What do we *produce*—to use a word wrongly foisted on education—what do we try to impart to the young to help them grow up human and equip them for rough seas ahead?

"We do believe that there are certain intellectual luxuries that perhaps we could do without," announced Governor Ronald Reagan in 1967, as he cut state support and called for tuition at the University of California: taxpayers should not be "subsidizing intellectual curiosity."[3] Thus was fired the opening shot of the war the right wing has been waging ever since, steadily and stealthily undermining public funding and confidence in education, not only postsecondary but K–12, where curricula have been stripped of the arts and humanities to make room for testing. Our poor beleaguered subjects—literature, history, philosophy, languages, the arts—where students learn that others have walked this way before, learn about the past and creations of our kind, about their culture and themselves, are "curiosities" we can do without. Higher education needs *transformation*, say the "disrupters," says Bill Gates, who is, of all the billionaires remaking education, the most interventionist.[4] A "technocrat," he sees education as a "a technocratic issue" (his words), as a system to be standardized and scaled to produce a workforce that will give US corporations dominance throughout the world.[5]

One of the shocking things I discovered, writing this book, is how much of what we read and hear about education is simply not true.

Mainstream media turn to business leaders, politicians, tech moguls, for "expert" opinions. They're more likely to accept a press release from a billionaire-funded think tank or foundation than ask an educator, so they perpetuate the narrative of higher education as a "broken fiscal model" that needs to be transformed, to be made more like business. They feature attention-grabbing stories of admissions scandals, athletic scandals, snowflake students, "cancel" culture—"if it bleeds, it leads"—stories that highlight what's wrong with higher education, but have little relevance to the experience of most undergraduates. The media give disrupters inordinate air time. Kevin Carey, author of *The End of College*, and Ryan Craig, author of *College Disrupted*, advocate doing away with "bricks and mortar" colleges and "unbundling" higher education into online learning and workplace-directed programs. For them, as for Gates, the "value" of higher education is measurable and monetary, training that yields maximum return on investment.[6]

Society has ceased believing in a liberal education, and educators are losing heart. Higher education has allowed itself to be defined by edu-crats, ideologues, politicians who would have us produce workers "job-ready on day one," in the words of former President Barack Obama,[7] whose Education Department was packed with Gates Foundation people.[8] We in the liberal arts watch as enrollments plummet and humanities courses and programs are replaced by degree programs with "product-market fit," as the Charles Koch Foundation advocates.[9] The assault on the liberal arts is bipartisan, one of the few things Democrats and Republicans can get together on; and it's been extremely effective.

Students are flocking to majors in STEM (science, technology, engineering, mathematics) because they've been told this is where the jobs are—when in fact, there are more STEM graduates than there are jobs.[10] They've been told the humanities offer poor job prospects—when, as Karl Voss explains in the *Hechinger Report*, "Employers consistently say that they are looking for employees who can analyze complex, multifaceted problems, are creative and innovative, have good communication skills, are willing to learn, work . . . with a variety of people, see the larger setting in which decisions are made, and understand the ethical dimension of decisions and interactions"—all of which the liberal arts develop.[11] "The difference between humanities majors and science majors, in median income and unemployment, seems to be no more than the difference between residents of Virginia and North Carolina," writes Benjamin Schmidt in the *Atlantic*: "If someone told to me not to move to Charlotte because no one there can make a living, I would never take them seriously."[12]

"Death Spiral," "Budget Bloodbath," "Extinction-Level Event" are familiar headlines for what is happening to the humanities. And it's not only the liberal arts, but higher education itself on the chopping block, denounced as "unsustainable," student debt exceeding credit card debt—"the public won't take it anymore," "the bubble's about to burst," an avalanche is coming our way, a tsunami is about to hit. A tsunami did hit, in the spring of 2020, though not in a form anyone anticipated: less than a year after the onset of COVID-19, by February 2021, US colleges and universities saw their workforce cut by 13%. Administrators leap at the promises of ed tech to deliver a future of online teaching, though now that we've had a taste of how alienating and ineffective this can be, most students and faculty appreciate more than ever the value of person-to-person teaching.

"Personalized learning" is what Gates calls computerized programs that have kids sitting at screens, following the prompts of an algorithm. He devises tech-heavy, standardized, test-driven programs for other people's children, while sending his own to the posh, private school he attended himself, Lakeside: "I had great relationships with my teachers. . . . Classes were small. You got to know the teachers. They got to know you. And the relationships that come from that really make a difference. If you like and respect your teacher, you're going to work harder."[13] Gates knows what works. Everyone knows what works: small classes where teachers can give students individual attention. Teaching and learning are things done with people, by people, for people, dependent on the trust and goodwill, presence, participation, responsiveness of human beings.

"If there is one thing that the educational research clearly and consistently demonstrates, it is that the most successful long-term results for students occur when they are able to develop close relationships with their faculty," writes Joshua Kim, director of Digital Learning Initiatives at Dartmouth Center for the Advancement of Learning. When asked, "Is there innovation/idea/movement methodology that excites you in terms of the future of education?" he advises, "Get a liberal arts education." If we hope to "reimagine and revolutionize education," we should recognize that "the most powerful personalized and adaptive learning platform ever invented is an experienced and well-supported educator": "Give me an oval table, an experienced and well-supported educator, and 12 curious students—and I'll rip out every single piece of campus technology."[14] Strong words, from a techie, but research corroborates that relationships are "central to a successful college experience," as Daniel Chambliss and Christopher Takacs conclude on the basis of a 10-year study of students and alums of Hamilton College, a small liberal arts college in New York.[15] Relationships matter more than the technology being sold to schools and colleges in the name of "innovation," more than the subjects studied.[16] They matter especially to first-generation students and students of color,[17] and they matter especially now, when students have been starved of human connection for too long. They matter in terms of "long-term life outcomes," as Richard Detweiler concluded on the basis of a study of 1,000 graduates of all kinds of colleges, "by educating people for lives of consequence, inquiry, and accomplishment," accomplishments that serve not only the individual but "the common good."[18]

Show and Tell

Surveying this scene, I decided to tell the inside story of "an experienced and well-supported educator" who taught 40 years at a small liberal arts women's college, Scripps College, Claremont, California, and to urge that we hold on to this kind of teaching, for dear life. Before Scripps, I taught seven years as an adjunct at Queens and Brooklyn College of the City University of New York (CUNY). I spent a term as a visiting professor at the University of Washington. I was a student for five years at Berkeley, a year at the University of Chicago, a semester at CUNY, a summer at Stanford, and several years at Columbia, where I finished my PhD. Nearly half a century teaching has convinced me that professor-student interaction is where the magic is, and that it's likeliest at a liberal arts college committed to education that's human-scale, relationship-rich, humanities-based, and sufficiently resourced to keep educators engaged.[19] ("Twice as likely," Detweiler discovered.)[20] Such colleges also have the highest and fastest graduation rates, and often the lowest rates of student debt.[21] And women's colleges are especially "productive": graduates have measurably higher levels of self-esteem, continue in disproportionally high numbers on to doctorates in science and math, and though they are only 2% of graduates, they make up more than 20% of women in Congress and 30% of a *Business Week* listing of rising women in corporate America.[22] Women's colleges also "claim more racial and socio-economic diversity than their co-ed counterparts," reports Marilyn Hammond, former president of the Women's College Coalition.[23]

But quality education can be had at colleges less pricey than Scripps—anywhere educators can find ways of interacting with students, enabling conversation, exchange, engagement. There are plenty of colleges you've never heard of chugging quietly away, opening minds and hearts, transforming lives, graduating human beings who make the world more livable. "My colleagues and I, out here in the provinces and far from ivory towers," writes Rachel Toor at Eastern Washington University, in an area that's "geographically and politically . . . [near] blood-red, gun-toting northern Idaho," "are building citizens who can read and write, think and analyze, ferret out alternative facts, and distinguish real news from fake."[24] And community colleges— which "prioritize student growth" over "institutional reputation," as Cathy Davidson says—are proof that this kind of education need not cost the earth.[25] So are the Historically Black Colleges and Universities (HBCUs). They spend two-thirds per student of what other colleges spend, but their graduates rank themselves higher than alums elsewhere in feeling "prepared for life" and "thriving in elements of well-being." Alums point to professors and mentors who made them feel supported as key to this success,[26] and the success is measurable: the percentage who enter from lower classes and end up in the middle or upper classes is twice the nationwide average.[27]

"Relationship-rich education" is more affordable than we've been led to believe, as Peter Felten and Leo Lambert demonstrate.[28] Compare the cost of a group of students at a seminar table to the expense of athletic centers and coaches or the labs and equipment required by the sciences, and you see why an English major costs about half as much to educate as an engineering student.[29] All we need is a room, some chairs, and a table. (Okay, we can do without the table.)

But HBCUs are reeling. So are community colleges and regional colleges like Rachel Toor's that serve low-income, first-generation, and minority students; many are being merged or shut down, especially in states with Koch-funded governors and legislators. And small liberal arts colleges are particularly endangered: in 1990, there were 212 small liberal arts colleges;[30] by 2012, there were 130. Between 2016 and 2019, at least 22 closed.[31] Half a century ago there were 230 women's colleges, wrote Joseph Traester in 2015; by 2018 there were 42, according to Carol Christ, UC Berkeley chancellor and former president of Smith College.[32] "Another Small College Closing" is so familiar a headline that we barely stop to inquire which one.

The public should know that these losses are their losses, are everybody's losses. Politicians, administrators, college counselors, students choosing what and where to study, parents writing tuition checks, voters electing lawmakers who will defend or defund higher education— all need to know. They need to see how liberal arts colleges, state colleges, HBCUs, community colleges contribute to the well-being of individuals and society; they need to understand the contributions the great research universities make to the health and wealth of this country. Educators must find a way of letting them know, of penetrating the miasma of misinformation surrounding education, of communicating what we're doing right. Our vast and various educational system is, as Marilynne Robinson says, "unlike anything else in the world": it "emerged from the glorious sense of the possible. If it seems to be failing now, this is because we have forgotten what it is for." What universities do is a "great and continuous gift to the culture" and "there's nothing elitist or non-utilitarian about what they are and what they do." What they need is "morale, a sense of confidence."[33]

"Perhaps the most daunting challenge," writes Andrew Delbanco, professor of American studies at Columbia and author of *College*, is the difficulty of conveying the value of a liberal arts education "to anyone—policymakers, public officials, and even many academics— who has not personally experienced it."[34] It's especially daunting now, when we've been blindsided by attacks, dumbfounded at having to defend ourselves at such an elementary level, when the very notion of "expertise" has been impugned and the words we reach for to defend ourselves—*value, use, outcome*—have been nailed to the material and monetary. Besides, as Delbanco emphasizes, it's the *experience* that's convincing, and that takes more than a sound bite or summary, more than abstractions or generalizations, to get across.[35]

Most attempts to defend the liberal arts are so abstract that you could read through stacks of books and hardly know there are students present, though the students are what the whole show is about. If they figure at all, it's as data points, numbers on a graph. We need to *show* how our teaching speaks to students' needs, how we give them something that serves them in their lives. And by *show* I mean *demonstrate* with the specificity, the particularity, the respect for persons that's the genius of the humanities, of humanism, of democracy. I can say, "the humanities is about the cultivation of the human and the creation of a citizenry capable of democracy"—I can repeat that till I'm blue in the face—but it won't communicate the lived experience; it won't tell you how or why it works or how it feels. It's complicated, what goes on in a class, the currents that get flowing, the feedback loops that get looping, the synergy that makes a class add up to more than the sum of its parts. You have to be there.

So I bring you into my class, where you meet the students, learn something of their strengths and needs, and experience the feeling and flavor of a class—for there is much flavor and feeling in a class, a class pulses with human interest, humor and nuttiness, and occasional magic, lively and unpredictable and full of surprises. You meet me, too, because—spoiler alert—*teachers are human too.* (That's what a student said she learned, reading Frank McCourt's *Teacher Man,* her very words.) "Professor as human"—something else you won't find in most writing about higher education. You'll feel what it's like to encounter, as I do, each semester, a whole new show, a room full of bristling egos, needs, interests tugging this way and that, as I try to capture their attention, communicate an appreciation of imaginative literature to kids who are increasingly a-literate, fixated on digital media, accustomed to instant and easy gratification, who arrive in our classes punch-drunk with pressures, more of them holding jobs than when I was a student, more taking on debt, more on medications. As we move through a semester, you'll see how a small class can build a complex human ecosystem that pushes students to discover interests and potentials of themselves they may not have known they had, and to recognize that others have views and values that differ from their own. You'll see how a college built to human scale, where students find community and a culture of engagement, speaks to human needs for connection and sociality and can be, in a modest way, a site of resistance against the dehumanization that's hollowing out our lives.

But why Shakespeare? He is, as we'll see, the heart of humanism, and humanism is the heart of the humanities. But what *use* is he? Why inflict this difficult material on kids whose own dramas seem so much more compelling to them than these old plays? There are easier subjects, for sure—every other course I teach is easier. But reading a Shakespeare play develops mental muscles that become useful for other sorts of problems, and talking about the plays in a class provides excellent training ground for living in the world. The challenges our students face, that we all face, navigating the human minefield, are of a verbal, social, interactive sort, learning to interpret our fellow human beings, to hear meanings behind words, read between the lines, to push back against agendas being pushed on us, so we're not *led by the nose as asses are*, as Iago says of Othello, like those poor fools whose bodies litter the stage at the end of a tragedy. There is never a time we don't need these skills, unless we move to a desert island or the deep woods—these are survival skills, not frills. They're decoding skills that have a longer shelf life than the coding Bill Gates is trying to push on K–12, than training in a specialization that may be automated, outsourced, or obsolete within a few years.

Actually, Shakespeare is *fun*, and that matters, because pleasure is the key to motivation, and motivation is the key to learning. These are *plays* we're reading, by a playwright and player who understands the uses of play, who plays with the idea of play, who knows he needs to engage his audiences so they keep coming back. Play is essential to learning, now more than ever, when kids have been ground down by a K–12 system that deprives them of recesses, the arts, and the pleasures of using their minds.

It's been the failure of so-called reformers to understand this that doomed No Child Left Behind, Race to the Top, and the Common Core State Standards, from the start. I hadn't given much thought to the "lower grades" until I saw the same joy-killing dictates that have done a wrecking job on K–12 moving up the system like gangrene, strangling even colleges like Scripps with what Jerry Muller calls the "tyranny of metrics" that's "engulfing an ever-widening range of institutions including the most elite."[36] In the early years of this century, the "outcomes assessment" regime hit Scripps College, demanding that faculty produce quantifiable "student learning outcomes" to demonstrate our "accountability." At a time when we need all our wits, nerve, heart to defend ourselves against charges that we're useless, we're made to devise "metrics," hire "officers," fill out spread sheets and "worksheets," reducing our students and subjects to numerical "learning outcomes," to show we have a right to exist.

When my search for the origin of this travesty led to K–12, I saw what corporate reform has done to public education, reducing schools to test-taking factories and routing public funding to private profits for producers of test materials, textbooks, educational technology, and charter schools. I thought nothing could shock me: I'd written a book about nuclear industry and government cover-ups of radiation risk—I thought I'd seen it all.[37] But when I saw the venality with which corporate America carved up education, I was amazed. And I realized—light bulb moment—that this reduction of teaching to testing has played no small part in the decline of enrollments in the liberal arts.

If you really want to know about our "student learning outcomes," ask the graduates, find out what they're doing with their lives—which I've done throughout this book. I've been collecting testimonials from students and alums for decades, from e-mails, conversations, informal interviews, the *Scripps Magazine*, posts on Facebook, Yelp, College Confidential. Alums tell me how their liberal arts education taught them to read, write, think, interpret, synthesize, how it's given them intellectual agility, adaptability, flexibility that's served them well in their lives and work, how it's sparked a social awareness that's kept them engaged with communities and causes.

"Scripps really did push me to be the best version of myself," writes Claire Ellen, '11. "Thanks to the humanities program, I have the ability as an attorney to look at what I am reading and see the people, money and implications of the cases before us. I ask, who is paying for this? What happens if it comes out this way or that? What's really important here? What will be the result of the precedent?" These are qualities that make a good attorney: knowing how to evaluate, to sort out what matters, to "see the people," to think through consequences, to ask, "who profits?" She goes on to say, "I learned hope. The professors who teach at places like Scripps are people who want and can see a better world. . . . When my friends say, 'what do you expect?' I say, *I expect better*. And I do, all the time."

Claire is describing an education that made her better not only at what she does but at what she is. The habit of hope, the capacity to imagine alternatives—these are "student learning outcomes" a college can be proud of, outcomes as immeasurable as a human life. "This college transformed me . . . opened doors for me . . . showed me there was more to the world than I imagined . . . taught me to trust my own voice"—these are things I hear. This is what transformation looks like, not the top-down imposition of a system that creates scale and efficiency, but the transformation of hearts and minds that a class or a college can bring about, the cultivation of the human that makes democracy more than a dream.

The challenges that young people face—climate change, the toppling of democracies, rampant inequality, refugee populations larger than ever before, recurrent pandemics—will require every bit of imagination, creativity, intelligence, inventiveness the human race can summon. Do we really think a degree in computer science or marketing will equip anyone to face this four-horseman horror show? Do we think the future is well served by graduates who know nothing about their fellow human beings, their world, their past?

This book tells the story of a Shakespeare class, a composite of many classes I've taught at Scripps through the years. Students' names have been changed, their identities have been disguised, though they are all true-to-life; the alums are, most of them, identified by name. You'll meet a richer mix, a more economically and ethnically diverse group than you might expect of a college that costs so much, more diverse than I found when I arrived 40 years ago. Multiculturalism lives, at least in Los Angeles County; 224 languages are spoken in this county.

It has given me great pleasure, revisiting these classes, bringing these moments back to life, moments I never doubted my students and I were doing essential work. So come on in and see what we do, see why it's worth saving.

ONE

First Day

> There are defenses of the humanities, lamentations about the state of
> the humanities, critiques of the humanities, and historical accounts of the
> humanities without number, but very little in the way of a positive
> account of what humanistic scholars actually do.
> —GEOFFREY HARPHAM, "Finding Ourselves"

First day of class, running late, halfway out my office door, when I
hear the ping of an e-mail. THANK YOU! pops up on the subject
line, big bold caps. I can't resist. I click on the message and read: "You
won't remember me. I did not do well in your class. I was pregnant
and miserable. Those novels we read gave me courage to have my baby.
She just left for college. I'm writing to say thank you."

Wow. I sit down, read it again. You never know. I know which
course that would have been—Contemporary Women Writers—but
this student, I don't remember. I had no idea. What they take from a
class, you really never know. Unpredictable. Unimaginable. Immeasurable, as a human life.

Humanities 120

Mad dash across campus, I catch my breath, walk in. Humanities 120, the English seminar room. The table is full. I glance around at the kids who are looking at me. They don't look like "butts," though that's what a North Carolina governor said he'd fund—"butts [that] can get jobs."[1] Nor do they look like widgets, though that's what Bill Gates suggested, defending the one-size-fits-all Common Core State Standards he inflicted on K–12 public schools. ("If you have 50 different plug types, appliances wouldn't be available and would be very expensive," he said. "But once an electric outlet becomes standardized, many companies can design appliances and competition ensues, creating variety and better prices for consumers.")[2] Nor do they look like products or consumer-producers that will give the United States a competitive edge in the global economy, contrary to those who would remake education to that end. They look human, younger each year as I get older, funny how that happens—kids, with that dewy eagerness of the first day of class, bright-eyed and fresh-faced as we set out on the adventure of a new semester, each bringing hearts, minds, hopes, expectations, talents, needs to this table, and baggage, more baggage than I hauled around at their age, that's sure.

Humanities 120, Scripps College, Claremont, California. A good room. Large windows look out on ivy, trees, and lawn. Amazingly important, this natural light, these gracious grounds with tree-lined paths, bougainvillea trailing up courtyard walls. The perks of privilege. Privileged we are to be here, none more privileged than I to have taught all these years at a college that still requires courses in the humanities, that names a building "the Humanities." Though this late in the day, the room's a bit tatty, trash bins overflowing, crumbs and sticky rings on the seminar table, the 4:15 fug of much-breathed air.

I throw open a window, look around, struck by a sudden and startling thought: I grew old in this room. I was 30 when I taught my first class in this room. Now I'm 70. I will soon, like Prospero, have to lay my staff aside.

I do a quick head count. 16, 17, 18. Not bad. Smaller than in the past—my seminars used to have 25–35. I thought it was just me getting older, then I realized it was English getting smaller. When I graduated in the mid-1960s, 1 in 5 graduated in a humanities subject; today, fewer than 1 in 20.

As always, I am struck by the variety. Our students come in all sizes, shapes, and colors—Asian Americans, African Americans, Latinas, children of immigrants from India, the Philippines, and combinations thereof. They're a heterogeneous lot, mostly female, but there are a few guys from the other colleges, and, these days, an occasional gender in flux. Scripps is part of the Claremont Colleges, a five-college consortium of about 5,000 students, an interesting mix: Pitzer, with its artsy creatives, some of the best students I've had, and the worst; Harvey Mudd, strong science and engineering; Pomona, rival to Harvard in wealth and selectivity; Claremont McKenna (CMC), known for government, economics, and parties, though more of its students seem to be drifting across the street to take literature courses at Scripps, while hedging their bets with a major they think is "safe."

I take out the book. Well-thumbed and worn, its cover fell off years ago, its pages are ragged and coffee-stained, but it's still solidly there. *The Complete Works of Shakespeare*. A book to conjure with. Lives have been made off these words, acting careers, scholarly careers, teaching careers, *my* career. I have done well by these words. Shakespeare did well by these words. Young man from Stratford, son of a glover, joins a group of players, makes his way to London, makes a fortune writing plays. There was no Globe Theater when he arrived in London; he and his fellows built it, owned it, profited handsomely from it. It was huge by the standards of the day, held 3,000—just think, in a week, a tenth of London might see a play. And did—his plays drew them in. A nobody from nowhere grows up to write *The Complete Works of William Shakespeare*. An algorithm-defying outcome, that—no "predictive analytic" could come near *that*. Bought himself a coat of arms, purchased three of the finest houses in Stratford, retired to Stratford, and, five years later, died.

And here it sits, having survived the acid bath of literary theory, the death of the author, the banishment of the text, the debunking of genius and dead white men; even the Common Core State Standards make room for Shakespeare. It has come through the canon wars, the culture wars, grand and monumental as the observatory dome in the ruins of Hiroshima, still standing after all these years, a piece of the past we can all, or nearly all, agree is worth saving. Alive and well and thriving in classrooms, on stages, in reading groups, Facebook groups, prisons, at conferences, at the center of flourishing industries, film, stage, festivals, adaptations, fanfiction, alive in the hearts and minds of human beings outside academia as well as in. "The Bard is big business," brings hundreds of millions of pounds into Britain, a tourist attraction that rivals the Royal Family.[3] Shakespeare, the beating heart of the humanities, of humanism, here in Humanities 120, Scripps College.

And here we all are, the start of a new semester, this many students wanting to read these plays, difficult as they are, drawn by curiosity, not careerism, just wanting to know, "what's this dude about?" While all around rage angry voices—what *use* is it, what product, what profit? Endangered species, we who care about the humanities. Me, "independent operator professor," as Andrew Delbanco calls a professor free to design her own courses, protected by tenure and academic freedom, a "relic" (his term).[4] They, the students, human capital fatted for the corporate crunch. This building that once seemed so solid, the Humanities building, the humanities, soon to be swept away.

Such dire things I read, such deafening detractions: "Who Killed the Liberal Arts?" "Why Are the Humanities Doomed?" If you want to major in gender studies or philosophy, go somewhere else, said Pat McCrory, the butt-funding governor of North Carolina.[5] Former presidential contender Marco Rubio mocked the idea of loaning students money "to study, you know—I don't want to offend anybody—Roman history? Are there any Romans here?"[6] As "consumer demand" falls off, legislators and administrators slash away, pushing for courses with "high-demand career paths" leading directly to jobs.

Accountability, accountability—the word thunders through the land—what good are you, what are you good *for*?

Can I deliver? I have only this tattered old book and these words, hard words, old words, and this is an age when words have lost their magic. Shakespeare had only these words, bare, wooden stage, no scenery, a few cannonballs rolling around the rafters to make thunder; words were all the special effects he had. But now, when students' most *awesome* experiences come from visuals—when, at the push of a button, their heads fill with light, color, sound, instantaneous excitement—shall these words live?

And *why*—why should it matter if they do?

"Accountability"?

I sigh, feel a stab of longing for last semester. Where do they go, the classes of the years gone by? Where is Annalisa, who sat at the far end of the table, whose mouth would go triangle when the talk got too abstruse; I'd see that frown and think, uh-oh, if I've if lost her, I've lost others, better do some summing up. Or Jocelyn, who I could always count on for a good guffaw to one of my asides. Or Gordon, the scruffy Pitzer student who looked like he'd swept in from the sixties, who'd say things like, *"Awesome!* you really think Shakespeare meant *that?"* Wonderful for morale. And Diane, who'd follow me back to my office, wanting to know, did Shakespeare really "invent the human," and what did Bloom mean by that, and did I really think he was "bi"? (She'd hinted that she was.) We begin to feel like family, then poof, they're gone, and I'm starting over with a whole new group.

"Tell me who you are," I say, taking out a piece of paper to make a chart. "Tell me—tell *us*—about yourselves. Then I'll tell you about the course." A primal instinct, show me yours, then I'll show you mine. I need to know their names. I am feeling, as I always feel the first day, massively outnumbered, more than a little unnerved by this room full of strangers that I must somehow make into . . . something they'll never forget. Will I ever get used to all these eyes on me, judging, assessing, sizing me up? I'm not a natural performer; many in this profession are—they just walk in and carry on. Me, I'm a let's-get-this-group-talking kind of teacher. It's a conjuring feat, teaching. You get the show up and running, it hums along, then poof, it's over, *melted into air, into thin air,* like Prospero's magic displays, only you hope it leaves more than *a trace behind.* The next semester, you crank it up again, a whole new show.

Accountable? You bet. You set foot in the door, all eyes on you, you're on, you're *it*, you're what makes it happen. Adrenaline rush, all stops out.

"Tell us who you are," I repeat. "Introduce yourselves not just to me but to the class. Say what your major is, year, school, college, experience with Shakespeare—you know, which plays you've read or seen or maybe acted in. Oh yes, and where you're from, what part of the world." Anything that helps us register one another as human beings. "Say a few words about why you're here, what drew you to this class—you know, like, what you hope to get out of it, what you'd like to learn. But if it's because you needed an English class Tuesday and Thursday afternoon and this is what there was—don't tell me that, okay? Even if it's true, don't say it. Make something up. Use your imagination."

I pause, let this sink in. It draws a few chuckles, a few perplexed looks, a few exchange glances, like "what'd she say?" What I'm saying is, it's about the morale, the spirit that breathes life into a class. What I'm saying is, it's about responsibility, yours to me and mine to you and all of us to one another. There are a lot of people in this room who are not you—me, for instance, I am a person who is not you, besides all the others. Best get the hang of it. Look around, take note who else is here, learn to play your part—don't hog the show but don't disappear, come in on cue, learn what a cue is. There's a lot of improv in a seminar—it's ensemble work, we're co-creators, we depend on one another, draw energy from one another. If you put yourself out there, something will come of it, you'll see.

This is what *accountability* is, you to me and me to you and all of us to one another. Only *accountability* is the wrong word. It's a blaming word, a bludgeoning word, a whipword to beat teachers into shape. Accountability refers to something that can be, well, you know . . . *counted*. A thing done with numbers. What goes on here is done with people. A class is a relationship, a crisscross of relationships, two-ways, multiple ways, fraught with the complexities that come with a relationship, times ten, times a thousand.

No, *accountability* is not the word for what goes on in this class.

Meet the Students

And so we go around the table, as I have for many semesters, same as always yet never the same—the students are different, I'm different, the way we go together is different, this class will be a whole new show.

Why, even the plays of Shakespeare become different under different eyes.

Ah, good, Barbara, a familiar face, an intense face, too finely featured for those large horn-rimmed glasses. First of her family to go to college, Latina, from east L.A. I had her in a Humanities course last year. I used to try calling on her, but she'd turn red and stammer, so I'd back off; but I could tell from her papers, she was taking in every word. When I asked her why she never talks in class, she said, "I don't know, I don't know what I think till I've thought it over." Fair enough. I'd have said that myself, never opened my mouth in class, would have been horrified to be called on (no risk of that at Berkeley, which was one reason I went there). Hers is a quiet intelligence that runs deep, and such fine-tuned empathy, I hear her sharp intake of breath as I read Macbeth's *full of scorpions is my mind*. If I can get her to feel even slightly less diffident about herself, that will be something.

But Barbara will add nothing to class discussion. If I get too many students whose right to remain silent I respect, I end up doing all the talking.

And here is a pair of very wary eyes—uh-oh, if that hoodie were pulled any lower, she'd disappear. All I can see is a pointy nose and eyes with a show-me look. Ruthie is from Chicago. She says she, uh, read *Hamlet* in high school and thought she'd like to read more. Major? Undecided. What baggage she is carrying to make that slouch, that desire to disappear, I will later learn. Next to her sits Sandra, long, sandy braid, dreamy gaze, impressive cheekbones, all jutting angles; too many of our students are thin like this. "I, uh, always really wanted to read Shakespeare," she says. Somehow that sounds unconvincing, since she, uh, as an English major, sort of has to. Shakespeare is not a required course—I'm glad of that—but English majors have to take a course in literature before 1900, and sometimes, this is what there is. She looks guarded, like she's sizing us up.

Me, too, I'm sizing them up, appraising my forces. Like a conductor sussing out the players, for I can be no better than the players—will they learn their parts, will they turn up on time, will they come in on cue, stay on key? If they miss their cue, if the trombones slide off note, if the drums are out to lunch, if the strings are, well, texting—what can I do? So far, signs aren't great.

"Generic blond," I jot down by Sandra's name. Boy, did I call that wrong.

And here is a Lizzie, round face beaming with goodwill and freckles, hair a frizzy goldish halo that bobs in agreement with what I or others say. Frizzy Lizzie, I don't need a memory prompt for her. "I, uh, don't know what my major will be. Either English or . . . chemistry?" her voice trails up, that upward lilt you hear in young women's voices that turns everything to a question. There's a hesitation, a catch on the word *chemistry.*

"There's a big difference," I say gently. I'm used to students saying they're trying to decide between English or French, or history or art history—but this?

I will later learn, in office hours, that she wants to major in English, but her parents want her to "do something practical, like chemistry." "What jobs would that open for you?" "Oh, you know, petrochemicals, pharmaceuticals." "Can you see yourself working in those areas?" She rolls her eyes. "You know, it's you, not your parents, who will have to live with this decision," I say, not sure I should go on, but I do: "A job is a terrible thing to hate." She comes in to office hours again, and again, and I try, really try, to get her to hear her voice, not mine. "Isn't it self-indulgent to major in English?" she says, and I think, for the millionth time, what a strange pass we've come to, that a student feels "self-indulgent" for wanting to study something she loves—she's 18, for chrissake! Especially when English majors are a lot more employable than people realize.[7] Anyhow, Lizzie's decision makes itself by the end of the semester. She falls in love with Shake-speare, and that's that.

Ashley is from New York, Upper West Side, my old neighborhood. "I played Juliet in high school," she says, sweeping a shock of reddish-blond hair out of her eyes, looking around to gauge the effect. "I hope to be an actress." Offstage as well as on, I see. She bristles with attitude. Tricky, these attitudes, they stick out like porcupine quills, something that needs to prove itself, to show itself off, handle with care, bruises easily as a ripe peach. It makes me so grateful for the straightforward kids, the ones who are just there: there's the kid, there's me, there's Shakespeare, and when we're talking about the play, we're talking about the play, not some complicated meta thing going on. But with an attitude, there's the kid and this dynamic you have to work around, work it so you get it working with the class. So much of what goes on in a class is not in the words, but in glances exchanged, an eye roll, a snicker, a smile, a slouch.

Beside her sits Cynthia, red, spiky hair, rings in ears and nose, tattoos up her arms, attitude comes off her in waves. Oh, no, please don't let her be all PC, tie my tongue in knots, have us all walking on egg-shells. Third-year, Pitzer, from San Bernardino, half hour east of Claremont but a world away. "I, uh, felt I sort of ought to read some Shakespeare, you know?" "Right." "Spiky," I write beside her name.

A few guys, funny how they huddle together, though they're nothing alike. Danny from Denver, large, scruffy senior at Harvey Mudd, majoring in engineering; good humor glints behind thick glasses, round, boyish face framed by Bob Dylan hair. Danny says, "I didn't think I should graduate without knowing something about Shakespeare." Good lad. Maybe he's making it up, whatever, good for morale. A good tongue in his head, too, like the day *The Merchant of Venice* inspired my rant about Silicon Valley fortunes, he cut in, "You do realize, Professor Greene, that Silicon Valley is where many of us are hoping to go?" Gotcha. Some self-deprecation in that comment, but a jab at me, too, like, "get real, Professor." Being a "Mudder," he just may get there. Though what he finds there may not be all he hoped for, not when you see *New York Times* headlines like "In the Salary Race, Engineers Sprint but English Majors Endure."[8]

And here is Trevor, also a Mudder. Thin, tightly wired, nervous, looks like he's marking the nearest exit, hair so close-cropped it looks shaved. He's from Boston, majoring in computer science. So many are majoring in computer science these days, but when you read about "en masse layoffs of midcareer programmers and IT professionals," you suspect, as Michael Anft warns, "the outlook for tech-knowledgeable people isn't all that rosy."[9] Next to him sits Brent, blond, natty, econ-government major, Claremont McKenna College, exudes confidence, takes up a surprising lot of space, considering he's not that large; says he wants to find out what all the fuss with Shakespeare is about.

And here's a Samantha—hang on, you'll be meeting these kids again—a first-year, from Fresno, black helmeted hair, slash of red lipstick like a 1930s film star. She looks like a "Samantha"; no memory prompt required. Tanya, by her side—that can't be a Chinese name—has been drawing out strands of long black hair, bringing them up to her eyes, searching for split ends, so close that her eyes nearly cross. She says, "I'm a sophomore." Major? "English. Maybe. Not sure." "From?" "San Jose." I try to engage her in small talk about San Jose, a sleepy agricultural town when I grew up not far from there, the capital of Silicon Valley today. She smiles, says no more.

Worrieder and worrieder. These are deep waters we're sailing into—are we seaworthy?

Brittany, whose eyes have barely left her lap, flings a mane of wavy, strawberry blond hair conspicuously out of her eyes (when did hair become such a big deal?) Zaftig, too much of her to fit into that skimpy tank top—c'mon, girl, button it up, your future does not lie that way. But then I remember, I do remember the complexities of self-presentation for a bursting-out-all-over 18-year-old girl, the bundle of self-conscious confusion I was. "San Diego," she says, her eyes meeting mine. Thank you, Brittany, good of you to join us, as though I can't tell you're texting—no, I am not a one-way screen, I see and hear and register all, just as you do, or would do, if you gave us your attention. *Be here now*, Brittany, face-to-face, the meat world, remember, can't change the channel or click on another link. Brittany says, "Uh, well, this class worked perfectly with my schedule," not having heard me say, please don't say that; naturally not, she was texting. Nor does she register the amused titters of several who *did* hear what I said.

Okay, I have to say something. "Uh, put it away, cell phones in off position." I feel like a flight attendant.

And here are one-two-three serious-looking, straight-haired brunettes clustered together—oh no, can their names really be Alice, Allison, Alicia? Alice is a Mudder, engineering; girls didn't used to major in engineering, good to remember, days I feel bleak about feminism. The other two are from Scripps. Alicia is in media studies; Allison's in . . . environmental science, did she say? no wait, was that Allison in media studies—gads, will I ever get them straight? "Listen, do me a favor, take out a piece of paper and write your name, big letters, prop it in front of you so all can see . . ." Eye rolls, groans. "C'mon, humor me." I squint at their scrawls. "Allie," well, *that's* no help. Nor is "Kit" or "Buzz." There are no names like those on my class roster.

And way to the left, where she sits, trying to disappear, is Lydia. She is plump, wears an oversize white T-shirt with a puppy dog on it; I look more closely and see a pair of luminous blue eyes under a tangle of unkempt hair, eyes that would be lovely if they didn't look so frightened. "I'm from a town you've never heard of in the Central Valley."

I wait. "Major?" "Dunno." "Experience with Shakespeare?" She blushes, shakes her head. Somehow the image of the puppy blends with the girl—"Puppy," I jot down.

And one-two-three auditors sit along the wall, huddled together, what we call "older women," though probably they're younger than I am. Edna, Edith, Bernice. Their body language communicates they don't feel they have the right to be here. Yup, that's how it is with older women, that diffidence about taking up space. It can be awkward, working older auditors into a class, so if they choose to sit silent, that's fine. Actually I enjoy them greatly, even if they say nothing; they seem to be the only ones who laugh at my jokes anymore.

Wait, there's one more, by the door, though Marianne, unlike the auditors, radiates the right to be here. Legs crossed, shown to advantage by classy shoes, leather attaché case propped by her chair, she looks ready to effect giant mergers, buy and sell corporations, primed for "leadership," a thing women's colleges are pushing. She flashes me a smile, the kind made with the mouth, not the eyes, says she's not sure about her major, "Uh, something to do with entrepreneurship or organizational management." "Do we have those majors?" I say, wishing immediately I had not. "Self-designed," she sets me straight. Her professionalism unnerves me—so many of our students come in with résumés, titles they put on e-mails, "associative assistant administrator to the" etc. Building a brand. I'll take the rough, unpolished, any day; "finished" means, well, like finished, over and done with.

What on earth is she doing in this class? (She does not stay.)

No Two Alike

So here we all sit, a room full of bristling egos, each bringing expectations, experiences, equipment to the table, all so different. The routes they have taken to this place, this small women's college east of Los

Angeles, are different, too. Some are here because they want to get away from home, some because they want to stay close to home, some because their mother graduated from Scripps, some because they didn't get into Stanford. "I fell in love with the campus," "My boyfriend goes to CMC," "I wanted to come to the West Coast"—these are the things I hear. I remember it well, the serendipity of my moves at that age. When I think of the energy that goes into marketing a college, defining a "brand" or "signature experience," and see the whimsical choices of 18-year-olds, I want to laugh.

Ruthie, slouched in her hoodie, will later tell me, point blank, "I don't know WTF I am doing in this class. My father told me I had no right to spend his money taking Shakespeare, so I—sorry, that is really why I'm here." She blurts this out in one of many tearful conversations we have when she comes to my office to apologize for missing another assignment, another week of classes. "He says he's not spending this kind of money on Shakespeare, only to have me move back home." I hear things like this all the time: either you major in econ or engineering and make a living, or you study literature and move back home. It's one of those lunk-headed either-ors that obliterates distinctions and allows no middle ground. I learn, in the course of our conversations, that she was two when her family moved to Chicago from Russia, an only child, all her parents' ambitions focused on her; and she is lost, one of increasing numbers of kids overly pressured and strung out on a pharmacopeia of medications. Some days, she sits silent and withdrawn, other days she won't shut up, depending on her meds.

Brittany, eyes glued to her lap, would rather be texting; I'm afraid I called that right. She's here because her father says she *must* take a Shakespeare class; she's just putting in time. So young, so disaffected— there seem to be more of them these days. Is it K–12 "reform" that's sucked the life out of them, or is it me they're bored with—that's always the question, is it them or me? But I've heard younger colleagues complain of student disengagement, too. And you never can tell. I once had a student who sat staring into space, I thought she hated the class; then one day she came to office hours and burst into tears, told me she was getting a C in organic chem, she'd blown her chances for med school, and ours was the only class she liked.

Some will need teasing out, others need damping down. Some are brimming with confidence, others, barely scraping by; confidence is a quality not always dealt out fairly, I have found. Ashley will be difficult to shut up, Barbara difficult to bring out, Cynthia with the spiky hair and attitude will make a force field, preppy Brent will make one too—how to get these two working together, working with me? Frizzie Lizzie brings so much energy to the table, she perks us all up, Brittany gives off waves of indifference like a blight. Tanya will spend the semester drawing out strands of her long black hair, examining them for split ends, saying nothing. Some will spend the semester working their butts off, others, drinking their brains out—not a lot I can do. They are so all over the place, this hive of human variables tugging this way and that, me trying to focus their attention, gently nudging them through complicated texts.

How can I possibly pitch to this disparate lot, find a level to pitch to, even know what ball to pitch?

What they have in common is that they are young, toggling between adolescence and adulthood, between family and the great wide world. An exhilarating time, their lives all before them, but scary too. We have forgotten, those of us whose lives have been shaped by decisions long ago made, how scary it was, how hugely consequential each move might be. It's a time of life when choices matter, when a word, a class, a book, a person may set them on a path, open up a future, or close one off. Take off those rose-tinted lenses we seem to grow like cataracts as we look back on our youth, and remember—it was hard. "These are the best years of your life," said the grown-ups, and I'd think, uh-oh, this could be a really rough ride. I was filled with anxieties—would I find love, work I cared about, a way in the world, would I be up to it, whatever *it* was. I had no idea what I was capable of, what "a good life" might be.

I don't want to hear what my students can do for the global economy. I want to know what I can do for them, how I can help them grow into sane, whole, responsible human beings who make choices that genuinely benefit themselves and the world. I want to help them grow themselves, not grow the economy or feed "the human capital pipeline" or fatten the profits of some multinational conglomerate— because the world they're coming into is no friend of theirs. I see so much potential in my students, but the world does not want the best of them or the best for them. It wants a kind of instrumental cleverness, a workforce "just smart enough" to read instructions, run the machines, "and just dumb enough," in the words of comedian George Carlin, "to passively accept all those increasingly shittier jobs."[10]

And that is why it does not want the liberal arts.

Responsibility, Not Accountability

This, then, is my *accountability*: to "make it possible for the students to become themselves," as Brazilian educational philosopher Paulo Freire says.[11] Only *accountability* is not the right word.

The word *accountability* was unleashed onto education in January 2002, by George W. Bush's "No Child Left Behind," which made standardized test scores the sole measure of performance and made teachers *accountable* for students' scores—as though any teacher could overcome the disadvantages of poverty, racism, unequal opportunity that bring test scores down. Teachers were fired if test scores didn't measure up, schools were declared "failing" and shut down by the hundreds, mainly in disadvantaged neighborhoods where kids don't test well—a dark irony, since leaving "no child behind" was the excuse for this draconian regime, but a neat deflection of attention from social problems inconvenient to address.

By 2009, No Child Left Behind was a demonstrated failure, but the Obama administration simply took it over, giving it a new name, Race to the Top, requiring that states adopt, as a condition for federal funds, the Common Core State Standards, a set of national "standards" nailed into place in 2010 by the billions and boosterism of Bill Gates. The Common Core "standards" were imposed with no trial runs, no pilot programs, without a shred of evidence that they worked. (They did not.) They reduced teaching to drilling in decontextualized math and reading skills devoid of any purpose other than passing the test. Since schools live or die on the basis of test scores, what does not get tested does not get taught, and curricula are stripped of "extraneous" subjects like literature, history, philosophy, the arts, languages, social sciences, and even, in some places, the sciences.[12] No wonder kids arrive in college with so little interest in the liberal arts. Most wouldn't know a "liberal art" if it smacked them in the face.

No, *responsibility* is the word I want. The dictionary defines *accountability* and *responsibility* as synonyms, both meaning "answerable to." But look at the words—they're very different. *Accountability* refers to something that can be calculated, *measured*, as in a tallying up, keeping score. Whereas *responsibility* is rooted in *respond, response, responsiveness*; it refers to the engagement of minds with other minds, of students with me and with each other and the plays of Shakespeare. *Responsibility* is the word for the living, breathing human quality of a class, the dynamic that develops between and among us, active, interactive, a current that gets flowing, me to them, them to me and to each other, a process one hopes will go on perking long after the class is over, inspiring curiosity and the desire to know. *Inspire*, to breathe spirit into, encourage, rouse, move, stir someone to reach beyond—a good word, but not a word we hear in ed-speak today. *Incentivize* is the word we hear, as though we were all Pavlov's dogs, salivating for the chow.

My responsibilities I well know—to the students, to the college that employs me, to the parents who trust me with their kids, to the material, which I work up every class, making it new. You can trust me to do my best—*trust* is a big part of it—because it feels so good when it works and so bad when it flops, like falling on my face in a public place. But accountability to some overseer that purports to have a way of keeping score, to some data cruncher making sure we measure up? No way. That is *surveillance*.

But it's responsibility *to*—not responsibility *for*. I am responsible *to* my students as they are to me as we all are to each other. But responsible *for* this disparate lot, this collection of bristling adolescent needs and egos, these human beings who are so very much who they are? No. What they bring to the table, how they feel about the subject and themselves and one another and me, how far they want to go—is not in my control. Contact must be made, a spark must be lit, but I am not Dr. Frankenstein, throwing a switch—the current flows both ways. They are not passive consumers of their educations, they have *agency*; they shape what goes on in this class, what the class becomes. *Motivation* is the heart, blood, and breath of learning, yet this is another word we hardly ever hear—because if you're trying to blame teachers for everything that goes wrong, the last thing you want to draw attention to is that kids come with vastly different desires, talents, drives.

I look around the room. Will you be the kind of class that puts a spring in my step, that feeds us lines we can work with, or will you sit dull and inert and gag us all? Will you be the kind of class I live to teach, energy surging as from a strong team of horses? Not that I've ever driven a team of horses, but I can imagine—a good team, you nudge a little, you breeze up the hill. Or will you be a class I have to drag along, all of us, horses, carriage, riders, and I could get trampled under sharp, unforgiving hooves?

It's like a blind date that goes on 14 weeks. For which I am responsible.

"The Best Kind of College"

Scripps is not the kind of college I went to or considered going to. Too small, too obscure. One of the few times this college got mentioned in the *New York Times*, we were described as "a tiny all-female institution in California"—those were the words in an article about the shooting of Arizona congresswoman Gabby Giffords, perhaps our best-known alum.[13] In a culture where size matters, "tiny" is no compliment, and "female" never is. On account of some science writing I've done—a biography of a radiation epidemiologist and an account of insomnia that delved into sleep science—I get queries from people who think I'm at the "real" Scripps, the Scripps Institution of Oceanography or the Scripps Research Institute. That's not us, though our founder, Ellen Browning Scripps, is the same. We rank, for what the rankings are worth, 23rd to 28th among liberal arts colleges in the country, 3rd to 6th among women's colleges. Three of the Claremont Consortium, Pomona, Harvey Mudd, CMC, regularly turn up among the top five. But there are no Nobel laureates on our faculties. We are required to show evidence of engagement with our profession, which means publishing, and that's been ratcheted up through the years—but we're here primarily to teach.

I'd never given much thought to colleges like these, except to decide not to attend one, but after a few weeks, I got it: this works. The measurable outcomes of such colleges are demonstrable. Only 1–2%

of graduates come from small liberal arts colleges, fewer than 100,000 out of 18 million graduates, but disproportionate numbers go on to advanced degrees and doctorates, including in STEM fields. They account for 20% of all US presidents, 20% of Pulitzer Prize winners, and 20% of the scientists elected in recent years to the National Academy of Sciences. They account for disproportionate numbers of Peace Corps volunteers and about 1 in 12 of the nation's wealthiest CEOs, as documented by Susan McWilliams and John Seery in *The Best Kind of College*.[14] Such colleges produce "a hugely disproportionately large percentage of leaders," writes Victor Ferrall, former president of Beloit College, "at the forefront in every field: educators, scholars, jurists, statesmen, diplomats, politicians, scientists, business executives, artists, musicians, writers, journalists."[15]

Nor had I given much thought to a women's college. But after a few months here, I got that, too; women really do take more initiative when they're the main event. I like having guys from the other colleges in my classes, but a few too many or even one "type-A" may take over (I could tell tales). I arrived at Scripps with a dissertation on rhetoric in Shakespeare's Roman plays, but I soon realized that arcana was not what students needed, and designed feminist courses more in line with their interests and my own. Feminist criticism of Shakespeare was the subject of my first book; my next book was on twentieth-century women writers, and the next was on Doris Lessing, with a few anthologies of feminist criticism and theory along the way. Teaching here gave me a keen sense that women's voices need to be heard not only in the classroom but in the literary canon and the world at large, and women's colleges help make this happen.

And lately I've been struck by the range of social class, ethnic backgrounds, and skin tones in our classes. "Actually, the diversity of Scripps students' personalities really surprised me when I arrived at the school," an alum said, when I asked her what she'd got from this college. Contrary to the popular conception of small private colleges as only for rich white kids, they "enroll approximately the same proportion of minority students as do public universities (about one-third of the student body) and a slightly *higher* proportion of low-income students and first-generation students than public and private doctoral universities," writes Georgia Nugent, former president of Kenyon College, in a report for the Council of Independent Colleges: "African American students, Hispanic students, and low-income students . . . graduate from private four-year colleges both at higher rates and more quickly than they do from public universities."[16] In a way, small residential colleges may provide more experience of diversity than schools with tens of thousands, where it's easier for students to self-segregate.

As for the *immeasurable outcomes* of a college like this, the qualitative benefits, these require a longer discussion. They take a book—*this* book. Here I'll just say, "education" is not about producing human capital, consumer-producers to fuel the economy—but human beings. Our "product" is an educated human being. You'll get a fuller sense of what this means as you read on.

The Liberal Arts as Liberation

Forbes writer Brandon Busteed describes the liberal arts as a clunky, unsalable brand that ought to be junked in favor of "industry-recognized credentials."[17] And yet the liberal arts *work*. Unlike what's being put in their place, their *value added* is tried and true. *How* they work is a much longer story. But here I'll say a few words about what they are, since the term is widely misunderstood.

Liberal does not mean politically progressive, and *arts* does not mean fine arts—let's get that straight. *Liberal* is from the Latin *liberare*, "to liberate, set free." The liberal arts are skills a person needs to take part in the world, *practical* skills. Cicero referred to the arts as *quae libero sunt dignae*—that is, "worthy of a free man," skills that prepare him to take a part in civic life, to be a citizen, not a slave. Yes, I'm afraid he meant "man," and not all men, either; only the elite could aspire to anything like self-determination. But the Romans got this right: freedom requires education. It takes knowing enough about yourself and the world to make choices that work for you, to steer clear of agendas that would have you buy or buy into something that may not serve you well.

Freedom does not mean the license to do anything. Freedom confers benefits, but it entails responsibilities as well. Education for freedom "is also education for human community," writes historian William Cronan in a widely read essay, "Only Connect" (1998); it makes us "ever more aware of the connections we have with other people and the rest of creation."[18] We are a species that "craves connection—to other people, to meaning, to the natural world," says Johann Hari, author of *Lost Connections*. We need "to feel we belong, to feel we are secure, to feel we are valued, to feel we have a secure future we can understand,"[19] needs that are violated by the ideology we live by. *Neoliberalism*, for lack of a better word, pits us against one another in a pursuit of profit and power, dividing us not only from others but from parts of ourselves that crave sociality and the cooperation crucial to our survival. The liberal arts are "all about connections," writes Audrey Bilger, president of Reed College, connections "among individuals . . . across time in pursuit of answers to the most difficult questions, and across boundaries and perceived differences."[20]

We have seen, in the pandemic, a society perilously close to losing the ability to live as a society, as a crisis that should have drawn us together has driven us apart. "We need doctors right now," wrote Frank Bruni, June 2020, in the *New York Times*: "My God, we need doctors. . . . We need research scientists. . . . But we also need . . . Homer. We need writers, philosophers, historians. They'll be the ones to chart the social, cultural and political challenges of this pandemic—and of all the other dynamics that have pushed the United States so harrowingly close to the edge. In terms of restoring faith in the American project and reseeding common ground, they're beyond essential."[21]

Where better to reseed the common ground than at a college where students find community and a culture of engagement that presents an alternative to the war of all against all we've been persuaded is inevitable? I do in this book what I try to teach my students to do: turn the tools of critical thinking on our culture, unmask ideology, expose assumptions so taken for granted that they seem "natural" but are no more natural than the shape of a bound foot. When they see how differently people saw things in the past, they realize there's nothing inevitable about the way we are, and since things have changed, so may they change again.

Shakespeare has been claimed by every trend, school, "-ism" that ever was, but *humanism* is the "-ism" that best fits.[22] His characters care about each other, listen to each other, love, hate, destroy, and are destroyed by one another; they find meaning, hope, perdition in their connections to others. The characters we love are defined by relationship to others, whereas his villains pride themselves on self-sufficiency, imagining themselves "self-made," like the Ayn Randian hero admired by politicians, libertarians, entrepreneurs today.[23] There are few writers who demonstrate so powerfully that human beings are part of a "network of mutuality," in Martin Luther King Jr.'s words, that "whatever affects one directly affects all indirectly."[24] And the questions the plays raise—*what a piece of work is man*, what *are* we, what might we be, what kind of a life do we want, what world do we want—are by no means academic to young people just starting out in life.

TWO

Once upon a Time in the Twentieth Century

How the Humanities Took a Great Fall

> It is a common sentence that knowledge is power; but who hath duly considered . . . the power of ignorance? Knowledge slowly builds up what ignorance in an hour pulls down. Knowledge, through patient and frugal centuries, enlarges discovery and makes record of it; ignorance, wanting its day's dinner, lights a fire with the record, and gives a flavor to its one roast with the burned souls of many generations.
> —GEORGE ELIOT, *Daniel Deronda*

> Only faculty who have lived through the loss realize what has been lost.
> —JANE JACOBS, *Dark Age Ahead*

In my day—don't you love it when someone begins a sentence like that?—back in the day when I was growing up, life was easier. I guess that's a reversal of the usual generational lament—"in my day, we knew the value of a dollar," "in my day, we had to work for what we got." But I do think I had it easier than my students, by leaps and bounds.

To show you how we got to where we are, I'll take us back to mid-twentieth-century USA, show how things were then and how, in the decades since, things have changed. In 1964, the year I graduated from Berkeley, Barry Goldwater lost the presidency to Lyndon Johnson;

Johnson introduced the War on Poverty, signed the Civil Rights Act, stepped up the Vietnam War; Martin Luther King Jr. won the Nobel Peace Prize; and that fall, the Free Speech Movement rocked the Berkeley campus. I know, I can count—to the class of 2023, 1964 is as far back as *Downton Abbey* days would have been to me in 1964. What could a person from that long ago possibly teach me?

What a person from a bygone era can give is a perspective on your own time.

When you think how complex growing up is, all the things that can go wrong, you wonder how anyone ever pulls it off. I mean, growing up whole and human, not bent out of shape by fear or deprivation or warped to someone else's agenda. Different people need different things, of course, and in different measure, but I think there are some basics for "human development" (once thought to be the purpose of education):[1] shelter, support, something to aspire to. For, as a young plant sends our shoots and tendrils in search of something to grow toward—a trellis, the sun—so too does a human being need something to reach for and trust that it's worth the reach. Those were the necessities of my life, anyway, and *time*, that's a big one—time to make mistakes, to risk doing it wrong and figure out how to do it better. And luck. Nobody tells you how important luck is, maybe because there's no moral to be drawn from it.

What luck it was to have moved through time at the time I did. Best time to be a kid, a student, a professor—if you were white, straight, and middle class, that is. And more of us were middle class those days; the middle class was thriving. When I look at the world my students inhabit, the competition, distractions, the many ways of riding off the rails, I know I'd never have survived. Whether I'd have learned to "drill, kill, bubble fill" or found a way of zoning out, developed an addiction to social media, video games, or something deadlier, I do not know. But I do know that whatever spirit was in me, whatever spark of creativity or imagination that might do myself or the world some good, would have been snuffed out before it could ignite. Oh, some maimed version of me might have limped through, but not *me*, the person I became, the person I'm glad to have become— *I* would never have been allowed. I'd have been a casualty of these times.

I suppose the world would have survived that loss, but *I* would not.

Easier in My Day, though Not Exactly a Walk in the Park

I landed in the sweet spot of history. The first half of the twentieth century was a bloody butchery, and the last decades, ushered in by Reagan-Thatcher, issued into another kind of war, a war of all against all. But the middle, that's where you wanted to be. Postwar prosperity made a wave, possibilities that lifted not all boats, but many. The country had come through a depression and a world war by pulling together, which made a feeling for the common good. I sailed through school before test-and-assess made kids hate learning, when the idea of committing suicide over a C was about as thinkable as pigs with wings. Many more things are possible when you're riding a wave than when the wave has crashed and you're scrambling for footing and breath.

Mid-century USA was the great age of public education. The GI Bill of 1944, which funded four years of higher education for any veteran who'd been drafted or volunteered before the age of 25, sent millions of vets back to school. The landmark 1947 Truman Commission Report, *Higher Education for American Democracy*, defined education as the cornerstone of democracy and called for the founding of community colleges and increased student aid. "America's golden age," as author of *The One Percent Solution* Gordon Lafer describes the decades following the war, was a time of broadly shared prosperity when "the economy grew, most people benefited . . . every segment of the population gained ground, but income growth was actually faster for the poorest households than for the richest."[2] It was no golden age if you were Black, Asian, gay, or a divorcée in the suburbs, like my mother. But income equality was at an all-time high, and it was generally assumed that the next generation would be better off than their parents.

The country was investing in education, health, and a social safety net that gave a larger majority a shot at climbing out. Chris Hedges, a social commentator not given to sentimentality, describes the America he grew up in as a country that

> paid its workers wages envied around the world. It made sure those workers, thanks to labor unions and champions of the working class in the Democratic Party and the press, had health benefits and pensions. It offered good, public education. It honored basic democratic values and held in regard the rule of law, including international law, and respect for human rights. It had social programs, from Head Start to welfare to Social Security. . . . It had a system of government that, however flawed, worked to protect the interests of most of its citizens. It offered the possibility of democratic change. It had a press that was diverse and independent and gave a voice to all segments of society.[3]

This was the country I grew up in. It was a country that paid high school teachers more than it paid most National Football League players ($8,000) and nearly as much as it paid engineers ($10,000).[4]

My parents had not had it so easy. By the time I was born, they'd lived through two world wars and the Depression. My father was in the war in the Pacific, away for two and a half of my first three years. He was on the healing, not the killing side of war, so he did not come home a shattered wreck, but his absence made a breach in our family. "Instability" doesn't begin to describe the late-night scenes, the shouting and stormings out. By the time they split up for good and Mother and I moved to Los Altos, a sleepy, semi-suburban town south of Palo Alto, I'd gone to six schools in six grades.

Los Altos was not, those days, the high-end boutique community it is today. In 1953, the Santa Clara Valley still had vestiges of the vast orchards that earned it the name "the Valley of Heart's Delight"; there were small farms, strawberry fields, and canneries that filled the air with the fragrance of fruit. The ranch-style house my father bought for $14,000 was on a block fresh cut from an orchard; that's about $147,000 in today's dollars, except you'd need three and a half million to buy that house today. Our block was on the wrong side of the tracks—there were still railroad tracks those days, soon to be torn up for an expressway—but we were solidly middle class. Next door lived a furniture salesman who sent his kid through Stanford and retired comfortably. At the end of the street lived the owner of Sam's Shoe Repair in Mountain View, where Google is headquartered now. In 1964, a CEO made about 25 times what a worker made; today, 361 times.[5] Not that I'd ever heard of a CEO—that word wasn't part of every kid's working vocabulary and the life goal of many. Billionaires were not heroes—did we even have billionaires? A graduated tax rate, as high as 90% at the top, put a brake on rapaciousness.

The greatest blessing of my youth was growing up without a TV. By the time we got our first TV, I was 12, and nothing on that little black-and-white staticky box could compete with the worlds I'd traveled in novels, 20,000 leagues under the sea, to the center of the earth. Today the media are where kids get their stories and aspirations, where they're bombarded by advertising that teaches them a "good life" is filled with goods, that they should buy more and want more, not useful messages at a time when wages are falling and the planet is being consumed by an orgy of wasteful consumption. And since anxious people buy more, it keeps us anxious and insecure, promising to feed the longings it creates by the purchase of things. Advertising today is, as Talbot Brewer describes it, "the largest and best-funded program of proselytism ever mastered in the history of humankind," with global spending totaling "about $650 billion in 2003, making it the world's second biggest industry (after weapons)."[6] It is a misery-making, mind-bending machine that traps us even as it creates the illusion of providing "choice." And the more persuasive and pervasive it becomes, the dumber we become, less able to distinguish infotainment from information, reality from make-believe.

The 1950s may have given us terms like "status seekers," "conspicuous consumption," "keeping up with the Joneses," but it was amateur night compared to the consumerism and craze for status fueled by advertising today. Sure, Los Altos had a country club, and there were people in the hills who had splendid homes with pools and stables, but they sent their kids to the same public schools I went to. Money and status weren't in our face the way they are today. Years later, I was shocked when a student described how her school chums made fun of a girl whose clothes came from K-Mart (ours came from the Salvation Army). I assumed the class would want to discuss this, but nobody was shocked but me. That was a while ago; nothing shocks me now. My students are so conversant with brand names that they use them as descriptors: "she was a Hermès chick with a J. C. Crew kind of guy."

Nor was race in our face, Los Altos was so white. So white that it might lead one to suspect, though only later did I suspect . . . and sure enough, a friend who grew up a mile and a half from us found a deed to a property her parents bought in the late 1940s specifying that the land could not be occupied "by any persons of African, Japanese, Chinese, Mongolian, or Malay descent."[7] If this was the same apricot orchard our development was cut from, the same developer, then my father, who was Jewish, would have had to sign a "restrictive covenant." A friend who's kept better track of her high school yearbooks than I have, wrote to me, when I asked her to look, that in our class of 430, there were two Black girls, one Hispanic, one Filipino, and five Japanese, one of whom was a track star.

So, yes, it was a sheltered cove, but for someone from a family as volatile as mine, shelter was no bad thing. There were no drug problems, of course—no drugs. But if I ever get nostalgic about those years, I remind myself of the whispers about witch hunts, blacklists, "visits from the FBI," which my aunt was said to have had. I remember "duck and cover" drills, where we crawled under school desks to brace for a nuclear blast. I recall the snubs and slights my mother endured because she had no husband, the friends she had who were closet gays, who led short, unhappy lives. Even women with live-in husbands couldn't face their lives sober, such was the blight of what Betty Friedan would call the "feminine mystique." Mother's drug of choice was her piano, a great giant grand that filled our small house with the rich, mournful chords of Brahms, Chopin, Schuman. I'd slam my door against that sound, so sad and full of longing. But later, I thanked her for that gift, not only the music but for teaching me, art could save a life.

So, no, not exactly a walk in the park.

The Golden Age of Public Education

I owe my life to public education. My father did, and I, through him, since the most reliable predictor of success in college is the educational level of one's parents. Education was my father's way out of the Lower East Side. He was the first of his family to be born in the new land, a family that fled the pogroms of Ukraine to a country that generously opened its doors and educational system to the castoffs of the world. He was one of many Jews who flocked to City College in the 1930s, the first free public college in the country; he did the rest on scholarship—the University of Chicago, Yale School of Medicine, at a time Yale had a quota for Jews

I fastened onto school like a barnacle on a rock, as kids from unstable families often do. It chills me to think how it would have felt, to come back from summer and find my school shut down, teachers and school chums scattered to the winds, as has happened to tens of thousands today. "Disruption," the dream of "creative destroyers," is a nightmare to a kid from a disrupted home.

My favorite courses were the ones most public high schools have had to eliminate to make room for tests—art, debate, theater, physical education. Band, orchestra, dance were there for the taking, though I didn't take them. In Home-Ec, we had our own little kitchenettes—imagine, a middle-class school, and all this. Mother's dislike of domesticity made me sure I'd hate it—she was certainly not priming me to be a wife—but it was thrilling to see a cake or a dress emerge from ingredients I'd thrown together; it was the kind of tactile, hands-on experience every kid should have. (My friend Rachel, who teaches math in a community college, tells me her students are lost when she tries to illustrate by example—"say you have two-thirds of a cup of sugar, what would half that be? Kids used to get it, but no more—everyone eats takeout, and Home-Ec's long gone.")

The basketball court and the soccer field got my competitive juices flowing, which was interesting to learn, since I hadn't thought of myself as particularly competitive or athletic. I'd entertained fantasies of being an artist, but sitting next to Jerry Bowden in sophomore art class, I looked over at his drawings, so full of life, and thought, Uh-oh, better stick with words. I had fantasies of being an actress, but, cast in a school play, I got up on stage and froze. Those sorting-out moments were important, steps toward figuring out what I could and could not do. Another such moment stands out, much later, at Columbia, when a friend looked at a paper I'd written and snorted, "Yuck,

all those *ibid.*s and *op. cit.*s—I could never do footnotes like *that*!"—
and I realized I'd actually sort of *enjoyed* doing those footnotes, and
maybe I had a touch of the scholar after all.

They say education is what's left after everything you've learned
has been forgotten. I retain so few factoids from four years at Los Altos High School, I'm embarrassed to say. But what my teachers left
me with was a sense of the world of knowledge as something that mattered, maybe not to me right then and there, but to somebody some-
time, even if I was a girl. Our teachers were allowed to teach as they
best knew how, and that was pretty good, some better than others,
but all were engaged, none of them mean. Only one course made me
feel really stupid. Chemistry. Nothing that teacher ever said explained
why some things sizzled and popped or why anyone should care.

Whenever I encounter a kid in Shakespeare who looks lost, I remember how baffled I felt in Chemistry, and later, at Berkeley, in
Physics 10—what if you felt like that in all your classes, that dull, ach-
ing incomprehension so complete you don't even know how to formulate the question that might pull you out of the fog. What if you
felt that way and your life depended on your test scores, parents breathing down your neck, teachers' jobs on the line? Could I have knuck-
led down for test prep in subjects I had no interest in? I doubt it. Luckily
I didn't have to find out—I think I took two standardized tests before my senior year, when I took the SAT. But reading and writing, I
could do forever; it never felt like work, it was pleasure, and I was
allowed to go with it.

My education was an amble, not a scramble, and not just because
I was a girl—the guys weren't racing either, though a lot of us were
college-bound (80% I heard it said). My sophomore year, 1957, the So-
viets launched Sputnik, which ratcheted up the pressure to teach science and engineering, but word didn't reach Los Altos until after I'd
graduated. Summers were long, you could barely see one end to the

other, and they were *ours*—no summer school, no summer "enrich-ment" activities or tutors, no extracurriculars to pad out a CV, no CVs. It takes time to figure out what you want to do, what you're capable of doing, and kids today don't get time. They arrive in college with goals and purposes fully formed, titles to put on e-mails, and an al-phabet soup of disorders. ADHD, ADD, PTSD must have existed back then, but they weren't household words. We had recesses and after-school sports, we could play in the streets, have fruit fights in the orchards, ride bikes and horses, and there were still wild places in the hills, abandoned railway trestles, dilapidated barns, fields and meadows where the grass grew tall and we could roam, free range, and our imaginations had room to wander, too.

A Gateway Drug

Left to my own devices, I read. I read weekends and after school, on school breaks, on school buses, in the back of the car, at the dentist's, the doctor's, at the dinner table, pausing only to turn the page. After the Nancy Drew series, the Hardy Boys, the Bobbsey Twins, I read every dog and horse novel I could find. Then I moved on to Jules Verne and Victor Hugo, and from there, to well-thumbed paperbacks that got passed around, *Peyton Place, Forever Amber, Marjorie Morn-ingstar, The High and the Mighty, From Here to Eternity, Atlas Shrugged* (that, too). The bigger the book, the heavier the hit. Schlocky as it was, all that reading transformed a pretty good student into a much better student, gave me a facility with language that made me easy with other subjects. Fiction, says Neil Gaiman, is "the gateway drug" to other kinds of reading; pleasure reading is the gateway to college success.[8] I see this all the time: I get a student who writes well and it turns out she reads a lot and she's doing well in her other courses.

If there'd been a pulsing color screen at the center of our house, the focal point of attention and my default babysitter, if there'd been video games and movies for streaming, I'm sure I'd have found easier escapes, escape artist that I was. If there'd been a Tiger Mom or tiger teachers on my tail, that might have nixed it, too. But Mother wasn't worried about my addiction to novels, and teachers didn't need my test scores to keep their jobs. Reading was just . . . reading. The great escape.

It was novels that I loved, not the kind of thing we read in history, informational texts about the Dred Scott decision, the New Deal, the Federal Reserve. They were slim little volumes, but deadly, with tall, double-columned pages. I'd force my eyes down the first column, then back up to the top to begin again, fixing each factoid in my mind. Those abstract, fact-clogged accounts of slavery, the Depression, the Dust Bowl, left me sleepy and uncaring, remembering nothing after the test. But give me *Uncle Tom's Cabin, Gone with the Wind, The Caine Mutiny, The Day Lincoln Was Shot, The Wall*, and I'd whip right through. There was history in those novels—slavery, Sherman's march to the sea, the Napoleonic wars, the French Revolution, the Holocaust—but it went down easy, along with the rest that fiction delivers, psychology, ethics, politics, philosophy, the whole human drama. And it wasn't a big leap from these to *Crime and Punishment, The Brothers Karamazov, Anna Karenina, The Red and the Black, A Tale of Two Cities*.

There was a lot of talk in my family about "the common man," the struggle for a living wage, but I didn't get what the talk was about until I read *The Grapes of Wrath, Les Misérables, The Dollmaker*, novels that made me *feel* the poverty. I used to feel guilty about needing a story to care, but now I think most people are like me, likelier to be moved by *Oliver Twist* than facts and figures about childhood poverty in nineteenth-century London. One death is a tragedy, one million is a statistic, as it's said. Novels are how we get to know one another, feel what it's like to walk in someone else's shoes. Stories can change lives; statistics rarely do.

Here's something I was allowed to do that no kid would be allowed to do today. A teacher in junior high (what's called middle school today) let me do a book report on a 1955 best seller, *The Day Lincoln Was Shot*. I wrote, as I recall, 40 pages. There's no way a teacher would allow that today, not with a standardized test looming up and her job riding on our scores. That led me to an interest in the Booth brothers, Edwin, the elder, the foremost Shakespearean actor of nineteenth-century America, and the younger, John Wilkes Booth, who found a way of upstaging his more talented brother by assassinating Lincoln. A 1955 film, *Prince of Players*, fueled my fascination: Richard Burton played Edwin Booth, who was playing Richard III—*Now is the winter of our discontent / Made glorious summer by this sun of York*. That may have been the first time I heard Shakespeare, really *heard* the words, spoken by a first-rate actor. I think this is what David Brooks means by an "annunciation moment," when "beauty strikes," when "something sparks an interest or casts a spell" and "a new passion is silently conceived."[9] And in another film of that vintage, Laurence Olivier as Richard III was sexier than he had any right to be, and his 1948 *Hamlet* and a 1953 film of *Julius Caesar* with James Mason and Marlon Brando set my heart pounding, too. The erotics of learning; it has to turn you on.

Deep and mysterious, the currents that feed an imagination, determine a life choice. What a mishmash of images and ideas I had floating around in my head, gleaned from novels and the big screen. But it was *mine*, not some pre-fab module clamped down from on high, telling me exactly what and when I had to learn, the way kids get cookie-cuttered today, no time for wandering, wondering, curiosity, surprise.

Today, the Common Core State Standards emphasize informational texts to the near exclusion of imaginative literature; only the analytical is deemed "useful." Teachers have to cut out novels and poems that might actually engage students' imagination and curiosity, to make room for readings like "FedViews," by the Federal Reserve Bank of San Francisco (2009), and "Executive Order 13423: Strengthening Federal Environmental, Energy, and Transportation Management," by the General Services Administration—these are suggested nonfiction selections for high school juniors and seniors, reports Lindsey Layton in the *Washington Post*.[10] I'd never have survived.

I went to the University of Chicago, barely 17, because I wanted to get away from home. Also because it was the school my father loved most—but I wasn't telling anyone that. When asked, at freshman orientation, why I'd come to Chicago, I said it was because I wanted to go east to college, which occasioned some amusement. I doubt you'd find a kid that clueless today, though you probably also wouldn't find many who'd read their way through the Russians. A year later, in 1961, I transferred to Berkeley, on account of a guy I met—but I wasn't telling anyone *that*, either. By September, we'd broken up, and I found myself back in California, too close to home for comfort, 50 miles from where I'd grown up. But as luck would have it, I landed in a sweet spot. Berkeley was where the great professors were, not pricey Chicago or Ivy League Columbia, but the huge state university in my own backyard.

I did not know it then, but the year before I got there, California put in place a Master Plan for Higher Education. And I was part of it.

The Master Plan: University of California

The Master Plan laid out a system of two-year and four-year colleges—the university, the state universities and colleges, the community colleges—making it possible for anyone willing to work for it to get a tuition-free, first-rate education. It was a grand plan, the first of its kind in history, allowing a person to get a BA from one of the finest universities in the country. What I paid, or my father paid, totaled maybe $1,000 for five years and two degrees. Now, for residents, tuition is over $14,000 a year, and for nonresidents, almost $44,000.

It is mind-boggling to think how recent this all was, this commitment from the state to provide free education to anyone anywhere in California. California's higher education enrollment tripled from 26,400 to 79,500 in the five years after World War II, reports Christopher Newfield in *Unmaking the Public University*. Most of the funding came from "taxpayers whose kids would be the first or second generation in the family to go to college." The university was bringing together children of blue- and white-collar workers who, though predominantly white, would make a massive middle class that enjoyed "the most egalitarian access to prosperity in recorded history." The plan did not entirely achieve its ideal of educational access and equality, but it came, as Newfield says, within a country mile.[11]

And it was an education that gave the liberal arts pride of place. The golden age of American higher education was the heyday of the humanities. "It was," says Wendy Brown, "a time in which a broad . . . education . . . inclusive of the arts, letters, and sciences—became an essential element of middle-class membership. More than an instrument of economic advancement, higher education in the liberal arts was the door through which descendants of workers, immigrants, and slaves entered on to the main stage. . . . A basic familiarity with Western history, thought, literature, art, social analysis, and science was integral."[12] Whether you call it a "rich humanism," as Brown describes it, or an "egalitarian humanism," as Newfield terms it, or "liberal humanism," as Jeffrey Williams calls it, it was *humanistic* in that it aimed for human development and "cultivated the humanities as the base of higher education, prompted wide cultural knowledge and understanding, and placed primary value on the flourishing of human lives."[13]

This was, says Brown, "nothing short of a radical democratic event"; "for the first time in human history, higher educational policy and practice were oriented toward the many, tacitly destining them for intelligent engagement with the world rather than economic servitude or mere survival."[14] By 1956, about 8.8 million vets had used the education benefits of the GI Bill.[15] The returning GIs, mainly first-generation students and farm boys, were expected to go for vocational or technical training, but they took more humanities and social science courses than nonveterans, reports Paul Tough; and they ran away with the honors.[16] Many GIs experienced "breathtaking transformations in their life circumstances," a coal miner's son becoming a geologist, a cobbler's son becoming an engineer.[17]

Education those days was a public trust. State and federal governments willingly supported it, trusting that the investment would pay off long-term in an educated citizenry who'd live better lives and make a more prosperous society for all. The state was accountable to the public to provide education, and the public, made wealthier and healthier because better educated, gave back to education, supporting it as an investment in the common good. Governor Pat Brown made expanding the University of California system a top priority, articulating his goal (in 1963) of a good society "for all": "We are here to prove that a civilization that can create a machine to fulfill a job can create a job to fulfill a man."[18] There was no contradiction between the enrichment of individual lives and the national interest. I never had to apologize for studying Shakespeare.

Did the trust pay off? Big time, judging from the longtime prosperity and power of this nation. GI benefits "issued a return of 7:1 for every dollar invested."[19] Direct payback came in the form of new knowledge, inventions, and discoveries. The University of California played a major part in making the Golden State golden: if California were a country, it would have the fifth-largest economy in the world.[20] Check out the websites of the Universities of Wisconsin, Michigan, Minnesota, Texas, and other flagship universities for similarly impressive contributions. The trust paid dividends in making a system of higher education that's led the world in the production of new knowledge.

To be honest, I didn't love Berkeley. I was painfully shy, and in those coliseum-size lecture halls, I got to know no one. The first (and last) time I tried to approach a professor, he scurried away like I'd pulled a gun. But they were the best, Henry Nash Smith, Mark Schorer, Norman Rabkin, Charles Muscatine, Stanley Fish; they were on fire. English was a vast, eclectic department that offered as many approaches to literature as there were profs. Historical approaches were alive and well, and so was "New Criticism" (as close reading was called); no one way of reading was promoted to the exclusion of others. I learned from those professors the same variety of approaches I now teach, to go at a literary text with whatever tool works.

There was a brief moment when I did feel I might want to be part of it, and it took me by surprise. On a bright spring morning, March 23, 1962, Memorial Stadium was packed full, 88,000. Governor Pat Brown was there, along with President Clark Kerr, and the faculty turned out in full regalia, a sea of royal blue robes. "Your faculty includes more Nobel laureates than any other faculty in the world," intoned John F. Kennedy: "This college from its earliest beginnings has recognized and its graduates have recognized that the purpose of education is not merely to advance the economic self-interest of its graduates. The people of California, as much if not more than the people of any other state, have supported their colleges and universities and their schools because they recognize how important it is to the maintenance of a free society that its citizens be well educated." Imagine, a public willing to support higher education to create a better society for all. Something else he said: "I sometimes think that we are too much impressed by the clamor of daily events. The newspaper headlines and the television screens give us a short view. They so flood us with the stop-press details of daily stories that we lose sight of one of the great movements in history. . . . Wisdom requires the long view."[21] Imagine, a politician talking about wisdom, the long view.

I think it was this event that made me want to be part of it all, though what *it* was, I couldn't have said. All that achievement, that sea of silky blue. Funny, because once I got a PhD, I never did get a robe, only ever borrowed someone else's for occasions, so it was never about the regalia. Do kids today get inspired—"incentivized"—by promises of jobs (pronounced "jawbs"), by the idea of advancing US corporations to global domination?

I should add that the UC system remains to this day one of "most effective drivers of upward economic mobility," as Miriam Pawel reported in the *New York Times*, 2019, with more than 40% of its undergraduates the first in their families to attend college: "More than half come from families with annual incomes of less than $80,000 and pay no tuition. Berkeley . . . educates the lower-income students at almost twice the rate of Ivy League schools—and Pell grant recipients graduate at roughly the same high rates as their wealthier classmates."[22] In 2021, Berkeley was ranked number one by the Forbes ratings—"The First Time a Public School Is Number One"—which I confess, gave me a bit of a thrill.[23] The rating system "gave extra credit to schools that educate the greatest number of students from the broadest range of backgrounds," and found that graduates "earn enough to pay back their college costs in 1.45 years on average"; grads from low-income backgrounds pay back college costs in 0.7 years.[24] This bumped Stanford, for all its wealth, down to fourth place.[25] The engine of social mobility is purring away, at my alma mater, anyway.[26] Go bears.

"The Real World": Open Admissions, CUNY

But I was tired of school. School was all I'd ever done, and in 1967, I was packing my car and heading east, really east this time, to "the city," the *real* city, setting out in search of "the real world." New York was where it had last been sighted.

The job I found was in publishing, but the look and feel of it, the office hierarchy, the dress, the locale, were right out of *Mad Men*. I'd sashay down Park Avenue, high heels smartly clicking, feeling ever so grown up, spending lunch hours and my salary in the midtown department stories. Luckily I got fired from that job; six months later, the project folded—there was incompetence and mismanagement in that office that wouldn't survive five minutes in academia. If this is "the business model" higher education is aspiring to, we are so lost.

I learned a lot from that job, mainly about what I was not. I learned what a huge chunk 40 hours takes out of a week, how you don't squeeze much else in on the side. I realized I was going to have to find something to do with my life that was not about generating profits, my own or anyone else's. The "real world" catapulted me straight back to grad school. Columbia had some pretty arcane requirements those days, Anglo-Saxon, History of the English Language, three languages, one ancient—but after that MadAve experience, bring 'em on!

Around that time, the late sixties, the City University of New York opened its doors to all high school graduates. CUNY needed adjuncts and I needed a job. My first day teaching, at Queens College, the secretary ordered me out of the mailroom—"students are not allowed in the mailroom." I was 23.

Nothing in my years as a student or in the work world prepared me for the challenges of teaching. Not that the kids were tough or ill-behaved, they were not—they did the reading, did not miss class—but that I was so ludicrously unprepared. They were from every background and ethnicity, young and old, and many were learning English as a second language. I remember a sea of smiling, expectant faces looking at me like I held the key to the American dream. Some would arrive at my 8 a.m. classes from night shifts, others went off from my evening classes to night shifts, working their way through college, weary but hopeful that a degree might make a difference.

I have never felt so terrified, so ill equipped. Remedial English was the "revolving door" of the Open Admissions program; three strikes and they were out, and they knew it. And I, as an adjunct, was part of CUNY's "floating bottom," kept moving every few years so we didn't make claims on tenure. Floating, revolving, all of us hanging on for dear life. Mondays and Wednesdays, uptown for Anglo-Saxon and a seventeenth-century doctoral seminar; Tuesdays and Thursdays, two subways and a bus to Flushing, and later, the A train to Flatbush. After several years at Queens, I was let go by Queens and hired by Brooklyn College, where I had two classes of remedial English back to back, 8 to 10 and 10 to 12, Tuesdays and Thursdays. I trapezed through those classes high on Chock full o'Nuts coffee, which is what there was before Starbucks, in a smoke-filled haze—those days, we smoked in class. The most intense feeling I remember from those classes was, would I make it to the break to pee.

But it was exhilarating, the presence of real live human beings staring back with looks of appreciation, bewilderment, amusement, disbelief—it focuses the mind marvelously, as Dr. Johnson said of hanging. I knew nothing about teaching but what I'd observed in my professors; Columbia was training us to be scholars, not teachers. But I, who had never opened my mouth in a class, opened it and found, to my surprise,

I had something to say. It came pouring forth—literature had saved me, it could save others, and though the particulars of the process were a bit vague, I took to teaching as to a vocation.

"This class was always a lotta laughs." Of all the student evaluations from those years, that is the one I prize most—it was an 8 a.m. class, and I am not a morning person. That was my first and strongest instinct about teaching, better get some morale going, an instinct I stand by to this day. I was winging it, making it up as I went along, learning by doing it wrong and then figuring out how to do it better—which is the way most people learn, I think. What those kids got from my classes, I'll never know, apart from a few e-mails that have dribbled in, one that reached me recently saying I was a California ray of sunshine that taught her school didn't have to be boring; and Kevin, who I ran into on a subway platform, years later, who told me *King Lear* had changed his life. I thought he'd hated the class, he'd sat in the back, chair tilted against the wall, face set in a scowl, yet he was teaching high school on account of *Lear* (not a reading I'd assign a freshman class today).

But what they gave me was an inkling that my years in school, my love of literature, might add up to something somebody might use, might even translate to a living wage. This is where I found "the real world," in those classes, face to face with human beings who needed something I had to give. I wasn't the stablest of creatures, but in front of a class, I knew who I was. They were marvelous, those teaching jobs, as a way of working my way through graduate school; they reminded me why I was suffering the long slog to the PhD. CUNY had a strong union, the pay was good, my apartment was rent-controlled, I didn't need a car. I lived well, hitting my father up only for tuition and dental bills. How anyone could survive in Manhattan on an adjunct's salary today, I have no idea.

Those days, when you were an adjunct you had the sense you were just passing through on your way to the full-time job you'd get when you finished your PhD. (Less than a quarter of the faculty were part-timers; today, three-quarters are.)[27] But the job market crashed just as I finished my degree, and it looked like I might be an adjunct forever. Those were grim months, the summer of 1974, spent frantically writing job letters and subwaying around five boroughs, interviewing for part-time positions I did not want; I'd been fine teaching beginning courses when I was a graduate student, but I wasn't, once I got my degree. I doubted I'd have been able to keep the morale going for long; no, I don't think my classes would have been "a lotta laughs" for long. Today, "subway schleppers" and "freeway flyers" teach five or more classes a semester, no security or benefits, a quarter of them requiring some form of government assistance. And many do manage, amazingly, to keep up the morale.

The Open Admissions program was, like UC's Master Plan, a grand and idealistic plan to make education available to all. There were grumblings about "declining standards" from some of the senior faculty, but there was also enormous will to make it work—and it did work, for many. According to a 1996 survey of students who entered the City University under the open-admissions policy, more than half received bachelor's degrees, sometimes more than a decade later, and went on to better-paying jobs.[28] David Lavin and David Hyllegard, authors of *Changing the Odds: Open Admissions and the Life Chances of the Disadvantaged*, conclude that the ambitious effort to promote educational opportunity paid off.[29] A 2007 study of minority women who'd received degrees from that program found that not only had they secured "more stable and better-paying jobs" than women who had not finished the program but tended to read more books, volunteer in community organizations, talk to their kids more and be more involved in their lives, all of which "influenced children's success in school and their likelihood of staying out of trouble."[30]

The engine of social mobility was humming along, the engine that propelled my father out of the Lower East Side, that gave me my real start in life. And still is, in spite of extreme cuts in funding. A "Mobility Report Card" issued in 2017 put City College near the top of the list. As David Leonhardt reported, "At City College, 76% of students who enrolled in the late 1990s and came from families in the bottom fifth of the income distribution have ended up in the top three-fifths of the distribution. These students entered college poor. They left on their way to the middle class and often the upper middle class. The new data shows . . . that the City University of New York system propelled almost six times as many low-income students into the middle class and beyond as all eight Ivy League campuses, plus Duke, M.I.T., Stanford and Chicago, combined."[31]

Backlash

That was the problem, you see: education was working too well. It was producing, as Newfield says, "wave after wave of well educated and potentially independent, intellectually active people who seemed to have lost their reflexive respect for authority," turning out, by 1980, "nearly a million graduates a year." By the late 1960s, corporate America was losing its hold. Public education had created "a restive middle class" that was laying "greater claim to the country's future."[32] It had to be stopped.

Look what happens when you educate people: they get uppity. They begin to assume they're entitled to a living wage, job protections, benefits. They start asking for government programs to improve their own and others' quality of life, "entitlements," to promote a fairer distribution of wealth. They join labor unions and protest the wrongs done to others and make social justice movements: the civil rights movement, the antiwar movement, the women's movement, the environmental movement. Higher education was creating a climate that was threatening, in its demands for regulations and a social infrastructure, to cut into corporate profits. The humanities, birthplace of gender studies and ethnic studies, have always been the most troublesome.

"The American economy is under broad attack," warned Lewis Powell, corporate lawyer and champion of the tobacco companies. Powell's memo, "Attack on the American Free Enterprise System," which he circulated to the US Chamber of Commerce in 1971, shortly before he accepted Nixon's nomination to the Supreme Court, was a clarion call to corporate America to rein in dissenting forces. It warned, "The overriding first need is for businessmen to recognize that the ultimate issue may be survival—survival of what we call the free enterprise system."[33] The memo galvanized Charles and David Koch and other wealthy conservatives to begin leveraging their fortunes to protect their interests. It "laid out a blueprint for a conservative takeover," writes Jane Mayer, in *Dark Money: The Hidden History of the Billionaires behind the Rise of the Radical Right*, "a brilliant battle plan detailing how conservative business interests could reclaim American politics."[34] Foremost among the enemies of free enterprise were the colleges and universities, dangerous not only because they were full of ferment, but because they were creating a powerful middle class that threatened conservative rule. To change the way people think, the right wing had to create opinion makers of its own.

This is where the think tanks came into play: the American Enterprise Institute, the Institute for Humane Studies, the Mercatus Center, the Heritage Foundation, the Cato Institute, Citizens for a Sound Economy (which became Americans for Prosperity). The Koch brothers, libertarians whose empire is based on fossil fuels, have been the major source of funding, if not the founders, of these and other think tanks which have been cranking out privatizing propaganda, "white papers," op-ed pieces, policy papers purporting to be scholarship, to counter the expertise of academics. Charles, an engineer with three MIT degrees, set about the organizational feat of changing political opinion as though it were an engineering problem, calling his project "The Structure of Social Change." The Kochs and a cadre of billionaires created a largely invisible network of corporate lobbyists, including the US Chamber of Commerce, the National Association of Manufacturers, the National Federation of Independent Business, the Business Roundtable, and the powerful corporate lobbying group, the American Legislative Exchange Council (ALEC), which coordinates lobbying groups, buys elections and legislators, and writes legislation aimed at smashing unions, cutting taxes for the wealthy, shrinking public services, and privatizing public resources, including education. About a quarter of state legislators belong to ALEC; all the major corporate powers belong or have belonged, including Amazon, Facebook, Microsoft, Walmart, Home Depot, Coca Cola, HP, Exxon, Chevron.[35]

"By creating their own private idea factory," business interests "found a way to dominate American politics outside the parties," Mayer documents. Reagan gave them a figurehead, but he was barely necessary: by the early 1980s, their propaganda had been so successful that "Americans' distrust of government for the first time surpassed their distrust of business."[36] Their behind-the-scenes maneuvering brought free market fundamentalism from the fanatical fringe, where it was when Barry Goldwater lost his bid for the presidency in 1964, to the center of power, and turned large portions of the public against government and all forms of public interest. Invisible opinion makers have been barraging us with propaganda for decades: government is bad, unions are bad, so are regulations, a minimum wage, taxing the wealthy, all bad; free market is good, private is good, and climate change is a myth. They've pumped up a politics of resentment, inciting rage at minorities and "others" claimed to be receiving unearned "entitlements," and at "elites," by which they mean "experts" and academics who contradict them. They've been jamming our circuits for more than half a century, waging war on education.

Reagan launched his political career by running not only against Governor Pat Brown but against the students and faculty of UC Berkeley. In May 1966, he railed, on television, against "a small minority of beatniks, radicals and filthy speech advocates." He vowed to "clean up that mess in Berkeley," warning of "sexual orgies so vile that I cannot describe them to you," complaining that "outside agitators were bringing left-wing subversion into the university."[37] He cut state funding and argued that if students paid their own way, "they'd value their education too much to protest."[38]

The Reagan years began a hollowing out of the public services and protections that the New Deal had painstakingly put in place. "Government is not the solution to our problems; government is the problem," said Reagan in his first inaugural address, January 1981, and he set about deregulating industries, breaking unions, cutting taxes for the rich. "There is no such thing as society," echoed his UK counterpart, Margaret Thatcher, who'd been busily slashing Britain's social infrastructure; there are only "individual men and women, and . . . families."[39] In Reagan's first administration, between 1981 and 1986, "economic inequality increased at an intensified rate."[40] Wealth and power concentrated into the hands of a very few, creating the plutocracy we have now.

Today the tentacles of the Kochtopus are everywhere. "Dark money," money of nondisclosed origins, floods foundations, think tanks, advocacy groups, and so-called nonprofit charitable organizations. The Kochtopus has made inroads in to academia, funding programs and institutes that train free-market lawyers and judges to step into powerful positions. It backs advocacy groups disguised to look grassroots, like those that brought us the Tea Party. It has waged what Paul Krugman calls "a war on the very concept of community," on the idea that society owes the most basic protections to its members.[41] We did not elect these billionaires, we barely know their names, but they are our invisible legislators, buying elections, writing legislation, stacking school boards, setting educational policy, pushing charters and vouchers. "Dark money" is unaccountable money. Schoolteachers and professors are under the gun to demonstrate "accountability," while those with real power are accountable to no one. None can call their power to account, to paraphrase the mad Lady Macbeth.

A 2018 Pew Research Center Survey found that 61% of Americans believe higher education is going in the wrong direction, 73% of Republicans and Republicans leaners, 52% of Democrats and Democratic leaners. It found that 57% of people between 18 and 34 felt college wasn't worth the cost, up 17% in four years.[42] Educators have watched public opinion turn against us, asking ourselves, with much hand-wringing, What have we done? Where did we go wrong?—unaware that there's been this powerful propaganda machine gnawing steadily away.

Trust Busting: Eviscerating the University

It's astonishing how quickly the tear-down was accomplished, how little resistance there was. In 1965, the year after I graduated, the University of California opened new campuses at Santa Cruz and Irvine, both on spectacular sites by the Pacific; in more than half a century since, it has opened only one new campus, though enrollments have increased and the state's population has nearly quadrupled. In 1971, Berkeley got 70% of its funding from the state. Today, state support has been estimated as low as 9–10%; "at the once-proud U.C. Berkeley, class sizes are ridiculous and desks are broken," reports a student.[43] Wastebaskets don't get emptied and faculty salaries are frozen. (The Forbes rankings seem not to have looked at details like this.) If the present trend continues, state funding will drop to zero by 2057, according to a study published by the Pell Institute for the Study of Opportunity in Higher Education.[44]

No longer a public trust, higher education has been turned into a commodity available to those who can afford its ever-pricier price. Colleges and universities raise tuition to make up for state defunding, then get excoriated for being "a broken fiscal model." No longer is there bipartisan belief in the value of learning and research. In states with Republican governors—Alabama, Florida, Iowa, Missouri, Oklahoma—higher education has been cast as the enemy. Governor Kasich said he would "take an axe" and slash funding of the public universities of Ohio if they didn't "deal with it."[45] Legislation to get rid of tenure has been introduced in Florida, Georgia, Iowa, Missouri, South Carolina, Wisconsin. Early in 2015, Scott Walker, the Koch-funded governor of Wisconsin, tried to slash $300 million from the University of Wisconsin budget (while committing $220 million to a new basketball arena) and attempted to rewrite the university's mission statement, stripping out public service, "improving the human condition," "the search for truth," and replacing these with "meet the state's workforce needs."[46]

But the governor who takes the prize, foremost among the wreckers, is Alaska governor Mike Dunleavy, who, in the summer of 2019, slashed the state university budget by a staggering 41%.[47] These cuts wield a blow not only to the university but to the International Arctic Research Center at Fairbanks, one of the world's leading research centers for the study of climate change. Dunleavy is a climate denier who's had significant Koch funding.[48] No matter that the summer he made these cuts, the sea ice off Alaska's coast disappeared entirely, millions of acres were consumed by wildfire, and coastal villages will be underwater within the decade; he won't be around to suffer the consequences. (Climate deniers tend to be white, male, and old.) Colleges in rural areas are always the hardest hit by cuts like these, institutions that have been economic and cultural ballasts to their regions, providing pathways for low-income, downwardly mobile populations and ethnic minorities to the middle class. The same pattern is being repeated throughout the Midwest and Rust Belt, with the same effects: anyone who wants an education who can afford to move does move, which leaves these areas further impoverished.

"We spent 150-plus years building a public higher education system that was the envy of the world," said Dan Reed, vice president for research and economic development at the University of Iowa.[49] "And we could in a decade do so much damage that it could take us thirty years to recover." Thirty years? I doubt universities will ever recover from blows like these, any more than Palmyra or Aleppo will reemerge from their rubble, ignorance destroying in an hour what took centuries to build. Fundamentalism is on a rampage, whether in the form of ISIS or bought-and-sold Republicans. "Make no mistake about it," as classics scholar Katie Billotte says, "the death of the humanities is an ideologically motivated murder, more like a massacre."[50]

It's well to remember that it was the power of education that made this backlash: it was because education was creating a middle class that demanded better lives for themselves and others, that it became a threat. Cold comfort, but good to keep in mind as the assault continues unabated.

Use to the Economy

What a falling off, from JFK's expansive vision of an educated citizenry making a free society, that morning I heard him in 1962, to Reagan's withering announcement five years later that intellectual curiosity is no longer worth funding. Another blow was wielded at education by the Reagan administration's report, *A Nation at Risk*, 1983, which blamed K–12 teachers for a "rising tide of mediocrity" that was putting the nation at economic and military risk.[51] And in 2006, a Bush administration report attacked higher education in similar terms, when the Spellings Committee Report (named for Bush's secretary of education, Margaret Spellings) declared that higher education was putting the country's ability to compete globally at risk: "our competitors . . . are passing us by."[52] The Spellings Report decries "the remarkable absence of accountability systems" (the word *accountability* rings through this document, no less than 36 times in 50 pages) and calls for the formalization of "learning assessments" and the collection of data (*data*, another incantatory word, occurs 30 times). It advocates national exams, "innovation," an emphasis on STEM, and recommends that learning assessments be made part of the accreditation process, including "value-added measurements that indicate how much students' skills have improved over time." The report acknowledges that "at first glance most Americans don't see colleges and universities as a trouble spot in our educational system." And why would they, since—as the report acknowledges—"American higher education has been the envy of the world for years." So what exactly makes the "public demand" for "accountability"? It comes from a few Republican business organizations, including the Educational Testing Service, which would profit hugely from national exams and assessments.[53] This is the origin of the outcomes assessment regime, the demand for "student learning outcomes" that's got a stranglehold on higher education (more on this in a later chapter).

The Spellings Report didn't get far in 2006, but with the financial meltdown of 2008 and the steady acid drip of right-wing detraction—and with the Gates Foundation at the helm of Obama's Education Department—the pressure to link higher education to economic growth was ratcheted up. In 2013, Obama released a "Scorecard," an online tool that ranks colleges "in terms of costs, completion rates, and average student-loan debt,"[54] a tool that has Gates's fingerprints all over it.[55] The Scorecard will show "folks" where they can get "the most bang for the buck," as Obama promised in his 2013 State of the Union address.[56] The message to higher education was clear: buff up your business and engineering if you want federal funding. You'll rise higher in the rankings for graduating a hedge fund manager than a teacher.

(What a disappointment, coming from Obama, who of all people ought to know better, who got his start at Occidental, a small liberal arts college not far from the Claremont Colleges that's a lot like us. "It's a wonderful, small liberal arts college. The professors were diverse and inspiring," he said of Occidental, adding, "those first two years really helped me grow up."[57] But such qualitative perks have no place in his Scorecard, nor do "the first stirrings of destiny, a sense . . . that he was brought into the world for a purpose," which his biographer David Maraniss says was kindled by Occidental: "Oxy lit a pilot light inside him." "In the development of the person he was to become, Oxy was significant, . . . helping him work through the complexities of his cultural identity," and his interaction with the professors and students "steered his interests toward politics and writing."[58] Yet Occidental is the kind of college most penalized by his Scorecard, since liberal arts graduates tend not to have high starting salaries. And since Obama didn't graduate from Occidental— he transferred to Columbia—he'd probably figure in Occidental's minus column for that. Nor would his starting salary as a community organizer have done much to enhance Columbia's ranking. According to the quantitative standards he advocates, our first African American president would have "counted" as a dead loss all around.)

"I promise you, folks can make a lot more, potentially, with skilled manufacturing or the trades than they might with an arts history degree," Obama said, a claim immediately refuted by critics who produced charts, graphs, and numbers to show it wasn't so.[59] No matter. With the humanistic base of education shattered, programs in the arts and liberal arts, majors leading to public service, social, or environmental work, fall away; if it doesn't enhance the institution's eligibility for federal funding, it won't be encouraged. Anything that doesn't provide immediate, measurable rates of return doesn't count in this system of accountability, whatever its long-term or qualitative yields. "Accountability" is accountability to the bottom line. "I'm only interested in result per dollar charged," said Mitch Daniels, president of Purdue and a former governor of Indiana; "that's the value equation."[60] Dollars in, dollars out, no more care about the development of a person or the public good. *Antihumanist* is Jeffrey Williams's word for this reorientation of education to job training.[61]

With market values dominating every sphere of our existence, what's at risk "is not only medieval English poetry, Sanskrit, and political philosophy," as Wendy Brown says, but all "thinking, teaching, and learning that pertains to questions of what, apart from capital accumulation and appreciation, planetary life might be about or worth."[62] There is no realm outside the market: "Business models and metrics come to irrigate every crevice of society."[63]

And what exactly are we supposed to be producing? "I hope you'll carry with you . . . a continuing commitment to build human capital," urged David Sorton, president of Cornell, to a 2014 graduating class.[64] Former University of California president Mark Yudof described the purpose of education as delivering "efficient instrumental systems"—"that's us," said Wendy Brown, gesturing at the faculty, in a UC teach-in—"to generate human capital—that's you," she said, gesturing at the students: "those are his terms for what UC does and what it offers to the state."[65] Students are human capital, more capital than human; professors are capital enhancers, all of us cogs in a chain of production-consumption.

What the free market makeover of education leaves out is the human being. "Drown the bunnies," said Simon Newman, who came in as president of Mount St. Mary's from a private equity management group, with a plan to make the college rise in the rankings: just identify the 20–25 weakest students and "put a Glock to their head."[66] Newman's logic may have made sense in the world that spawned him, but it did not in a college committed to the liberal arts. He was asked to leave.

This has been the most profound change I've seen in my lifetime. No longer is higher education about human development and the betterment of society; it's about use to the economy. Not only has our conception of education shrunk, so has our sense of ourselves and what we live for been degraded. Greed was not good in the years I was growing up. Corporations prided themselves on fairness and accountability to their employees and communities. Civic services were not seen as "handouts" to "moochers"; "public" and "welfare" were not dirty words.

Now income inequality is the highest it's been in 50 years.[67] The family of former Secretary of Education Betsy DeVos owns 10 luxury yachts, while "an estimated half of all college students struggle with food insecurity, even at elite flagship universities" like Berkeley, according to a survey of nearly 86,000 students reported in the *New York Times,* 2018: 56% of these respondents had been "housing insecure" in the previous year; 17% had been homeless.[68] Millions of people are so burdened with student debt that they'll never be able to buy a house, have a family, or retire. In 2020, the United States ranked 27th of 82 nations, just below Lithuania, in terms of social mobility.[69] In key indicators of the well-being of a society—social trust, health care, longevity, education, help for the poor, elderly, and children—we rank somewhere between Poland and Cyprus.[70] "It's called the American dream because you have to be asleep to believe it," as George Carlin said.[71]

That young organism, sending out shoots and tendrils, seeking a way to grow—what do young people encounter today? How do they grow up in a world so shrunk, a country whose only interest in them is as producer-consumer yielding profits for corporations? Somebody, somewhere has to say, there are other ways to be. Contrary to Margaret Thatcher's blighting assertion, "there is no alternative," there are alternatives.

This is where the humanities come in, and a small liberal arts college like Scripps.

Human Scale

Toward the end of the summer of my discontent, 1974, as I was scouring the five boroughs with my shiny new PhD, in search of part-time teaching, I got a phone call. Somebody knew somebody who knew of a job. "It's not in your field, but if you fly yourself out, we'll interview you," said the voice on the phone, a man I'd met once. "Sure," said I, "no problem." How I was so sure I could teach Modern British Literature, when I'd just emerged from years in the Columbia library with a 500-page dissertation on Shakespeare, I'm not sure. I'd taken Modern British Literature from Mark Schorer, that's how, and though that had been a decade and a half before, it was unforgettable. Scripps kept apologizing for dragging me all the way out west for a one-year appointment, assuring me I'd have a crack at the tenure-track position the following year. "No problem," I said, confident that I'd be back in New York by then.

Coming to a small college town in Southern California from the Upper West Side, I was in culture shock. Scripps had 580 students;

I was used to universities with tens of thousands. And what a contrast, this pastoral campus, from the stony gray monumentality of Columbia. I soon realized I was going to be bumping into the same people again and again—uh-oh, no more road rage in the parking lot; the anonymity of Berkeley and New York had suited me fine. At a small residential college, you live with the consequences of your actions. Something the students learn, too: "That guy you made out with on a Thursday night at CMC—you may be running into him at Pomona Sunday night and it's probably a good idea to start thinking about what kind of reputation you want to cultivate for yourself," as Claire Ellen, '11, realized early on. *Consequence* is a useful concept for a twenty-year-old to get into her head, the lesson that what she does may come back to bite her. The word *college* comes from the Latin *collegium*, "partnership," association, a group of people living together, as in a residential college; it's related to collegiality. I came to see how community fosters development and responsibility.

But what impressed me most was the way faculty sat around talking about students, comparing notes: how's she doing? she hasn't been to class, I think there's a problem at home; she missed my midterm; she was talking in class the other day, I think she's okay. I never heard a single conversation like this at Queens or Brooklyn College. True, I was a lowly adjunct, but I think it was the same if you were full time; you rarely saw a student again once she'd left your class. Now I was at a college where faculty talked about students as though they were—gasp—human, people with problems and personalities that affect how they're doing in our classes, not just a set of numbers tallied up into a final grade. What a change, and how much more complicated to relate to a human being than a name in a gradebook, and how much harder it becomes for a student to slip through the cracks. We get to know our students and they get to know us and each other, and—this was a pleasure I realized only as the years went by—we get to watch them grow, perhaps play a part in their growing up.

It's so obvious as to be easy to miss: the kind of teaching to human scale that goes on at a college like this, the relationships students form with other students and faculty, can be a kind of humanism in practice, a site of resistance against what Douglas Rushkoff calls the "anti-human agenda" that's turning "our major cultural institutions . . . from forces for human connection and expression into ones of isolation and repression."[72] Humanity is, after all, our subject in the humanities, and one hopes a little of it rubs off.

And the beauty of the campus, which first seemed so exotic, came to matter to me more than I'd have thought possible. Scripps regularly turns up on lists of the top 10 most beautiful campuses in the country, though to my mind, there's none lovelier. On those raw, skinless days that come along from time to time (the thing about teaching is, you show up—your father died, your lover left, you show up), on those days you're not sure why you're here in class or on this planet, the landscape is a benign, healing presence. Its founder, Ellen Browning Scripps, planned it that way: "I am thinking of a college campus whose simplicity and beauty will unobtrusively seep into the student's consciousness and quietly develop a standard of taste and judgment," she said.[73] New buildings are built in 1930s Mediterranean style, none of those concrete, cinder-block monstrosities that blight most campuses.

I read what Corey Robin posts on Facebook (May 20, 2016) about Brooklyn College, and I want to weep: "There are leaky ceilings, clogged toilets, stagnant salaries, and ballooning class sizes, [while] the state yawns. It's difficult to explain to people who teach on tonier campuses how wearying and dispiriting this relentless shabbiness can be. While you're striving to inculcate excellence in your students, to get them to focus on the lyrical beauty of a passage in Plato or the epigrammatic power of a line from Machiavelli, you have to literally shut your eyes to the space around you, lest its pervasive message of 'What's the point? Give up' get inside your head. Or the students' . . ."

I see that I began this chapter extolling the great institutions of public education and ended up praising the small liberal arts college where I landed, sheer luck. UC Berkeley worked for me. I learned from the best in the profession, and I learned street smarts—nobody was looking out for me at Berkeley. But I had a supportive family 50 miles away, and I came to Berkeley knowing what I wanted of my education—to learn everything about literature I possibly could. I saw kids slip through the cracks who might have made a go of it if they'd been at a college like Scripps, where they'd have had small classes with engaged students and found a group of friends or a prof who took an interest in them. When I see the spirit and loyalty of alums who come back for reunions, when I see how many daughters of alums choose Scripps, I think I really missed out on something. I don't have a shred of this kind of fondness for Berkeley or Columbia; prone to nostalgia as I am, not a shred.

But the Claremont Colleges feel like islands in a rising sea, and even here the ground's a bit soggy, students fleeing the humanities for what looks like safer ground.

✂ ✂

THREE

What's Trust Got to Do with It?

Some of the best courses I have taken . . . have been the ones that are small, and where the professor and students develop a sense of trust with one another. This trust can only be attained by person-to-person contact. . . . The college experience is truly about making human connections.

—STUDENT QUOTED BY PETER HERMAN,
"Online Learning Is Not the Future"

I thank you for the trust you had in me, Professor. I think you believed in me more than I did myself. You and the other professors I had taught me to trust myself, and that may be the most valuable thing I got from Scripps. —NANCY, '02

They are waiting, first-day excitement, notebooks out, pens poised, laptops open, iPads . . . oh, dear, I really do have to say something about those devices. No, not yet, don't put a damper on it yet—this is the honeymoon period, before I get their first papers and they get their first grades. A time to build trust.

The trust in this room is palpable. Here they all are, committing time, energy, resources to this class. If I were untenured and worried about enrollments, I'd need a jazzier title: "Sex, Death, Gender Blending in the Plays of Shakespeare," something like that. But this is just

Shakespeare, and still they come, committing 45 hours to class plus time spent reading, writing, viewing. That's a lot in lives so busy; we all have other things to do.

They are trusting me to take them through the mazes of a difficult writer, trusting that they'll come through the next 15 weeks with something they didn't have before. They are trusting me with the power of the dreaded grade. Some cannot afford to get less than an A, though they will. Some cannot afford to be here at all. And I am trusting them to do their bit. Leaps of faith all around, and for parents, too, some of whom have taken out second mortgages, cosigned loans, emptied out trust funds (trust fund, a fund of trust).

Here we all are, committing ourselves to a new relationship, for that's what a class is, and not just one relationship but many, a crisscross of relationships, theirs to me and to each other, face-to-face, here and now. A plunge into unknown waters, no telling what tides and currents we'll encounter, which way we'll be swept.

There has to be trust for a class to work. It's that simple, and that complex. Trust is the cornerstone of a class, of a relationship, of a society. Distrust breeds loneliness, suspicion, fear. Trust is a terrible thing to lose, and young people are losing it. Betrayed by a society that requires them to have a college degree yet drives them into indentured servitude to get it, a government that bails out bankers but burdens them with crushing debt—what's to trust? Look at the way they thrill to *The Hunger Games*, where a corrupt ruling class pits the young against one another in a fight to the death, or at the 2021 hit survival drama, *Squid Game*. Look at the post-apocalyptic and fantasy fiction they're drawn to. I've had students who've read the Harry Potter novels six times. They never want to come back from Hogwart. Anywhere but here.

Trust comes up a lot in this class. In the plays of Shakespeare, disloyalty and betrayal bring death and worse. So let there be trust. Let this class model, in its workings, the ideals I hope to get across, re-weave a piece of our tattered social fabric.

Classroom Chemistry

"This is a seminar," I say. I guess that's pretty obvious, since there are fewer than 20 of us in the room.

"What is a seminar? It's a conversation. You get to ask questions, test out ideas, hear your own voice and the voices of others. That's what a seminar is. If you want a lecture, there are lectures online. Some people claim online is all you need—check it out. But this is a reading and thinking kind of course, a trying-out and talking-through kind of class. A space where we can converse. You are paying a lot of money for this chance, your parents may have mentioned—best take advantage." A few nods.

"A seminar is as good as you are." I point to where this is written on the syllabus, in bold type and underlined. I read: *"A seminar is as good as you are."* I'd like to say but dare not say—it is *you* who will make this class soar or sink, not me. If it's boring, you've made it so. But I could say this till I'm blue in the face and it would make no difference: they are who they are and it will be what it will be.

"You can find me in Balch Hall, across the quad, office hours Tuesdays and Thursdays right after class, on the third floor."

"Elevator or stairs?" says one of the serious-looking brunettes. That strikes me as so funny, I can't resist: "Yes, those are the customary ways . . . though you could try levitating, I suppose." She looks bewildered, then bursts out laughing. Good. Allison, or is that Alicia, has a sense of humor. So do a few others, but there are some perplexed looks—huh, "levitate," what'd she say? Oh no, let it not be one of those classes. I can always tell if a class is with me by whether they get my jokes, not jokes, exactly, more like asides—I can't help it, they just bubble out—if they don't get these, they won't get me. Lately, it seems fewer do. Studies describe a loss of humor in the young; students are so deadly earnest that stand-up comics are reluctant to book performances on college campuses.[1]

And this is the single most important determinant of how a class goes: *Will they like me?* This is what it comes down to. It's a terrible tyranny, but it's true. This is what student evaluations tell, pretty much all they tell, as studies show, as teachers know. There's a bellwether question on our student evaluation form: "Was the professor available outside class?" I get high marks from the class that loves me, a middling response from the so-so class, and a low score from the problem class. Same semester, same prof, there in my office the same number of hours (office hours kept faithfully, whether anyone shows up), same everything—and these wildly different responses.

Was it always this kind of popularity contest? When I've read professors' evaluations (as I have on review committees), I find things like, "I love, love, love prof X," with exclamation marks and hearts, along with descriptions of what she wears. I don't recall having such feelings for my profs. It never occurred to me to *love love love* a professor. True, I'd get crushes, I'd look forward to some classes more than others, but profs weren't there to *please* me; they were just . . . professors.

Maybe it's the celebrity culture, the cult of personality. Maybe it's all those "like" buttons kids get to click, all those easy ratings—rate this film, rate this recipe, rate this prof. Maybe they've got the message that they're "consumers" and we're here to deliver customer satisfaction, that is, an easy A. Education as business, student as customer, degree as a ticket to a job, each wrong-headed notion spawning a worse. Students are not here to purchase an education—they're here to purchase the *opportunity* to get an education. Such misconceptions mean that anything I do that makes a course difficult, like assigning a lot of reading or writing, may get me trashed in evaluations. Nontenured faculty can't risk this, most faculty are nontenured, so we get grade inflation. "At Berkeley, a student can slap a suit on you on the grounds that the grade you gave him kept him from getting into medical school," a prof told me. "He may not win, but he can make your life miserable."

And it's hard to admit, but not everybody will like me, for that is the way of human beings with each other—not everyone's equally keen on everybody else. Why should this be a surprise? Not everyone likes the same books, the same films, the same food. People are really very different—we know this—yet somehow it doesn't get factored into conversations about teaching. Maybe we don't talk about it because we don't like to admit there are going to be kids who are just not that into us. Classroom chemistry, invisible, uncontrollable, a current that sweeps us along or sucks us down. And unpredictable: sometimes I'll see eyes glaze, glances slip away—and I'll think, *What?* How can they not find this fascinating? Sometimes I'll see eyes light up—and I'll think, *What?* What did I just say that was so interesting?

Something else crucial to whether a class sinks or swims is whether the students like each other. A class is made up of individuals with unique personalities who also form a group identity with a personality of its own. This is rarely discussed, maybe because there's so little we can do about it, but a big part of classroom chemistry is whether they find each other interesting. We're social creatures, energized, excited, defused by one another, different in the presence of different people. They're playing for each other as much as for me, maybe more. If I see a student roll her eyes when someone else is speaking, I can call her aside, tell her to show respect, but I cannot force respect any more than I can force her to fall in love. Oh, sure, I can put a lid on open expressions of contempt, and I have tricks for setting a group at ease, getting them to speak to each other and not just to me; but mainly, there's this chemistry. I used to go to great lengths to try to change it when I felt it go wrong, call students in individually, ask them to write anonymous evaluations about what they'd like to see changed. Now I know there's no changing it, there's only riding it out.

I can sometimes feel if a class has that energy the minute I set foot inside the door. Actually, I can tell *before* I step inside—if I hear talking and laughing as I approach the room, there's an energy I can harness; I step in, become part of the flow. If they're not lively and engaged with each other at first, that's okay, but it's not okay after a few weeks. Cell phones don't help. I walk in and find them glued to their phones—*talk* to each other, dammit, I want to say; I do sometimes say.

So I approach each new class with humility and hope, hope that this random group of people will have the chemistry to make it work. It's a leap of faith for me as well as them, riskier for me, in a way, since whatever dynamic gets going, I get the blame.

The Syllabus: It Is Short

"Okay, let's talk about the course. You know, nuts and bolts. Take out the syllabus." Rustle of papers as they shuffle through the handouts.

Most students have never seen a syllabus so short. Two pages, no rules or warnings, percentages, grading formulas. Syllabi these days are usually 18–20 pages, mostly boilerplate, rules and regulations for anything that could go wrong, penalties and policies for any infringement imaginable (some probably unimagined until the syllabus planted the idea), grade appeals, and only on page 10 do you get to the readings—by which time, who cares? Students from K–12 public schools come to us from a testing regime based on distrust. "It's all about distrust," laments a middle school principal in Tennessee, "not trusting principals to judge teachers, not trusting teachers to educate children."[2] "My profession is being demeaned by a pervasive atmosphere of distrust," declares Gerald Conti, former high school teacher, whose denunciation of "'data driven' education . . . standardization, testing and a zombie-like adherence to the shallow and generic Common Core" was published in the *Washington Post*: "I am not leaving my profession, it has left me."[3] To students unaccustomed to trust, this class will be a new experience.

Among other things you won't find on my syllabus is an attendance policy. I don't have one. If you don't want to be in class, don't come. If you think you can read these plays on your own, best of luck. If you don't want to be here, you should find somewhere you want to be. I mean that—life's short. Don't sit here taking up space someone else might use. You bring us all down. In a class this small, I can tell who's not here, and I get in touch after a week. But a student can be physically present and be a million miles away. Brittany, for example, is here at the table but nowhere in the room. Tanya, examining her split ends, looks like she's not here, but turns out to be. Attendance is not just about being physically present—it's about *attending*, paying attention. There's no way I'm going to reward students for just showing up. Then they go out into the world thinking all they have to do is show up, and employers are right to complain.

"Participation counts," I've written on the syllabus. But only if you have something to say, I'd like to add. A student who never opens her mouth but is attentive can be more a part of the conversation than the nonstop talker who's so busy preparing her next remark she hears nothing anyone says. Shut up and *listen*, I'd like to say, but I can't, of course, since I've urged them to talk. I remember wondering, in classes at Chicago, why doesn't the prof shut that motormouth up? Now I know, it's not so easy. I take them aside and urge, gently, uh, someone else might like to talk, and they may pipe down for a week, but never for long.

"Papers, several, topics to be announced," I have written. No due dates. I never know what the class will be like when I make up a syllabus. A class is a living, breathing organism with a mind, heart, and energy all its own. How long we'll take on a play depends on how engaged they become.

Something else not on the syllabus: a late paper policy. I'd rather have a good paper that comes in late than shoddy work turned in on time. I don't advertise this, but word gets out. Student papers thrown together the night before do brain damage, I swear, to *my* brain, I mean. Or, you get those slick, say-nothing pieces that sound computer-generated and may well be, voiceless as a drone; better a rough paper that shows signs of grappling than one of these. Students seem so terrorized about deadlines; they come up after class, timid, guilty, "Could I please have an extension, I've, uh, been sick, I'll take the grade reduction." Oh, no you won't, not from me; if you need more time, take more time. But if a week goes by, I warn, I have to start marking down. "Students need to learn about punctuality from us," a colleague said. Not from me, they don't; they can learn that as needed. People have different pressures on them; we don't know what their lives are like.

Of the two tools teachers have to work with, I say, go with the carrot. Do not let go of the stick, but I can tell you from long experience, you'll get farther with the carrot—and there's a vast literature that bears this out.[4] Besides, in a pinch, someone could eat the carrot, but there's nothing much you can do with a stick, except beat the kid. Which is what so-called reform is all about; corporal punishment is not allowed, but the pummeling of minds and crushing of hearts— that's okay. "No pain, no gain," say the reformsters, modern-day Malvolios, descendants of those joy-killing Puritans set against the arts. "No gain with pain" is more like it. Oh, you may get kids to jump through hoops and over hurdles, raise test scores a digit or two, but unless they *want* to learn, save your breath.

Here's the kind of thing you see on syllabi: 10% oral participation, 60% written work, (10% each for the first three papers, 30% for the final paper), 30% for exams (5% quizzes, 10% midterm, 15% final exam). If your cell phone rings in class, that counts as a tardy, two tardies count as a nonattendance, two nonattendances bump your grade down a half; if you're caught texting, that counts as a cell phone demerit, two demerits is a nonattendance; if your car breaks down, you must show me the towing receipt; if you're ill, I need a note from health services; if you attend a funeral, bring me documentation . . . and on and on. "Course-specific expected learning outcomes" all spelled out, exhaustively, font style, margins, spacing, footnote form, all so air tight no judgment can squeak through, nothing that might be subjective or (gasp!) human. It is infantilizing, this language. It reeks of risk aversion, computationalism, the mentality that brought us "outcomes assessment." Syllabus as contract, legally enforceable, to cover our backsides in a court of law. Well, my backside has been uncovered so long, I'm not going to start worrying now.

I try to imagine how it would work. I'd sit here, grade book open, tallying up points—walked in late, down a point, but she raised her hand and made a comment, up a point, but wait, it was a dumb comment, didn't have anything thing to do with what we're reading or talking about, besides, she talks too much—so, make that a plus? a minus? ignore?

How we doing? Somebody someday will no doubt devise a software program, probably somebody already has, so we can sit here logging in this junk, which is called "data." In *Getting Schooled*, a delightful memoir about teaching in a Vermont high school, Garret Keizer struggles with a software program he's required to use to take attendance; it is slow and inefficient, and if a kid wanders in late, he has to change "not here" to "here," which wipes out everything he's entered, and he has to start over. It eats up gobs of time and requires that he begin each class with the question, "Who did not do the homework?"—a bad-news question to greet a class with.[5] But by god, we'll get the data, we'll know, like Santa, if you've been bad or good—you, the student, you, the teacher, everyone trained up in compliance, no judgment calls allowed.

"If there is one single artifact that pinpoints the degradation of liberal education," writes Mano Singham, in "Death to the Syllabus," "it is the rule-infested, punitive, controlling syllabus"; it's like "something that might be handed to a prisoner on the first day of incarceration."[6] Starting a course like this screams, I do not trust you. As I am not trusted, I will not trust you; as I am micromanaged, so will I micromanage you. It sets me in an adversarial relation with my students. Suspicion breeds suspicion, breeds no good.

I have seen syllabi so airtight they take my breath away, I mean knock the wind right out of me. From 2:15 to 2:30, we will discuss time in *The Winter's Tale*; from 2:30 to 2:45, we'll talk about atonement; from 2:45 to 3:00, wonder. No kidding, *wonder*, 2:45 to 3:00?—don't you think that might be cutting wonder a little short? Wonder is a big theme in *The Winter's Tale*, also in *Midsummer Night's Dream*, when Bottom wakes out of his marvelous night in the woods, eager to *discourse wonders*, his mind boggled *past the wit of man to say what dream it was*. What if something comes up, you know, like you or I say something interesting, could happen, and we start riffing and discussion wanders off—sorry, no time for spontaneity, for the unexpected turns that make a class soar, no time to soar. As though a class could be mapped out like this. This is the liberal arts, remember? *Liberare*, to make free.

Wonder. I would be so happy to inspire *wonder* in my students. The noun means "a sense of awe, surprise, amazement, marvel." The verb means "to have desire to know," to think or speculate curiously, to be filled with admiration, amazement, to be curious, to conjecture, meditate, ponder, question, marvel at. It would be wonderful to engage students' curiosity, their desire to know. *Awe.* That was a good word once, till *awesome* got so done to death that it was banished from Jewish prayer.[7] But awe is what I'd like to inspire, what literature can inspire, stretching the imagination to conceive of the inconceivable, to envision something new. *And take upon us the mystery of things / As if we were God's spies.*

I would love for my students to find in the plays even a fraction of the pleasure and sustenance I have found. "What we have loved, others will love, and we will teach them how," writes Wordsworth in *The Prelude.* Wonder can inspire *enthusiasm*, which is "one of the most beautiful words in the language," said Louis Pasteur. The word is from *en theos*, a god within: "Happy is he who bears a god within, and who obeys it."[8] Maybe that should go on my syllabus, under "student learning outcomes": "Find the god within. Figure out what you'd do even if nobody paid you or paid you attention for doing it, what you do that puts you in the zone." "Whoever . . . can no longer wonder, no longer marvel, is as good as dead," said Einstein, adding that wonder is "the fundamental emotion that stands at the cradle of true art and true science."[9] Hear this, ye politicians and policymakers who are dismantling the arts and humanities and raising STEM in their place: the cradle of art *and science.*

So from me, students get a list of the plays we're reading plus a dozen or so critical essays I put together in a reader, the old way, printed and bound. And, what a surprise, they're likelier to read a short syllabus than a long one, brevity being the soul of wit and all. Oh, yes, and a handout, "Writing a Paper," 18 pages of tips and explanations I've put together through the years: the difference between a thesis and a topic, a paragraph, transitions, referents, dangling participles, issues that come up in their papers. Nothing about footnote form; I only care that they give me enough information to track a reference down.

That, I do care about.

Papers, Finals, Films, and, Oh, Yes, Grades

I direct them to a few sentences on the last page that deal with grades. This gets their attention. "Papers, several."

"How many is several?"

"That depends. You'll be writing on every play we read. Topics grow out of discussions. Most will be short, some written in class— I'll tell you when." But no preassigned topics. Assigning topics too far in advance is a sure way of inviting bought work; there are so many ways a paper can get itself written. Lead them not into temptation. "You'll have warning," I say. "Anyhow, you'll be able to figure it out— after we've spent a certain number of days on a play, you'll know that a paper's coming soon."

"Will there be a final exam?" This from Brittany, who raises her eyes from her lap to ask. It's the first question she asks in this class, and the last.

"Maybe," I say. "It says on the syllabus, 'there may be a final exam.'" I truly do not know, at the beginning of a semester, whether I'll need to give a final, so I keep my options open. "You'll have warning. Questions will evolve out of class discussion, so if you've been following discussions, you'll be fine. Also, mark up your books and always bring them to class. No, you may not read the plays on an electronic device." Students may prefer reading on screens, but research shows that they retain less;[10] from what I've seen, they retain nothing. "Except," I add, "when you're on stage. Did I mention the acting assignment? It's on the syllabus, look under *Midsummer Night's Dream*."

"I can't act," comes a moan from . . . Allison? No, that's Alice who groaned, the engineering student from Harvey Mudd.

"Good. You'll play one of the characters who can't act—there are several in *Midsummer Night's Dream*. And by the way, make sure you watch at least one film version of each play." I used to make a big deal about their getting hold of tapes and listening to the plays, but the library seems to have *de-accessioned* its recordings, along with its books; some administrator's bright idea that libraries would be more efficient without books. (What logic drove this policy is a mystery: just when reading has dropped off so precipitously, start tossing out books or shunt them to a distant storage bin where they take days to get hold of. It prompted outrage from the faculty, but it was a done deal by the time we got wind of it; and it's happened at many colleges, not just Claremont.) So I rely on the films. There are excellent films, easily available—what a difference from when I was a student, when seeing a Shakespeare play was such a big deal. I don't police their viewing, but I can tell from discussions, they watch them; they catch on fast that seeing a play makes reading it easier.

"But hold off watching until you've read the play a couple of times. Try to form your own image of what the characters look like—once you see Branagh as Hamlet, you'll always see him as Hamlet. Watching a film, you're giving yourself over to someone else's interpretation, and you don't want to do that until you've developed some sense of the play yourself."

"How much does the final count—I mean, would it count, if we had one?" Brent, an econ major, wants numbers.

"A lot," I say. "Assignments are weighted more heavily at the end of the semester than at the beginning—makes sense, right? To see if you've improved. Things count more as we go along."

"How much more?"

"Well, that depends." Depends on what? he wants to ask, but has the sense not to. Anyhow, I wouldn't tell. Depends on what you came in with, how much you've learned. With most students, the final more or less confirms what the papers already show. But with a student whose writing skills aren't great, but who's tuned into class discussions and shown understanding—if she comes through on the final, that weighs a lot. And with a student who comes in knowing how to write but coasts through on skills she already has—if she bombs the final, that weighs too. There are no absolutes, not in a course like this.

It is unbelievably complex, grading. The hours I've spent anguishing the difference between a B+ and an A–, a B– and a C+, the hundreds of thousands of judgment calls that go into making those distinctions—if I could have those hours back, I'd be young again. I pick someone who's clearly, unambiguously earned an A or a B or a C, and then compare; I put a ruler under the line of grades, getting the general drift—up? down?—weighing which assignments count more, which less—hmm, worse on that assignment, better on this, shows progress here, nope, she bombed the final. Then too there's a general sense of the person—has she been attentive, alive, curious, or dead weight that the rest of us have had to drag along? Has she pitched in, been *responsible* to me and to the others, to the course, to herself? Have I seen a spark of interest, a glimmer of improvement, any indication that she's leaving with more than she had when she came in? Or has she made me trudge through paper after paper that's pointless, purposeless, nothing glaringly wrong with it but nothing right, just pointless—I wish there was a P grade, P for perfunctory, pointless, purposeless, waste of time, hers and mine. We none of us have that kind of time.

Get used to it, I want to say. You have to settle for a lot of uncertainty in life. You cannot read Shakespeare if you can't deal with uncertainty. Punctuality, you can pick up on your own, but this I really care about. Learning to deal with uncertainty is one of the most important things the liberal arts can teach.

What I do say is, "If your grade is borderline, the final may push you one way or another, and in that case, it would count a lot." Brent is looking like he wants to bolt.

"Keep your eye on the drop date," I say cheerily.

"The Rule-Infested, Punitive, Controlling Syllabus"

No way could I get away with this if I were just starting out. But you see, I come from a distant land. I come from the past, bearing witness to the way things were.

"I too wish I could have a shorter, less legalistic syllabus," commented a reader of the *Chronicle of Higher Education*; "I just cannot . . . and keep my job." This is one of many comments on an article by Paula Cohen, who keeps her syllabus to one page.[11] And another:

> At the community college where I taught . . . , there were several pages
> of material that were required to be on any syllabus, much of it
> boilerplate from the administration that had to be included verbatim.
> ADA notice, emergency procedures, notices about using the library
> and the student counseling center, etc. . . . It is also required to tie the
> course into larger "learning goals." . . . Also . . . we were required to list
> all assignments, grading scale, etc. And all syllabi had to be submitted
> in advance for approval, and they would be returned with markups if a
> required section was missing or not up to date, and a corrected version
> had to be submitted and approved before being allowed to start classes.

And another: "Yes, and our syllabi must include grade breakdowns, paper expectations, etc. by university fiat. They are not allowed to change after the second class unless the class votes unanimously. . . . Some of my colleagues even made 'a-know-your-syllabus-quiz.'"

"University fiat"? A "know-your-syllabus" quiz? Submit your syllabus for approval, revise and resubmit for final approval? This is not the profession I signed on to. This is not a profession at all. This is not quality control; it's control, plain and simple.

And yet the idea of syllabus as contract keeps getting reinforced more literally, as Paula Wasley says, "down to a proliferation of fine print and demands by some professors that students must sign and attest that they have read and understood."[12] When John Warner started teaching as an adjunct, he was told on no uncertain terms that a syllabus was a contract. "I honestly didn't know I was allowed to act according to my own judgment." He soon realized that the point of syllabus as contract is to relieve faculty of judgment, which destroys the agency of both teachers and students.[13] A commenter on Paula Cohen's article describes "a New York phone book of regulations trying to anticipate every possible question and difficulty and to codify same so that the teacher or administrator *never has to exercise judgment* or make a tough decision." It replaces responsibility with a checklist of categories, boxes to mark off, as three Lindenwood University faculty write: "A bewildering array of acronyms and abbreviations— OA, SLOs, PSLOs, and ISLOs—dictates a template for all syllabi and covers 'outcomes.' . . . These documents are now sufficiently complex that department chairs have to provide us with a checklist for the eighteen expected categories to ensure that they have been included. . . . For one department, the mandatory syllabus information now comprises nineteen pages."[14]

Some faculty welcome the relief from responsibility. At a conference of college teachers, Mano Singham describes a session that "promised to provide a stress-free method for 'managing' students— an odd word choice that presumes students are like employees and we their bosses. . . . The presenter's idea of being 'stress-free' was to create a set of rules so detailed that everything about assessing students could be quantified on a micro level. The presenter advocated an intricate structure of points and penalties to ensure that every possible excuse a student might present . . . could be dealt with by invoking the appropriate rule, thus avoiding having to make judgments that might be challenged by a student." The session "had an overflow crowd."[15]

A set of rules to "manage" students, to alleviate stress? "The more detailed, the better," says Linda Garavalia, associate professor of psychology at the University of Missouri, Kansas City, who has studied the way students see syllabi. "Students tend to be anxious about what it is that's expected of them. Spelling out as comprehensively as possible what types of activities students will do in class, how they will be assessed, and how much each assignment counts toward a grade reduces that stress." Her syllabi "range from 10 to 20 pages and include examples of written assignments, along with policies on punctuality, participation, and classroom visitors."[16]

Risk aversion institutionalized.

Generation . . . Anxious

"Students tend to be anxious." I don't like to generalize about students, but this is true. They have a lot to be anxious about.

People who find it easy to generalize about students do not, I suspect, know many students. I sit at the table with them 30 weeks of the year, 135 hours a semester, besides time spent in office hours, advising, directing senior theses, talking them through breakups, a death in the family, plus godknowshowmany hours spent reading their papers, plus e-mail exchanges that go on more or less continually—and I don't find generalizations at all easy. Ask me how I feel about my students after a bad class, and you'll get a rant. Ask me after I've spent an hour with a Lizzie, a Danny, a Barbara, and I'll gush about how bright and bold and caring they are. Ask me after I've got an e-mail that says, "I couldn't make it to class today, did I miss anything?" and stand back for the blast. My feelings about my students swing wildly, from proud to perturbed to piqued to protective to plagued; fond to amused to annoyed, disappointed, exasperated, outraged—sometimes within the same day. I imagine that range of feelings is not unknown to parents.

When people generalize about "kids today," it's almost funny, their generalizations are so all over the place. I read about the Me Generation, the Medicated Generation, the Dumbest Generation, the Organization Kid, and I think, yes, I've met a few of those. I read about Generation Materialistic, Generation Wired, Generation Entitled, Generation ADHD, and I've met those too. Then there's Generation Nice, Generation "Like," Generation Sold Out, Stressed Out, Checked Out, Disengaged, "Educated Sheep, "Entitled Shits," Snowflakes, Generation Coddled—I sigh and nod, yes, those, too. But some have dealt with difficulties beyond anything I've ever known, and some are amazing. Generation Super Accomplished, Super People, Socially Engaged, that, too. Generation All Over the Place.

But "Generation Stressed"—yes. Faculty, counselors, deans, parents agree, the kids are anxious. A 2018 report from the American College Health Association found that over 60% of college students said they'd experienced "overwhelming anxiety" and more than 40% said they'd felt so depressed that they'd had difficulty functioning in the past year.[17] A dean of students told me, "I'd say 40% or more come to college already taking psychoactive medications." Many are "self-medicating," a euphemism for taking drugs or binge drinking. "Here in Claremont the counseling services are so overwhelmed that the colleges have had to add a back-up counseling service with private providers in town and additional emergency on-call service," a Pomona professor posted on Facebook (Victor Silverman, May 23, 2016). He speculated, "I don't think this is because they've been pampered and just need to toughen up, but rather, it's our times." His post inspired a flood of comments citing the causes I've mentioned, pressure, competition, debt, social media, helicopter parents, being deprived of play. And this was pre-pandemic.

Here are some reasons for late papers I had in the space of a month: my roommate tried to jump off the roof and I had to sit with her all weekend, my mother has cancer and needs me at home, I had to call my aunt to intervene with my mom's drinking, our house was foreclosed and I had to help my family move, I've been fighting with Financial Aid and don't know if I'll be back next week. When they write about their lives, I read of families disrupted, jobs lost, debts accumulating; of depression, eating disorders, drugs, self-harm, suicide attempts. How can we imagine that an ironclad set of rules will address problems like these?

One semester, three of my students took medical leaves "for mental health reasons," and one tried to kill herself. Whenever the subject of suicide comes up, the room goes quiet, then it comes out, how many students know someone who's tried, or succeeded. When a student told us her high school was called "Suicide High," there were nods of recognition all around. Suicide rates among 15- to 24-year-olds nearly tripled since 1960, the year I graduated high school.[18] Two schools near where I went to high school, Gunn High School and Palo Alto High, have had rashes of suicides—the "Silicon Valley suicides," the media calls them.[19] There was one at Scripps in 2017, and two within the same week at CMC in February 2019.

MIT had seven suicides in a 14-month period. MIT professor Daniel Jackson speculates, "Today students feel much more that they're being assessed by a bunch of metrics: grade-point average, the scholarships they've received, how prestigious their summer internships are, and so on. These measures sort of become proxies for meaning and purpose in life," displacing such satisfactions as "feeling that you were learning interesting, exciting things, that you were broadening your mind, and that you had a life ahead of you of purpose, of doing good things in the world."[20]

As for the large public universities, 43% of them do not collect data on suicide.[21]

Students are punch-drunk with pressures, scattered a million ways, hurtling from task to task, taking too many courses, working too many hours. "They're breathless," said Julie Lythcott-Haims, former dean of students at Stanford and author of *How to Raise an Adult*. "They're brittle. They're old before their time."[22] I once asked a class, "If I could give you a pill that eliminated the need for sleep and had no side effects, would you want it?" I assumed they'd leap at it—they could party all night and get straight As. But there were groans. "No way, sleep is my only escape." "They'd just make us work more. I went through high school on 4–5 hours' sleep, I'm good if I can get that much now. They'd make us work around the clock." (That unspecified "they" signals a sense of victimization. I hear it a lot: these kids do not feel in control of their lives.) The class went on about how little sleep they get, how they're always working, always behind. A student once told me, "What we talk about in this class is really interesting, Professor. I've never thought about it. But I literally don't have time to think about it now." A dean of students at Pomona described it this way: "Their sense of entitlement has been pumped sky high, while their actual prospects are falling, and that makes for a kind of craziness."

Student debt has reached $1.71 trillion—that figure is well known, widely advertised by our detractors. Less well known is that the government let this happen, turning much of the student loan program over to a privatized student loan industry. "A generation ago," explain James Steele and Lance Williams, "Congress privatized a student loan program intended to give more Americans access to higher education. In its place, lawmakers created another profit center for Wall Street. . . . Today, just about everyone involved in the student loan industry makes money off students—the banks, private investors,

even the federal government."[23] Former Education Secretary Betsy De-
Vos, the wealthiest of Trump's billionaire cabinet members and a major
investor in the debt-collecting company Performant, did everything she
could to roll back the loan forgiveness protections Obama put in place
for students defrauded by for-profit colleges. Time was, the government
tried to help with education. Today, "You're on your own," as Paul
Tough says. "You figure out how to get the skills you're going to need.
And by the way, here's the bill."[24]

I get it, how telling students exactly what to do to get an A might
alleviate some anxiety. So would a lobotomy. But a rule book that relieves them and me of responsibility is not what any of us needs.

Not long ago, I asked my class to watch the Ian McKellen film of
King Lear and write about whether it made them see the play
differently—"did it show you something about the play you hadn't
thought of, make you feel differently about the characters, show a new
angle?" I got a plagiarized paper. The student was deeply humiliated
when I called her on it, but said, in her defense: "I didn't know what
you wanted. There wasn't a rubric."

"A *what*?"

"You know, like guidelines, like, what you expect."

"It was a *response* paper, I wanted to know about how you responded, how the film affected your reading of the play."

"But where are the guidelines?"

"For your *response*? You want me to tell you how you *responded*?" I
hoped she'd see the absurdity of this, but she would not meet my eyes.
"Well, if you really didn't know what the assignment was getting at,
you should have asked me, but look, *response*, that means the way you
responded—did you *like* the film, did it make you see anything new
about the play, anything you hadn't seen reading? A response is *how
you feel and think*, you know, your own view."

"But I didn't know what you wanted."

We weren't communicating. She looked exhausted, close to tears. She was so used to being given a "rubric" that spells out exact steps to an A that when asked for her response, she was at a loss. "The hardest transition from high school into my college life at Scripps," wrote an alum, "was not being told what to do. . . . Spending the majority of my life in an educational system that gave a to-do list to me, I lost the ability to trust myself. . . . After being told what to do for so long, I stopped trusting my own ideas. . . . My education at Scripps has forced me to adapt to an entirely new form of education . . . where there is no list or required facts to memorize. . . . The transition from high school to college is a stepping stone into the uncertainty that is the real world."

There has to be something to take the rule book's place. That something is *trust*, says Mano Singham. Students have to feel "they can trust us . . . that we have the competence to make judgments about their performance and meaningful criteria for doing so, and that we have the impartiality to be honest and fair."[25] Singham puts a lot of effort into building trust, creating a sense of community. So do I. It's important that students feel the class is an environment we're all in together, that they have a part in making it what it becomes.

How, if we trust nothing about our students' judgment or character, can they develop judgment or character? Treat them like adults and they may behave like adults. At least it increases the chances.

The Humanization of Stereotypes

So here we all sit, checking each other out. They're sizing me up, reading me according to their experiences and preconceptions, slotting me into categories they bring from their pasts. It's what we do when we encounter new information, reach for our categories, our stereotypes. Me, too, I'm doing it too. Me reading them reading me; it gets complicated. And they happen fast, these first impressions, and they stick. Two Harvard psychologists found that the ratings students assign lecturers after watching a 30-second video are remarkably similar to what they turn out to be after 15 weeks.[26]

They are liking me, disliking me, according to some principle that has little to do with me. I remind them of their mother, I do not remind them of their mother. I remind them of a third-grade teacher they loved, or loathed. I am foreign to some, familiar to others—urban, Jewish, East Coast, is the way I come across (actually, I'm suburban, West Coast, half-Jewish). For some students, any or all of these qualities will be a draw; for others, not. It could paralyze me, thinking about what they are thinking of me—best not think. But my mind whirrs on: Damn, why does the first day of class always have to be a bad hair day; maybe I ought to get a new book, one that has a cover.

I know that whatever else they are seeing, they are seeing old. As young as they look to me, that's how old I look to them. Back in the day when I wore leather miniskirts and cab drivers mistook me for Joan Baez, affection flowed easily; oh, I still have groupies, but fewer. It's painful to realize, that loving energy just isn't there like it used to be, hard to admit it probably had more to do with my youth and appearance than my skills as a teacher. I think I'm a better teacher now, but "old" trumps all.

And whatever else they are seeing, they are seeing authority. Authority sits more easily on a male; so does age. Recent studies find that teaching evaluations are biased in favor of males, white males.[27] Any female prof could tell you that, and I daresay, any person of color. I've team-taught with men and seen what they get away with. There's no way public school teachers would be getting the bashing they're getting if they weren't 75% female. Young, male, good-looking, easy graders— these are the most likely to be liked. Old, female, not easy graders, not so great. Whatever problems kids have with any of these, they'll have with me.

So here I stand, aged, female, visible, and in a position of authority, as older women are expected not to be. On bad days I think I should get out of the way, make way for the young—but then the gray panther in me rears up and roars, hell, no, that's what we're expected to do, disappear. It's good for students to see age, no airbrush or facework, good for them to see that life goes on past 30. Diversity is good for a college, everyone agrees—well, that means diverse ages, too. Academia is rife with -isms and anti-isms, but ageism is the big one that's rarely discussed. All the other -isms have been done to death, but ageism is as invisible as age.

Ease off, Gayle. Remember the profs you were drawn to, charismatic, male, attractive. In all my years as a student at Chicago, Berkeley, Columbia, I had *one* female professor. True, there were not a lot to choose from, but there were more than that.

And me, too, I'm stereotyping: generic blond, intelligent-looking brunettes, spiky red hair, spill-all top. But that's the beauty of a small discussion class: it gives us the chance to test out first impressions, to dislodge our stereotypes. Sometimes I'll look back at notes I scrawled the first day—"big hair," "looks smart"—and think, boy, did I call that wrong.

How Not to Make It Safe

Something else you won't find on my syllabus: trigger warnings. I first heard of these several years ago, from a friend who was teaching a class on vampires. "May contain disturbing material," she was ordered to put on her syllabus. "It was a class on *vampires*, for chrissake," she laughed, "it's *supposed* to be disturbing! that's the *point* of vampires."

"Yeah, and how about those television shows they're glued to," I shot back. "*Game of Thrones, Breaking Bad, House of Cards*—no disturbing material there? Women are raped, burned, stabbed, beaten, strangled. To say nothing of reality TV shows or *Fox and Friends*, rot to the brain, brick to the head."

That was back when we were still capable of laughing about this. Today it is no joke. And amazingly, the call for trigger warnings comes from students. Students call on administration to police faculty—they have no idea what a bad idea this is—and administrators often all too readily comply. Kids used to have more sense; Frank McCourt describes, in *Teacher Man*, how his students would instinctively side with him if the principal walked in and gave him trouble.[28] I get it, students are in a low-level hysteria about their futures, and it's easier to complain about that insensitive thing somebody said, that upsetting thing we read, than to tackle the forces that are stealing their futures. I get the hysteria; I just wish it were more productively directed. But I guess that's the thing about hysteria—it is rarely productive.

I wish I could say, lighten up, guys—this classroom may be the safest place you'll ever be. You want "unsafe," drive a few miles south or west of these pastoral campuses, walk a few blocks from major urban campuses—Yale, Chicago, Columbia, Penn, USC, Johns Hopkins— you'll find unsafe. If you want to talk about racism, check out the public schools in those areas, look at the shuttered buildings, read about the theft of public education and public resources, the wealth gap, the opportunity gap; then we can talk about how unsafe you feel here. "Burn down Pomona College," screamed a student at a demonstration. Oh, no. Your enemy is not this college, where most of the staff and faculty are earnestly working for social justice.

Yes, of course, the classroom should be a safe space, no bullying, no hate speech; that goes without saying. But safety does not come from a set of rigid rules policing everyone's every word, so a presumed infringement of speech or behavior sparks the fires of the Inquisition. It doesn't come from an ironclad contract disallowing controversy— that is the "safety" of a police state. You don't combat distrust with distrust; you combat it by building trust. Trust that students have room to try and fail and try again, to find their own way through.

Anyhow, discomfort comes with the territory of learning. As magician Raymond Joseph Teller says, who taught high school Latin for six years before becoming part of the famed partnership Penn & Teller, there's a kind of discomfort that "creates an energy and a spark that is extremely exciting. . . . When I go outside at night and look up at the stars, the feeling that I get is not comfort. The feeling that I get is a kind of delicious discomfort at knowing that there is so much out there that I do not understand and the joy in recognizing that there is enormous mystery, which is not a comfortable thing. This, I think, is the principal gift of education."[29]

A Growing Space

It's extremely interesting, getting to know a class. It's like watching a Polaroid photo come into focus: at first it's a blur, then the features begin to take on definition, emerging in clear, sharp relief.

Sandra with the long, sandy braid seems so vague and distracted— sometimes her eyes light up with attention, then they flicker off mid-sentence, as though she switches to another channel. Love trouble? Trouble with her courses? Then one day after class, she asks, would I mind if her paper came in a few days late, her mother died last summer, she's having a hard time concentrating, and I get it—*that's* where her attention goes, how can she focus on anything but that ache, so soon after? I tell her to come in and talk if she wants to; she nods and smiles vaguely; toward the end of the semester, she finally does.

Those three serious-looking brunettes who I can't tell apart: I'll soon see they are nothing alike, they don't even look alike—how could I not have seen? And Cynthia of the spiky red hair sets my teeth on edge, till I see that beneath that bristliness is the kind of seriousness a teacher would pay to have in class. Samantha, whose gash of red lipstick I mistook for a smirk, gets a C- on her first paper (I didn't want to demoralize her with the grade it deserved). She comes in to office hours, and I see from her second paper, she knows how to take suggestions. She says she feels out of place at Scripps, everyone seems to know more than she does, she's thinking of transferring. But six weeks or so into the semester, I see her sitting by Allison, talking and laughing. Later in the semester she tells me she'll stay at Scripps.

It's revelatory, really, watching real live human beings emerge from the categories we've cast them into, individuals so very much who they are. As I get to know them, they get to know each other, and discussion flows more easily. At first, they tend to sit with people they know. The older auditors clump together, ignored by the others, age being an embarrassment. Then an auditor will loan a student a DVD; or she'll ask, "Where do you get your hair cut?" and I'll see them chatting after class. I overhear a girl comment, after a class that was an intense discussion of sex and death in *Measure for Measure*, "I wonder what sex was like before we had to worry about AIDS," and an auditor you'd type as "little old lady in tennis shoes" tosses over her shoulder on her way out the door, "It was . . . *fabulous!*" Gales of laughter, including mine, after which, Edna is sitting among the students. The same thing happens with the guys, and with ethnic groups that stick together at first but then begin to mingle. It's more than seating arrangements that are shifting around—stereotypes are breaking down, "others" seeming less "other." Fifteen weeks in a class like this allows for the humanization of stereotypes. The hope is that this will spill over into the rest of their lives.

We have our students for four years. That doesn't seem like a long time to me, but remember how long a year once seemed: four years at their time of life counts a lot. That young organism sending out shoots and tendrils—these classes, these colleges, offer support. We help with the transition from family to the world, help them grow into themselves. We offer a space where they can try out selves and ways of looking at things, where they can hear their own voices apart from the noise in the air, begin to see how they might fit into the world.

Back when I first started teaching, I saw the 1969 film *The Prime of Miss Jean Brodie*, Maggie Smith's first great role. The Edinburgh schoolteacher is too over-the-top to offer much by way of tips on teaching, but she said something I'll never forget. As she was being called to account for one of her many infractions, she said in her defense: "The word 'education' comes from the root of *e* from *ex*, 'out,' and *duco*, 'I lead.' It means a leading out. To me, education is a leading out of what is already there in the pupil's soul." Miss Brodie's superintendent retorts that surely teaching also has something to do with putting in. "Oh no," she replies, "that is intrusion, from the Latin root prefix meaning *in* and the stem *trudo*, I thrust." That is also indoctrination, stuffing full of unexamined beliefs or opinions. Education is, of course, a putting in as well as a leading out, a fine line a teacher treads, one of many. As we tease out what is there in students, we try to slip stuff in, not just information, but how to use it.

Education Is Not Indoctrination

A word about indoctrination, since higher education gets accused of it by right-wing media and politicians. Betsy DeVos told the Conservative Political Action Conference, February 2017, "the education establishment" is set on a course of "indoctrinating" students and turning them against Trump: "The faculty, from adjunct professors to deans, tell you what to do, what to say, and more ominously, what to think."[30]

Whoa there, Betsy. This is a woman whose family is a major donor to conservative think tanks, part of that vast ALEC opinion-making apparatus churning out fundamentalist ideology, chipping away at the wall between church and state. In 2001, she stated that she sees education reform as a way to "advance God's kingdom."[31] *That's* what indoctrination looks like. The Heartland Institute, a think tank affiliated with her family and with ALEC, has done a mass mailing of "Why Scientists Disagree about Global Warming," 200,000 copies to science educators, K–12 and postsecondary, to undermine belief in climate change, attributing it to natural causes.[32] *That's* indoctrination.

This is a myth in need of busting, that higher education is a hot bed of liberals using their authority to silence conservatives. We're the ones who are trying to steer young people *away* from indoctrination, away from a fundamentalist adherence to one sole truth, to free them to think for themselves. We try to teach them to deal with ambiguity, to exercise judgment in face of uncertainty, resist simple formulations, keep questions open, avoid premature closure. We try to teach them to understand the views of others, and we succeed. After only one year of college, "many students view both liberals and conservatives more favorably than when they arrive on campus," according to research summarized by Scott Jaschik.[33] A report released in October 2020 by the Georgetown Center on Higher Education and the Workforce found that a liberal arts education, exposing students to different kinds of people, cultures, attitudes, and practices, enables them to see others as less threatening.[34]

It's a major aim of education, or ought to be, said David Foster Wallace in a 2005 graduation talk at Kenyon College, to jostle us out of our "default position" into a less self-centered view. "Everything in my own immediate experience supports my deep belief that I am the absolute center of the universe"; this is "our default setting, hard-wired into our boards at birth."[35] When we're young, our parents encourage it, and if we're lucky, we get to develop lots of lovely ego strength; then if we're really lucky, our parents gently nudge us into an awareness that other people exist in their own right, not as props in a drama with us in the star role (this is where helicopter parents fail). College furthers that process, pushing us beyond infantile fantasies of autonomy and self-aggrandizement, making us abler to appreciate that we are one of many. If, in becoming more educated, students lean left,[36] that's because they've been made to support opinions with evidence, been asked, "Where do you find that, how do you back that up?" They learn to question assumptions, their own included, to form their own judgments, which makes them less vulnerable to dogma or mob rule.

Here is another myth in need of busting, that academia selects against right-wingers. Actually, conservatives are more likely to select themselves out. The PhD is a long haul; work in academia is hard and the pay is low for all but a few superstars. And conservatives have other fish to fry. A 2007 study drawing on national surveys of freshmen and seniors by the UCLA Higher Education Research Institute found that conservatives are more likely to pick majors that put them "on the fast track for an M.B.A. (or for a job) . . . than a Ph.D."; they take themselves "off the track for academic careers well before graduate school." The survey found that of students considering the PhD (only 13% do), more than twice as many were left-leaning than right-leaning—42% as opposed to 20%.[37]

A liberal education is not in the business of telling students what to think. We try to "make it possible for the students to become themselves," as Freire says.[38] And we succeed. I've seen students arrive at Scripps awash in the clichés of the culture, their styles and minds plucked off a rack—the Farrah Fawcett look, the Jennifer Aniston look, the happy hooker look. I've seen it all, peasant skirts to power suits, overalls and oversize T-shirts to skinny jeans and naked midriffs. Then I watch as a person begins to emerge from the type she's cast herself into, that I too may have cast her into. It's not only that my perception changes—students actually do grow into themselves.

They develop minds and imaginations they can call their own. "My liberal arts education helped me grow into myself," Dorothy Shapiro wrote from Harvard Law School. "This college helped me find out who I am," wrote Nik Jay from Georgetown Medical School.

Sometimes I play a part in the process, but even when I don't, I see it happen. As with Sylvia, who showed up as my advisee from a hypercompetitive prep school in the Northeast, foot-jiggling nervous, and wanted me to help her map out her courses for all four years, get the requirements out of the way so she could do two majors (this was her second day on campus). "Don't you want to see how things evolve?" I suggested. She did not. She was planning to spend a semester abroad, do a second major, in French, and she needed to know exactly what she was doing. So we made a plan. She took Shakespeare her sophomore year, seemed not to connect with the subject or me; I'd have given her the P grade, perfunctory. She did not major in English or in French; she did a politics major, got another adviser, but kept me for her English minor. I saw little of her until she turned up in Contemporary Women Writers her senior year. And it was as though somebody or something had plugged her in, some faculty, friends, activity—I never knew—but there she was, paying attention, writing with such passion and intensity I could scarcely believe this was the tuned-out student I'd had in Shakespeare. The last I heard, she was on a Fulbright scholarship in a country I'm not sure I could find on a map.

Or Zoey, from a large high school in San Bernardino, who showed up with glitter on her nails and lashes, flash of thigh and cleavage, perfume so strong I had to open the window. She decided to major in Spanish, found another adviser, and I didn't see her again until her senior year, when she appeared in my creative nonfiction writing workshop—and her papers were stunning, whimsical, reflective, self-aware. Something had happened in her years at Scripps, some prof or course had turned her around, and there she was, present, engaged, fully feminist, and fully clothed. When I last heard, she was teaching Spanish and theater at a private school in Pasadena.

And this, from a student who I remember grumbling a lot:

> Scripps wasn't my first choice. Scripps wasn't my second or third choice, either. . . . But I was soon proven wrong. . . . Here I see a wide range of women, some determined and straight-laced, some spontaneous and rebellious, but most not so easily defined. There's room at Scripps to be whoever you want to be.
>
> After spending the first semester spiteful and full of disdain, I realized . . . [this is] an environment that allows them to define who that woman is for herself without being doubted or judged. My professors have been consistently engaged and enthusiastic about their roles as educators . . . not only interested in seeing students succeed, but willing to appreciate them on a more personal level . . . respect my opinions, listen to my frustrations, indulge my interests.
>
> In my four years here, I've witnessed myself and many of my peers undergo a complete transformation. Those who entered judgmental and insecure, unsure of who they were, have since become unique individuals who embrace and celebrate their differences.

The transformation she describes—students growing into themselves, becoming more who they are, embracing and celebrating their differences—is not indoctrination. It's education.

FOUR

"The Reading Thing"

Attending, Remembering, Connecting

The reading thing—you learn to read a newspaper, hear a news story. It's like you're reading between the lines all the time, you just are. All that analysis we did in our classes—you never forget how.

—LORALYN CROPPER, '84

I feel like I can relate to my patients better on account of the stories we read and those discussions we had. I can hear what they're saying. Sometimes that's all people really need, for somebody to hear what they're saying.

—ELEANOR, '96

The part of the mind that reads a story is also the part that reads the world; it can deceive us, but it can also be trained to accuracy; it can fall into disuse and make us more susceptible to lazy, violent, materialistic forces, but it can also be urged back to life, transforming us into more active, curious, alert readers of reality.

—GEORGE SAUNDERS, *A Swim in a Pond in the Rain*

"Goals of the course—look here, it says on the syllabus—goals of the course are 'to learn how to read a Shakespeare play and show that you can in your writing.' Best get this clear at the outset. Simple, yes?" No. There's a question on the student evaluation form, "Goals of this course made clear?" I get less than a perfect score.

I say it again. "I want you to learn to read the plays, so you'll be able to pick up a Shakespeare play and find your way around it." And again: "The goal of the course is to get you easy with the plays, so you'll find a way through that wall of words, see what the fuss is about—you know, like what's so great about Shakespeare." A few nods. "So you'll know how to read a play on your own, so you might actually *want* to read a play on your own, you know, for pleasure, go see a play, take your kids." So you'll have something in your head besides the garbage the culture pumps into it, I'd like to say, but do not. So you'll learn how to read people and what they're up to, not be *led by the nose as asses are.*

"That's all we do, read the plays?" says Brent, who takes up a surprising lot of space. "Aren't we going to get theory? You know, post-structuralism, queer theory?"

"Get theory"—sounds like an injection, a shot, an energy drink. "Not . . . as such. Some of the plays raise theoretical issues. We can't talk about *Hamlet* without bringing in Freud, or *Lear* without talking about Marx, or *Taming of the Shrew* without feminist criticism. We'll bring in theoretical approaches as they apply." *As needed,* as it says on the pill bottle. We have so little time on each play, why would I spend precious moments unpacking some critic's argument when we could be talking about the play? (My problems with theory I keep under wraps, but I'll say here, I quit writing about literature around the time the "great books" and "humanism" became words that could only be used in scare quotes, when the books I loved were denounced as carriers of oppressive ideology; that had not been my experience of them. I guess I have theory to thank for making me a generalist.)

I draw their attention to these lines, which I've put on the syllabus in large print, and bold:

Reade him, therefore; and again'e, and againe:
And if then you doe not like him, surely you are
in some manifest danger, not to vnderstand him.

They're from the preface to the First Folio, the first printed collection of Shakespeare's works. His fellow players and partners in the Globe, John Heminges and Henry Condell, put this collection together seven years after his death, not for fame or profit but as a loving "office to the dead," "to keep the memory of so worthy a friend, and fellow alive, as was our Shakespeare."

"Don't worry, there's plenty in the plays to keep us busy. These plays cannot be read, they can only be re-read. I mean that. There are easier courses. Try the American short story." Cheap shot, but I know, anything contemporary goes down easier. Twice as many sign up for my contemporary women writers as for Shakespeare, three times as many for creative nonfiction writing. Go figure. How can they write if they do not read?

Words, Words, Words: The Hardest Things

"Okay, let's talk about reading a Shakespeare play. What are some of the challenges?" Silence. Nobody wants to go first on this, show how dumb they are. But we're all dumb with a Shakespeare play, at first. "Anybody?" Silence.

"Okay, open to act 3, scene 2, *Taming of the Shrew*, the play we'll be reading next week. Start with the horse."

Huh?

"Petruchio's horse, the one he rides to his wedding when he finally shows up, having kept Kate waiting at the altar. The wedding takes place offstage, but we hear what he looks like, crazily dressed, and here's his horse: *swayed in the back, shoulder shorten . . . possessed*

with the ganders and like to moose in the chine; troubled with the
lampas . . . full of windgall, sped with spavins, rayed with yellows, past
cure of the fives.

Lizzie's eyes widen. "It's like a foreign language."

"Why? On account of the complexity of the verse, the subtlety of
thought?"

"I, uh, don't know anything about horses."

"Right. What was familiar to Shakespeare is foreign to us. He'd
be lost in a conversation about shock absorbers and transmissions. We
have to cast ourselves back more than 400 years, journey back to meet
him in his world so we can bring him into ours. Which is why you
need an edition with good notes. The first time through, you're just
translating. And he used so many words, 15,000 by conservative estimate. He loved words, cavorted with them like a colt in spring grass,
and boy, could he rap them out, twist them and turn them and make
them do somersaults, arabesques, and flips, turn them upside down
and inside out, make them sparkle and flash, verbing his nouns and
nouning his verbs: *he childed as I fathered, whored my mother, lip a*
wanton, out tongue your griefs. His characters riff into verbal fireworks
for the sheer, intoxicated fun."

"Sounds like rap," comes the comment.

"Sort of. And if a word didn't exist, he made one up—take out that
sheet I gave you, words Shakespeare made up. Renaissance humanists
did a lot of this, translating classical manuscripts; if there was no word
in English for what the Latin was saying, they made one up. *Neologism.*
We do it too, invent new words. Googling, cyberspace, blogosphere,
infotainment." "Mansplaining," says Ashley. "Manspreading," says
Cynthia. "Crapification," from Danny with the Dylan hair.

"Seventeen hundred—that's how many words Shakespeare invented that made it into the language. Assassination, accommodation,
alligator, acutely—and we're still in the As—frugal, fitful, inauspi-

cious, lonely, obscene, unreal, worthless, zany. Many words he made up didn't make it into the language. *Incarnadine*, to make red—Macbeth imagines his bloody hand turning the seas red. *Intrinsicate*, combination of intrinsic and intricate—*this knot intrinsicate*, says Cleopatra, holding the serpent whose bite will untie hers."

"Then there's the wordplay. *Ask for me tomorrow and you will find me a grave man*—who says that?" Ashley, who has played Juliet, recognizes Mercutio's dying lines. Grave puns, serious puns, deadly puns, lighthearted puns. Resonant puns, as when Bottom, waking, reaches for words to describe his wondrous night in the woods: *I shall call it Bottom's dream because it hath no bottom*. Biting puns—*A little more than kin and less than kind*, Hamlet quips about his uncle, Claudius. Lots of wordplay in these plays, lots of play in these . . . plays. Play on that word *play: thou playst most foully, you cannot play upon me, the play's the thing*. Play on *lie*: *Lie . . . with her, on her, what you will*, says Iago, lying. *I lie with her and she with me, / And in our faults by lies we flattered be*, Sonnet 138. Play on the word *will*: intend, desire, please, also, of course, Shakespeare's name. Dr. Johnson called his punning 'the fatal Cleopatra for which he lost the world and was content to lose it.'"

Uh-oh, I am losing some of them. I find this more interesting than they do. It's hard to get them worked up about words.

It's actually the hardest thing about this course, to get them to attend to the words on the page, read the words with attention, let alone enthusiasm. How to get them to thrill to the enchanted woods with *green sour ringlets* and *midnight mushrumps*, to Caliban's vision of clouds opening up to reveal riches, *that, when I waked, / I cried to dream again*, to Ariel's *sea change into something rich and strange*? How to get them to imagine, when they're used to having their imaginations done for them: out of a steaming pool rises a screaming skull, fangs dripping stalactites, morphs into a pillar of fire, cities crumble, worlds collide, and more, much more than I can say—how can words compete? We're as blunted in the brain as Bottom and the benighted literalists who think that *to bring moonlight into a chamber,* you need an actual moon.

It's a big deal even to get them to bring their books. I know, *The Complete Works of Shakespeare* is heavy, in all senses—yes, you may use a paperback, as long as it has notes; no, you may not read the plays online; yes, you must bring the text to every class. Mark it up, don't save it for re-sale. Interact with it, react to it, write in it, make it your own. You may need it later, for reasons you can't fathom now.

Then to get them to actually *open* their books, find the passage, pay attention to the words. I cannot tell you how resistant they are to this. They'll come in full of indignation about Petruchio or Lear, ready to share their responses (a good class, that is). "I don't like Lear." Okay, that's a place to begin. I let discussion wander awhile, we talk about what a bad father Lear is—this is the easy part, where they get to say how they feel. "Can we turn to the play, see what's there, come back to how you feel after we've worked through the play? You may still not like him but at least you'll be able to say *why* with more, uh, evidence, so we're talking about the play and not so much about . . . you. There's a difference," I say (and say again), "between an opinion and an informed opinion—Where do you find that? What is your basis for saying that? Show me where in the text." But then, when I say, turn to act ɪ, what does Lear say? what does he do? I feel the energy drain from the room.

"Look at the words, stay with the words, it will repay. Trust me, it will."

Interpretation

"Let's back up a bit, talk about reading a play. What are some differences between plays and novels? Actually, no, first let's talk about fiction—what is fiction? Which do you prefer, fiction or nonfiction?"

Silence. Uh-oh, here's a distinction that's getting lost. Such odd things I've been finding in their papers: "in the essays Shakespeare wrote," "in Shakespeare's text books," "in the novels of William Shakespeare"—text books, novels, essays, all tossed on the same heap. A dangerous blurring in a post-truth age. Better sort this out.

"What is fiction? What makes a short story different from an essay?"

One hand, tentative, Lizzie. "You mean, like fiction isn't . . . true?"

"Good. Whereas nonfiction, an article you read in a psychology course or a newspaper is true, or presumed true, right? By which we mean . . . anyone?" "Like it really happened." "Based on facts." "Right. Fact-based, evidence-based, actually happened, as opposed to something made up. Whereas fiction is, well, it didn't really happen. If you say someone's telling a fiction, what are you calling them?"

"A liar?" Lizzie with the frizzy halo and the upward lilt.

"Right, they're inventing. Fabricating. So is that what we're doing in a literature course, reading lies?" Uh-oh, it may be too early for this question. Then a hand goes up, tentative, a voice barely audible, "Does it need to 'really happen' for it to be true?" Sandra of the sandy braid and dreamy gaze. "Good. You mean, like, fiction might tell a different kind of truth. 'The lie that tells the truth,'" I say, quoting Neil Gaiman.[1] I look around, nobody's picking up on this. "Let's file this away for later."

"There were people who condemned the theater for being lies— anyone know who?" "My father," says Brent, setting off chuckles. "Right. Who else? There was a whole class of people in Shakespeare's day, trying to close the theater." "Oh right," says Danny, "the Puritans! like in *Shakespeare in Love* . . ." "How many of you have seen *Shakespeare in Love*?" About half the class. "See it, or see it again. What did the Puritans have against the theater, besides untruths? Think about it: boy actors dressed as women." "In drag!" says Danny. "Yes.

They called it 'an abomination, to show themselves otherwise than they are, and so within the compasses of a lie.' They saw it as a subversion of the natural order, and of the social order, too, actors pretending to be kings and nobles, subverting hierarchy and rank. A pleasure-hating people, the Puritans, they made war on theater, music, poetry." They made this country, too; they're in our DNA, Republican governors cutting out the arts.

"So which is easier to read, a story or an essay?"

"Story." "Essay." The words come simultaneously from several directions.

I turn to Alice, the engineering student, who said "essay." "Why essay?"

"Because it's, like, you know, all laid out. You don't have to figure out what it means or anything."

"Yeah, but that's *boring*," says Allison. "A story's more fun." (How could I ever have had trouble telling these two apart? Alice is sharp-edged and self-assured; Allison is soft, round, tentative.)

"Why fun?"

"Well, you know, it pulls you in."

"Pulls you in—you mean, engages you, emotionally?" I push on this.

"Yeah. It makes me care." "How many of you feel a story makes you care?" Most hands go up. "More than an essay?" Heads nod. "Me, too," I confess. "Something else: when I teach nonfiction, I find it . . ." I'm groping for words that don't say "less interesting." It's interesting in a different way, of course, but the challenge, teaching *The Feminine Mystique* or *The Second Sex*, is remembering where the key passages are, seeing how the author brings in evidence to support her points, how she builds an argument. I say, "Once you've figured out what the author's saying, see her main points and how she supports them, there aren't a lot of surprises. What you see is what you get.

WYSIWYG"—I write it on the board, sound it out, "whizzie-wig— love that word. Whereas imaginative fiction is full of surprises. It requires, well, imagination. It's a creation of the imagination that calls on our imagination to piece it together—Why does this character say what she says, and why here, where she says it? Why is a drunken porter hammering at the gate, and why here, just after the murder? We have to tease it out, decipher, decode, fill in the blanks, read between the lines—*interpret*." I write the word on the board, alongside WHYSI-WYG. *Interpretation*. "That's what makes it interesting."

"Yeah but that's what makes it hard," Alice insists.

"You're right. If you lose the thread of an essay, what do you do? Page back and find a paragraph that gives the main point, probably at the end or beginning. But if you lose your way in *Middlemarch*, you're really lost. Your sense of the characters, where the story's going, what it's all about, requires that you hold lots of pieces in mind, figure out how they go together. But hard is good, right?" Silence. Some shifting in seats. I look around for a pair of eyes to meet, find none. Uh-oh, maybe they don't think hard is good.

"Okay, so we're reading fiction, specifically, plays. How is a play different from a short story?" Nothing comes back. "Which requires more . . . *interpretation*?" Still nothing. "Look at the page—tell me what you see."

"Words," says Danny with the Dylan hair. I do sort of love these wise asses. But I wish they weren't always the guys.

"Right. *Words, words, words*—but what kind of words? Look here"—I read—"Kate: *Where did you learn this goodly speech?* Petruchio: *It is extempore, from my mother wit. . . .*" "What do we call this?"

"Dialogue," says Ashley, who has played Juliet.

"Right, the characters are talking to each other. But they talk in a short story or a novel, too, don't they? What's the difference?"

"Uh, in a play, that's pretty much all there is." Ashley, again.

"Right, everything comes through the dialogue. What the characters say to each other has to say it all, has to get across—well, you tell me what sorts of things it has to get across. What kinds of information does a reader need to have?"

"You mean, like the backstory?" Ashley has a head start on this.

"Right, everything in the past, what went on before, to bring us where we are. What else?" I look hopefully around, trying to catch a pair of eyes not Ashley's, but she's back again: "About the characters."

Uh-oh, she's turning this into a conversation between her and me, please, somebody say something—"Yes, what about the characters? What's a soliloquy?"

"You mean, like, what they're really thinking?" Go, Lizzie. "Good, the whole realm of a character's inner life, interiority, the conversation inside, the dialogue has to get all that across. You know, I'm sure, that what we're saying here is only a small part of what's going on with us. Think—where are you now? In your head, I mean—where are you *really*?" A few exchange glances—does she really want to know? "Fess up, what were you thinking just now? About what happened last night? What you'll do when class is over? Memories, desires, hopes, fantasies, all that inner conversation. A novelist can pause the action, let you in on what a character's really thinking, spell it out. But the playwright has only what the character *says*, only the dialogue to get across everything going on inside. Can you pause the action in a play?" Heads shake. "Why not?"

"Well, you just can't stop a play. What would the actors *do*?" Ashley again.

"That's right—there's people present. A performance is people on stage doing and saying things—you can't hit a pause button. You've got real live people on the stage and in the audience, too. And real time—a play takes place in real time—you can't pause it and tell everyone to come back later. *Living theater*—you've heard that term?"

Come to think of it, this might be a good time to ask: "How many of you have actually *seen* a play, a live performance?" Most raise their hands, but not Barbara or Lydia in the puppy dog T-shirt or Samantha with the black helmet hair. Here's where you see a difference in cultural capital.

"Theater is the most human of the literary arts. It depends on the presence, energy, engagement of real live human beings. The actors can only act, the audience can only attend, for so long. A play has to keep moving. A live performance requires enormous energy—it's a strenuous act." Ashley nods vigorously. "And it goes by fast. A performance is for one night. Think of all the work that goes into preparing for those few hours, then poof, it's over. It's a labor of love, really; people act, dance, sing, write stories, draw, paint, for love, not money. And it's risky, no second chances—miss your cue, forget your lines, you don't get to go back and do it again, no retakes, not like film. Unforgiving, over before you know it, a bit like life." Like this class, I'd like to say, which also takes place in real time, which requires your engagement, your imagination, your generosity; which is also a living thing with limits, human, as we are. Except that in this class, you're both actor *and* audience; and so am I.

"So when we read a play, we're reading dialogue. A script. We have to picture what's going on, imagine how a line would be said, how the actor would look while he's saying it, imagine who else is on stage, how they might be reacting, interacting. Watch for the silences—there are eloquent silences in Shakespeare, they're more noticeable when we're watching a play than when we're reading. We have to imagine, to tease out the meaning—*interpret*. There's no authorial voice telling us what it means, no voiceover to direct our feelings, which leaves lots of ways to read a line, a character, a situation, a silence, lots of room for interpretation. A Shakespeare play never unfolds the same way twice; it assumes a different life with each new director, cast, audience. Which is why directors love to direct these plays and actors love to act them, and people like me write about them."

The class is with me, though not enthralled. I forge on. "Take out that handout by Oscar Eustis, artistic director of the New York Public Theater, and follow as I read." At the festivals of Dionysius, I read, there was storytelling:

> At some point, legend has it, right at the time when [the Greeks] were first inventing that idea of democracy, somebody named Thespis got the idea that instead of just talking to his audience, he, being on stage, could turn and talk to somebody else on stage. That changed everything, just as the Greek idea of democracy changed everything.

This was the moment theater was born, the same time, same place, as Athenian democracy, in the elimination of the authority of a single voice.

> As soon as Thespis turned and spoke to someone else, as soon as he invented dialogue, everything changed. The storyteller—who has had this authorial, god-like, unified perspective—isn't "right" anymore. . . . He is one of two points of view that are on stage. At that juncture we realize that truth resides not in the storyteller—truth resides somehow in the dialogue, in the space between two people. You're imagining that you're in my shoes: You empathize with me, and then empathize with whoever I'm talking to. That act—that empathic leap of imagination— is the democratic act. In order for a democracy to work you have to believe that nobody has a monopoly on truth.

I love the idea that the "truth" of theater, like that of democracy, is in the elimination of the authorial voice, that Shakespeare's theater, like the Greeks', was born of a democratic spirit, of an audience "diverse in class, in education and in every other way":

All of those people, from the aristocracy to the illiterate ground-
lings . . . are demanding to be entertained. They're insisting that a
writer show up who can speak to all of them at once. . . . So, in a way,
that democratic audience calls Shakespeare into being. . . . What you
see . . . is the exciting artistic result of democracy in action.[2]

"Just think, an audience calling an artist 'into being' . . ." It may be a
little early in the semester for the class to find this exciting, but it fas-
cinates me.

What Shakespeare "Meant"

"What did Rosemary's baby look like?" That question used to call
forth interesting responses. Now hardly anyone's heard of *Rosemary's
Baby*, or of Polanski or the Sharon Tate murders. But there was a time
when most of my students could tell me what the baby looked like,
and they all had different versions. The point is, we never do see the
baby. Mia Farrow walks over to a crib draped in black, her face fills
with horror, she gasps, "What have you done to his eyes?" Polanski
knows that our imaginations can conjure eyes more horrific than any
special effect.

Imaginative literature calls on the reader's imagination, challenges,
exercises, develops our imagination, and drama, of all imaginative literature, asks the most. One of the pleasures of teaching Shakespeare is to
see how differently people read lines, characters, situations—"How can
you think this is funny?" "How can you not?" "How can you say this is
not an anti-Semitic play?" "How can you say this is not a chauvinist pig
play?" "How can you like this character?" "Where do you get *that*?"
Students are surprised at the range of responses, and me, too, I can still
be surprised, though I know, ever since people have been talking or
writing about Shakespeare, they've found things to disagree about.

"Cleopatra really loves him, she gives up everything for Antony." "She's a bitch. He's a fool to give up Rome for her." And Kate, in *The Taming of the Shrew*—is she beaten into submission? Does she really place her hand under Petruchio's boot? We can argue endlessly about these things. And Isabella in *Measure for Measure*, who refuses to sacrifice her virginity to save her brother's life—how do we feel about her? Is she cold and brittle or principled and heroic? Students practically come to blows over Isabella. How do we read Gertrude, or Shylock—how did "Shakespeare's audience" see them? Was Brutus right or wrong to murder Caesar? (Students get more riled up over Kate and Cleopatra than they do about this assassination that turned the course of history.)

Arguing about these plays in class, we see that other people have ways of thinking that are nothing like our own. These moments of recognition can startle us into registering what Sheila Heti calls "the true singularity of others."[3] And they can teach us something about ourselves: I am nothing like that, or, I hope I'm not like that, or, I might like to be like that. They can be steps in sorting out me from "not me," toward knowing ourselves as we come to know others.

"Does this mean any reading is as good as any other, anything goes, texts are as we interpret them? How do we know one reading's any better than another—*is* there a 'right' reading?"

"One that agrees with you." Brent the preppy, Brent the cheeky, better get that guy on my side.

"Absolutely, for sure. But apart from that?"

"You mean, how do we figure out what the play really means?" says Lizzie.

"I was trying to avoid that word *means*. But okay, wouldn't we like to know what the play 'really means'?"

"Does it have to *mean* something?" asks Brent.

"Not in a 'take-home message' sort of way. More . . . exploratory, like the questions it's getting us to think about. But yes, I do think the plays 'mean' something, or why are we bothering with them, all these ages later? Look, Shakespeare was an entertainer, an entrepreneur, but that's not all he was. He was a pusher and mover, a showman, up to his eyeballs in showbiz, the show must go on. It was a tacky business, theater, consigned to the red-light district outside the city, disreputable, dangerous. His fellow playwrights were a dissolute lot, one step ahead of the law—Ben Jonson was in and out of jail. Christopher Marlowe, atheist, homosexual, spy, was killed in a tavern brawl under suspicious circumstances. Thomas Kyd was arrested and tortured. Yet somehow out of these madly chaotic conditions, Shakespeare managed to create something amazing, something that . . . draws us back again and again."

Brent looks unconvinced. So do a few others. "Well, look, why can't we just say, 'Shakespeare says, *this above all, to thine own self be true—* what's wrong with that?"

"Because it's a character who says it, not Shakespeare, strictly speaking." Ashley, who has played Juliet.

"Right, it's Polonius—and how does that complicate the line?" We tease this out. He's a windbag and a fool. "How about those lines we often hear, *life's but a walking shadow, a poor player / That struts his hour upon the stage*? Macbeth says this, on a very bad day. Shakespeare wrote the words, of course, as he wrote all the characters in the plays—but which of the many voices in a Shakespeare play is 'really' Shakespeare? Sure, there's more of him in Hamlet than Horatio, in Prospero than Miranda, but you can't take a line out of context and say, 'Shakespeare says.' Though we do it all the time."

"Google 'wisdom of Shakespeare,' see what comes up." "Wow, 36 million hits!" "Read some." "Here's a site that says, 'Words to motivate, challenge, inspire.'" "Which words?" *"This above all—to thine own self be true."* Right. Polonius. *"Love all, trust a few, do wrong to none."* Polonius again. *"Give sorrow words."* "That gets quoted in grief groups. Fine words, stirring words, but when you're quoting like this, is this reading? Or *raiding*?"

"You mean, like, it's out of context?" Thank you, Lizzie.

"Right. Reading requires context, connecting the lines to the speaker, the speaker to the play, trying to grasp the whole. So. How do we figure out what a play 'means'"?

How Does a Play Mean?

"Google 'why is Shakespeare important.'"

"Wow. More than 147 million hits," says Cynthia.

"Read some." "Homeschooling . . . Christians?" She looks up— "Seriously?" "Yes, and that's not daft—his plays are saturated in the Bible. But whether that makes him a Christian or a Catholic . . . we'll come back to that." "Here's a book called *Power Plays*, leadership advice," says Allison, and reads, 'What is *Julius Caesar* if not a very hostile takeover attempt by disgruntled stockholders? And is not *King Lear* a warning to all executives of family businesses on the perils of divestiture and early retirement?'[4] For real?"

"A CEO could do worse than read the plays of Shakespeare. Power is a big theme. But for how-to tips, there are books I'd go to first. So, Shakespeare as evangelical teacher, Shakespeare as corporate consultant, Shakespeare as life coach—are these all valid ways of reading the plays?" I let the question hang.

"I dunno. I guess," ventures Sandra. "Equally valid?" "Well, I guess, if you see it that way. I mean, isn't it always just us reading in?"

"Sure, in a way. We bring ourselves as readers. Our backgrounds, experiences, expectations, prejudices filter the way we read. We can never transcend the personal reference point. Every reader constructs her own Shakespeare, and every age. But does this mean anything goes?" Silence. I try another tack.

"Imagine if you did this in life. Say you meet a person you have a strong take on, want to hire or fire or go to bed with, or say that person is your boss and you need to finesse that. Do you say, oh, well, it's just me making stuff up, might as well go with the flow, anything goes?" Heads shake. "Why not?"

"Delusional," says Danny. "Dangerous," adds Cynthia.

"Right. So what do you do? You start paying attention, trying to figure out what's pushing your buttons or ringing your bells. You *read*. You know how to read. Tell me how you read." We tease this out. You listen to what the person says, watch what he does, watch body language, expressions, see how he is with others, find out what others say about him, try to figure out what makes him tick. "You try to get yourself out of the way, damp down your feelings and responses, open your mind and senses to register what's there. You pay attention. As a matter of fact, we'll be reading about characters who fail to do just that."

I stop, lest there be spoilers, but we'll see that Othello, Lear, Macbeth, Brutus read badly and so are easy prey, *led by the nose as asses are.* Malvolio, too. It's hilarious to see this joy-killing Puritan, so full of *self-love* that he's sure *all that look on him do love him*, played for a fool. But it's not funny watching Brutus being manipulated into a political coup for which he's wildly unsuited, or Othello, Lear, and Macbeth trusting people who lead them disastrous ways. The problems of interpretation we face, reading a play, trying to attend to what's there, are writ large in the failures of the characters, failures that lead them to tragic ends. The tragedies are object lessons in reading badly.

"Okay, so what can you say about the difference between reading and reading in?"

"I guess, if you're reading in, you're finding . . . what you're look-ing for . . ." comes tentatively, from Sandra, "like what you expect or want to find?" "Right. Call that *raiding*. And reading is . . . ? The question hangs there. "Can we find a way of reading the play that isn't . . . raiding?" Finally, Sandra: "Aren't a lot of those readings, uh, raidings, sort of . . . simple? I mean, there's a lot going on in a Shake-speare play."

"Good, a lot going on. Say more." "Well, there's the characters, the plot . . ." She trails off. "Let's list the parts of a play. Someone write this on the board." Ashley leaps from her seat, stands ready at the board. Dialogue, she writes. "Yes, dialogue, what the characters say, that's the heart of a play. Action, what the characters do. Only one plot? Nearly every play has a subplot, sometimes two or three, and a question we'll ask is, how does each plot relate to the other plots, are they parallels, contrasts, variations, commentaries? How does the pres-ence of a subplot affect the way we see the main plot? Why does Shakespeare graft these particular plots together? This is a question that comes up on exams, so listen up."

"Character, yes, characters"—I'm fast-forwarding here—how do we get to know a character? By what they say and do and what other char-acters say about them. The way we do in life. Structure—what do we mean by structure? How the play moves, where it starts from, moves to, develops, for always there is movement in drama, which is . . . well, dramatic. Dynamic. It has to move. Why does this scene follow that? How about imagery? Certain images recur, as, for example . . . ? "Light in *Romeo and Juliet*," says Ashley, who has played Juliet. "Right. Night in *Macbeth*, the ruined garden in *Hamlet*, animals in *Lear*. When a word or image recurs, pay attention, it's telling you something."

"So. There are all these working parts. When we're reading a play, as opposed to raiding, we take into account as many parts as we can, see how they go together. The more parts a reading takes in, the more complete and convincing, the more *responsible* it is. We'll see how images recur, building meaning." We'll see—they'll see, when we get to *Lear*—*Hence and avoid my sight. See better, Lear. We / Have no such daughter, nor shall never see / That face of hers again. . . .* Does Lear ever see her face again? Turn to the final scene, Lear searching the face of Cordelia for signs of life, *look there, look there. . . .* Does anyone besides Lear fail to see? Gloucester stumbled when he saw, sees better when he's blind—sight, insight, vision, these themes recur, gathering associations.

"Performances moved faster in Shakespeare's theater; scene followed scene in quick succession, no scenery to drag on and off, so it was easier to hear echoes, to get a sense of parts working in concert. As you begin to see patterns, you see *there's magic in the web of it*, as Othello says of the handkerchief he gives Desdemona, as there is in the weave of a text." *Text*, a good word. Literary theory has landed us with a lot of clunkers—*hegemonic, heteronormativity, hybridity, intersectionality*, and (my least favorite) *interrogate*, as though the text is on trial. But *text*, I like—it suggests textured, tactile, wrought, worked, woven like a textile or tapestry. It gets at an important quality of the plays, their patterns, designs. *Intrinsicate*, that word Cleopatra used that never caught on, there would have been a use for such a word. Each text weaves a world of meanings beyond what prose summary can say.

"If we attend to a play, really attend, the play can teach us how to read the play. Look at the words, say them aloud, hear them, open yourself to the sound and sense of the words, attend, remember. But you have to be paying attention to do this kind of reading, you have to remember when the image or idea occurred before, to see how meanings build, develop, intensify. Memory and attention . . ."

"Do you really think they got all this stuff we're digging out?" says Brent, unconvinced.

"Probably not. We bring a lot to the plays they didn't have. And we are reading—the plays weren't written to be read. But they got something, those original audiences, or they wouldn't have kept coming back. Just think, a mass audience, most of whom could not read, yet they loved these plays. Of course it was their world, so they wouldn't be thrown by Petruchio's horse. But I think you can do this with people, smarten them up or dumb them down, bring out their better or worser parts." I guess, as an educator, I would have to think this, wouldn't I?

"So now, what can you say of those evangelicals and corporate consultants and inspirationals who extract lessons about leadership or homeschooling for Christians?" "They're not seeing all the parts," ventures Lizzie. "Right, they're stripping the plays for parts rather than seeing them whole. They're raiding."

"But raiding's okay, isn't it," says Danny, "when you're just getting the gist of something, like a blog or article." "Sure, we need to know how to grasp information from the floods of information that come our way. When we read online, we're usually raiding. Online doesn't require the concentration that deep reading does; we don't need to connect ends with beginnings—there are no ends and beginnings, it's a continuous scroll. When we're skimming or snarfing up information or link leaping, we don't immerse ourselves so deeply, which is why we remember less."[5]

"But to come back to Sandra's question—yes, it is always us reading in, to some extent. The Shakespeare you'll encounter in this class is Shakespeare according to Gayle Greene. I read as a woman, a feminist, an academic who hales from a time when we believed in close reading. There will be parts I'm blind to, that the 'interpretative community' I'm part of is blind to, that another critic, another age may bring into focus. No single reading or critical analysis can fully take in a play. That doesn't mean anything goes or any reading is as good as any other or that we should quit trying. But the only final statement is the play itself, which is a lot more interesting than anything I or you or anybody can say about it."

One day, when a missed connection made me late to class, I called Becky, my right-hand woman at Scripps, and asked her to find the DVD of *Othello* on my desk and run it over to my classroom and get it playing, so the time would get used. When I got there, half an hour late, the students didn't even hear me come in, so lost were they in the Branagh-Fishburne film. So I took a seat by the wall and let it go on, and when class time ended, those who could stayed and watched to the end. Hmmm, I thought, maybe I should use class to show the films, maybe we should all just sit back and enjoy the movies. I think of William Hazlitt's snarky comment, "if you want to see the wisdom of the race, read Shakespeare, if you want to see folly, read his commentators."[6]

But then, maybe they were capable of that level of engagement because we'd spent three classes talking about the play, and that gave them a way in. One can hope.

The *Yin* of Reading, the *Yang* of Raiding

Deep reading requires that we get quiet, slow down, shut out other claims—and that's a lot, in lives so full of distraction. Deep reading requires *yin*, and we are a culture bursting with *yang*, better at asserting ourselves than immersing ourselves in something outside ourselves (as in, many more students wanting to take writing classes than literature). *Yang* comes more easily to us, fixated as we are on the ratatat of me-me-me. When we're raiding, snatching up information, skimming, we're in *yang*. It's important to know how to do this, but if it's all we do, other things atrophy, or never develop. Like memory and attention.

Everything in our culture works against attending and remembering. The media bombard us with a steady stream of "breaking news," spectacle, celebrity, sports, disaster. Each day's shooting or scandal is reported without context or connection with the day before. MTV, action films, scriptless films, those long, shapeless TV series we're addicted to, jerk attention from one high point to another, inducing amnesia: there is only the moment, and why try to remember, there's always more to come. Buzzed by the moment-to-moment stimulation of sensationalist news, blockbuster films, click bait, we may never develop the capacity to remember and connect.

Learning to read a complex literary work, to see how the parts go together and build a whole, we are learning to see patterns, relationships. This is what understanding is, making connections, contextualizing, so we can apply what we learn to other problems. Until we can do this, information is just information, not very useful. "Data is overrated" says a geek friend of mine, "useless, unless you know what to do with it." Knowing what to do with it requires understanding, seeing how things go together, and that takes the kind of attention and memory developed by deep reading.

Deep reading is hard, which is why everybody looks for ways of avoiding it. Literary theory offered marvelous ways of evading it: get a grid—Marxist, feminist, postmodern, postcolonial, queer—clamp it down and crank out a reading; the "great" books aren't worth reading anyhow, except to "interrogate" or "deconstruct."[7] Digital humanities offers whole new vistas of evasion: build a web page, make a 3-D model of the streets Shakespeare would have walked, way cool.

The Common Core State Standards have a very effective way of avoiding the challenges of imaginative fiction—just don't assign it.

"Only Disconnect"

Reading was in decline before the Common Core turned kids off to it completely. A 2007 National Endowment for the Arts report, *To Read or Not to Read*, found a "universal falling off of reading" that begins around age 13, with "the percentage of 17-year-olds who read nothing at all for pleasure" doubling in a 20-year period.[8] This is bad news, because the report also turned up strong correlations between pleasure reading and reading well, and correlations between reading well and doing well in school *and* making contributions to society, developing a "social and civic sense."

"Reading has really died," said a 2014 Scripps graduate; "nobody reads, except what they have to." "Assign a project that involves an extra book, it's like you're sentencing them to hard labor," lamented a colleague; "English used to be seen as a 'soft' major. Not anymore." The buzz my generation got from reading, kids now get from video games, TV, the Internet. Since they don't develop the habit of reading, reading is hard for them, and a downward spiral sets in: the less they read, the worse they read, the less they want to read. Everyone I know complains about how little students read, how badly they read, how short their attention spans have become.

Reading for pleasure declines precipitously around ages 13 to 17, reports the NEA study. This is when the culture gets hold of kids, but it's also when they get hit with a curriculum that kills their desire ever to pick up a book again. No Child Left Behind and Race to the Top delivered body blows to pleasure reading, narrowing what is taught to what is tested. The Common Core dealt it a death blow, giving primacy of place to informational over imaginative texts and reducing reading and writing to the acquisition of decontextualized skills: "identify the grammatical errors," "generate a thesis statement," "find the main idea," "name the literary devices," "draw a conclusion."

Bill Gates was keen on the idea of "national standards" before 2010, when he made the Common Core a reality. "The standards will tell the teachers what their students are supposed to learn," he told the National Council of State Legislatures, July 2009, "and the data will tell them whether they're learning it."[9] (By "data," he means test scores, multiple-choice exams, which he sees as measures of learning, though most educators do not.)[10] Gates financed the Core and chose David Coleman, a man with no experience teaching, to devise the English Language Arts Standards.[11] Coleman's repeated directive is, "stay within the four corners of the text"; whether you're dealing with an imaginative or informational text,[12] make no connection with anything you've read or thought, just drill down on those skills. The Gettysburg Address without the Civil War sort of thing; Martin Luther King Jr.'s "Letter from a Birmingham Jail" without the civil rights movement. As in this assignment for juniors and seniors: "Analyze Thomas Jefferson's Declaration of Independence, identifying its purpose and evaluating *rhetorical* features such as the listing of grievances . . . [and] compare and contrast the themes and arguments found there to those of other U.S. documents of historical and literary significance, such as the Olive Branch Petition."[13] With Shakespeare, the only writer specifically required by the Core, students analyze Polonius's speech, *This above all—to thine own self be true.* No attention to the speaker or the play (the play is not assigned)—just drill down on those rhetorical features, no connections allowed.

But kids read for same reasons grow-ups read, because they're seeking fun, fantasy, escape; because they care about the characters and want to see how things come out. Drills in skills kill all that. The Common Core locks teachers into standardized modules, no thought, judgment, creativity allowed, no point to the exercises except test prep. "It's like a checklist we check off. Then we assess ourselves, remediate ourselves, and gear up to take another test. I feel like I'm killing something I love," lamented a friend who teaches fifth grade. "We used to be treated as professionals who were allowed to have autonomy in our classrooms and play to our strengths," said Rebecca Simcoe, a high school English teacher who resigned in 2014: "Now we're expected to be automatons following robotic instructions, just getting these kids to pass tests."[14] Teachers are made to march kids through preset steps to predetermined right answers; kids are taught to follow orders—dangerous, in times inclined to authoritarianism. "Frankly, the more I bludgeon my middle school students with the Common Core skills, the more I turn them off from reading," commented a reader of Diane Ravitch's blog. "They're purely mechanical . . . the last thing a struggling reader will care about." (Ravitch was a prominent member of the education departments of both Bush presidents and a supporter of "reform"; she turned whistle-blower when she saw that its goal was privatization, and has written and organized against it ever since.)

Deep reading, writes Maryanne Wolf in *Reader, Come Home*, is all about connecting, connecting what we read to who we are and what we know, connecting what we know and feel to others, seeing relationships between ourselves and what's out there in the world.[15] Understanding comes this way, as we've seen, from perceiving relationships, connecting new knowledge to what we already know. Restricting reading to the "four corners of the text," the Coleman way, "leaves the reading floating, isolated and disconnected from everything that gives it meaning," writes teacher-blogger Peter Greene in *Forbes*.[16] Students "need to spend more time outside the four corners, not less," if they're going to learn to read. But No Child Left Behind, Race to the Top, and the Common Core have eliminated the "outside," cutting out courses that teach about the world, to make time for drill and kill.

Also disastrous is the Core's foregrounding of informational texts over imaginative literature, which drives fiction to the margins or out of the classroom altogether. The Core recommends that K–8 teachers spend 50% of reading time on fiction and 50% on informational texts; in high school, that division becomes 30% fiction, 70% informational texts.[17] California high school teacher Michael Godsey was advised by a consultant to ditch literature since "literary fiction is not critical to college success." And sure enough, "none of the state assessments has a single question about the content of any classic 'literature.' They only test on reading skills, so teachers now prioritize these skills over content."[18]

"With informational texts, there isn't that human connection that you get with literature," said Jamie Highfill, 2011 Teacher of the Year. "And the kids are shutting down. They're getting bored. I'm seeing more behavior problems in my classroom than I've ever seen."[19] And even imaginative fiction is modularized so it can be computer scored—which is where all this is leading, to computerized learning. "My students experienced *Frankenstein* . . . not as a gripping monster story that prompts questions about what it means to be human, but as a lifeless fragment on a practice test, from which they were required to extract and regurgitate specific information that corporate test-makers deem important," writes high school teacher Nora de la Cour.[20] "It's like taking something done by humans and having it done by a machine," a teacher posted on a *Washington Post* blog.[21]

"Done by a machine" is no bad thing, according to Gates, who has thrown billions at computerized teaching programs. But what his remake of K–12 leaves out is the human being. "I don't want to be a teacher anymore," wrote a teacher in the *Washington Post*; teaching is about "teaching children, not standards . . . seeing them as human beings."[22] Teachers who know what teaching is know this is not it, and they're leaving in droves.

And the Common Core has failed, even at its own narrow, reductive goal, to raise test scores. Test scores have flatlined.[23]

Decline in Reading, Decline in Empathy: Cause? Correlation? Chance?

A large-scale study by researchers at the University of Michigan, 2011, found a significant decline of empathy among college students, a rise of narcissism and materialism, a marked falling off in the capacity to imagine the experience of others. The researchers asked tens of thousands of students such questions as, "I often have tender concerned feelings for people less fortunate than me," and "I try to look at everybody's side of a disagreement before I make a decision." Nearly 75% of students rate themselves as less empathic than students in the 1980s.

The study attributes this in large part to the decline in reading.[24]

You can see how the slow, full, prolonged imaginative engagement that makes a good reader may also cultivate the capacity to register the existence of another person, to enter into that person's perspective, the experience of otherness Keats called "negative capability."[25] The alum who gave me the words I used in one of the epigraphs to this chapter—"Sometimes that's all people really need, for somebody to hear what they're saying"—is an oncologist whose work requires the kind of end-of-life conversations shunned by most doctors. "Lack of empathy in caregivers—doctors, nurses, even loved ones—is one of the most widely voiced complaints in the health care field," writes Sandeep Jauhar.[26] Rita Charon founded Columbia's program in Narrative Medicine, which draws on the humanities to teach physicians the art of "being able to listen as a reader," to register the human being, not just the illness, "to see the complex lived experience of the person."[27] "Active listening," hearing the patient's story, improves medical outcomes.[28] Empathy has been advertised as "a career power tool"; crass as that sounds, it may make you a better teacher, doctor, researcher, scientist, a more successful CEO or international kidnapping negotiator, should your career path lie that way.[29]

In *The Better Angels of Our Nature*, Steven Pinker describes a study that presented one set of participants with a radio broadcast about the effects of catastrophic events on the personal lives of the people involved and asked them to "focus on the technical aspects of the broadcast," "take an objective perspective," and not get caught up in feelings—the Common Core approach. A second group was asked to "imagine how the person who is interviewed feels about what has happened and how it has affected his or her life." Those who were asked to attend to the emotional impact were more likely to sign up to help the victims, offering babysitting to a woman who'd lost her parents in a car crash, for example, than those who'd been told to take a technical, analytical approach,[30] which is what the Common Core teaches.

Now we're dealing not only with the decline of reading, but the reduction of reading to disembodied, alienating skills. Consider this high school assignment described by Nicholson Baker in *Substitute*, his account of being a substitute teacher in the spring of 2014, a few years after the Common Core was set in place. In a chilly classroom at 8:30 a.m., students are shown, with no preparation, a documentary of Oprah Winfrey and Elie Wiesel strolling the bleak Auschwitz landscape, discussing the Holocaust. The film shows stacks of bodies in ditches and invites the viewer to imagine further horrors. Their assignment reads, "In an essay decide which of the mediums we have looked at is the best for telling a survivor's story. Defend your decision . . . be sure to use varied transitions to link your ideas and develop cohesion." If students did that, they got a score 3. To get a 4, they had "to consider the problem of which medium is best for a specific audience. Every essay had to have a thesis statement, and the students were allowed one spelling mistake." They were given a blank chart "to be filled out with the several qualities, or 'criteria,' that a Holocaust survivor's story must have, each of which was to be multiplied by a factor of importance, one through four, called 'the multiplier.' Students were asked to assign values to each format and figure out its overall score." Mechanical and dehumanizing as this exercise is, it targets Core standards "Text Structures Level 6, Opinion/argument Level 7, and Writing Process Level 5," and that's what matters. Hit with this the first thing in the morning, the kids dissociate, break off into groups, giggling and chattering about the Teletubbies.[31]

If you set out to devise a more effective way to make human beings disengage from their fellow humans—a better "disimagination machine," in Henry Giroux's term—you could hardly come up with a better one than this.[32]

"Reade Him"

So, to return to the question I raised at the beginning of class, "Goals of this course made clear? *Read him.* Get up close on the words, make sure you know what they mean, then stand back and try to see how each part relates to other parts. Read close and read whole."

I glance around the room, the blond with the big hair, the serious-looking brunettes, the preppy who takes up a lot of space. "Work with it, stay with it, it will repay. It won't be easy. Shakespeare is not for the faint of heart. But hard is good, right?" Nothing comes back.

I guess they don't think hard is good. And maybe I wouldn't either, in their shoes. I think back to the hardest course I ever took as an undergraduate, Physics 10. For a month, I went to class and tried doing the assignments, but it was a brick wall, and it was draining my energies from courses I cared about; so I stopped going and put it out of mind. (If I hadn't heard by chance that the final exam was multiple-choice, I'd have skipped it. I sashayed in 10 minutes late and out 10 minutes later, every eye in the room on me. I got a C. So much for multiple-choice exams.) Hard was not good with Physics 10. Hard is why students panic, copy, crib, buy work. The stakes have been ratcheted up so high, they're not looking for mountains to scale but slopes to slide down.

"Look, when you read *The Hunger Games*, the *Twilight Saga*, it's all there on the surface. What you see is what you get. Whizzie-wig. But what's easy to access may soon go stale. Whereas, when a work doesn't yield up everything all at once, when you have to dig through layers, the yield may be richer. It may get better each time through."

A few nods. I try a different tack. "You've heard of the glycemic index?" *That* gets their attention. It gives Allison a chance to tell us, "It's like the way foods act different ways in your body. Foods that break down slower stick with you, give better nourishment." "Exactly. Think of it this way: great literature has a lower glycemic index. You don't get the instantaneous rush you get from junk, it doesn't go down so easy, takes longer to digest, but it gives more lasting energy, does better things to your body and brain."

Brittany looks up from her lap—is that a spark of curiosity? Something I've said is more interesting than her phone? Dammit, put that thing away, girl. I'll grab her after class.

"Hard is good," I say again, but it comes out feebly. "Look, the first time through a Shakespeare play, you're just translating, figuring out what the words mean. The second time, it's easier; third time, it starts getting interesting, you begin to pick up patterns of words and ideas, connect the parts, and little by little, it opens up. Meanwhile we'll be doing close readings in class. You'll watch others do it, then try it yourself. It's a process, a slow and seeping-in kind of thing. And if you stick with it, it will repay. We're reading some of the . . . greatest works ever written." *Great*—even I stumble on that word, so trashed has it been by literary theory. Yet greatness exists, and genius, too.

I wish I could bring in Dorothy Shapiro Lund, Pomona '09, now a law professor at USC, to tell them what she told me, how her first

English class sent her "reeling": "my professor was pushing me to really think deeply. I went to a large public high school where I got by with memorization—deep thinking was not required. It took a long time for me to break the habit of just putting words on a page, and instead, sitting and thinking critically about something and being deliberate." Focus is what she's talking about. "Being a lawyer is a lot like that. You have to take regulations, statutes, briefs, and opinions and really give them a deep look. You have to wrestle with the language and look at it 15 different ways, and be ready to defend or tear apart each reading. I can't think of a better way to prepare for law school than being an English major."

I direct their attention again to these words on the syllabus, I read them out loud: "*Reade him, therefore; and again'e, and againe.* Then when you are 30, read him again, and when you are 50, again, for as you get wiser, so will he."

I look around. They're so young. "Making 18-year-olds read Shakespeare is like having toddlers watch porn," said novelist Jess Walter, describing "six Spokane writers and professors who read Shakespeare and meet in bars to talk about the plays. It's been amazing. I'm starting to think everyone should have to read Shakespeare in their 40s or 50s, when you've lost parents and had children and really know failure, when you can appreciate all of that paradoxical insight. . . . That part of it is wasted on high school and college kids."[33] Maybe, we should require students to live another decade before they take this course. That'd do wonders for enrollments.

"Just think," I say, patting my book, "it's all in one volume. Anyone ever seen the complete works of Dickens or Trollope? They fill shelves. But with Shakespeare, there's just this, *The Complete Works of Shakespeare.* Okay, so the print is small and the pages double columned, but still . . ." (Actually, 37 plays in 20 years is amazing, considering that no play is like any other play and Shakespeare was doing lots of other things, acting, managing the Globe, traveling back and forth to Stratford.)

"And maybe, just maybe, we can *pluck out the heart of his mystery*, I mean, figure out, what the fuss is about—why Shakespeare?" A few nod sagely. But I'm suddenly out of steam. Because, honestly, if I had to bet, I'd say deep reading is going the way of the dodo bird. And with it may be going the kind of intelligence we need to deal with the future, the capacity to remember, to connect, to think things through, to imagine beyond the here and now—all this and more.[34]

"Yes, actually, hard is good," I say firmly. I do not say, but I will find a way of saying, I've seen how good it can be. It's why people graduate from this college with a confidence they didn't have when they came in—because they've stretched themselves to take in something larger than themselves, because they've written a senior thesis they may have thought beyond them, they've fulfilled a boatload of requirements and come through. When, in office hours, the conversation turns to self-esteem, as it often does, I try to change the channel from the Oprah talk they're used to hearing ("you're the best," "you can do anything") and say, "Do something you respect yourself for, that's how you gain self-respect. It's no mystery." And a BA you've worked for is something you can respect yourself for. Because it gives you a sense of accomplishment, authority, the confidence to take on more. *Mastery*, I would say, groping for a female equivalent—Misstery? Ms.tery?

I stare down at the book, still open to Petruchio's horse. A heap of words, black scratchings on a page, old words, hard words, strange words.

Shall these words live?

FIVE

The Play's the Thing

Taming of the Shrew, A Midsummer Night's Dream

Let my playing be my learning, and my learning be my playing.
—JOHAN HUIZINGA, *Homo Ludens*

Never in my wildest dreams could I have imagined that we would have
to defend children's right to play.
—NANCY CARLSSON-PAIGE, "How 'Twisted' Early Childhood
Education Has Become"

"Why did you assign this play?" This from Cynthia of the spiky hair,
sounding like a moan—like, how could you inflict this on us? "How
can they call this a comedy? He tortures her, starves her, humiliates
her—what's funny about that?"

"Yes, but . . ." I bite my tongue. No, Gayle, let it come from them.

"Maybe that's the way they saw women back then?" Lizzie of the
upward lilt.

"Yes, that's a real question with this play—how did they see women
back then? But wait—who's 'they'? Who was Shakespeare's audience?
'They'"—I fill in—"were . . . diverse. All classes and ranks, common-
ers, courtiers, aristocrats, Catholics, Protestants, women. 'They' were
not all of a piece any more than a modern audience is. Well, a bit more

monolithic, more Christian, more conventional about women, but 'they' included lots of different . . .'"

"Yeah, but why do we need to read it?" Cynthia, again. "If it's just history . . ." *Just history?* Oh boy, is history ever in trouble. But she has a point. Here we are at a women's college more than 400 years later—why should we read about the "taming of the shrew," if it's only testimony to how bad things were back then?

It will take the next few classes to tease out some responses to this.

The Headless Woman

"Google 'quiet woman,'" I tell them; "go to 'Google Images.'" Huh? "That's right, 'quiet woman.'" Gasps and giggles as the pub posters come up—they can't believe what they're seeing. The quiet woman is a headless woman. There are still Headless Woman pubs in England; there's one right here in Southern California. History lives.

"Not funny!" says Cynthia.

"Funny to somebody," says Danny.

"Let's talk about how 'they' saw women 'back then'—what was the Renaissance ideal of woman? Anyone?" "Dead," comes from Brent, setting off chuckles; "I mean, if she's headless . . ." "That's not far off, actually; we'll see in *Othello*. But really, what was the ideal? Give me some words." Words drift in . . . "Obedient." "Yes." "Silent." "Yes. *Chaste, silent, obedient*," I summarize; "those were the cardinal female virtues, according to conduct manuals and guidebooks for women in early modern England; those were the qualities becoming a woman, and not only for that period, but for centuries."

"Chaste, you mean, like, a virgin?" Trevor. "No. Yes. Well, a virgin before marriage, not after, obviously—but faithful to her husband, women's fidelity being a much bigger deal than a man's. Why? Why the fixation on female sexuality?"

"Control." Cynthia practically spits the word. "Right. This is a society that's *patriarchal, patronymic, patrilineal*"—I write the words on the board. Rule of the father, name of the father, lineage through the father. "How does this make for a need to control?" "Inheritance," says Allison. "Yes, property, making sure your property goes to your legitimate heirs. Control of female sexuality is about making sure your kids are really yours. The double standard—know what that is?" Of course they do. "Guys don't get called slut," says Cynthia. "Guys don't get called lots of things we get called," from Samantha of the black-helmeted hair. "Yes, and are there parts of the world where woman is still *my ox, my ass, my anything*, as Petruchio boasts?" Discussion wanders off to the Taliban, honor killings.

"Let's talk about chastity, silence, obedience—what kind of virtues are these?" "*Boor*-ring," says Danny. "Contrast them to male virtues. What makes a hero?" Words drift in: "tough," "strong," "adventurous," "macho." "Active, assertive qualities. Female virtues are, by contrast, passive, negative, what a woman is supposed *not* to do—do not talk, do not disobey, do not be unfaithful." "Control," repeats Cynthia. "Yes, and you see who's writing the rule book. A woman's place is in the home, where she's supposed to perform domestic duties, be quiet, obedient, and bear heirs you're sure are yours. The virtues assigned her assure her subordination in a patriarchal system arranged by and for the benefit of men." WHO PROFITS? I write on the board. "You must always ask." A few write it down.

"What's a cuckold?" One whose wife has been unfaithful, and we bat this around, why a man's "honor" resides in "his woman," why cuckolds have horns.

"So, if the cardinal female virtues are passive and negative, what makes a female hero? Are there female heroes in Shakespeare's plays?" Too early for this question; but, yes, there are. "Were there female heroes in Renaissance life?" Silence. "C'mon, who was on the throne in the Age of Elizabeth?" And we're off on to stories about Queen Elizabeth, why she never married, what kind of ruler she was, how men must have felt, having to bow down to a woman, and how there may be ideology on the one hand and actuality on the other, and they don't always line up. Back to the text.

"So where in *Taming of the Shrew* is the doctrine of female subordination stated explicitly?"

"That long speech at the end?" Lizzie of the upward lilt.

"Yes, the longest speech in the play, where Kate lectures her wayward sisters on their wifely duties. Let's look at it. Start with *Thy husband is thy lord, thy life, thy sovereign.*" I read the lines through. See how the argument rests on analogies: *as* the subject is subservient to the king, *as* the limbs obey the head, so must the wife obey her husband. What's an analogy? A comparison of things unlike that points out likenesses, suggesting that if these things are similar in some ways, so will they be in other ways. *"As* we are weaker in our bodies, so are we weaker in our minds, in need of guidance from *our lord.* See how these analogies lock woman into a system of subordination. And that word *lord*, what a loaded word that is: husband is like the head of the body, is like the ruler of the land, is like . . . God?"

"That's in the Bible." A voice floats up unexpectedly from my left. I peer around, struck again by Lydia's luminous blue eyes. "St. Paul." She takes a Bible from her backpack, finds Ephesians, and reads: "Wives, be subordinate to their husbands as to the Lord. For the husband is head of his wife just as Christ is head of the church. . . . As the church is subordinate to Christ, so wives should be subordinate to their husbands in everything."

"Good! Woman's subordination was inscribed in scripture, divinely ordained: as Christ is head of the church, so is the husband to the wife . . . yet another analogy to lock her in to a system that brooks no opposition. Analogies are powerful; they're impossible to refute because . . . well, why?" "They're not an argument. A comparison's not an argument. You can't refute a comparison." "Right." Brent will make a good lawyer. "They're only illustrations. Yet they're often used as argument. Anyone ever heard of 'a Munich moment'?" The 1938 agreement that ceded control of part of Czechoslovakia to Hitler. "It's like Munich" has been used as an argument for just about every war since. Discussion wanders off. They're a good sign, these digressions—not all classes are so lively. But back to the play.

"Anyhow, Kate's lines are a summing up of the Renaissance ideology of woman, a compendium of conventional wisdom, every cliché in the book, woman's obedience as the cornerstone of social order. The doctrine of obedience was proclaimed in official Tudor documents, royal edicts, tracts, homilies, sermons: everyone in their place. But, as we saw the first week of class, people were moving out of their places, social hierarchies were breaking down. We talked about this as a time of great change, economic and social upheaval, a new merchant class gaining social mobility. The doctrine of obedience was asserted more emphatically as it was losing its hold. This happens. Ideology gets more virulently asserted as the old order loses its grip, to stem the tide of change. ("Elizabethans talked a lot about order because they didn't have any," my dissertation advisor, Ted Taylor, was fond of saying.) You've heard of the "feminine mystique"? A few nods. I take a few minutes to describe the 1950s ideology of submission clamped down to counter women's new Rosie-the-Riveter muscle. "Yeah," says Cynthia, "women start getting power and men start killing them." Which leads to a discussion of soaring rates of *femicide*, a word most of the class had not heard. The guys are silent.

"So is this the last word of the play, the moral of the story, simply that?" Cynthia nods vigorously. A few others nod, a few look dubious, waiting for cues from me. Most abstain. "It's the last word for many readers and viewers." I tell them about a comment I heard, coming out of a London performance, "That Shakespeare sure knew how to put a woman in her place, guffaw, guffaw." I do not mention the CMC student who muttered, "Works for me" (not long ago).

"But look, we've taken Kate's sermon out of context—we don't get to do this with Shakespeare, take some lines and say, 'Shakespeare says . . .' even with a speech as long and convincing as this. So how would we go about figuring if this is really the last word, the moral of the story?"

"You mean, like put it in context?" says Sandra. There's a lot going on behind that dreamy gaze.

"Good. Let's go back to the beginning. Let's read the play, not raid it. Open to act I."

Marriage: The Only Game in Town

"What is Kate's situation at the beginning of the play? Any of you have a younger sister who's perfect, who all the guys want to date?" Lizzie's hand shoots up, a few nod vigorously. "Now imagine that your father says she can't get married until you do, even though there's no one you want to marry and no one wants to marry you."

"Good marketing strategy," quips Brent.

"That's exactly what it is. How would it make you feel? How does it make Kate feel? What's a shrew? Give me some words . . ." Loud. Aggressive. Pushy. "Yeah, I've been called all that," says Cynthia. "Every feminist has," I say. "What's a stereotype? What work does it do?" We come up with a description: reduces a person to a type or category, in order to . . . ? "Control," Cynthia repeats. "Right. If you reduce a person to a type, you don't have to deal with them as a person, their humanity. Why is Kate called a shrew?" "Well, she does slug her sister," Danny points out—"I mean . . ." "She's furious," interrupts Cynthia. "Yes," I intercede; "How might her situation account for her . . ." "Rage!" says Cynthia; "Her father sells her off, everyone calls her names."

"So, is she or is she not a shrew?" I press. "I mean, is she 'really' a shrew or is she just . . . angry? Is Petruchio a shrew?" "Nah, guys don't get called shrew," snaps Cynthia; and discussion wanders off into the social construction of gender, the social construction of shrewishness.

"Along comes Petruchio—back to the text." Here's a scene I can't resist reading. Later, I'll ask students to read, but first they need to get easier with the language—and they will, next week, when they act scenes from *Midsummer Night's Dream. Kate*, he calls her. She corrects him: *They call me Katherine that do talk of me.* Why does she insist on *Katherine*? "*Kate* is too intimate," offers Ashley. "Yes, it's as though he's trying to appropriate her by appropriating her name. She tries to repossess herself, taking back her name—does she succeed?" "He goes right on calling her *Kate*." "But so do we." Barbara surprises me, speaking up. "Call her *Kate*, I mean." "Gads, you're right." "He won," grumbles Cynthia. They're . . . right. I feel there's something interesting I should be saying to this, but can't think what it is. Back to the scene: She calls him a *moveable*, playing off his, *moved to woo you.* He says, *What's a moveable?*" She says, *A joint stool*, which he turns sexual—*come, sit on me*—and she retorts, *Asses are made to bear, and so are you.* And he comes back with, *Women are made to bear, and so are you.* Ashley and Lizzie are chuckling along; they've seen the Taylor-Burton film.

> KATE: *Where did you study all this goodly speech?*
> PETRUCHIO: *It is extempore, from my mother' wit.*
> KATE: *A witty mother. Witless else her son.*

"You see the humor?"

"No," says Cynthia. "C'mon, they're enjoying themselves. It's like a duet, a war of wits, their terms volley back and forth, they're on a wavelength, it shows there's a potential for . . ." I trail off, hoping someone will supply the word, nobody does, so I say, "a relationship." Ashley and Lizzie nod vigorously; a few look intrigued.

"Okay, but Cynthia has a point—what is not funny about her situation? What is definitely *not* funny?" We coax this out. She's forced into a marriage she has not chosen, never consents to, hasn't even met the guy. He drags her away from her home and family, she's totally at his mercy. "And then," I summarize, "she spends the rest of her life having babies till she drops dead." A few look up, surprised at this so not happily-ever-after ending. "Well, that is the way it would probably have gone for a woman in the Renaissance. Either that, or grew old as a spinster in her father's house, where she becomes another mouth to feed, *a commodity [that] lay fretting* (like wool in storage, *fretted* by moths), as someone says to her father, congratulating him for getting rid of her. A commodity that's lost its value."

"Horrible," mutters Cynthia. "Yes, it was. Marriage was the only game in town. Kate marries the only man who'll have her. And what goes on at Petruchio's *taming school*?" He deprives her of food and sleep. "They do that to torture people," insists Cynthia. "Or brainwash them," adds Trevor, flashing her a sympathetic look. They're right, of course. And what is it about me, I ask myself (not for the first time), that I insist on salvaging this play?

"Yes, but does he literally beat her into submission? Is he physically violent with her? She strikes him in that first scene, he threatens to strike back if she does that again; but she doesn't and he doesn't. You want to see brutality, read the shrew-taming play Shakespeare drew on, *The Taming of a Shrew*, a folk play in which the wife gets pummeled. 'Rule of thumb'—you know that expression, where it comes from?" Amazingly, most do: a man was not supposed to beat his wife with a rod thicker than his thumb. Barbara looks chagrined. So does Lydia. A few others look . . . perplexed. Brittany looks up from her lap.

"Petruchio does strike other characters. Where? Find the scene." Rustling of pages. "We don't see it; we hear about it. Keep looking." Lizzie's hand goes up. "Where are they?" I ask. "On their way to his house." "Journeys are usually symbolic in Shakespeare. Plays are so short—every detail has to count. Who does he strike? And how does Kate react?" He strikes a servant; Kate intercedes. Twice, she does this, pleads with her husband to show pity. "What does this tell us about Kate? Kate, who's been locked into a perpetual tantrum, is capable of fellow feeling. Petruchio's behavior is so outrageous, it calls forth an empathic Kate who reaches out to help a servant. What does this imply about character?"

"You mean, how different situations make us different people?" This from Samantha, who's been quiet, but tuned in.

"Right. Selves are not set in stone. So, no, he never hits her. Do they have sex?" Embarrassed looks. "Well, they're married," says Trevor. "Yes, but what goes on in their bedchamber? What do we hear about what goes on? Find the lines." Rustle of pages. "Here," says Samantha, "It says he's . . . preaching sermons to her? About continency?" "Yes. That word meant self-control, not . . . bladder control. Why does it matter, this detail? What if we were left to assume he was having his way with her?" "That would . . . be rape, I guess, since she's so clearly not into him," ventures Sandra.

"Marital rape," interrupts Cynthia. "More common than you think."

"Right. It doesn't happen. He doesn't force her, doesn't hit her. But he does deprive her of sleep and food, and he won't let her have the gown and cap she wants—*gentlewomen wear such caps, when you are gentle you shall have one too*—at which point she protests,

My tongue will tell the anger of my heart,
Or else my heart concealing it will break,
And rather than it shall, I will be free
Even to the uttermost, as I please, in words.

Free . . . in words—file that away."

Luck and Laughter

"There's another journey later in the play, another scene that takes place on a road—find it. Where are they going?" Back to Padua, for Bianca's wedding. And here is another exchange I can't resist reading. Petruchio: *Good lord, how bright and goodly shines the moon.* Kate: *The moon? The sun! It is not moonlight now.* He, threatening to turn back: *Evermore crossed and crossed, nothing but crossed.* She: *Sun or moon or what you please. . . . I say it shall be so for me. What you will have it named, even that it is.*

"What's going on?" "She's so brow-beaten, she'll say anything," mutters Cynthia. But I am so obviously enjoying this, and so are Ashley and Lizzie, and Allison and Danny are beginning to see the humor, that she's outnumbered. "Are you sure you'd want to read these lines as browbeaten, Cynthia? Somebody help me out here . . ." "I think it's hilarious," chimes in Lizzie. "Why?" "She's just playing along." "Yes, *play. Free in words*—remember? *What you will have it named, even that it is.*"

Cynthia is unconvinced. "Okay. So does anyone else say anything in this scene that tells you how her lines should be said? Remember, we talked about how stage directions are sometimes embedded in the dialogue." Silence. "C'mon, guys, there's only one other character in this scene, besides Kate and Petruchio."

"Yeah, the old guy, what's his name, Vincentio." Trevor reads: "*your merry mistress.*"

"Yes, *merry*. Our Kate, *merry*? Who's Vincentio?" We go back and recap the subplot, which we've ignored. Lucentio has been wooing Bianca. He needs his father's permission, so he finds an old man who pretends to be his father, to give his "consent." "Now along comes the real father, Vincentio, on the road to Padua, and Petruchio greets him: *Good morrow, gentle mistress, where away? / Tell me, sweet Kate, and tell me truly, too / Hast though beheld a fresher gentlewoman?* And she responds: *Young budding virgin, fair and fresh and sweet . . .* and Petruchio replies: *Why, how now, Kate, I hope thou art not mad! / This is a man, old, wrinkled, faded, withered,* and she, not missing a beat: *Pardon, old father, my mistaking eyes, / That have been so bedazzled with the . . . sun?*"

"What's going on here?"

"It's like when they first met," says Ashley, "that back and forth, only now she's really into it."

"No, she's not, she's a Stepford wife," grumbles Cynthia, whose scowl darkens the room.

"Lighten up, Cyn," snaps Ashley. These two are oil and water.

"Look," says Cynthia, "she says, *you mean to make a puppet of me. That's all she is—a puppet.*"

"Yes, she did say that," I intercede—"but *when* did she say it?"

"A few scenes back."

"Right. That was then. This is now, we're on the road—journeys, symbolic, remember?—physical movement, psychological change. Look, she's not only caught on to Petruchio's game, she does him one better when she addresses Vincentio, *young budding virgin*—she outdoes Petruchio in outrageous invention. Vincentio calls her *merry*—*and you, my merry mistress.* Are Stepford wives *merry*?" I push gently. "*Merry* is the way she seems to him."

"It's like my mom with my dad," says Lizzie, "'whatever you say, Dear.'" "Secret to many a lasting marriage," say I. Trevor snorts.

Cynthia shakes her head. Barbara glares. Samantha of the helmeted black hair looks dubious. The rest look . . . intrigued.

"Look, not only does Vincentio refer to Kate as *your merry maid*, Petruchio calls this *our first merriment. Merry*—the word occurs how many times in the play?" Blank looks. "Know how to find out? Google *Taming of the Shrew*, mit.edu, full text, do a word search, and bling, in the upper right corner you'll see a number. *Merry?*" Nine times. "How about *merriment?*" Twice. I love how easy it is to come by this information—in the old days you had to schlep to a library, where, in the recesses of the stacks, you'd find the Shakespeare concordance, flip through the dusty old tome till you came to the word you wanted, see where and with what frequency it occurs. Now in a few keystrokes, there it is. It's a game students get into, calling out the number of times a word appears. The down side, of course, is that I can no longer give the kinds of assignments I used to, asking students to find all the occurrences of a word, *merry, bond, nature*, make them really comb the text to find each place the word occurs.

"Why *merry?* Remember, this is a comedy, a 'festive comedy.' What is a comedy?" That's not a simple question, but for purposes of now, let's say comedy is a play that ends well, tragedy is a play that ends badly. "Festive comedy" is a particularly jolly form; its origins are in holiday, full of fun. *Shrew* is an early play, early 1590s, the decade of Shakespeare's festive comedies. He got less lighthearted as time went on.

"And what does *merriment* tell us about how Petruchio should be played?" Playfully, as *a madcap ruffian*, an over-the-top jokester so outrageous as to bring forth a merry Kate who catches on to his game and realizes she can make it work for her, becomes playfully, inventively, imaginatively *free in words*—it is the sun, the moon, whatever. Released from the confining role of shrew, she learns to play. Of course she also happens to have had the good luck of falling in love with the guy. Women in real life were not often so lucky. But in comedy, people get lucky, and that's the fun of it—we watch characters get into all sorts of trouble and know it'll come right. The comic world provides a safety net—nothing bad happens that can't be put right.

"Kate learns the lesson of comedy: to play."

Play: The Lesson of Comedy

"Okay, let's see if her *merriment* holds up in the final scenes, as her sister's plot unfolds. The real Vincentio, father to Lucentio, arrives and confronts the fake father; disguises are off, identities revealed. "Thanks a lot, Shakespeare, for making the names so easy to keep straight," mutters Brent. I pounce on this: "That's the thing about comedy—characters are not so individualized. Bianca and Lucentio are generic young lovers, eminently forgettable. Kate and Petruchio steal the show; they always do. Why?" "They're . . . interesting," ventures Samantha; "they're drama queens." "Yes. Dramatic. Dynamic—they move. The eye follows movement. Whereas Bianca and Lucentio are . . ." "Boor-ing," comes the word. "Static. Conventional," I add. "So the point of grafting the two plots together is . . . ?" Contrast. We see Kate and Petruchio better by seeing what they are not.

"Let's watch Kate's reaction as her sister's plot unfolds. Look at her lines—*husband, let's follow to see this ado.* She's enjoying herself, and . . . she calls him *husband.* He says, *kiss me Kate.* This is the second time he says that—can you find the first time?" Rustle of pages. While they're looking, I ask, "Anyone seen *Kiss Me Kate*?" Ashley has. Nobody else has heard of it or of Cole Porter. "Is there a difference between the first time Petruchio says it, and now?" The first time, they walk off in separate directions. This time she says, *Now pray thee, love, stay.*

"What else about that line?" "She calls him *love.*" Bingo, Lizzie! And no upward lilt. "Do you think she kisses him?" Nods all around.

"Maybe that's why everyone calls her Kate," says Barbara, still chewing on this. "I mean, the musical." "Interesting. Could be. Though we'd have to look at how people wrote about the play pre-1948, to see if that's true. Project for a senior thesis—why not?" Barbara looks . . . intrigued.

"So this brings us to Kate's last long speech, her sermon on subordination. Does this context make those lines seem . . . different?"

"Very different," says Trevor. "Like, she could be just pretending."

"*Playing* might be a better word. What exactly prompts the speech?" Baptista commiserates with Petruchio for being married to *the veriest shrew* (the word *shrew* or its variant *shrewd* occurs—how many times?—15, wow). "Petruchio says, we'll see about that, and proposes a contest to see who has the most obedient wife, as in, *my ox, my ass, my anything*, as in trophy wife. How is he so sure of her?"

"He's seen her . . . *merry*?" Trevor's got it.

"And Kate, who has by this time caught on to how to play his game, rises to the occasion—*and* gets to speak the longest speech in the play *and* to upstage her obnoxiously perfect sister, who's not looking so perfect anymore."

"But she puts her hand under his foot." Alice, who's said not a word this whole time, weighs in on Cynthia's side.

"Does she? She offers to. Are you sure she does?"

"She didn't in the production I saw," says Ashley. "She winked when she said this, and he took her hand and raised her up."

"So it depends on how it's staged. How it's interpreted. Obviously if you stage it playfully, you'll find a way to signal playfulness in that last speech, whether with a wink or some other sign. Here's a question: Is Kate better off at the end of the play than at the beginning?"

"Better, definitely," says Lizzie. A few nods. "Think back to her situation at the beginning. She's moved out of a dysfunctional role, a role that made her miserable, into . . ." "Another dysfunctional role," mutters Cynthia. "Or, might you say she finds a release into a playful self? No longer locked into an unhappy role, she's released into laughter, love, fellow feeling. But there has to be chemistry between her and Petruchio for this to work. And it takes luck, the luck of falling in love with the guy. But hey, that's why we enjoy comedy, people get lucky."

"I don't buy it," says Cynthia.

"Well, let's imagine Kate as a Stepford wife. I have seen it played this way: she and Petruchio walk off in opposite directions at the end, as they did before. What's the effect?" "A downer," says Trevor, as much to Cynthia as to me. "Not one bit of fun, not even on the road to Padua—that scene was played with Kate sort of dazed, echoing back whatever Petruchio said; it made nothing of her lines to Vincentio, *young budding virgin,* or Vincentio's, *your merry mistress.* And the second time Petruchio said, *kiss me Kate,* she did not kiss him. Besides being a downer, is this interesting?" "You mean, like, nothing changes," offers Lizzie. "Right, she starts out as a victim of the patriarchy and ends as a victim of the patriarchy, miserable at the end as at the beginning. A static character, a static play, a single-mindedly grim display of brute authority."

"But a play has to move. It has to move to move us, and it has to move us because Shakespeare needs his audiences to keep coming back. Comedies generally move to some kind of release. They begin badly, with characters caught in an unhappy situation, but the happy ending brings release. *Liberation* may be too strong a word for what Kate experiences—but can you see it as a kind of liberation?" Silence. Oh please, somebody say something, this is the main point I've been trying to get across.

"Okay, think what 'liberation' might mean for a woman of this time. She couldn't move to the city, get a job. There weren't even nunneries in England after the Reformation. Marriage was truly the only game in town, and marriage was an arrangement between men. Even perfect Bianca has to play by the rules—remember, we looked at the bartering scene between father and suitors, each suitor strutting the size of his estate, the father choosing the suitor with the biggest. Bianca is not even onstage; she is, like Kate, chattel passed from father to husband, *my ox, by ass, my anything*. But against this grim social reality, both sisters find a way of exercising choice, Bianca by trickery, Kate by finding a way of manipulating that role so she has some . . ." I trail off, searching for a word.

"Wiggle room?" Lizzie offers.

"Yes, wiggle room. *Free in words*, remember? Of course the happy ending can only be had by getting lucky, and by playing within the rules of the patriarchy. But what is freedom?" We bat this around awhile. I go to the board, write the words, "Freedom is what you do with what's been done to you." Jean Paul Sartre. "How's that for a definition? Seems like the best any of us can do."

"Best of a bad deal," mutters Cynthia.

Players, Onstage and Off

"You mean she's just acting?" This from Barbara, who's been looking chagrined this whole conversation.

"Aren't we all? C'mon, what role are you playing now?" She looks dismayed, like I've kicked some prop out from under her. "Look, aren't we all sort of acting, all the time—I mean, you're playing student, I'm playing professor, but is this *really* who we are?" I'm making things worse. "I mean, the *whole* of who we are? Who will you be when you leave class, when you meet your boyfriend, when you call your mother—you'll be somebody else, no? What role will these audiences call forth, which self will come into play? Can you say which is your *real* self, your 'authentic' self? Which is the *real* you? *All the world's a stage . . . and all the men and women merely players,*" I quote.

"But I believe I *am* . . . I really am the person I am now." I have to honor Barbara's seriousness, it's one of the things I most like about her. But it's also one of those moments when a chasm opens between me and my students. The young are so deadly earnest; maybe they've always been, maybe humor is a gift of age, but I sense a new . . . grimness.

"Yes, you are who you are now, and you are not." That sounds riddling; somebody help me out. Tanya glances up from under her long, black hair with a knowing grin, I catch her eye, flash her an encouraging smile, but she pulls back. "Look, who are you on Face-book?" That, they can talk about. "That brag book, I hate it." "Yeah, but you can't take that stuff for real; everybody's just making it up." "I don't like that I'm always thinking of my life as scenes on Face-book." I would happily spend the rest of this class talking about Facebook. I bet they could tell me a thing or two—never has a gen-eration been so practiced in the art of self-presentation, on camera from the day they were born. But . . . back to the text.

"You know, there's an entire plot we haven't talked about. We've talked about the Kate plot and the Bianca plot, but there's a third plot."

"You mean that guy at the beginning, what's his name . . ."

"Christopher Sly. What's he doing in the play? That's always a ques-tion we have to ask, Why does Shakespeare graft this plot onto that plot?" And with one eye on the clock because we're running late, I summarize: remember, he's drunk and a troop of actors comes along and tricks him into believing he's a lord. "They really screw with his head," says Danny. "Who's *they*?" I press this point. "Uh, the actors?" "Right, actors who are putting on a play—*what* play?" Silence. "*This* play!" exclaims Sandra. "Right, the play we're watching. Which makes *The Taming of the Shrew* a play within a play, which draws attention to the play as a play. To the self as . . . role. Right?"

"Okay, so, self as a staged performance. Gender, you've heard, is a performative art"—amazingly, most have heard—"well, so is identity." I write on the board, *The Presentation of Self in Everyday Life*, Erving Goffman. "Getting along in society is about presenting a side of yourself that's . . ." I trail off, hoping someone will find a word. "Appropriate?" ventures Sandra. "Something like that. Appropriate to the situation, to social expectations, norms, conventions. People would rather deal with your social self than your 'authentic' self, believe me." Tanya flashes me a knowing grin, but immediately ducks beneath a strand of long black hair, scrutinizing it for split ends.

"*All the world's a stage*—that line is from . . . anyone know? *As You Like It*. We're all actors upon the stage of the world. And the name of Shakespeare's theater was . . . ? The Globe. And the inscription on the theater—does anyone know?" *Totus mundus agit histrionem*, I write on the board. "It means, 'All the world plays the actor,' something more interesting than *all the world's a stage*. Anybody know the ancient Greek word for actor?" One of these days someone will surprise me and know; so far, nobody has. I write it on the board: H-Y-P-O-C-R-I-T-E. Eyes widen. "What's interesting about that? An 'actor' is somebody playing a part, pretending to be someone he is not. If 'all the world plays the actor,' that means we're all pretending to be someone we are not?" They're with me.

"The art of happiness . . ." I hate it when I say things like this; I rephrase, "The challenge of living well in society is finding a role that allows expression of your . . . fullest self, so you don't lop off essential chunks of yourself. Maybe that's the most we can hope for, finding a role that lets us express the most and best of our selves, maybe that's what 'freedom' is."

Cynthia's scowl darkens. "I don't see how you can call this freedom—it's just brute force."

"Well, there are lots of people who'd agree with you, Cynthia; you're not alone. George Bernard Shaw called this play 'disgusting.'[1] But if you read the play as grim social realism, how do you play the scene on the road to Padua? What do you do with the words *merry, husband, love*? You can always cut them, of course . . ." A few nod. I can't tell if they're agreeing with me or with Cynthia.

"Let's talk about play, not the play, but play in general. Why do we play? Does play make life . . . better?" Nothing comes back. "Google 'polar bear and husky.' That's right, 'polar bear and husky.'" They can't believe what they're seeing. Polar bear comes charging up to a dog that's tethered to a post. The owner, watching from a distance, too far away to intervene, assumes his dog is toast. But then the dog goes into an appeasement routine—butt up, ears back, tail wag, signals for play—and the bear catches on and they have a jolly romp. And the bear comes back for the next few days, to play.[2]

"Did play change things for the husky? You bet. It disarmed the polar bear, eliciting a playful, not a killer response. Maybe with another bear, it wouldn't have ended well. Maybe with a different husband, Kate would have been raped and beaten and never merry. That's why you have to play Petruchio for laughs. Kate is like the lucky husky—she learns to play and it saves her life. Play won't alter Christopher Sly's reality—he'll wake out of his drunken stupor, his riches will fall to rags again—why? How is his situation different from Kate's?" "Well, he really *is* a beggar. You can't just go around making stuff up," says Danny; "It's gotta be . . . real." "Meaning?" "Like, other people have to agree." "You mean, reality is socially constructed?" "Sort of. But he really *is* a beggar, I mean, it's not just people agreeing." "You mean, there's bedrock beneath the social construction?" "There's gotta be . . ." (This conversation went on awhile.)

An assignment pops into my mind: write a prose paraphrase of what happens in *The Taming of the Shrew*. That's the easy part, they can find that online. But here's the part that might be interesting: What gets left out of your description? Play, that makes the fun, that makes the play, that comes across on stage better than on the page. On second thought, I'm not sure I'd give this assignment, afraid I'd just get a lot of mangled versions of what I've been trying to get across. Students are not, I think for the hundredth time, in a playful mood. A woman published a satirical piece in the *Chronicle of Higher Education* about how many grandmothers seem to die around finals time, and got death threats for disrespecting students.[3] Hair-trigger tempers all around.

Lizzie ventures, "I mean, like, sometimes you just gotta laugh, and that makes you feel better." Bless you, girl. "Something like that. Yes, always assuming luck. Assuming you're not about to be gobbled up by a bear."

"So, what if you got this question on a multiple-choice exam. *The Taming of the Shrew* is, choose one: (a) a critique of marriage in a patriarchal order, or (b) a celebration of marriage in a patriarchal order?" "Critique." "Celebration." The words come simultaneously from different directions. "What makes you call it a critique?" Woman as commodity, sold to the highest bidder. "Why a celebration?" There's a happily-ever-after ending, feast and marriage, the traditional ending of festive comedy. And though Kate and Petruchio have been married since the middle of the play, only at the end, after she's called him *husband* and *love*, are they *really* married; only when her consent is earned and mutuality achieved, can their marriage be celebrated.

"So it's a celebration?" "Yes." "And a critique?" "Yes. That's how it is with Shakespeare, always both-and, never either-or, you can never say *never* or *always* with Shakespeare—oops, I just said *always* and *never*. Okay, so, it's *almost* never either-or with Shakespeare, *almost* always both-and; his plays defy either-or categories. Of course that won't get you far on a multiple-choice exam, but then a multiple-choice exam won't get you far in life."

Coleridge called him "Our myriad-minded Shakespeare."[4] Something for everyone. This play can satisfy a chauvinist pig and can please a reader like me. Well, not quite everyone; Cynthia's still scowling. But most feminist readers find ways of salvaging this play. I draw their attention to an essay I've put in the reader, Marianne Novy's "Patriarchy and Play."[5] Once you read this essay, you'll never unsee the play in this play.

"Shakespeare is so good at having it both ways. There's the high-spirited fun and high jinks, but tilt the angle and you see a grim social reality, a woman bartered, shunted from the home of father to husband. But imaginative literature lets us play, lets us imagine *what if . . .* This is a play, I mean, we're watching a play, right?"

"A play within a play," corrects Sandra.

The Fox Knows Many Things

So, yes, *The Taming of the Shrew* is a critique of marriage, and yes, it is a celebration of marriage. The play asks us to hold more than one possibility in mind, to open our minds to more than one way of viewing the characters and situations. This is what Keats means by Shakespeare's "negative capability," "when a man is capable of being in uncertainties, mysteries, doubts."[6] It's what F. Scott Fitzgerald means by *intelligence*: "the test of a first-rate intelligence is the ability to hold two opposed ideas in the mind at the same time, and still retain the ability to function."[7]

Or, as Norman Rabkin used to say, "The fox knows many things."[8] I lucked into Rabkin's Shakespeare seminar my first semester of graduate school. A Shakespeare play, he said, is like a Rorschach ink blot where you see first one image, then another, first the rabbit, then the duck. It's difficult to see both images at once, but once you've seen that each is truly there, neither can be unseen; the figure will not resolve into one clear and certain shape again. Rabkin was fond of quoting Aesop's fable, "The fox knows many things, the hedgehog knows one big thing." He had a wry, playful wit and agile intelligence that made him very like a fox.

The semester I took his course, I audited a Milton course where I encountered a surefire hedgehog, two of them—Stanley Fish and John Milton, about as hedgehoggy as they get. In Rabkin and Fish, I saw how different types of sensibilities draw us to different authors. Rabkin was felled by a tumor that put him in a wheelchair, retired early, wrote no more books. Fish is still going strong, full of zealous self-assurance, pumping out pronouncements and op-eds showing us the error of our ways, as he showed us students how our misreadings of *Paradise Lost* were signs of a fallen intellect.[9] Fish had a pipeline to Milton and Milton had a pipeline to God. I wonder, if Rabkin had gone on writing and teaching, could his wise, gentle voice have made itself heard? You don't meet a lot of foxes these days. People want certainty, the authoritative, authoritarian; the middle ground, the nuanced, is going the way of the polar icecaps.

Cynthia, I later learn, has a history of trauma that won't let her see the lightheartedness of this play. A few weeks from now, when we get to *Merchant of Venice*, I'll see Allison tense up that same way. I'd jotted down, "mid east? Latina?" the first day. She turns out to be from a family nearly wiped out by the Nazis; she can see only anti-Semitism in this play. *The Merchant of Venice* is another of those lightning-rod plays that provokes wildly different responses, that requires historical context, that needs us to get ourselves out of the way and let the play teach us how to read the play, which may be impossible since the Holocaust. This is a play that, like *Taming of the Shrew*, makes us see double, see the stereotypical Jew that made the play popular with the Nazis and see, simultaneously, the critique of the stereotype, the contextualization of "the Jew" in a world full of "gentiles" no gentler than he.

But that is too long a story to tell here.

Evolutionarily, What's the Point?

Shakespeare was a player before he was a playwright, a player the whole time he was a playwright. All those years he was writing, he continued to act. He well knew the uses of play, the pleasures of play, the many kinds of play, lighthearted play, sinister play, manipulative play, sexual play. *Go play boy, your mother plays*, says Leontes, whose jealousy convinces him his wife's playing him for a fool; *Thou playdst most foully for't*, says Banquo of Macbeth; *you cannot play upon me*, says Hamlet to Rosencrantz and Guildenstern. We are all of us actors upon the stage of the world, our deeds are *actions that a man might play. The play's the thing.*

Why do we play? Children, left to their own devices, play all the time, making up games, inventing rules, negotiating territories. Animals play, birds play, especially those at the top of the food chain. Evolutionarily, what's the point? The more a species has to learn, the more it plays, and the more creative its play. Human beings have a lot to learn. No species plays as much as we or with as much imagination. We are *Homo ludens*, the title of the study by Johan Huizinga, *Homo Ludens: A Study of the Play-Element in Culture.*

Play is about learning, a rehearsal for the real thing. Given more toys, ladders, wheels, and other creatures to play with, animals "develop more rapid response, faster processing, swifter recovery times, better coordination," reports Brian Boyd in *On the Origin of Stories.*[10] Children who are the most active players in kindergarten become the most active learners in elementary school.[11] Play is where kids test bodies against bodies, wits against wits, learn what they can and cannot do. Play is where we learn what is "fair" or "out of bounds," learn to take turns, resolve conflicts, control impulses, as Peter Gray explains in *Free to Learn*.[12] Play teaches us to negotiate, to cooperate, to develop as social beings "capable of living with others," writes Martha Nussbaum in *Not for Profit*, making us less likely to see others as "looming threats."[13]

But play needs a space that's free, so kids can try things out without needing to control or dominate or fear being dominated, can form relationships and networks without being afraid. "Here, then, we have the first main characteristic of play: that it is free, is in fact freedom," writes Huizinga.[14] And play needs to be pleasurable, so we want to come back to it, do it again, because that's how we learn—the more often we repeat an activity, the better it sticks.

At Waldorf, a low-tech school in Los Altos where many high-tech Silicon Valley CEOs send their kids, creative play is allowed to develop naturally into learning. "Our teachers let our play just sort of evolve until it became learning," said my student Tess Williams, '16, who'd attended this school. Play is also where kids get to develop imagination, creativity, to act out fanciful "what ifs," entertain new possibilities—"let's pretend." "Children who pretend more have a distinct advantage in understanding other people," writes Alison Gopnik in *The Gardener and the Carpenter*.[15]

"Play is the primary engine of human growth. . . . Play is the way children build ideas and how they make sense of their experience and feel safe," writes Nancy Carlsson-Paige, early education development expert and author of *Taking Back Childhood* (who happens to be the mother of a famous player, Matt Damon); but "play is disappearing from classrooms."[16] The Common Core has brought its regimentation all the way to preschool. In a letter of resignation she made public, Susan Sluyter wrote, "We kindergarten teachers . . . have found ourselves fighting to keep play alive in the kindergarten classroom."[17] Recesses are eliminated; new schools are built without playgrounds; art, music, and theater are cut, and kids are suffering a mental health crisis. What minimal play they're allowed is supervised, structured, regimented, which is not the same as free or spontaneous play. Deprived of the development they get from play, they don't build confidence; they feel unsafe.

"Kids don't know how to play anymore," says Noam Chomsky. "They can't go out . . . like when you were a kid or when I was a kid, you have a Saturday afternoon free, you go out to a field and find a bunch of other kids and play ball or something." Now "it's got to be organized by adults, or else you're at home with your gadgets, your video games. But the idea of going out just to play with all the creative challenge: that's gone."[18]

When supervised play takes the place of free play, kids don't get a chance to develop skills of social cooperation. The loss of these skills, argues economist Steven Horwitz, flips "our default setting" from, "figure out how to solve this conflict on your own" to "invoke force and/or third parties whenever conflict arises." People's first instinct becomes "invoke coercion by other parties to solve problems they ought to be able to solve themselves through democratic self-governance," which lays the ground for authoritarianism.[19] They reach for the rule book, the iron-clad syllabus, the "rubric" that tells them what to do; they call in administrators to make regulations to govern the behavior of fellow students and faculty. And when they're monitored so closely, they learn by example to patrol one another. To bully.

When I was a kid, age seven to nine, we lived in South Miami. There was a canal across the street, where we swam. Alligators swam there too. We'd post a sentry on the bank who'd keep an eye out and shout "alligator!" "snake!" (Did I mention the snakes?) Today a mother who let her kid do that would be arrested. But you know, if I had to choose between the alligators or constant adult supervision and being pumped full of drugs to make me sit still, I'd take my chances with the alligators.

Playtime for Grown-Ups

"Do we outgrow the need for play, or learn different ways to play? Name some ways grown-ups play." Video games. Sports. Yes, but that's organized. Spontaneous play, batting a ball around a field, has no ulterior motivation, is not goal-oriented. What are some ways adults play that's not goal-oriented? We play with our kids, our dogs, our cats. We make videos of our cats and dogs playing, we put them on YouTube, we watch other people's videos of animals playing—dogs doing goofy things, cats beating up on dogs, interspecies play, the husky and the bear, the orangutan and the hound, the dolphin and the dog—these get millions of hits.

And . . . what else? We watch *plays*. The arts are how we keep the experience of play alive in our adult lives, nurture our capacities for play, as Martha Nussbaum suggests, drawing on Donald Winnicott's description of the arts as preserving and enhancing a "play space" and "nourishing and extending the capacity for empathy."[20] Let's pretend I'm a princess, you're a frog—that's a first step toward symbolic thought, right there. And what are stories but grown-up versions of "let's pretend," a chance to try out roles and situations? A play or novel is an elaborated "what if," a hypothetical situation that allows us to explore possibilities in a space free from consequence. Fiction, says Boyd, is "a kind of cognitive play"; it provides "stimulus and training for a flexible mind, as play does for the body and physical behavior." It engages and activates the brain, making us more adaptable to situations and other human beings. Our "compulsion to tell and listen to stories with no relation to the here and now or even to any real past," says Boyd, "improves our capacity to think in evolutionarily novel, complex, and strategically invaluable ways. . . . By developing our ability to think beyond the here and now," imaginative play allows us "to be less restricted by [the given], to cope with it more flexibly and on something more like our own terms."[21] It enables us to imagine what might be.

I tell the class about a study that found that just five minutes of watching a screwball comedy improved problem solving on tests requiring creative leaps: 75% of those who saw the comedy solved the problems, compared with only 13% of those who'd seen no film.[22] If five minutes of humor improved the creative leap, facilitating flexibility and the imagination of new possibilities, imagine what 15 weeks of Shakespeare might do.

Think of the theater as a "play space"—well, obviously it's that, a place to put on plays—but it's also a play space in being set apart in time and space from everyday reality, where laws of logic are suspended and players play kings, and (on Shakespeare's stage) boys pretend to be women. "Subversive," said the Puritans, this topsy-turvy world where clowns mocked their betters and kings were brought low; it upended the laws of the land. And maybe it really did: maybe the spectacle of so many kings dethroned and dying—Richard II, King Lear, Macbeth—made thinkable the public beheading of an actual king, Charles I, in 1642, a few decades after Shakespeare's death. Life imitates art. We become what we watch.

So, let's pretend I'm a princess, you're a frog, and let's pretend to take this pretense for real. "Suspension of disbelief"—Coleridge coined this term in 1817. We know these things never happened—why do we bother? If a writer could impart "a human interest and a semblance of truth" to a work, says Coleridge, the reader would grant a "willing suspension of disbelief for the moment, which constitutes poetic faith."[23] His term "a human interest" is key. We have keen human interest in the lives of others, an insatiable curiosity to know how other people live, an appetite for reality shows, talk shows; the hook of the human draws us every time. And we have a strong need for the arts. We're seeing the mental health crisis that results when kids are deprived.

Next week, I tell the class, you'll be performing *A Midsummer Night's Dream*. I point them to scenes from the beginning, middle, and end of the play. They choose their roles, and it's up to them to find time to rehearse, figure out how to act the scenes.

A Midsummer Night's Dream: Playing the Play

Sometimes we use the courtyard or lawn outside. If the Humanities auditorium is empty, we may use that—it's cavernous, intimidating, but it gives a sense of what it's like to be up on a stage. This time, we choose the space that's easiest, at the front of our room, the several feet between the seminar table and the board.

I'm always amazed at how easily this space, with its tatty gray carpet, wastebasket, and backpacks propped against the wall, can be transformed to a forest—tell us it's a forest, and poof, it's a forest, we're right there with you. I look around at the rapt faces of the "audience," the half dozen or so of us who are not performing, totally caught up in the scenes we're watching, engaged, amused, and I'm struck—what a lunatic enterprise this is. Here we are, half the class pretending to be characters they're not and the other half pretending to take them for real—and for this, students get course credit and I get paid. They oughta lock us up.

There's some resistance to this assignment at first, but most of the students get into it. Some bring props for the ass's head, the fairies' wings, a magic cloak for Oberon. One semester I got to class to find they'd fastened ropes and pulleys so they could swing down into the courtyard from the second floor of the Humanities building—oh no, you don't, I intervened, imagining broken heads and limbs. Before they leave "the stage," they have to tell us what they learned from act-ing out the scenes; "you know, like the 'special features' on a DVD." Some things they say: "At first when I tried to say the lines out loud, I thought, oh no, this stuff makes even less sense than I thought; but then when I said the words over and over, they started to make sense, more than when I just read them." "I hadn't realized how hard it was to say the words so the audience could hear them." "It never occurred to me you'd have to worry about what to do with your body when you're onstage and someone else is talking." "Don't just act, *interact!*" I said to one particularly wooden group that just stood there, reading their lines. "Talk *to* each other—it's ensemble work, you're working together"—and they admitted they'd been boring, when they saw how inventive others had been.

It's a bonding experience, this assignment—if they loosen up and laugh, it bodes well for the semester. It leaves us all with increased appreciation for what goes into a good performance. "And you don't even have to memorize the lines," I tell them. I tell them what Ben Kingsley said, that he got it, why Hamlet asks, "Should I commit sui-cide . . . ? What should I do? The actor doesn't know whether he has the strength to finish the play." No wonder he's carried offstage at the end—"he's exhausted."[24]

They love the Monty Python zaniness of the scenes where the ar-tisans rehearse *Pyramus and Thisbe* for the wedding of Theseus and Hippolyta. Danny shows us a clip of the Beatles performing *Pyramus and Thisbe*, which he found, googling around. He admits to feeling some uneasiness at first, playing Snug the Joiner (carpenter): "When I first read the play, I thought Shakespeare was making fun of these guys, putting down the lower classes for being ignorant. That made me uncomfortable. But when I got into the role, I saw that Snug and Bottom are so likeable, there's a lot of respect, actually; I think he really loves them. I don't think we're laughing at them, well, maybe a little." Right, not laughing at them, well, maybe a little, having it both ways.

"But Shakespeare *is* elitist, isn't he?" asks Cynthia. I'm glad she asked. "He gets called that often enough, but so does anything that requires study. But look, he wrote for a popular audience, most of whom could not read. His father was a glover who ran into debt and couldn't pay for his education. His acting company had origins in the artisan class. When they had trouble with the landlord of their first theater, they dismantled it and ferried the beams across the Thames and rebuilt it as the Globe. James Burbage, brother of Richard Burbage, the company's lead actor, had been a carpenter. (Richard Burbage is the actor we have to thank for Hamlet, Lear, Othello, and Macbeth—Shakespeare couldn't have written these roles without an actor who could play them.)

"Have you ever come out of a high-spirited, imaginative performance of a play or a show, feeling exhilarated, like you've been transported?" A few nod, and launch into descriptions of *awesome* performances that I've (naturally) never heard of. This gives me an excuse to tell them about a mind-blowing performance of *Midsummer Night's Dream* I saw when I wasn't much older than they are. I had not particularly loved this play when I read it, but this production by Peter Brook was transcendent. The fairies were trapeze artists, streaks of vivid color against a stark white stage, particles of flickering energy that seemed scarcely to have bodies. I felt transported to a wondrous realm where the laws of gravity and logic had been suspended, a trippy place of magic and make-believe. There was a dark side, too, young lovers lost and warring in the woods; they'd have killed each other, left to their own devices, but in comedy, as we know, as Puck assures us, *all shall be well.* I came out of this performance dizzy with elation, transported: this was the play itself, play itself, the essence of play, enchantment.

I came away feeling, that's what we love about Shakespeare, he makes us feel good about being human. It was a feeling more than a thought, a flash more than a feeling. I don't know how else to say it, just glad to be a part of it, humanity in all its silliness, splendor, squalor, sordidness, grandeur, outrageousness. Not the warm, fuzzy feeling of a feel-good movie where the bad guys turn good or turn out not to have been bad, "triumph of the human spirit" sort of thing. Not like that. Because he gets it all, the whole wide range, the greed, nastiness, brutishness, along with what's fine and noble in us. Something to do with what Marilynne Robinson calls "the old humanist joy in what people are."[25] Something to do with living theater. I do think this is a reason we love him so, this validation of humanity, *our* humanity.

I've brought in some quotes: "Watching live theater can synchronize the heartbeats of an audience," says award-winning playwright Ayad Akhtar. The communal experience harks back to a primal sense of connectedness to our kind, of our common humanity, which makes living theater "an antidote to digital dehumanization."[26] Acting, says Ben Kingsley, is "about getting close to other human beings, real or imagined. It's about overcoming the distances between us. . . . It is a way of keeping the human landscape open and alive," of exploring "the joy of that landscape which . . . seems to be shrinking" as technology takes over our lives.[27] Film can't touch the effect of a live production when it gets off the ground like this, can't come near it. Here's an actor to tell us what it feels like:

I feel so lucky to have work that I love. . . . In my earlier years I felt
terrible that I "failed" to become famous, or successful (in our culture,
meaning rich). But when I get to be on stage, in a collaborative effort
with other artists, in communion with an audience, as part of a profound story of our common humanity (I do a lot of Shakespeare) . . .
nothing can make me happier. I'm respected in my field, and only play
roles I'm dying to play. Why waste my heart on anything else? I'm
spoiled, grateful, humble. The actors I work with are the bravest people
I know, walking out on a ledge every night, for "a dream, a breath, a
bubble."

. . . When I go to work I get to wear a crown and a velvet robe, and
speak, well, poetry. So fools like me will keep my art alive.[28]

This is why theater will never die: actors love to perform, audiences
love to attend. We come out of a high-spirited, high-quality performance feeling better in our bones. I've felt this at concerts, too, watching players subordinate selves to working with a group, seeing them
set aside ego and play together to create harmony. Look at what
humans are capable of when they pull together—why can't we be like
this all the time?

I think it's *awe* I'm describing, an experience of awe. Awe, says
Dacher Keltner in *Born to Be Good*, is a binding emotion that has an
evolutionary purpose, "binding us to social collectives," "improving
our odds for survival." As humans evolved into a social species that
needed to work in groups, awe helped us "to act in more collaborative ways."[29] And art "opens up new dimensions of possibility," as
Boyd says; "by fostering our inclination to think about possible worlds,
art allows us to see the actual world from new vantage points. It therefore enables science."[30] Art *enables science*—listen up, Gavin Williamson, UK education secretary, who, in May 2021, praised students for
pivoting away from "dead-end courses that leave young people noth-

ing but debt" and urged them toward "higher technical qualifications, modular learning, and our flagship Institutes of Technology."[31]

Several years ago, King Ethelbert School teamed up with the Royal Shakespeare Company to implement an unusual program of teaching and performing Shakespeare. The experiment transformed a "nonselective school" in a deprived area of Kent "from one of the worst in the country to one of the best of its type," reports Kate Greig, head teacher, "thanks to Shakespeare": "it has transformed teaching in all departments, raised aspirations and increased parental involvement." This was a town that felt Shakespeare wasn't really for them, but the school was bold enough to try this out: "maths lessons covered iambic pentameter while science lessons involved detailed investigations of deaths in the plays." Getting "students and teachers to think like actors and directors" had striking effects, reports Annie Holmquist. Students arrived in history "keen to study the history of the plays they have performed," and the school saw "an improvement across all subjects. . . . Proficiency on the school's exit exams has risen from 14 percent to 55 percent."[32] And in Los Angeles, Rafe Esquith has used Shakespeare to galvanize students in an inner-city fifth-grade class. Each year his classes perform a Shakespeare play. Check out the 2005 documentary, *The Hobart Shakespeareans*, filmed the year the class put on *Hamlet*.[33] Sons and daughters of first-generation Asians and Latinos overcome their difficulties with this formidable writer, pull together, do something extraordinary (and, by the way, their test scores go up).

Negotiated Knowledge as Agency

So. You could see a seminar as a kind of play space, a place where you get to play with ideas, test out your voice against other voices, open yourself to other points of view. A space where you're free to entertain alternative possibilities and perspectives, free to contradict yourself and to contradict others without fear of reprisal, without fear that someone's keeping score. A safe space, not in the sense that it's free of controversy or views that contradict yours, not that kind of safety, but safe in the sense a play space is, where you're free from harm, from dire consequence.

What comes of a discussion class is not right or wrong answers, but ways of going at problems, thinking with others as we work out ideas. What comes is not "some definitive historical or philosophical truth about the past," as Michael Roth says, but ideas worked out in negotiation, in the exercise of "intellect and imagination."[34] Discussion "can envelop the mind in multiple perspectives," says Andrew Delbanco, give a sense of "truth in flux, in the making rather than the ready made," a creating students have a part in.[35] That does not mean that anything goes, anybody's "personal belief" or "personal opinion" is as good as any other, but it does mean that the kind of knowledge that comes from a discussion is qualitatively different from what comes from a lecture. Negotiated knowledge comes from a process of thinking together, a process that's alive, exploratory, interactive, provisional, open to change, that gives students an active role in their education. "It's not what 'we cover' but what you discover," as Chomsky is fond of saying.[36]

There's a lot of talk about agency lately. Everybody agrees it's a good thing, but there's not much said about how kids come by it, the secret sauce. Agency is feeling you have a say in what happens to you, that you're an active participant in your life, a producer of events. It's not developed by marching students through a set of predetermined "learning targets," prescribing the exact steps to master them; that makes them the butt end of forces beyond their control. I like the idea of agency better than leadership, though "leadership" is the word *du jour.* Leaders require followers, winners require losers, make a zero-sum game, whereas agents may become fit to rule themselves.

But it's harder to engage students in this kind of play of mind when their schooling beats play out of them, stunts their willingness to entertain multiple possibilities or fanciful "what ifs." Berkeley English professor Alex Zwerdling told me he got this student evaluation of a course he team-taught with a historian, "Problems in Western Civilization: "The professors seemed to disagree with each other. I don't understand why they didn't get together ahead of time and work their answers out." A student told me ruefully, "I'm an econ major, I need something more cut and dried," as she handed me her drop slip. And I'm not sure I'd have got this semester's reading of *Shrew* off the ground to the extent that I did if it hadn't been for Lizzie and Ashley, who'd seen performances they thought hilarious and got the humor, and who, coming from comfortable backgrounds, find it easy to lighten up.

I leave the class with this to think about: "In *Midsummer Night's Dream*, as in *Taming of the Shrew*, Shakespeare grafts a player plot onto love plots. How do the plots go together? How might art relate to . . . love? Think how engagement with a work of art might draw on and develop the same qualities required in a relationship." They know, when I leave them with a question like this, they're likely to encounter it again.

SIX

✣

Teaching Is an Art,
Not an Algorithm

Teaching remains a mysterious, magical art. Anyone who claims he knows how it works is a liar. No one tells you how to do it. You walk into a classroom and try to remember what worked for the teachers who impressed you, or, later in the game, what seemed to work best for you in the past. Otherwise, it is pure improv.
—JOSEPH EPSTEIN, "Who Killed the Liberal Arts?"

In many ways, teaching is the most difficult of professions. In other occupations, professional success lies in the skills and knowledge of the practitioner. . . . But teachers depend on students for their success. Teachers can only be successful if students choose to learn. Surgeons operate on clients who are unconscious, lawyers represent clients who remain mute; teachers need to find a way to motivate students to learn.
—DAVID LABAREE, "Targeting Teachers"

Teaching is a daily exercise in vulnerability.
—PARKER PALMER, *The Courage to Teach*

"I thought all you did was walk in and start talking. You made it look so easy," said Anne, back from a year at UC Davis as a teaching assistant. "Boy, was I wrong."

Boy, was she wrong.

"Like being a conductor, you mean—just get up there and wave your arms around?"

People can see skill on a basketball court, admire the footwork and fine-tuned moves of an athlete, but teaching—that's "just talking."

I can give you analogies to say what teaching is *like*—it's like conducting an orchestra, driving a team of horses—but really, there's nothing "like" it. Even the term "teaching a class," is misleading—*which* class? I can only tell you about *my* class, nobody else's, and then only about my class this one time, because next time will be different; each class is as unlike every other as human beings are from one another, some so lively I can barely get a word in, others seem not to have been wired for sound.

Here are some things I know.

What Goes In, What Goes On

First I have to tell you about the preparation, what goes on before I step into class that first day, back up to the stuff nobody sees, the massive amounts of preparation that go into a course, invisible as paper grading, those endless hours.

First there's the months, years it takes to master a subject, reading, researching, finding a way around a field. Then, from this whole vast area, select a set of readings, carve out an approach accessible to 18-year-olds: What do I want each play, poem, novel, memoir to get across, what do I hope a young person will take from it? Will it make her life richer? Is it within her reach, but not too easily within reach? Then there's charting a path, deciding the order of the readings, figuring out the most effective way of getting the reading across, where to begin, how to present the material so it can be grasped not just by one mind but many different kinds of minds.

The problems are not unlike those encountered in writing: what points am I trying to make, how best to get them across, what details are most effective, how long to spend on each point? Questions of shaping, timing, suiting the material to the audience, constructing a narrative, only trickier, because teaching takes place in real time, rapid time. It's not just about knowing, as Mike Rose says in *Possible Lives*, but being able to draw on knowledge on the spot, presenting it in a way that clarifies and inspires: "Knowledge plays out in social space and this is one of the things that makes teaching such a complex activity."[1]

Teaching a seminar is harder than lecturing (for me, not for everyone). When you lecture, you're the sage on the stage, delivering the word, unlikely to get interrupted or derailed. If it goes well, you can use it next time, updating, of course, keeping it current. Teaching a seminar, you sit at a table alongside the students, asking questions to open up discussion, trying to get the material to come from them. Comments come zinging every which way, any kind of question from any direction—in a lively class, that is. You have to work up the material, get it all in your head, every bit of it; those pesky details you're most likely to have forgotten are the details students are likeliest to ask about. You dare not *not* reread, though you might risk it when you lecture. And you have to get back into the *experience* of the text, remember what it was like to move through it the first time, so you can convey the excitement, make it new.

I go in with a plan. I know where I want us to go, know the best routes to get there, but I set my notes aside. I have an opening gambit. *Who's there?*—the opening line of *Hamlet*—who says this? Why so jumpy? Who else might be there? Why might a ghost be prowling the land? Where is this ghost from? Any of those questions might lead in any number of directions. If nobody's responding, I change tack— what *is* a ghost? Anyone here ever seen a ghost? If anyone has, she's usually from another culture, and why is that, we wonder, and we're off into a discussion of the cultural construction of ghosts. Let it wander, but not too long

Again and again, back to the page: Where do you get that? Why do you say that? Can you be more specific? Where in the play? What makes you say Gertrude is as slutty as all that? Ah, yes, Hamlet says so—are you sure you want to take his word for her? What do we see her do, hear her say—do her words and actions corroborate his view? Can you say more, I push, can you find other references to gardens in the play, poisoned gardens, polluted gardens, withered blossoms, weeds, compost. Are there ruined gardens in anything else you've read?

I go in with a girding, but it has to bend with the interests, engagement, energy of the class; it's the students who set the pace, determine which way and how far we go. I kick an idea out onto the table, hoping someone will pick it up; I toss in more questions, edging us the way I want us to go. The students who are paying attention see that the questions I ask are not random. But they have to be listening, picking up the threads, and that's increasingly difficult for kids used to having "the four main points to know for the exam" laid out with bullets on a PowerPoint presentation. Then someone comes in with a question that has nothing to do with anything—should I deflect it or try to fold it in? Can I incorporate it and stay on track? Uh-oh, they find this interesting—okay, let's talk about Kate Winslet's Ophelia, maybe it will lead somewhere. Dammit, 17 minutes to go and we're still in act I.

Plans and backup plans: Plan A, get them wondering about that question, "who's there?"; Plan B, get them thinking about who knows what when; Plan C, talk about the films; Plan D, divide them into groups; if all else fails, F, film clip. "Creative chaos," Parker Palmer calls class discussion.[2] It is sheer dumb luck, the things they toss out for me to work with. I try to find a thread, pick up something from 20 minutes before and relate it to what's just been said, weaving their comments together so they see the connections, the contradictions, trying to construct a path that lifts us to a higher plane, takes us somewhere new.

In a good class, we go slow, dig deep, tend to fall behind. In a class not so engaged, I feel their impatience and pick up the pace. Lately it seems their interest is more easily spent, it's harder to hold their attention for the time it takes to go deep. When we move on without covering what I wish we'd got to, I try to leave them with some points to think about. But they never stick; when I lay out points like this, they don't get them, I can tell from their writing. They have to put the questions to themselves, do some grappling, figuring out. This is what Chomsky means, "It's not what we cover but what you discover."[3]

Judgment Calls

And always, the judgment calls, calculations, hundreds in a class—how to bring out the shy, smart one, tone down the blatablat. There was a student I'll call Sophie who took a lot of classes from me, smartest girl in the class and never let us forget it, hand always waving, first with the answer, trying to turn the class into a conversation between her and me and sometimes succeeded—how can I *not* call on her when nobody else's hand is in the air? "Uh, could we hear from someone else?" I'd say, but careful—they're not with her, but the slightest hint of a rebuke could turn them against me—and off she goes again, and sometimes it's not a tangent, sometimes it's brilliant, how long to let her go on? I take her aside and suggest gently, it might be good to let someone else talk, and she points out that nobody else has their hand up, and I refrain from saying, yes, but they might if you weren't hogging the show; and she contains herself for a week, but then she's back, rattling away.

Hit a wrong note and feel them tense up. Like the time I was handing back papers and told Brenda hers was excellent, and saw Annalisa's face fall. Those two always sat together, roommates and friends, but rivals, too, I saw too late—how many times do I have to learn to be careful with praise? Or the time I was trying to get the class to imagine what night was like before electricity and said something like, "in northern Europe, where most of our ancestors are from, the nights were long," and saw a few exchange glances and looked around and registered, oops, most of this class did not hale from northern Europe. If it had been a class I felt easy with, I'd have made a joke of it, but it was not, and I did not; foot firmly wedged in mouth, I trudged on. You could put a generous construction on that lapse, I had simply not registered the variety of colors and ethnicities in the class. It would be considered a microaggression today; kids are not in a generous mood.

You develop a feeling for what works with a class, what they're capable of, the speed at which they move, how deep they can go, how to nudge them along. You learn how to seed the ground, how they need to know X before they can understand Y. I have tried, when a class works, to go back to my office and write down exactly what I did, so I can remember the moves and repeat them the next time I teach the play. THIS WORKED, I scrawl in the margin. BEGIN HERE, then use the third-act act soliloquy to segue to the end, be sure to mention . . . But what worked with one group rarely works with another: the kids are different, the context is different. You adjust your movements to the players at hand, then the players change, and it's a whole new show.

"How can you *stand* it, teaching the same plays year after year?" asked a lawyer friend. "But it's never the same," I replied, surprised both at his question and my reply: "The conversations, the way we go together, are always different." It's true, I have taught *Romeo and Juliet* maybe 20 times, many of them in this room, Humanities 120, but it's the faces I see, and they're never the same. One class wants to talk about the macho thing; another, the generation gap; another gets caught up in questions of fate or free will; another can't stop talking about which film was better, Baz Luhrmann's or Franco Zeffirelli's. You never know which topic will take off, and you'd be crazy to cut off a discussion that's full of juice, though you'd have to if you were locked into a roboscript, prepping students for a test—*that* would go stale fast.

A judgment call every time I open my mouth, every time I call on a student: if I call on him, I'll get the answer I want, but then how to shut him up? if I leave act 3 now, I must remember to make this point before we get to act 5, oh please, no more about Ophelia. Meanwhile, I have my eye on every corner of the room, scanning for signals, attuned to every twitch, sigh, snort, snicker, my antennae moving between the kids and the clock, making constant calibrations—should I leave this question for later or bring it up now, how much time is left, time in this class, time in the semester, do they have a paper coming up, will they be prepared—should I call out Ashley for that eye roll . . . dammit, that's the third time she's left the room, why can't she sit still? Alison's scowl tells me we've talked enough about Ophelia; Barbara's frown tells me we're wandering; the clatter of Lizzie's fingers on her laptop tells me she got that point, but when her keys go silent, I tense up—if she didn't get it, nobody did, better get back to where we were before, if I can remember where we were before— oh yes, Polonius, *or you'll tender me a fool.*

You see why *response* is the word for what goes on in a class, why *responsibility* is the word we want, not *accountability.* In fact, you could call teaching an *art of response,* responsiveness to the moment, to streams of information, verbal and nonverbal, moves too complex to calculate, except that I am calculating them at a level deeper than words. A teacher once described teaching as constantly "'just zapping away,' making rapid, real time decisions."[4] "Real time," that's the challenge, split-second calculations every move I make, in conditions of uncertainty constantly changing, attention scooting from the student to the clock to the text to the random comment tossed into the mix, trying to take it all in. Judgment calls requiring "a feel for the whole and a sense for the unique," macro and micro, are "precisely what numerical metrics cannot supply," as Jerry Muller says.[5]

Start the Stretch . . .

The first time I taught *King Lear*, I began by talking about the commercial revolution of the late sixteenth century, the transition from feudalism to early modern capitalism. That put everyone to sleep. Now I start with something like, "How does it feel when someone asks, 'how much do you love me?'" We natter on a while about what a bad father Lear is, what he does wrong, then move on to talk about implications for family, society, the body politic, easing gradually into the Big Themes—*is man no more than this, a bare forked animal? Are we as flies to wanton boys . . . to the gods?* What gods? Are there gods?

Students want to find themselves in the work, to "relate," but I do get tired of hearing, "I don't like Lear." "There may be more important issues in a literary work than whether you like the protagonist," I once snapped, then relented: "Of course, it's important. Me, too, I need to 'relate.' The novels I don't finish, the films I walk out of, are where I simply don't care how things come out because I don't care about the characters." My admission led to an interesting discussion— how much of ourselves can we or should we expect to find in a work?

But students don't use the word *relate* anymore—they say, *relatable*. A play is relatable, or not. There's a big difference. To say you can't relate to a play is to say that you haven't found a way in that makes it meaningful to you, but to say the play is not "relatable" shifts the problem to the play—how does it measure up in terms of *you*? You make yourself the yardstick by which the work is deemed worthy. Radio personality Ira Glass tweeted, after watching a performance of *King Lear*, "Shakespeare sucks"; then, after watching Mark Rylance in *Twelfth Night* and *Richard III*, "Shakespeare is not relatable."[6] Ira Glass has not found a way of relating, so he decides the plays are not "relatable." He makes this Shakespeare's problem, not his, when maybe he just hasn't put in the effort. Try harder, Ira.

What we find "relatable" tends to be narrow when we're young; it will stay narrow if it's not stretched. My job as an educator is to widen the bandwidth of response, not funnel the work down into students' expectations and let them stay as they are. If I'm not stretching them, I'm not teaching; if they're not stretching, they're not learning. There may be resistance, just as there is when you move your body in an unaccustomed way, but there's no change or development without it. In my day—there I go again—we did not expect long, complex works to size themselves down to the dimensions of our inexperience, to be like selfies. We were told certain books were "great," and we believed it, perhaps too readily and docilely believed it, but it spurred us to some effort; they were mountains to scale that might make us stronger, smarter, more grown-up. I trod mazes through some pretty trippy stuff, *The Faerie Queen*, *The Rape of the Lock*, *Moby Dick*, and I did find a way through most. It would never have occurred to me to dismiss a work because I couldn't find myself reflected there, because there was no *me*, white, female, Californian, twentieth century, mirrored back. We were expected to make leaps of the historical imagination, and we did, and that made us capable of other kinds of leaps.

No leap was so dizzying for me as the *Iliad*, University of Chicago, freshman year. I was barely 17, far from home, and it was like being drop-kicked to the far side of the moon. I trudged through every word, every description of every shield and battle. I can't say that I ever found much to relate to, but it did not occur to me to say, "Homer sucks." Would I recommend the experience to others? I would. I was learning that the world was a lot wider and weirder than I'd any idea of, that I was not the measure of all things.

In Humanities 1-A at Chicago, we had primers, *Learning to Look*, *Learning to Listen*, and *Learning to Read*. We were told to find our way to the Art Institute and write about assigned paintings. I remember standing in front of *Guernica*, bewildered. I can't say I got it, but I never forgot it, and years later, when I had more scaffolding, I could connect it to other things. We were assigned a paper on Beethoven's violin concerto; I had to listen over and over before I could begin to write, and as I did, I grew to love it; there was even a Bartók concerto I warmed to, though it seemed alien and off-putting at first. We looked at Frank Lloyd Wright's Robie House and read *Richard II* and *Pride and Prejudice*, and we were supposed to pull it all together and say profound things about "art." It was a wildly incoherent course and I got a B, but the experience of those works, I never forgot. I could not name the works encountered in any other class from that long ago, but these stayed with me, *Richard II* especially; I set out to follow that ravishingly beautiful sound to its source.

Now I know how many faculty hours must have gone into patching together that committee-designed camel of a course, now I have a sense of what goes into making a course required of all freshman, having sat on committees hashing out the humanities program at Scripps, which we used to revise every few years. Now I can imagine the haggling, the compromises—if you teach that, I get to teach this. But I'll tell you something Chicago got right that Scripps in recent years has missed: it plunged us into an experience of the senses, listening, viewing, reading. Scripps throws a lot of theory at our first-year students, analyses of race-class-gender, diversity, disability. I say, throw art at them, let beauty strike, as *Richard II* struck me—that's how you grab attention, not with abstractions. What can be felt upon the senses, the sensory, the concrete—that sticks. When we feed our students the thin gruel of theory, we surrender the field of the senses to popular culture, the dazzle of special effects, the thump of rap; we offer nothing to compete. Hit them with Beethoven, Bartók, *Guernica*—that might be competition. At least it would get their attention.

When you stretch to take in a great work of art, you're larger for it, having experienced something larger and other than yourself; you've learned that much more about the world. That's why we bother with great literature, that's why some of us still call it great. Go ahead, start the stretch. Stay with it, try to take it in, feel how the language transports you, makes you see anew. Stretch!

Gads, I could be teaching yoga, and that's not a bad analogy, since I'm trying to extend the reach, broaden the range of movement, improve flexibility. A literary work may provide a *growing point*—I like that term. I got it from Toni Morrison's *Sula*; Sula and Nel, best friends, "used each other to grow on."[7] A relationship may be a growing point; so may a teacher, a course, a calamity. In Doris Lessing's novels, situations that seem catastrophic offer opportunities to grow, as loss does for Lear. Keep an eye out for people or situations that push you new places.

"A key job of a school," says David Brooks, "is to give students new things to love," to extend imaginative sympathies beyond the here and now, transport them beyond where they've been, to imagine others and other ways to be.[8] To make the mind large enough for paradoxes, as Maxine Hong Kingston's narrator says in *Woman Warrior*.[9] It may not happen overnight. Or it may—sometimes I feel the moment an idea or insight clicks into place for a student or a class, I almost hear the click. But sometimes, as Brooks says, "professors pour more into the class than the students are able at their ages to receive. And in that way good teaching is like planting."[10] A seed gets planted, unnoticed at the time, but later it connects with something, finds a scaffolding, and the person realizes, *that's* what that poem or story meant, and *voilà*, the seed bears fruit.

Fine Lines and Fancy Footwork

It's a balancing act, teaching, many balancing acts, fine lines to tread and fancy footwork. Teaching is an art of treading fine lines.

Fine line between bringing some students out and damping others down, fine line between leading out—*e-duco*—and planting. You want them to express themselves, but you also want them to listen and take in the ideas of others. Fine line between spontaneity and plan, letting the conversation unfold and nudging it the way you want it to go. Fine line between bringing the material over to them and bringing them over to it. Start from where they are, find points of intersection between their experience and the work, then start the stretch.

Fine line between fun and challenge—you're their pal, then their judge, you slap a grade on them, friend no more. Fine line between being "myself" and the persona I construct, a persona that contains parts of me but not all of me. How much of myself should I reveal? Depends on the class, of course, how interested they are; and that, I've discovered, changes with age. Back in the day when taxi drivers mistook me for Joan Baez, students were more likely to be amused and interested when I let slip things about myself; but at my age, a vulnerability revealed can seem more dotty than charming. Or maybe

I'm just too sensitive, leery of becoming one of those blowhards boasting of laurels long since withered. When I first got to this college, there were a few of those on the faculty; I vowed never to become one. Though it is gratifying when a student comes across an article or book I've written and realizes I've had a life, a writing life, anyway.

Teaching guru Doug Lemov, author of *Teach Like a Champion*, was surprised to find, studying videos of teachers, microgestures that are not on the radar of what's measured in teacher evaluations: "How long [teachers] waited before calling on students to answer a question (to give the less confident students time to get their hands up); when they paced about the classroom and when they stood still (while issuing instructions, to emphasize the importance of what's being said); how they moved around the room toward a student whose mind might be wandering." Lemov concluded that these moves are an essential part of a teacher's effectiveness, though they're not measured or even mentioned in evaluating teachers.[11] He's right, of course, but there are countless moves so micro as to be invisible—how long you let a discussion go on before moving to the next question or directing their attention back to the text, how you deflect a go-nowhere comment—and there are no rules for these.

Bill Gates has a bright idea that a videotape would give teachers a "real feedback system," an "objective" assessment system, and suggests teachers ought to video themselves so they can see what they're doing wrong—they'd see, for example, there was a hand up that they missed.[12] Nonsense. There may be a million reasons I might not call on that student. To judge my judgment calls, why I'm calling on this student and not that or calling on no one, you'd need to know who my students are, the myriad signals I'm processing, what went on last week—you'd have to be me. And to know if these moves have been wisely made, where they will lead, what will ripple out and make a wave, for that, you'd need a crystal ball.

Teaching is not rocket science, wrote a rocket scientist turned teacher—it's harder. Ryan Fuller, aerospace engineer who became a teacher, admits to experiencing more failure every five minutes of teaching than in a week as an engineer. In engineering, he had time to make decisions; in teaching, he had to move right on the spot.[13] Real time, no pause button, no retakes. It gives you plenty of opportunity to make a fool of yourself, which you are sure to do—the question is not *if*, but *when*, and when again—and if you can't deal with that, find another line of work. "Everything I did before was a vacation by comparison," says Bob Shepherd, who came back to teaching after he'd worked (very hard) as an executive in publishing.[14]

Teaching is a high-wire act without a net.

"In the high school classroom you are a drill sergeant, a rabbi, a shoulder to cry on, a disciplinarian, a singer, a low-level scholar, a clerk, a referee, a clown, a counselor, a dress-code enforcer, a conductor, an apologist, a philosopher, a collaborator, a tap dancer, a politician, a therapist, a fool, a traffic cop, a priest, a mother-father-brother-sister-uncle-aunt, a bookkeeper, a critic, a psychologist, the last straw," writes Frank McCourt in *Teacher Man*, of the high schools and community colleges he taught in.[15] What he says is as true at every four-year college where I've taught. But I'd add to his list: you're a wizard, a magician—you pull stuff out of the air, make stuff disappear, make something of nothing, sense of nonsense, order of chaos. You're a parent, a pal, a mentor, a role model, a guide, a taskmaster, a judge, a trained seal. You're there to delight and instruct, to capture kids' attention, spark their imagination, to deliver and get them to deliver, all at once. You make nice one minute and stern the next, and you turn on a dime, slipping in and out of roles like a quick-change artist, keeping your footing on a high wire without a net, now and then managing to say something that may change a life.

You need bells and whistles to compete with Facebook and Snapchat and Instagram and gchat and godknowswhat; you need the entertainment value of Lady Gaga and the energy of Michael Jackson and the hide of a rhinoceros—for teaching, like old age, is not for sissies. You need the intuition of a psychic and the charm of a salesman, for always you're selling, aiming to please, because, as veteran teacher Rita Pierson famously said, "kids don't learn from people they don't like."[16] But never pander. That's another fine line to walk—to please but not pander. It takes the wisdom of Solomon and the patience of Job. It takes everything you've got, and some days it takes more. There are times I miss a cue or come on weak when I should have come on strong, let a discussion drag on too long or cut it off too soon, or maybe an unexpected ray of hostility zaps me out, and that spark just doesn't catch. Tough luck. The show must go on.

Grace

There are days I drag in with too little sleep, cannot imagine how I'll get this off the ground, but they're there, they're on it, and the energy lifts me like a bird in an updraft. Someone kicks off the ball, someone else picks it up, and they're off and running, then someone comes in with a question that takes us magically to the point I was hoping to make, and I reach in myself and find an eloquence I didn't know was there, find the right words, make the connections. When a class finds me wise, witty, wonderful, I become those things, a current gets flowing, a positive feedback loop—this is what athletes mean by being in the zone. When it works, something marvelous happens. I feel the atmosphere relax, they're joking more, risking more, speaking because they have something to say, not because they're trying to impress me.

"Do you think Shakespeare really knew all that, I mean, do you think he really plotted it out, all the stuff we talk about?" That could be a go-nowhere question, only this day, we are talking about *Mid-*

summer Night's Dream, and a riff on the mysteries of artistic creation is not a tangent. "Are there any poets, artists, musicians in the room?" A few hands go up. "You know how there are days when you feel the notes just coming, your fingers have a life of their own, the juices start flowing?"

"I know, I improv on guitar . . ."

"The other day, I was writing an e-mail and it turned into a poem . . ."

"How about your dreams—ever get inspiration from a dream? Are there any dreams in this play?" Silence. "Well, yeah," says Samantha. "It's, like, called a dream."

"Right. Is there any way it sort of is like a dream? What goes on in dreams that's like this play?" "You get turned into an . . . animal." "Everyone gets changed into something or someone else." "Do dreams leave us changed sometimes for the better, knowing something we didn't know before? Is Bottom changed by his dream? What does he say when he wakes up? *I have had a most rare vision.* Is he different?"

"He's—lost the ass head."

"True. And is he really . . . not an ass? He reaches for words to express *a most rare vision*, he calls it *Bottom's Dream*—why that? *Because it hath no bottom*, and because it's *his* dream, Bottom's. What has he done there?" "He's made a pun." "Right. What do you have to know, to make a pun?" "You mean, like, words can have more than one meaning?" "Right. Remember, this is the guy who thought, you want moonlight, you open the window to bring in moonlight, and if the moon's not shining, you get a man with a lantern. His pun shows he's moved beyond the literal, is using his imagination. Then he says, *I will get Peter Quince to write a ballad of this dream.* Why a ballad? Because that's when you turn to art, when you have a *vision past the wit of man to say*—that's when you reach for poetry, painting, music, to express . . . stuff too complex, too wondrous, for just plain words.

How does Shakespeare bring the moonlight in?" "Poetry," says Lizzie. "How many times does the word *moon* occur?" "52—wow!" "*The watery moon, her silver visage in the watery glass,* her *liquid pearl.* The moonlight gets beamed in on Shakespeare's words and our imaginations."

When it works, the class feels like a spontaneously evolving conversation, a team working together; it's a heady thing. Allison passes the ball to Danny, Danny says this is something he's been wondering about, where inspiration comes from, Lizzie comes in with, "it's like Kate and Petruchio riffing off one another. I lean back, enjoying this, knowing that if I'm enjoying it, they are too; I feel like I could leave the room and they'd keep going. I am jotting down notes, hoping I can pick up the threads and weave them together. We're building this together, they're feeling their power, hearing their own voices, stretching to take in Shakespeare, becoming more.

We have only one class left on *Othello*, there's so much we haven't talked about—which parts to let go? I focus in on Desdemona—why is she so defenseless? What became of the spunky, outspoken woman who addressed the Senate so boldly, who leapt over barriers of class, race, nationality, age, to defy her father and marry Othello—where did that woman go? We look closely at a scene in act 4, we're longing for her to speak and be heard, but Othello's *horrible . . . imagining* has staged the scene as a brothel and cast her as *that cunning whore of Venice*; and though he asks, *what art thou?*, he's so far into his *horrible fancy* that he cannot see or hear the woman before him, only the projection of his poisoned mind. We see how defenseless she's become, how incapable of speaking or acting on her own behalf. But *why* has she gone so limp, so passive?

"She's like a battered woman. You go numb like that." Who said that? I look to my left and see Lydia, blushing at what she's just said. Tears spring to her eyes, and to mine, too. This is one of those moments I am humbled by how much some of these kids have gone through, how little I know of them.

We skip to the end, time is running out. I direct their attention to Othello's final lines, where he describes himself as *one who loved not wisely but too well*. His language is lyrical, he's got his groove back. But is it true, he loved Desdemona *too well*? He adored her, was besotted by her, but remember when he said, early on, *she loved me for the sorrows I had known / And I loved her that she did pity them*. Really? Is that love?

"*What is love?* Remember, Feste asked this. We talked about love in *Twelfth Night*, saw the difference between loving and *doting* there and in *Midsummer Night's Dream*, Helena doting on Demetrius, Titania doting on the ass (yes, that has been known to happen, a woman dotty for an ass). What would it mean, to love *wisely*—is it possible to love wisely?" And we're off into a discussion of how hard, maybe impossible, it is to see clearly, how we're always "making stuff up," spinning our own versions, seeing what we hope or fear to see, especially when in love. "Love is blind"—can you ever really know someone you love? Can you ever really love someone you do *not* know?

These luminous moments that come along like grace, when students are fully engaged, are like moments in writing when the muse reaches out, only better, because the gratification is instant and in concert with other minds. I don't want to get all New Age-ey about it, but something magical happens. "Every true teacher understands," says Andrew Delbanco, "that, along with teacher and students, a mysterious third force is present in every classroom." When that force is working in favor of learning (it isn't always), "the Puritans' word for this invisible and inaudible force was grace."[17] *Grace* is as good a word as any, or maybe it's sheer dumb luck, the great good luck of being on a wavelength, having rapport, whatever it is that sparks affection, regard, interest among human beings.

Bounty

I have to admit, I don't know how it happens, but I do know *that* it happens from time to time, that classroom magic, moments when the class is fully present, tuned in, freed, momentarily, from the pressures that weigh on us all.

And you never know when it will happen. Last semester, it was Macbeth's lines, at the end of the play: *I have lived long enough.* I so nearly didn't read these lines, there were only a few minutes left, that class-is-over feeling when they're packing up books, shuffling in their seats, stealing glances at the clock, but because this was our last class on *Macbeth*, and because I love these lines, I held them over a few minutes, and read:

> *I have lived long enough: my way of life*
> *Is fall'n into the sear, the yellow leaf;*
> *And that which should accompany old age*
> *As honor, love, obedience, troops of friends,*
> *I must not look to have.*

This, they heard, these stunningly simple lines—I could tell because of the hush that fell, all shuffling ceased. Macbeth finally gets that what makes life worth living is people, relationships, and having murdered these, he's killed love, friendship, honor, the qualities that give life meaning. It's funny, I'd talked myself blue in the face trying to get this point across in *King Lear*, how Lear's *give me words of love and I will give you land* was a confounding of quantity with quality that tore his world apart. And nobody heard.

But Macbeth's words, they heard, and that opened their hearing to other plays, so when we came to, *Tis paltry to be Caesar*, Cleopatra's dismissal of Octavius Caesar though he's ruler of all the world,

Barbara, who's begun to speak up, made the connection—"*paltry* because, like Macbeth said, the point is people?" Right. Relationships. Caesar may have won the world, but as a human being, he's a dead loss, a calculator, a strategist who sacrifices his sister to a marriage he knows Antony will betray so he'll have an excuse to break with him. *Kingdoms are clay*, says Antony, pronouncing on the power politics he's played at and lost. Though Antony has lost the world, he retains qualities of magnanimity, generosity, humanity that command the loyalty of his men and the love of Cleopatra. He has a *bounty*, as Cleopatra says, that *grew the more by reaping*. That word *bounty*, Shakespeare reserves for his most admirable characters, a generosity of spirit that's the opposite of mean-spiritedness. Hamlet has it; Juliet, too: *My bounty is as boundless as the sea, / My love as deep; the more I give to thee, / The more I have, for both are infinite.* A quality that grows *the more by reaping*—how is that possible? How can a quality *grow the more by reaping*? The paradoxical possibility of non-zero-sum exchange. Teaching is like this—the more I give, the more I have, the more that comes back to enrich me. A commercial transaction, on the other hand, where you try to give less and get more, is zero-sum. Yet another reason business is no model for education.

Lately, fewer students are impressed by Antony's *bounty*; more see him as a "loser" for letting go of power. I look around the room and see brand names and logos blazing forth from jackets, backpacks, T-shirts, human billboards for Nike, Adidas, North Face, REI. Branding used to be something done to cattle. Now students talk seriously about finding a signature brand, building identity capital, maximizing their human capital potential, no qualms about serving up self to the market. And yet many do yearn for something beyond the snatch and grab of money and status. I get this on a student evaluation: "What sticks in my mind is *Kingdoms are clay*, from *Antony and*

Cleopatra. Power is nothing compared to human connection. Shakespeare's understanding of humanity will never leave me. I thank you, Professor Greene, for bringing him to me."

On a good day, or night, when I feel our discussions opening up the play, I feel like I'm channeling the writer. I am a cupbearer, a host, inviting them in to partake of a feast. Edward Said described literary criticism as a prolongation of the work.[18] Mark Edmundson says teachers are *disciples*, in the sense that we immerse ourselves in the work, merge with the writer, bring the writer into the present; our job is "to continue the lives of the poets on in the present, to make them available to those living now who might need them," to "offer past wealth to the present."[19] I like that word *disciple*; it has connotations of both learner and teacher, and it relates to *discipline*. And it *is* a discipline, what we're doing, subduing the self to a master, to a text, trying to get ourselves out of the way, to teach students to attend and remember. When asked why they remember certain teachers, students will often say, he or she has "a passion for the subject," "brings the subject to life." "I always thought that passion made a teacher great because it brought contagious energy into the classroom," says Parker Palmer; he now realizes, "Passion for the subject propels that subject, not the teacher, into the center of the learning circle—and when a great thing is in their midst, students have direct access to the energy of learning and of life.[20]

The kind of energy that gets released when minds are thinking together, this mysterious, ineffable, even mystical thing that sometimes happens—it does feel like grace. Once upon a time on the Scripps website, Victoria Podesta, '78, when asked, what was her favorite Scripps memory, wrote, "Shakespeare with Gayle Greene. I remember thinking, after I left class one day, that this must be what some people went to church for: joyful enlightenment through engagement with a text . . . and a teacher." (That was a long time ago; students don't use words like *joy* or *enlightenment* anymore.) Technocrats hate it when we talk like this, but I tell you, it happens, and there is nothing from the data-driven world of "performance indicators" or "best practices" or "benchmarks" or markers of "teacher effectiveness" that can capture it, no algorithm that comes near it. Devise a metric for the ruffling of a complacent mind, the kindling of the imagination by a work of art so a person never sees or feels the same again, or for joy, wonder, wisdom, enlightenment, empathy, humanity. You cannot. These are matters of the spirit, not the spreadsheet.

And with a good class, the conversation continues through the semester. We develop a backlog of understanding that lets us refer back to earlier discussions, earlier readings—they remember Malvolio when we get to Brutus, they remember Macbeth when we come to Octavius Caesar. There was a *New Yorker* cartoon a student brought in: a man on a plane reading a book, slaps his forehead, "Oh no, not another recurring theme!" That became a leitmotif of that class—"Heads up, guys, Another Recurring Theme." That cartoon has been on my office door ever since. Students get to know the ideas I'm big on: reading, not raiding, growing points, both-and perspectives.

It is night and we have the building and the campus to ourselves. I used to love that feeling; on warm nights, the doors open, the sound of crickets, the class is a pool of light surrounded by dark and quiet. All eyes turn suddenly to a creature at the window, nose on the pane, staring in. "What is *that*?" says one. "You've never seen a raccoon?" says another; "It's an . . . *oxymoron!*" says another; and the class dissolves into laughter. We'd been talking about the oxymoron in *Romeo and Juliet*, a figure of speech like a paradox that yokes together opposites in a logically impossible conjunction; there are lots of them in this play. Students always find the word amusing, riffing off on "morons who go to Oxy" (Occidental College). Someone walking in on us would have had no idea why we're laughing. We develop a language, become like, well . . . families get like this, giggling at things not funny to anyone else. There have been semesters when I've felt closer to my students than my colleagues, because, face it, who in my grown-up life cares whether Antony is a fool to give up Rome for Cleopatra, whether Hamlet grows up or down. In a good class I get to talk seriously about the ideas that brought me to this place, Humanities 120.

Actually, that raccoon at the window was years ago, back in the day when I could get students to stay past 10 p.m. if we were on a roll. Not anymore—they all have a meeting, a study group, a date to rush off to. I'm not sure I could get that kind of high hilarity going today, not with Shakespeare. It can still happen in creative nonfiction, occasionally in contemporary women writers, where they relate more easily to the material. And lately, well, I can't help worrying, the large plate glass window, the doors wide open, we're completely visible, vulnerable. I never had to think such thoughts before.

Gagged

It's not always so wonderful, of course. One semester, I had a class I had to brace myself to walk into, duck the poisoned darts. An afternoon class in that same room found me witty and wise, but the evening class—if looks could kill, they would, and some days I wished they would, rather than have to walk through that door again. Same room, Humanities 120, different planet. Lucky them, I'd think, they can drop this course, I cannot. I haven't had many classes that bad, maybe half a dozen in nearly half a century, but I could tell you about them in more vivid detail than the dozens of good and fair classes that fade with time. Every female faculty I know has such horror stories; male colleagues tend not to. Go figure.

A few students, or even one, can bring a whole class down, turn off a student I might have reached. I had a student in a lively class where it was cool to be engaged; she worked hard to keep up, and her writing got better. That same student later turned up in a dicier class, and I lost her. She bonded with a girl who hated the class and the two huddled together, reinforcing one another, eye rolls and glances communicating how sucky it all was, and I thought, uh-oh, that's the last good work I'll see from her. I wanted to shout, get away from that girl, find some other friend. I've seen this time and again, how the students in a class can sway a marginal student one way or the other. And that is why, when you're thinking about where to go to college or where to send your kid, find out what kind of students go there, hear how they talk about their classes, how seriously they take them; this tells you more than test scores. If you hear a school's a "party school," give it a pass. Yes, it matters that classes are small, that profs are engaged and bring material to life—that matters hugely—but the students matter more than anyone ever tells you.

If students sit, mute and unresponsive, it defuses me as surely as a good class buoys me up. I have read that a teacher can dumb her students down or smarten them up—well, students can do that to a teacher. Indifference, disinterest, strike to the heart. I trail off mid-sentence, forget what I'm saying, hard to keep caring when nobody else does, can't remember why I ever found this subject interesting. *When a man's verses cannot be understood . . . it strikes a man more dead than a great reckoning in a little room.* Those lines from *As You Like It* are Shakespeare's homage to his fellow playwright Christopher Marlowe, struck dead in a tavern brawl over a quarrel about the reckoning (the bill). But they resonate beyond Marlowe's death to state a principle actors know so well, that "a circular energy" gets going, as Mark Rylance calls it, a feedback system that can make or break a performance.[21] Imagine, if actors feel this vulnerable, and they're up on stage with a script, think what it's like to be sitting amidst the audience, no script, trying to get the performance to come from them.

I kick the ball out into the center, it sits there, made of lead. I hobble up beside it, give it another kick. I want to hang my head and cry. I have sometimes stopped and said, "I can't do this all by myself, you know." A few students pitch in valiantly with forced remarks, but the class soon slides back to baseline. Toughen up, I tell myself, firm up your boundaries, but I cannot be a good teacher to a bad class. What I'd like to say but dare not say is, if this class bombs, blame yourselves, because I can tell you, it has enthralled others, this very class.

And when you're saddled with a class that dislikes you, it's hard to muster much affection for them. These kids are spoiling something I know can be wonderful, and, adding insult to injury, I'll get the blame. They will make me look awful and inept, do a wrecking job on the class, then savage me in evaluations. It's a noose I drag around for 15 long weeks; I haul it everywhere. Usually I like it that I'm thinking about my classes in the grocery checkout line, on the freeway, storing up stories, clipping out articles, sending links; but when a class goes dead, it's like dragging a corpse around. Until finally the semester is over and I can breathe again, and the memory fades, but never entirely; these days, it hangs around in cyberspace, those online venues for vengeance.

And imperturbable, always imperturbable, summoning every trick I can to delight and instruct, giving giving giving, no matter how depleted I feel. Though a class has me pulling my hair out with rage and disappointment, keep on giving, forgiving; though a student is yanking my chain and wasting precious time and pushing me to make a policy that will penalize everyone, suck it up, let it out with a friend but never with a class—well, nearly never, anger has its uses, but careful.

I can tell by a colleague's body language, when I see her coming out of class, I can tell from her stride, her expression, what kind of class she's just had. If she flashes me a smile, it's been good; if she slouches by, gaze on the ground, I think, that bad, eh? I'm sure I'm just as transparent. A therapist friend in Berkeley tells me she has clients who bring their teaching troubles into therapy.

Grace under pressure. That was scrawled on a note from an auditor the last night of class, an older woman who'd sat in on a particularly dismal Shakespeare class, a three-ring circus that never cohered, two guys who took pleasure in what I'd call baiting behavior, testing my limits, showing off for a babe who was paying more attention to her reflection in the plate glass window than to them or Shakespeare. Why this auditor stuck around, I have no idea, though I was glad she did, grateful for a compassionate, comprehending presence; she'd catch my eye, flash me a look; she'd taught high school, she'd seen it all. She slipped me this note the last night: *You have shown grace under pressure.* It was one of highest compliments I ever got.

A learning teacher, that's what Frank McCourt says he is.[22] Always learning. That's what makes it exciting, humbling, heart-rending. I think in other lines of work, you figure out how it's done and it gets easier, but in teaching, you can never rest. "Teaching is not something one learns to do once and for all and then practices, problem-free, for a lifetime," as Bill Ayers says; "It is practiced in dynamic situations that are never twice the same. I marvel at academics and policy makers who so glibly prescribe . . . who offer the 'magic wand' for classroom success, try to capture and tame teaching into a set of neat propositions."[23] Me, too, I marvel.

"Teaching at the Claremont Colleges is a blood sport," said a colleague, as she left for a UC campus, preferring a podium between her and her students to the cheek-by-jowl interaction of a seminar. Me, I cringe when I walk into one of those huge lecture halls, the long banks of seats, the big blank screens where PowerPoints serve up neatly bulleted take-home messages. They give me the willies, those caverns. They reek of alienation. And as tempting as it sounds to have a "reader," how would I know if my students are getting what I'm trying to get across, if I didn't read their papers?

"Blood sport" it may be, but I'll take this kind of teaching any day. And studies and "anecdata" show, as we'll see in the last chapter, that this is where sparks get lit, where learning is likeliest to happen. But if it's this challenging at a place like Scripps, all these complicated moves at a selective college where students are here by choice, supposedly, imagine what K–12 teachers deal with. Piss-poor salaries, pissed-off students, meddling parents, whip-cracking administrators, everyone telling them what to do. There may be other lines of work where the risk of burnout is as high, but not many.

Are There Rules?

Of course there are volumes of rules and regulations, but the kind that matter are the ones you work out for yourself. Here is my bag of tricks, for what it's worth.

Begin at the beginning (except with *Taming of the Shrew*). That only sounds simple. Students always want to jump to the middle or the end. "Why don't you ever want to begin at the beginning?" I moan. "Can't we hold off on the ending till we've moved through the play?" Do not let discussion get hung up in generalities before you get grounded in specifics. Try to move from particulars to the general, the simple to the complex, concrete to abstract. I've learned, teaching Shakespeare, there are certain cliffs not to go to near, bogs not to get backed into. Leave Shylock for last; he runs away with the show. Stay away from the question of fate in *Romeo and Juliet* until you get something in place about the characters.

Never say anything as a statement that you can phrase as a question. Make it a teaser. "What does Antonio say when Prospero forgives him? Prospero's brother, who deposed him and would have killed him, Shakespeare's last villain, his last play. Prospero says, *I do forgive thee*—what does Antonio say? Nothing? You sure? Keep looking." Silences are important in Shakespeare, as they are in a class. Keep looking, go on, all the way to the end . . . what does Antonio say? (Spoiler alert: His eye lights on Caliban, he declares him *marketable—no doubt, marketable.* That's right, the last word of the last villain in a long line of Shakespeare's villains—*marketable.* Remember Iago? *Put money in thy purse.*)

It's hard, allowing silences. But if you want the material to come from the students, you must. Silences leave them a space to figure out what they're thinking. It can be excruciating. You ask a question, nothing comes back; you rephrase it, still nothing; it makes them uncomfortable, it makes me uncomfortable. I'm not very good at this, nor are the students—I feel their impatience, and I share it, foot tapping invisibly under the table, restraining myself from rushing in to finish sentences. The less easy I feel with a class, the more likely I am to rush in with words. But it's good for us to wait out the slow, garbled response of a student trying to find the words for what she means, help her shape her thoughts. It takes patience. It takes trust.

That's why the blatablats can do such a wrecking job—they make silences impossible. One motormouth can drive a whole class under cover. Sophie, hand waving in the air, even if I don't call on her, there's her hand wagging; Sophie, racing off in directions nobody can follow, occasionally brilliant but as likely not to be—do I take the time to try to unpack that monologue or simply nod and smile and call on someone I hope will say something that pulls us back on track? Sometimes I do one thing, sometimes the other.

And always and ever, be kind. Give the benefit of the doubt. If you're going to err, as you surely will, err in the direction of kindness.

It's a short list. There aren't a lot of rules. Can it be taught? I don't think so. It can barely be described. If even I can't make my own successes work for me a second time through, how could I assume they'd work for anyone else? What works for you won't work for me because I'm me and you're you, and the way I relate to the material and the students, the style, the energy, is mine. There is no one size that fits all, no recipe, no prescription. It's a disaster when somebody imposes something that's worked for him on everyone. Much of the trouble of the world comes from someone trying to impose his bright idea on everyone. Yet "every single adult citizen of this country," says Sarah Blaine, who tried teaching but found being a lawyer easier, "thinks that they know what teachers do. . . . So they prescribe solutions, and they develop public policy, and they editorialize, and they politicize. And they don't listen to those who do know . . . the teachers."[24]

You learn by doing it wrong and then figuring out how to do it better. And by imitating someone who's doing it right. I used to enroll in writing workshops just to watch teachers teach. "It's the ancient practice of people imitating people," writes Douglas Rushkoff in *Team Human*, "one human learning by watching another, observing the subtle details, establishing rapport. . . . The human social engagement is the thing."[25] Students learn that way, too. Watching me open up a text, watching other students do it, they may, in the course of a semester, get the hang of it, acquire a skill that enables them to read not just Shakespeare but much else.

"It takes years," says McCourt. "And it's like writing or like any art, or any human endeavor—you have to find your own way. You have to find your own techniques and style."[26] It takes trial and error and the chance to learn from mistakes without fear of losing your job or being docked in salary or publically humiliated, which is impossible when teachers are penalized for students' test scores. It takes "familiarity with the materials of one's field," writes Mike Rose, "a ready stock of illustrations and analogies, a grasp of the ways particular concepts and operations are typically misunderstood and a repertoire of responses to facilitate understanding."[27] And that takes time to build. The weakest teachers are in their first two years. But with teaching conditions as they are, or were, pre-pandemic, 50% were leaving within their first five years;[28] many more, since the pandemic.

Teaching is an art as well as a profession—this needs repeating, since only those who've done it seem to understand. Some people have a gift for it, as for anything else. I think it has to do with an interest in people and love of subject, yet I've seen people who were not naturals work at it over the years and become excellent teachers. But you have to really want to do it and trust that you'll get better, to give it the effort it needs. Trust, that's a big one, and faith, which is a kind of trust, and love. Motivation is the sine qua non of teaching, as of learning. Call it devotion. Call it sheer bloody stubbornness.

What is certain is that teaching at any level requires a set of complex, highly developed professional skills built up through the years. All this talk about "innovation" makes me want to weep, as though we weren't "innovating" all the time, trying new angles, testing out what works, seeing if we can make it better, always starting over, every day, a whole new show. Walking our tightropes, dancing on high wires, dangling our carrots and waving our sticks. As for "best practices," which policymakers seem to think can be codified into hard, fast rules, decontextualized from the specifics of students and teachers—a teacher's "best practices" are the practices she can get to work best.

And yet at some colleges, the pressure to "innovate" (that is, use technology) has been so strong that faculty are required to give an account to administrators of keeping up with new teaching techniques and trends. Here to help us understand the "new learning technologies" is "innovative educational leader" Richard Culatta, former director of the Office of Educational Technology at the US Department of Education, currently CEO of the International Society for Technology in Education, with a glossary of terms:

> Competency-based learning: you move when you show you can do.
> Adaptive learning: technology assigns educational resources.
> Individualized learning: adjusts the pace of instruction.
> Differentiated learning: adjusts the instructional approach.
> Personalized learning: adjusts pace, approach, and adds student agency.[29]

Adjust the pace and approach—ya' think? Move on when you think you've got the point across—outstanding! Never would have occurred to me.

In *The Teaching Brain*, Vanessa Rodriguez and Michelle Fitzpatrick draw on neuroscience to describe the complex dynamic of a class, to challenge the reductive notion that teaching is a simple input-output system. A class is "a dynamic system [that] has many variables. Each variable is constantly interacting with other variables within the system, as well as with those belonging to other systems. They are all affected by and affect one another." Expert teachers "recognize there are multiple systems in play all at once, and they have the ability to decode those that are directly and indirectly affecting the learner. Expert teachers think, behave, and change in response to the various needs of their students, the classroom environment, and their own personal contexts." The authors call this "systems thinking."[30]

What do you know, I've been doing "systems thinking" all these years! I feel like Monsieur Jourdain in Molière's *The Bourgeois Gentleman*, delighted to discover he's been speaking prose all his life: "Heavens, for more than forty years I've been speaking prose! I never would have suspected it!"

While we're on neuroscience, here's another analogy. Think of a brain, where a whirlpool of synapses connects billions of neurons into myriad pathways and feedback loops, where the flow of everything affects everything else. It is infinitely complex, the workings of the brain. So is a class. It may not have quite these billions of interconnections, but it's got that life and mystery and complexity. You could not possibly diagram those cascades and currents, those loops, flows, and currents, and why would you, since they'll never be the same again.

Teaching and learning depend on the trust and goodwill, the morale, spirit, energy, enthusiasm, engagement, of all concerned. These are precious, perishable qualities that are destroyed by the sledge hammer of measurement/management that's smashing its way through education at every level. Teachers are the most crucial resource of any school, college, university. We are more important than buildings and grounds, lab equipment, athletics, coaches; yes, even Information Technology, that buzzing hive, is a mere limb of the enterprise of which we are the heart. We are more important than trustees or administrators or assessment officers, more than all these together. Without us, it's a no-go. We are the authors and engines of innovation, the innovators, believe it.

You want to know how teaching works? Put a teacher in a class, a small class, provide her with resources so she's not an embattled mess, with kids who are not so damaged that their problems become the main event, and let 'er rip! Learn from her. Don't go telling her what to do.

And let this chapter provide weaponry for the millions of teachers whose professionalism has endured so many blows.

✻

SEVEN

De-grading the Professors

Outcomes Assessment Assessed

I for one would welcome what is quite possibly among the most easily measured metrics. Lost faculty/student/staff work time required for "outcomes assessment." Heck, we could even flip it around and measure additional personnel/costs required for "outcomes assessment."
—READER COMMENT, *Chronicle of Higher Education*

Whatever their purpose, outcomes-assessment practices force-march professors to a Maoist countryside where they are made to dig onions until they are exhausted, and then compelled to spend the rest of their waking hours confessing how much they've learned by digging onions.
—LAURIE FENDRICH, "A Pedagogical Straitjacket"

"It can't happen here." Those were my very words. Spoken with the complacency of one who lives slightly higher up the hill and imagines herself safe from the rising seas. Rachel had dropped by my office on our way to dinner, just come from a meeting where her college had been informed of the new system to make faculty "accountable." She was livid, muttering about "the Bush juggernaut come to college," violations of academic freedom. This was some years ago; I had no idea what she was talking about.

"We're supposed to make up a bunch of SLOs, put them on our syllabi, proof that learning has taken place," she spluttered. "What,

you've never heard of an SLO? You will. Student Learning Outcomes."
To which I replied, "It can't happen here." My gaze drifted out the
window. I'm always slightly embarrassed about this office, when I
think of the windowless cubicle Rachel has inhabited all her years at
her community college. The view from my office could be a post-
card from Tuscany, red-tiled roofs, cypress trees, mountains in the
distance.

"No way," I said.

"You'll see," said she. "Batten down your hatches—it's coming your
way. They say other kinds of workers get assessed for their productivity, so should we. They want *outcomes assessments* . . ."

"Oh, assessments. If that's all they want, no problem—we do assessments all the time. Grades, comments on student papers, final
exams—and *that*!" I pointed to a pile of papers on my desk, requests
for letters of recommendation, a 300-page manuscript to be read for
a tenure review. We write letters on students; they write letters on
us. We evaluate colleagues for promotion and tenure; they evaluate us.
We solicit letters from faculty at other colleges and universities, we
meet on committees to review their evaluations, reading them carefully, inferring as much from what they do not say as what they say.
We sit on standing committees and ad hoc committees, evaluating
our programs, departments, curricula. We review articles and books
submitted for publication, and our own work is reviewed; we ourselves
are peer reviewed—reviewed, that is, by professionals. I'm afraid to
open my e-mail for fear of finding a request for a letter, a blurb, a book
review. But that's what a profession does, monitor itself; that's what a
profession *is*, trusted to keep track of itself.

"Oh, no, this is different," said Rachel. "This is coming from outside. They want student learning outcomes they can *measure*. They
want *numbers*. There are whole new systems, metrics, rubrics, benchmarks. You'll see."

"Who's *they?*" I bristled. "We don't have the state breathing down our necks. Anyhow, numbers are not what we do in English. Maybe in your field . . ."

"No!" Now it was her turn to bristle. "You cannot boil a math class down to 'outcomes'; it's as reductive in my field as in yours. I mean, you can measure whether students can do fractions or differential equations, but there's a world of difference between their getting the right answer on a test and understanding the principle. What you really want is to teach them how to *think* mathematically, approach a problem mathematically, so they can go on and apply what they know to some other problem."

"You mean, even in math, numbers don't . . . tell the story? I'd have thought . . ."

"Nah. There's no way I could boil a course down to a set of numbers to show an outside evaluator. Only the teacher can judge whether a student has learned to think mathematically. But faculty are no longer *trusted* to judge our own students."

"Right," I laughed, "what does the professor know? All we do is design the course, teach the classes, make up the assignments, do the grading, get to know the students—what do we know?"

Rachel was not laughing. "You cannot imagine what a ton of work this will make, the meetings, reports, like we don't have enough to do." Rachel is a fiercely dedicated teacher who prides herself on how many of her students go on to graduate from four-year colleges; she puts in 14-hour days. "*Rigor*, they call it," she practically spits the word. "*Rigor mortis* is what it is."

We were silent. I was thinking about my Shakespeare class, with its wild, wooly unpredictability, where I try to help students find a way into the plays, experience the pleasure of using their minds. I tried to imagine how I'd go about whittling this complex, living dynamic down to a set of measurable learning outcomes, reduce our open-ended, exploratory discussions to the numerical system Rachel was describing. *Outcomes?* I can tell you what I hope they'll learn in my course, but what they actually take, take to heart, take through life, I might as well try to predict the weather on the day they graduate as try to tell you that.

"You'll see," she said. "As we are, you will be." Rachel had been much impressed by the bone chapels, crypts, and catacombs she'd seen in southern Europe the summer before, heaps of empty-eyed skulls with idiot grins, mocking, "as we are, ye shall be."

Godzilla on Our Backs

Sure enough, several years later, it came to pass, just as she warned. The accountability police swooped down in the form of WASC, the Western Association of Schools and Colleges, the West Coast accreditation organization. Every six years, colleges and schools in California have to go through reaccreditation. (Accreditation bodies are regional; there's a Southern, a New England, a Western, etc.) Every college and university in the country has to be approved by a federally recognized accrediting agency in order to receive federal student-aid dollars, the lifeblood of a college. The process used to take a couple of months, generating a flurry of meetings, self-studies, reports to demonstrate we're measuring up. We'd write a WASC report—"wasp," we called it, for the way it buzzed around making a pest of itself— the WASC committee would come to campus, much hoopla, more meetings. They'd write up a report on our report, and after their visit, we'd write a report responding to their report; the reports would be circulated, more meetings. Then it was over and we could get back to work. It's fairly pro forma with us; this college runs a tight ship, what with our nonstop self-evaluations. Just one of those annoying things to be got through, like taxes.

But that's how it used to be. Now that the reaccreditation process is tied to state and federal demands, it's morphed from a wasp to Godzilla, a much bigger deal, more meetings, reports, interim reports, committees sprouting like mold on a basement wall. WASC demands that we come up with "appropriate student outcome measures to demonstrate evidence of student learning and success," then develop tools to monitor our progress and track changes we've made in response to the last assessment. There are pre-WASC preps and post-WASC pow-wows, a flurry of further meetings to make sure we're implementing assessment plans, updating our progress and updating those updates. Every member of the college has to be involved, every professor and administrator, every course and program brought into the review. The air is abuzz with words like *models and measures, performance metrics, rubrics, assessment standards, accountability, algorithms, benchmarks, best practices.* Hyphenated words have a special pizzazz—*value-added, capacity-building, performance-based, high-performance*—especially when one of the words is *data: data-driven, data-based, benchmarked-data.* The air is thick with them, a high-wire hum like a plague of locusts, never has the likes been heard. And lots of shiny new boiler-plate to put on our syllabi, spelling out specifics of style and content, penalties for infringements, down to the last detail.

It is perceived to be so complicated that a Director of Assessments and Institutional Research is hired. Yes, there are such things—it's a burgeoning industry, it's where the jobs in academia are—though they have different titles at different colleges: Assessment Officer, Officer of Institutional Effectiveness, Director of Assessment and Regional Accreditation. Our new "director" has "areas of expertise [in] WASC, course evaluations, survey administration and analysis"—no teaching experience, of course. At a time when the college can ill afford new appointments, when every faculty opening and sabbatical replacement is carefully vetted, suddenly there's this new administrator. Administrators require staff and offices, and though they don't have tenure, they might as well; they're here to stay. And the less real work they do, the more make-work they generate for faculty. When I came to this college, there were a dozen or so administrative offices whose functions I understood, whose staff I knew by name, who genuinely facilitated the work of the college. But between 1993 and 2009, administrative positions increased by 60%, 10 times the rate of tenured faculty.[1] Now their offices and functionaries outnumber faculty, a bureaucracy that drains resources and drives up costs.

We are required to work up an "assessment plan and logic model." As specified in a memo intended to clarify, this means we have to work up "rubrics for student learning outcomes," "assessment method type(s) to assess each SLO," "measurement tools to assess the selected student work assignment(s)" and suggest "potential work assignments your department could collect to measure your SLOs." There are "worksheets" with comment boxes, a results box, an action summary box—that's right, worksheets, like schoolkids fill out. "Additional Design-Tools— provides extra space to include more entries of design methods, additional student work product(s) to collect, and other measurement tools(s) to assess your SLOs." "Results/Actions—includes a recap of each SLO, design method, selected student work, and measurement tool in the Logic Model worksheet tab."

"Unbelievable!" sighed a colleague after one of our meetings. "If I'd wanted this kind of crap, I could have gone into business and be making money."

"After you have conducted your assessment you will need to complete the Results and Actions Summary boxes for each SLO." This is to be incorporated into an "Educational Effectiveness Review Report." "By applying the rubric to last year's senior theses enables you to evaluate both the rubric and your results to help fine-tune the assessment of this year's theses." (That sentence is why some of us still care about dangling participles.) All written in a language so abstract and bloodless that it's hard to believe it came from a human being. But that is the point, phasing out the erring human being and replacing the professor with a system that's "objective." Except that it's lunacy to think you can do this with teaching, or would want to.

My colleagues roll their eyes, roll up their sleeves, set to work. Awfully good sports they are, also awfully glad to have jobs. This is a faculty that works very hard. Each year I've seen demands ratcheted up, committee work proliferating, more pressure to publish. Students at colleges like ours expect a lot in terms of faculty availability, advising, mentoring; they have a right to—they pay a lot. We're forever being asked to participate in weekend events with parents and trustees. It's funny how people see professors getting away with a mere 6 or 12 hours work a week—what do we do with the rest of the time? I read there's a move in some places to make faculty provide documentation that they work 40 hours a week. 40 hours? Oh, *please*, that'd be a holiday.

Now this assessment rigmarole adds a whole new layer of bureaucratic make-work; reports and meetings bleed into one another like endless war. Forests die for the paperwork, brain cells die, spirits, too, as precious resources of time and energy are sucked into this black hole. And this is to make us more—*efficient*? Only in an Orwellian universe could this be called *efficient*. And this is to compile a "culture of evidence," we're told. Evidence of *what*?

We are given deadlines. By February 28, we are to produce the first phase of the plan, and a second phase by April 1, then on to a next phase, and a report. We're not entirely sure what we're being asked to do, and we get the sense that the assessment officer is not too sure either—and how could she be? How could she possibly understand the zillions of decisions that go into planning and teaching a course, orchestrating each class so it builds on and leads into the other classes, the countless judgment calls involved?

"So, said a colleague, storming into my office, "let me get this straight. We give them a number instead of a letter—no, we give lots of numbers— and that makes it 'objective'? But we give them a letter grade—and that's not objective?" He was waving a new directive that instructs us to "assess randomly selected students by number, assigning numbers 1 to 3, exemplary to unacceptable, initial to highly developed, and, using an Excel spreadsheet, rate their work numerically according to things like design process, argument or focus, authority, attribution, evaluation of sources, "communicative effectiveness." "I thought this college prided itself on *not* treating our students as numbers," he spluttered. "And w-t-f is a 'design process'? What are we *doing*?" and he did that gesture they make in Italy, pretending to pull out his hair, signifying, *loco*.

"Because the Accreditor Makes Us"

Nobody seems able to tell me where this is coming from. Even administrators seem baffled. Responses to an *Inside Higher Education* article offer speculations:

> Faculty members just want to keep the assessment office off their backs, the assessment office wants to keep the accreditors at bay and the accreditors need to appease lawmakers, who in turn want to be able to claim that they are holding higher education accountable.[2]

> My school's assessment guy brought in each department's assessment liaison and asked, "So why do you think we do annual assessments?" Each liaison answered with some BS-y variant of "to discover what we do well and what we can do better."
>
> "Nope," said the assessment guy. "We do it because the accreditor makes us."[3]

"Welcome to the world of elementary teachers," commented an elementary school teacher on an article in the *Chronicle of Higher Education*—"it has finally hit the universities." So that's what Rachel meant, "the Bush juggernaut come to college." Remember Bush's Spellings Report, 2006? It endorsed "outcomes-focused accountability systems" for higher education, calling for standardized assessments, standardized testing metrics, value-added metrics to be made part of the reaccreditation process. Now these directives have filtered down to the regional accreditors, making "performance outcomes" central to reaccreditation. This is what's hit us.[4]

There were a few warning voices, but they were unheard. Diane Ravitch alerted the Modern Language Association in 2014 but was ignored.[5] Paul Horton, a history teacher at University High School, Chicago, wrote a response to a cheerleading article about the Common Core (in the *Chronicle of Higher Education*, June 2014), cautioning that "the professoriate is beginning to hear the same sorts of messages that K–12 teachers have heard for twenty years." Now when state legislatures are beginning to demand "value-added measures" for professors, "when the chancellors of major universities begin to send messages embracing the Common Core Standards like those recently published in *The Chronicle*, my guess is that the same foundations that are pushing for K–12 reforms are beginning to push for undergraduate education reforms. The Gates Foundation has sponsored a lot of research and dozens of named professorships, and . . . can make itself heard very easily."[6] Horton's warning elicited comments from six readers, two of whom were concerned about his overlong paragraphs. "Higher education is really asleep at the wheel on this," said a friend at the American Association of University Professors, the watchdog of academic freedom.

"No big deal," say my colleagues; "if we don't do it, outsiders will." That same logic suckered faculty into policing colleagues during the

McCarthy era. And yet they have a point: as problematic as reaccreditation agencies can be, they're at least made up of academics, mainly. Congress has been gearing up to take reaccreditation away from regional accreditation agencies and shift oversight to government bureaucrats. Department of Education officials have been saying "they are going to pay greater attention to student outcomes in their oversight of federally recognized accreditors . . . [and] take a more aggressive approach."[7] Now that the Gates Foundation has established its new lobbying group, the Postsecondary Value Commission, to "educate" Congress about the "value" of higher education, "aggressive" may get real. The foundation has poured half a billion dollars into accountability schemes for higher education and is likely to spend that much more with this lobbying effort, in which Margaret Spellings—yes, *that* Spellings, of G. W. Bush's Spellings Report—is playing a key role. (More on this in a moment.)

The Language of Assessment

Our new "director of assessments" is a pleasant young woman, only it's hard sometimes to figure out what she means. Colleagues huddle in the halls, bent over the latest memo—could she be saying . . . might this mean . . . look, it says here, no, that's *goals*, not *objectives* . . . wait a minute, it says *outcomes*, not *objectives* . . .

I swear that *O* stood for *objectives* when these directives first started appearing. There's a big difference between *outcomes* and *objectives*. An *objective* is a goal, a purpose aimed for, aspired to, sought after, whereas an *outcome* is a result, conclusion; and, as used here, it must be *measurable*.

Okay, "department goals," we can do that, make up a bunch of goals. But wait—now we're told to recast these to fit "goal/outcome" structure. And that requires a lot more verbiage. What was before

"Students will learn basic skills in literary studies" is now, "Student exhibits the ability to read primary texts closely. Student is able to pose effective questions about form, content, and literary devices. Student engages with relevant critical approaches and with secondary material in literary studies." (That's the kind of garbage I try to purge from my students' writing, but never mind.) "Students will learn to see their argument in historical context" becomes "Student demonstrates an awareness that her arguments participate in a long-term conversation about the nature, function, and value of literary work." "Students will learn to recognize and construct well-formed arguments" becomes "student recognizes well-formed argument, including recognition of argumentative structure, use of evidence, and a disciplinary framework. Student constructs such arguments."

Student in her right mind will flee this major and find another, except they're all drowning in this gobbledygook.

A guideline is circulated explaining the difference between outcomes and objectives, to make sure we know it's *outcomes*, not *objectives*, we're being asked to produce. "Objectives are generally less broad that [*sic*] goals and more broad than student learning outcomes." I do a Google search to learn more, and sure enough, there's a boatload about this online. Outcomes are "what a student must be able to do at the conclusion of the course," explains an online source, and in order to assure these, it is best to use verbs that are *measurable*, that avoid misinterpretation. Verbs like *write, recite, identify, sort, solve, build, contract, prioritize, arrange, implement, summarize, estimate* are good because they are open to fewer interpretations than to *know, understand, appreciate, grasp the significance of, enjoy, comprehend, feel, learn, appreciate.* Verbs like *know, understand, comprehend, feel, learn, appreciate* are weak because they're less measurable, more open to interpretation.

Wait a minute, I thought getting students to *understand, feel, learn, appreciate, grasp the significance of, comprehend, enjoy*—was sort of the point. No more. A friend who teaches poetry at a community college was instructed to take the word *appreciate* out of her SLO. Now we're supposed to be teaching students to *prioritize, arrange, implement, summarize, recite, sort, solve, build, contract*—because these verbs are less open to interpretation? And here I was, thinking *interpretation* was kind of central to . . . what I teach.

Anyone who wishes to know more about assessment-friendly verbs, I refer you to a 27-page typology, *To Imagine a Verb: The Language and Syntax of Learning Outcomes Statements*, by Clifford Adelman of the National Institute for Learning Outcomes Assessment. It is staggeringly specific. The document explains that "non-operational verbs" are not useful because they do not refer to outcomes: "These verbs do not produce observable behaviors or objects: recognize, develop, relate, consider, prepare, comply, reflect, realize, anticipate, foresee, observe, review, extend, work. . . . Unless the learning outcome statement specifies what kind of 'work,' e.g. construct, build, model, shape, compose, it cannot be observed and judged."

The author gives a list of 16 categories, A through P. This gives the gist:

> F) Verbs falling under the cognitive activities we group under "analyze": compare, contrast, differentiate, distinguish, formulate, map, match, equate
> G) Verbs describing what students do when they "inquire": examine, experiment, explore, hypothesize, investigate, research, test
> H) Verbs describing what students do when they combine ideas, materials, observations: assimilate, consolidate, merge, connect, integrate, link, synthesize, summarize
> I) Verbs that describe what students do in various forms of "making": build, compose, construct, craft, create, design, develop, generate, model, shape, simulate

J) Verbs that describe the various ways in which students utilize the materials of learning: apply, carry out, conduct, demonstrate, employ, implement, perform, produce, use

K) Verbs that describe various executive functions students perform: operate, administer, control, coordinate, engage, lead, maintain, manage, navigate, optimize, plan

L) Verbs that describe forms of deliberative activity in which students engage: argue, challenge, debate, defend, justify, resolve, dispute, advocate, persuade

M) Verbs that indicate how students valuate objects, experiences, texts, productions, etc.: audit, appraise, assess, evaluate, judge, rank

N) Verbs that reference the types of communication in which we ask students to engage: report, edit, encode/decode, pantomime (v), map, display, draw/diagram

It goes on. The list is "by no means exhaustive," says the author, concluding, "you folks do a good job, but all of you—not just some of you—have to be far more explicit in your student learning outcome standards than you are at present."[8]

Remember Scholasticism? The medieval theological-philosophical system that strangled knowledge with dogma for six centuries. Scholars debated how many angels fit on the head of a pin as the Turks were battering down the gates of Constantinople. A reader comments, astutely, on Erik Gilbert's article on assessment: "So while we are agonizing about whether we need to change how we present the unit on cyclohexane because 45 percent of the students did not meet the learning outcome, budgets are being cut, students are working full-time jobs, and debt loads are growing."

Get those deck chairs rearranged—the ship is sinking fast.

"Academics are grown-up people who do not need the language police to instruct them about what kind of verbs to use," writes Frank Furedi in a blistering denunciation of "learning outcomes" in the *Times Higher Education*. Warning faculty against using words like *know*, *understand*, *appreciate* because "they are not subject to unambiguous test" is fostering "a climate that inhibits the capacity of stu-

dents and teachers to deal with uncertainty."[9] And dealing with uncertainty, with ambiguity, is one of the most important things the
liberal arts can teach.

A Culture of Compliance

And the assignments keep coming, and we keep on complying, drop-
ping our assessment plans like doggie bones at our masters' feet.
We're given an assignment to assess our senior theses from the year
before. Mind you, these theses were handed back with grades and
comments months ago, and the students have graduated, so this is just
an exercise to make sure we're all on the same page. The senior thesis
is the college's capstone requirement, required of every student in every
major. It is labor-intensive, involving qualitative evaluations in the
form of two or more readers' written and oral comments. It occasions
much grumbling, especially in the weeks just before it's due, when
there are mutterings about making a senior requirement that would
be less work for everybody; but we always come back to the thesis as
the best demonstration that students can do an extended piece of research and writing, can think through an issue and support arguments with evidence. Completing it gives them a sense of pride and
accomplishment; some tell me it helped them figure out what they
wanted to do after graduation. Awards are given for the best theses,
and there is a "Capstone Day," a sort of mini-conference that a colleague organized out of the goodness of his heart, some years ago, which
was so successful that it became a yearly event. Students feel honored to
be chosen, and it's excellent experience for them to present their work to
an audience of their peers, parents, and professors.

Now we are ordered to subject this qualitative assignment to a system of quantification. The assignment asks us to tally up the rubric
ratings, counting how many students earned each rating in each ru-

bric, and to summarize our quantitative findings, giving percentages, not raw numbers, showing the percentage of students that earned each rating, and . . . the memo goes on. Then we are asked, at the end of it all, what did we learn from the exercise? Oh boy, is that ever not a question you should ask me. I shot back an e-mail, "I learned there is no end to the idiocy . . ." words to that effect. My chair tactfully omitted my comments, submitting a report that said, "Well, we learned that the A's were really good and the B's were not so good. The five good theses were really good, and the two bad theses were really bad." The drain of faculty time, energy, and resources for this task, particularly for the chair, who had to write up an assessment of the assessment exercise (professing what we learned digging onions in the Maoist dirt), would make the gods weep.

Now I have to tell you, teachers are a self-directed lot, also a self-scrutinizing lot, forever asking ourselves, what did I do wrong, how could I have done better? The self-questioning "exists for few adults with the same remorseless constancy as it does for a teacher," writes Garret Keizer in his memoir *Getting Schooled*.[10] This may explain why faculty let "outcomes assessment" slip in with so little protest—we're so accustomed to self-monitoring, what's a little more, if it keeps Admin off our backs?

But there's a world of difference between being judged by professionals, assessed by peers with experience of teaching and scholarship—the peer review that comes from within the profession—and being assessed by outsiders who claim to have a "science" of assessment more reliable than we are. This is a problem with outcomes assessment that's rarely discussed, as assessment insider David Eubanks points out: the assumption "that grades given by people with disciplinary knowledge and training don't tell us about student learning, but measurements developed by assessors" who lack this expertise do.[11] When you place authority in outside overseers, boards, policymakers, lawmakers, managers, you are saying that we cannot be trusted to monitor ourselves, that we are not a profession, since a profession is entrusted with authority to govern itself, to regulate its own affairs, develop its own standards for promotion and advancement, as long as it adheres to certification practices and regulations established by law: this is what a profession is, by definition, *entrusted* by virtue of the long training of professionals and its service to society, to govern itself.

This is just "another expression of widespread erosion of trust," as Stefan Collini says. "What's being asked for is not any insight into how learning happens or how minds may be enlarged, but a confirmation to third parties that the announced procedures have been followed."[12] The process tells us nothing about the value of the educational practices being assessed, only that the procedures have been complied with. This is not quality control: it's control, plain and simple. You know, the word *assess* comes from the Latin *assidere*, which means "sit alongside, assist." It does not mean cudgel—but that's what this is. The "culture of evidence" being built is evidence of compliance.

Another highly questionable assumption, also a legacy of K–12, is that the outcomes of a class lie solely with the professor. "Current assessment models habitually and almost obsessively understate the responsibility of the student for his or her own learning, and . . . overstate the responsibility of the teacher," writes Christopher Nelson, former president of St. Johns College, Annapolis.[13] Surely the student has some responsibility. But, blame the teacher: it worked with K–12, deflecting attention from larger problems and delivering the educational system to federal control. So bring the same wrecking ball on up to higher education.

Who's to Blame?

Do not think I am singling out my own college for special criticism or targeting the evil genius of administrators, many of whom are reeling from this as much as faculty. This is a regime that's been foisted on all institutions of higher education. If we want accreditation, we comply. It hit the state colleges and community colleges before it hit us, but when Pomona's English department balked, some years ago, WASC made it go through the process all over again. It's even hit Stanford. But not Berkeley, from what faculty tell me. A 2018 report by the National Institute for Learning Outcomes Assessment, *Assessment That Matters*, finds that "the larger the size and greater the selectivity of the institution, the less likely it is to employ a variety of assessment activities." "Why size and selectivity are negatively associated with assessment activity is not clear," says the report.[14] Oh, I think I can guess why any institution with the clout to do it would bar the doors against this scourge. Go Bears.

Scripps faculty have had mainly cordial relations with administrators in recent years, far more cordial than at many other colleges. I think most of us see our dean and president as indefatigable women who work for and not against us and genuinely respect the liberal arts. I for one feel very lucky that we don't have managerial administrators or heavy-handed trustees trying to make us over on the corporate model. But now that we're being made to hop through these hoops to prove that we're measuring up, some of us aren't so sure we're still on the same page. Morale is not what it used to be. "We don't have the dumfuk politicians to deal with, but this—from our own college?" wailed a colleague.

But it's worse elsewhere. S. Robert Shireman quotes San Diego State's 2015 self-review: "Course Learning Outcomes (CLOs) are required for all syllabi; curricular maps relating Degree Learning Outcomes (DLOs) to major required courses are now a required component for Academic Program Review; programs are being actively encouraged to share their DLOs with students and align DLOs with CLOs to provide a broader programmatic context for student and to identify/facilitate course-embedded program assessment." Shireman comments, "All this SLO-CLO-DLO gibberish and the insane curriculum map database is really crazy."[15]

Here are some faculty responses to articles in the *Chronicle of Higher Education*: "Every form forced upon me makes me feel a little more a part of some Orwellian enterprise. Every assessment kills a little piece of my soul, my passion for teaching." And another: "The more educational buzz words included, the more valid the assessment 'rubric.' I've come to loathe that word. . . . The effort it takes to create, and fill out, and debate, and revise, and submit, and re-revise, and re-submit, and revise (get the picture?) the assessment RUBRIC (!) is a God-awful time-suck that subtracts from what we are supposed to be focusing on in the first place." Yet another: "The iron frame of student learning outcomes that has been foisted on us by campus administrators, accreditation agencies, and know-it-all, high-charging 'consultant' and 'experts' has produced such a deformation of the teaching and learning process that it becomes a parody of what once it was."[16]

Crazy, nuts, delusionary are some of the milder words I hear. *Absurd, make-work, insane, outrageous, fraudulent, charade* also ring out, along with lots of unrepeatables. *Soul-killing, soul-sucking, time-sucking, demoralizing, B.S.* are descriptors we've long been hearing from K–12 teachers, as well as comments like this: "Besides the possibility that we may be harming education by using reductionist approaches to the art of teaching, there is the possible harm caused by the demoralization of faculty whose accreditation agencies ramrod their assessment approach down the throats of well-meaning faculty. I, for one, intend to leave the profession earlier than originally thought. . . . My love of education has been permanently blighted."[17]

Nuts or not, this is now the law. Tenured faculty have been fired for not complying. (Not at this college, but by now I know better than to say, "It can't happen here.") When faculty protest, they are criticized for being troublemakers. Shireman describes "countless examples of colleges that have been coerced down the SLO path. . . . San Jose State University reported to its accreditor that it was finding 'faculty resistance.' . . . To address the problem, the campus adjusted its faculty reward system to force faculty participation, a step the accreditor praised."[18] When Texas Tech tried to propose alternative kinds of learning outcomes more consistent with their real teaching goals, their proposal was rejected by the southern accreditation board, "and the entire university placed on probation, under threat of a loss of accreditation that would lead to every student on campus being denied access to federal financial support," write Gordon Hutner and Feisal Mohamed in *A New Deal for the Humanities*.[19]

"What this stuff steals is our aliveness," says Ann Lamott; "grids, spreadsheets and algorithms" steal "everything great and exciting that someone like me would dare to call grace."[20] And even if you don't believe the word *grace* belongs in educational parlance (I do, though not in the Christian sense Lamott means), it drains the lifeblood out of teaching. It kills the art of teaching, which, as Furedi says, "depends on exercising judgment based on experience . . . presupposes the capacity to respond to unexpected and unpredictable questions and problems . . . requires a willingness to extemporize, change direction and even introduce issues and questions into the course that were not anticipated."[21]

Ticking Off Boxes

And it all goes—where? Faculty often wonder—what do they *do* with it? It goes into a "warehouse of materials" that are dumped into a giant database, never reviewed, never analyzed. Here is an account from John Powell, a philosophy professor "elected" to oversee assessment at Humboldt State:

> These efforts began with people who are off campus—systemwide administrators, the board of trustees, influential businessmen, legislators, staff in the governor's office, accrediting agencies, the U.S. secretary of education, and national education organizations operating at a level of abstraction to which one must bring one's own oxygen. Not one of these is going to look at a single document my department generates, nor will my department's results even find their way into a summary of all the documents written by my committees or my college. . . . No one will ever read outcome assessment reports unless someone pays for it and requires doing so as part of some poor soul's position description.[22]

A reader comment in the *Chronicle of Higher Education* gives a similar testimony to futility: "I've filled in sections of prefabricated curriculum maps to show where my courses fit into any of the 57 (I kid you not: 57!) learning outcomes in the college curriculum. I've used alternate rubrics on my final exams to report findings to someone who promptly reported them to someone else, and so on up the ladder, in a process which I can only assume terminates with the data being boxed up in some warehouse." There's comfort in that, I suppose, that this junk will never be looked at again. Let the madness end.

And apart from draining time, energy, and morale, there is no evidence that it accomplishes anything. Laurie Fendrich, a major player "in constructing the rubric for outcomes assessment in my department," concludes that "outcomes-assessment practices were, at best, misguided and, at their worst, detrimental to higher education itself. . . . Oh sure, they make numbers and graph lines go up and down, and give education think-tankers something to cluck about, which in turn gives them more billable hours and conference fodder. But they haven't made the teaching any better . . . or shown up in the form of improved performance by any students I've encountered."[23]

Other insiders have begun speaking out. Natasha Jankowski, director of the National Institute for Learning Outcomes Assessment, says, at a meeting of assessors, it's time we "own up" that this has been a "hot mess": it's not about "crabby" faculty who "hate change"; "There are good reasons why faculty hate it. It's real and it's earned."[24] "People in the assessment world have known for some time that their work was not producing results," summarizes Erik Gilbert; "this has been an open secret for awhile."[25] So why does it go on? "Studies that demonstrate its lack of effectiveness are either ignored or met with the claim that what is needed are more data," says Jerry Muller. "Metric fixation, which seems immune to evidence that it frequently doesn't work, has elements of a cult."[26]

And anyone who cherishes the illusion that assessment measures can ferret out fraudulence, consider this: In the summer of 2015, Joe Palermo reports, the president and vice president of WASC "admitted that their 'metrics' completely failed to pick up on Heald and Corinthian colleges' egregious predatory lending, ethics violations, and fraud aimed against students (many of whom were combat veterans). . . . Indeed, WASC continued to give its seal of approval to Heald and Corinthian *right up to the moment those schools were exposed (not by WASC)* as being out of compliance with even minimal federal standards, but by the US Department of Education."[27] Just think, the West Coast accreditation board gave for-profit predators Corinthian and Heald its stamp of approval. Those are big fish to let slip through the net.

Outcomes assessment has produced "outcomes," alright—outcomes like "despair, rage, crushed morale, . . . shrunken creativity, numbed affect, distorted collegiality, and cynicism . . . debased standards, and unhappiness," writes Mark Hulsether in *Academe*, who describes outcomes assessment as "probably the single greatest factor in dumbing down college education," perhaps "the single worst thing about higher education today, and that's a tough competition to 'win.'"[28] "It's taken a huge toll," sighed my friend Rachel, a few years after she gave me the heads-up that this was on the way. "I've watched the heart and soul go out of my college as we've tried to resign ourselves, to re*design* ourselves to fit these absurd standards." It's never a good idea to demoralize your workforce—corporations know this, or at least they used to, before they turned cannibal. But for colleges to inflict this on faculty at a time when higher ed is already so embattled, fighting for its life—this is a *really* bad time. As Collini cautions, academia runs on enormous expenditures of goodwill—drain that away, and you're left with a robo workforce following orders.[29]

Most disturbing, as Furedi notes, is the "culture of cynicism and irresponsibility" that's being bred: "What matters is whether the formal outcomes have been achieved, not what students have actually experienced or learned. It promotes a calculating and instrumental attitude where responsibility becomes equated with box-ticking."[30] As Alka Cuthbert writes of health care, "if every task is broken down into a discrete isolated act, then eventually we tend to feel responsible for only that act. . . . So if a checklist is complete and targets reached, then the substantive work, which is often longer-term, more difficult and less empirically visible, disappears."[31] See what's happened: responsibility, which is the lifeblood of any class or institution, gets reduced, in the name of "accountability," to the ticking off of boxes.

Faculty dutifully fill in worksheets, tally up columns of figures, offering them to administrators who are themselves hopping to the tune of reaccreditation agencies who are themselves following orders of legislators, politicians, policymakers. No good can come of this.

Creativity Killers

Outcomes assessment works against everything the liberal arts work for. We in the humanities try to teach students to think, question, analyze, evaluate, consider more than one perspective, reckon costs and benefits in human terms, weigh alternatives, tolerate ambiguity. Now we are being forced to cram these complex processes into crude, reductive slots, to wedge students' imaginations and our own into narrowly prescribed goal outcomes, to make premature closure. We are saying, "You, the student, will learn what I have determined that you know: here is the outcome, here is how you demonstrate you've attained it, here is how I demonstrate to my overseers that you have done this." And students will not object because they come from the death-dealing pedagogy of the Common Core, which we are on our way to emulating.

I'm sorry to put it so bluntly, but we are being asked to be as simple-minded as those who are laying these demands on us. We're being asked to obliterate what David Labaree calls the "zone of creativity and exploration" higher education can provide: "The danger posed by this accountability pressure is that colleges, like the K–12 schools before them, will come under pressure to narrow their mission to a small number of easily measurable outcomes."[32] That's the way it works with metrics: once you've established numerical targets, you adjust your behaviors to meet those targets. You start to make assignments that are safe, as John Warner warns, requiring "students to make the moves we can measure and quantify," that have nothing to do with those mind-blowing moments when a teacher "causes you to suddenly see the world in a new and different way."[33]

Creativity doesn't come this way. It comes from "divergent think-ing," being allowed to follow out divergent possibilities, wander in dif-ferent directions, as in the freewheeling, open-ended conversations we have in a liberal arts seminar. This is how students learn to make connections, bring disparate thoughts together in new combinations, envision new possibilities. Checking off boxes gets you doctors who can read numbers on a screen but can't hear what a patient is saying; architects who fail to imagine how a housing project affects a neigh-borhood; engineers who fail to ask how a dam affects the population downstream; software makers who have no idea if their program can be used by nonexperts. You get technicians who've mastered a skill or technique and can follow lines laid down by others, but not scientists who can launch out in new directions and create new knowledge.

In *The Pleasure of Finding Things Out*, Richard Feynman describes scientific discovery as "born of a struggle against authority": "if we say we have the answers now . . . [we] doom man . . . to the chains of authority, confined to the limits of our present imagination." New dis-covery originates in "freedom to doubt," in keeping questions open to allow for the possibility of new discovery.[34] It does not come from checking off boxes.

The Dumbing Down of Higher Education

"It is not to the credit of higher education that we have tolerated this external assault on our work," says John Powell, assessment overseer at Humboldt State: "Its origins are suspect, its justifications abjure the science we would ordinarily require, . . . and it displaces and distracts us from more urgent tasks."[35] This is the unkindest cut of all: the com-mittees enforcing this madness are staffed by colleagues, faculty po-licing faculty. Some are drawn to these committees because assess-ment metrics promise a system that elevates the humanities above the swamp of subjectivity, give us a claim to "rigor" and "objectivity." Here is a chilling description of a faculty debate at Swarthmore: "In a 2014 faculty debate on the college's mission statement, faculty members from all three divisions criticized the notion that the college should aim to teach virtues such as courage, a sense of justice, a feel for beauty, and perseverance on the ground that there are no discrete, objective tests for possessing these things."[36] You see how thoroughly "metric fixation," defined by Jerry Muller as the belief that "it's possible and desirable to replace judgment with numerical indicators," has colonized the thinking of a faculty that ought to know better.[37] Faculty have overestimated their ability to implement this system without being taken over by it. Younger faculty are particularly vulnerable, since they've grown up in an assessment culture and have no memory that we were once a profession trusted to monitor ourselves. "Every day, there are fewer who remember what campus once was, or would want to fight for it," writes Frederick de Boer.[38] Autonomy, trust, respect—that's a lot to lose.

And this in the name of "efficiency"? Is anybody actually keeping track of how much the extra administrators, the consultants, the wasted faculty time add to the cost of running a college? "As managerialism embeds itself, you get entire cadres of academic staff whose job it is just to keep the managerialist plates spinning—strategies, performance targets, audits, reviews, appraisals, renewed strategies, etc.," says a former academic dean at a prominent British university (quoted by David Graeber); and this goes on "almost wholly and entirely disconnected . . . from the real life blood of universities—teaching and education."[39] If we reckoned the dollar amount lost, we might put an end to the madness—though, as Muller warns, in his article "The Tyranny of Metrics," academics may lack the business sense to cap it: "Businesses have a built-in restraint on devoting too much time and money to measurement—at some point, it cuts into profits. Ironically, since universities have no such bottom line, government or accrediting agencies or the university's administrative leadership can extend metrics endlessly." Now that there are so many stakeholders, officers, offices, an entire assessment industry, it may be too late to pluck it out.

The liberal arts offer students ways of understanding their culture, of challenging and revitalizing it and envisioning a future that's not more of the same. By instilling "the metrics—and morality—of technology within ourselves as individuals and into the texture of society," writes Andrew Hacker, we are narrowing "the kind of nation and people we are to be."[40] "Humanists," writes John McCumber in the *Chronicle of Higher Education*, "build humanity, one work of art at a time," one course at a time, one year at a time. Humanity is built, not born, and it's a strenuous act: "For humanity doesn't just exist; it has to be created, over and over again. . . . Cultures which do not teach the humanities to as many people as possible . . . are inviting serious trouble, for continuation of the current dystopia is not the worst possibility before us. . . . Consider this: Is it possible to have a society full of young people who are creative, energetic, entrepreneurial, technologically informed—and wholly comfortable with mass slaughter? I know the answer. I'm in a German department."[41]

Where It Leads

To faculty who see outcomes assessment as trivial, who dismiss it as bureaucratic twaddle—"just make up a buncha rubrics, go to the meeting, no big deal"—heads up! Look at higher education in the United Kingdom, and be worried. Back in the 1990s, when UK academics were called upon to participate in what they thought was "just some form they had to fill out, an annoying scholarly bureaucratic exercise that would not really affect us," says Tarak Barkawi, they thought it was too silly and trivial to take seriously, to think that scholarly research could be ranked like a restaurant or hotel. Barkawi describes where this has led:

> A decade later this five-yearly exercise completely dominates UK academic life. It determines hiring patterns, career progression, and status and duties within departments. It organizes the research projects of individual scholars so as to meet arbitrary deadlines. It has created space for a whole class of paid consultants who rank scholarship and assist in putting together RAE (Research Assessment Exercise) returns. . . . UK professors have become intimately bound up in administering and legitimating a government-run exercise that now shapes more of university life than they themselves do. They have actively ceded their power.

The author warns US academics that even directives for a syllabus can be an entering wedge: "Something as apparently innocuous as an accreditation agency demanding that syllabi be written in a particular format, or majors justified in a particular way, can wind up empowering university management to intimately regulate teaching."[42]

Where it leads is to the "audit culture" Simon Head describes: "The audit culture requires academics to squander vast amounts of time and energy producing lengthy and pointless reports, drenched in the jargon of management consultancy, showing how their chosen 'processes' for the organization of teaching, research, and the running of academic departments conform to managerial 'best practice' as laid down by HEFCE, the QAA, or the university administration itself."[43] HEFCE, that would be the Higher Education Funding Council for England, and QAA, the Quality Assurance Agency, for any of you still awake, reading of this garbage, all part of the RAE or Research Assessment Exercise. The effect on faculty has been spirit-crushing.

They're now evaluated by the number of their publications and the number of times they're cited, not the quality—and the result is shorter, sloppier books, less readable, and less read. Swept up in a frenzy of monitoring, measuring, and surveillance, British academic life has been transformed into what Collini calls a "distracted, numbers-swamped, audit-crazed, grant-chasing" enterprise that hardly recognizes itself.[44] This is the legacy of Margaret Thatcher, who made war on universities in her country, as every US president since Reagan has on ours. She got farther, eliminating tenure. But we're catching up.

Without tenure, say good-bye to academic freedom. "When the University of California adopted revised language on academic freedom, it said 'faculty must form their point of view by applying professional standards of inquiry *rather than by succumbing to external and illegitimate incentives such as monetary gain or political coercion.*'"[45] Outcomes assessment directives are *external and illegitimate incentives* and *political coercion*—how is this not a violation of academic freedom? And with academic freedom goes the production of new knowledge.

What has made the US higher education system exceptional is the cultivation of individual development that fosters originality and imaginativeness. "By embracing a broadly divergent array of knowledge and experience," as Karin Fischer says, "we bring diverse and unexpected perspectives to any problem or situation, allowing us to adapt rapidly to change." But we will lose these "capacities for creativity and innovation" if we bend to a "close-minded, bean-counting approach to accountability."[46] Yet here we are, moving toward an assembly-line education that strives for standardized, interchangeable "outputs," bowing to the dictates of technocrats incapable of imagining otherwise. Here we are, making ourselves over into a regimented system like China's, a standards-based, test-driven system that rewards "obedience, compliance, and homogeneous thinking," as Yong Zhao writes in *Who's Afraid of the Big Bad Dragon*, warning of "a rising tide of authoritarianism."[47]

And if we had any illusions that our self-policing would neutralize the animosity of politicians, that if we produced "evidence" of our outputs, they'd get off our backs—guess again. Attacks on higher education have only intensified, with the humanities taking most of the heat.

I am trying very hard not to agree with Christian Smith, when he says "higher education is so drowning in BS" that it's no longer possible to believe in it: "I have long believed that, despite its flaws, American higher education should, could, and often did stand as an elevated island, a protected reserve for the practice of open inquiry, reasoned debate, critical and self-critical reflection, persuasion through argument and evidence, and genuine progress in shared learning." But now, "under the accumulated weight of the mounds of BS, the island has been swamped, the reserve polluted, by many of the destructive outside forces that the academy exists to hold in check and correct. Much of American higher education now embodies the problems it was intended to transcend and transform: unreason, duplicity . . . *incapacities to grasp complexity and see the big picture, and . . . semimasked forms of coercion.*" Smith singles out for special mention "administrators' delusion that what is important in higher education can be evaluated by quantitative 'metrics,' the use of which will (supposedly) enable universities to be run more like corporations, thus requiring faculty and staff to spend more time and energy providing data for metrics, which they, too, know are BS."[48]

If higher education has a hope of seizing back the narrative, we need to get this Godzilla off our backs. Which is not to say that education is above accountability, but that we need to account for ourselves "in terms that actually capture what is distinctive and valuable about what universities do," as Collini says, in his heart-rending account of the wrecking job neoliberal management has done on higher education in Britain.[49] That is, in terms that actually represent the *value* of what we do (as I try to do in this book), rather than acceding to some bogus "system" that measures our compliance.

And yes, let's talk about *accountability*, who has it, who does not, who needs to own up; only let's be clear about what it is. Because when you see who is genuinely concerned with holding unaccountable power to account, you'll see it's the writers, journalists, academics I've drawn on in this book—Kurt Andersen, Joanne Barkan, Wendy Brown, Anthony Cody, Stefan Collini, Henry Giroux, Gordon Lafer, Jane Mayer, Christopher Newfield, Diane Ravitch, John Warner, and the teacher bloggers I've cited who are speaking truth to power, exposing the abuses of power, demanding accountability of those who owe it most. (And, by the way, most have backgrounds in the liberal arts.)

And if you really want to know about "student learning outcomes," look at what our graduates do with their lives. Ask the graduates. Which I do, in the last chapter.

Postscript and Warning

But first I must be the bearer of some bad news. The Gates lobbying group, the Postsecondary Value Commission, has big plans for higher education, plans for more elaborate and punitive measurement systems.

The Gates Foundation has always, before forming this commission (May 2019), exerted its influence from behind the scenes. But this new lobbying group will enable it to "talk directly with legislators about laws" for the "transformation" of higher education, explains Nick Tampio.[50] In May 2021, the foundation published a 117-page report, *Equitable Value: Promoting Economic Mobility and Social Justice through Postsecondary Education*, to "guide" congressional conversations about the reauthorization of the Higher Education Act.[51] The Higher

Education Act is the federal law governing higher education policy, including accreditation and standards that qualify colleges and students for financial aid. The Gates report will "aid policy makers in gauging what the public gets for its investment in higher education," provide them with data about which degrees lead to better earnings, and generally guide their understanding about the value of college.[52]

The report is draped in the rhetoric of social justice. Nothing new here—corporate reform always makes a brouhaha about "equity" and "access"—but this document, aimed at Congress, is drenched in it: "From the steps of the Lincoln Memorial in 1963, Dr. Martin Luther King, Jr. reminded America of 'the fierce urgency of now' when discussing how the United States has defaulted on its 'promissory note . . . that all [people] would be guaranteed the inalienable rights of life, liberty, and the pursuit of happiness.' And yet, nearly 60 years later, the insidious ways that racism, classism, and sexism continue to play out in modern-day American society have been laid bare by a national reckoning with pervasive racial bias and the COVID-19 health crisis."

And who is to blame for this "default"? Higher education, of course. While acknowledging that there may be other factors, poverty, discrimination, etc., the report targets postsecondary education as the primary offender and insists that it "*dismantle* its own inequitable policies and practices." Blame the educators. It worked with K–12, bringing public education under federal control. Higher ed has been harder to get hold of, what with its Nobel Prizes and reputation for excellence (also, it's not 75% women); but, undermined by a half-century of right-wing detraction, defunding, and now by the pandemic, it's never been more vulnerable.

And how, exactly, do we do this *dismantling*? By creating "a data system that captures key outcomes" and provides "more robust performance metrics," by devising "systems for gathering and reporting those metrics," collecting ever-more fine-tuned data to make sure we're "ameliorating inequities."[53] Dig down through the layers of rhetoric in this (formidably unreadable) document, and you'll see, this is its pitch: higher education needs to provide "actionable data" to federal policy-makers, "better measures to gauge how taxpayers' dollars are being spent." Colleges and universities must create "systems . . . dedicated to using data," "leverage data assets, develop a culture of data-use," "use data to reorient institutional strategic plans and institutional self evaluations required by accreditors toward the goal of providing equitable value," "revive accreditor data dashboards," and so on. The word *data* thunders through the report, 280 times, more than twice a page.

As a snow job, this report is brilliant. Its ringing call for justice appeals to progressives still shaken by the summer of George Floyd; its excoriation of higher education resonates with practically everyone; its insistence on data, buttressed by graphs, charts, "visually engaging slide decks and graphics," gives an air of incontrovertible scientific "objectivity."[54]

"The higher education system is ripe for disruption," says Anthony Carnevale, a writer of this report, a former Reagan appointee to Health and Human Services and a Bush appointee to the Educational Testing Service (ETS is hardly a disinterested party when it comes to "data"). "This unbundling could . . . be brutally efficient for higher education," he explains. "By providing students what they need without all the extras, programs leading directly to earnings, we could chip away at the waste, duplication and misplaced incentives." "Chipping away at the waste" means stripping out the lowest-earning majors. These are, as determined by Carnevale in his 2015 study, "The Economic Value of College Majors," early childhood education, elementary education, human services and community organization, social work, studio arts, visual and performing arts, theology and religious vocations. No "need" for these; they're "waste."[55] "Brutal," indeed, these eliminations, and suicidally short-sighted, since these are areas essential to the well-being of individuals and society, qualitative needs. Many of us would dispute the notion that human "need" is as bare-bones as Carnevale suggests—King Lear, for example, who comes to understand that human "need" is complex and qualitative, as we'll see in the next chapter.

If the accreditation of colleges and universities becomes contingent on their ability to demonstrate "value" in these terms, if Gates idea of "value" gets codified into law and federal funding gets routed to majors that lead directly to higher earnings, then humanities majors may find it impossible to get loans or grants. As Michael Itzkowitz, formerly director of Obama's Scorecard, now a senior official of the (Gates-funded) think tank, Third Way, states, "Students shouldn't be able to take out loans at programs that show no return on investment."[56] "No return"? What about smaller returns, or returns that take longer, or returns that enhance the quality of lives? Such nuances are obliterated by a standard that defines "need" as a top-paying job.

And how exactly will more stringent data gathering and measuring "dismantle racist practices and structural inequities"? It won't. But it will burden postsecondary education with measurement systems that bring it into the vise grip of management—measure to manage, that's the ticket. It will assure that funding is routed to the jobs Gates sees as vital to the economy, to give US corporations a competitive edge. (For a sinister use of "measurement" to further the corporate reform agenda, see the account in *Free City!* of a community college's fight for its life against an accreditation board's attempts to close it down.)[57] Like every policy Gates has pushed—the College Scorecard, the Common Core, computerized learning—this drives a nail in the coffin of the liberal arts and into the social infrastructure of society. And what about social justice? Even if more elaborate metrics and data collection were to lead to higher earnings for graduates (they won't), this kind of blow at the liberal arts is also a blow at ethnic and gender studies, the programs most concerned with social justice. Gates's plan places him squarely in the camp of Republicans who would eradicate social justice programs, which makes the high-flown rhetoric of this report a sorry sham.

The way to greater social equity is not by heaping more accountability demands on a faculty already groaning under them. It is to give greater numbers of people greater access to quality education, well-resourced schools with small classes and engaged faculty. Once upon a time, this was common sense and government policy. The GI Bill, the California Master Plan, CUNY's Open Admission program, the idealism that had community colleges expanding, in the 1960s and 1970s, at the rate of about one per week,[58] went far to break down social and economic barriers to higher education and improve social mobility; not far enough, obviously, and it was no match for the plutocracy that torpedoed democracy in subsequent years.[59] It is not higher education that creates the injustices this report condemns. It's a society that feeds the fortunes of the likes of Gates while forcing the young into indentured servitude to acquire the education they need to survive.

Imagine what Gates might have accomplished if he'd routed the billions he's poured into "transformative" schemes like this—this is one of many—to where they might have done some good. MacKenzie Scott, Jeff Bezos's former wife, figured out where her money could have the most effect, simply by looking at the situation. She gave more than $5.7 billion to "two- and four-year institutions successfully educating students who come from communities that have been chronically underserved," as she says, among which are California state colleges and HBCUs. Her gifts have been "Overwhelming. Transformational. Game-changing" to these struggling schools; and no strings attached.[60] This is the kind of "transformation" to be proud of, when it's hailed as such by the educators.

"The Bill and Melinda Gates Foundation may be the most destructive force in education," writes John Warner in *Inside Higher Education*.[61] If Gates has his way—as he may, since his foundation "has influence everywhere . . . federal, state . . . local," writes Tom Loveless of the Brookings Institution[62]—we may be seeing increased pressure on higher education to transform itself into a system that works for students motivated primarily by the drive for earnings. People are rarely so single-mindedly bent on gain, except in the eyes of those who are so motivated themselves; though in desperate times, "incentivized" by the reward system the Gates Foundation proposes, they may be pushed to be so.

EIGHT

Growing Up Human

Hamlet, King Lear

What a piece of work is man . . .
     —Hamlet

Is man no more than this?
     —King Lear

"What do the characters learn?" I ask. "Where do they start from, where do they end?"[1]

"Dead," says Brent, enjoying, as usual, the chuckles he sets off.

"Well, yeah. So do we all. But in the meantime? Life takes place in the meantime—that's where you find out what you're made of. Would you hurl your body in front of bullets to save us or crawl under the table to save yourself—how many of you know?" Everyone looks around, hoping someone else will go first on this one. "Me either, I don't know," I say finally. "It's a big thing not to know, isn't it?"

"You'd know if it happened, I guess," ventures Sandra of the sandy braid, whose gaze seems less distracted these days.

"Yes, that's how we'd find out. That's what the tragedies do, put characters up against the wall, let us imagine it without having to go through it."

The Heart of His Mystery

Would you pluck out the heart of my mystery? Hamlet challenges Rosencrantz and Guildenstern, the schoolchums Claudius has brought to Denmark to spy on him. "Let's see if we can pluck out the heart of this mystery—what is it about this play, what's its appeal? It's not the plot we go to *Hamlet* for; the plot could be *Game of Thrones*. It's not 'relatable' in an obvious way—I mean, how many of you have had an uncle murder your father and marry your mother . . ."

One hand goes up. "Don't you hate it when that happens?" Brent is on a roll.

I draw their attention back to the question. "What *is* the *mystery* of Hamlet?"

The responses come slowly. "Is he mad?" "Good—who thinks he is?" A couple of hands go up. "I mean, who *in the play* thinks he is?" The hands go down.

"How many characters are trying to figure out Hamlet?" Everybody in *Hamlet* is trying to figure out Hamlet, and so is Hamlet trying to figure out Hamlet, and so are we. It's a dangerous game. Polonius's spying gets him . . . offed. Rosencrantz and Guildenstern's spying gets them . . . offed. What are they trying to figure out about him? Why he's behaving so strangely. How do Rosencrantz and Guildenstern account for his behavior? Thwarted ambition; Claudius beat him to the throne. Social-climbing courtiers themselves, they read him as they are. How does Polonius read him? *Mad for . . . love. And truly in my youth I suffered much extremity for love; very near this.* Polonius reads his son Laertes this way, too, sending a spy to Paris to check up on him. These readings tell us more about the characters who are reading than about Hamlet. And we who are reading the play—do we too see as we are? Of course we do. Our challenge is to find a way of reading that isn't just us reading in.

"Who really needs to know what's troubling Hamlet?" "Claudius," says Brent. "Why?" "Skin in the game." Ghastly expression, but it fits. "Claudius needs to know if Hamlet knows he killed his father. That makes his question different from the others'. Think about who knows what in this play: Claudius and Hamlet are the only characters who have any idea what's going on. Claudius is watching Hamlet who is watching Claudius who is watching Hamlet watching Claudius. None of the others has a clue. It's an interesting situation, isn't it—imagine you're living in a story where what you thought was happening wasn't at all what was going on."

"Like when your best friend's shagging your boyfriend," mutters Cynthia, whose spiky red hair could be porcupine quills when she says things like this; she hasn't had an easy life.

"That'd do it."

What a Piece of Work Is Man

"Hamlet too is trying to figure out Hamlet, only the questions he's asking aren't the same as anyone else's. What does Hamlet want to know?" We tease this out: why, since he's determined to kill Claudius, since he resolves to do it, does he not? And the questions for us, the reader or viewer—what are these? Pretty much the same as Hamlet's, since our perspectives are allied: we know what he knows. Why, having vowed to carry out his father's command, does he not sweep to revenge with *wings as swift as meditation*? Oceans of ink have been spilled on this question, and it's a real question because Hamlet asks it, and asks it again—he says he wants to, has *cause and means and will to do it*, so why doesn't he? "He swears he'll rush right to it, then does nothing for . . . four more acts. Why not?"

"Short play," says Brent.

"Right. And not so interesting. So why do you think he doesn't?" I press Brent on this, wanting to see if he has more in him than one-liners.

"He's not sure about the ghost."

"Where do you get that?"

"He says it."

"Where?" "Something about the devil . . ." "Where?" Barbara finds it, reads, *the spirit I have seen may be the devil.* "Good. Though he's also said, *it is an honest ghost.* But then he decides he needs proof—can you find where?" She finds this, too, the soliloquy prompted by the long lament of the Player King, Hecuba mourning the death of Hector and the fall of Troy. "Only here does Hamlet mention not trusting the ghost—and we're how far into the play? End of act 2. And at what point in the soliloquy does he mention it?"

"About halfway through," says Barbara, "Or more. Seems like . . . an afterthought." "Like he's grasping at straws," agrees Samantha, "like, 'maybe this is why I haven't done it,' but he doesn't really know." "Good." Good to hear their voices.

"You know the word *rationalization?*" A few nod. "Somebody define it."

"It's like, excuses. You're making up reasons, but you don't know the real reason," says Allison. "Right. Hamlet's 'reasons' seem like rationalizations, excuses for inaction he doesn't understand. The word *rationalization* was coined by a disciple of Freud, Ernest Jones, who applied it to *Hamlet* in 1910. Jones, like Freud, saw Hamlet's problem as his unacknowledged desire for his mother and desire to kill his father, which complicates his feelings for Claudius, who beat him to it."[2] Some perplexed looks. "That's the Oedipus complex?" Lizzie. "Right. He can't acknowledge this, of course, has to repress it, which leaves him conflicted and unable to act." They look unconvinced. I turn them to Hamlet's line about Claudius: *He that hath killed my king and whored my mother, / Popp'd in between the election and my hopes.* "*Popp'd in!*" repeats Trevor, "Phew! But . . ." He trails off. "But what?" "Well, he never comes out and says that's why he's not doing it, does he? I mean, all those soliloquies." "But if it's repressed, he wouldn't know it," says Allison. I turn their attention to his last soliloquy, when he's watching Fortinbras, son of the king of Norway, marching his army off to conquer a patch of land not large enough to bury his dead. Hamlet sees Fortinbras's bravado as a reproach to himself and asks himself, again, why he's done nothing, and concludes, *I do not know.* "Rather late in the play for him not to know, isn't it? End of act 4. *I do not know.*"

They're looking mystified. "Usually a soliloquy reveals a character's inner motivations, but all Hamlet's reflections and self-questionings bring him (and us) no greater clarity about why he's not acting. Shakespeare is doing something interesting with these soliloquies . . ." "But, if he never says why he's not acting and doesn't know," says Allison, "then Freud could be right?" "Or you or I could be right, or anybody," I say. Nothing comes back. "My problem with the Freudian reading is that it reduces the play to personal neurosis. That loomed large for Freud, but there may be issues that loom larger for Hamlet, and I think his lines give us clues. Let's read on."

"Is there a turning point in the play, an event that changes everything?" We talked about this in *Romeo and Juliet* and *Julius Caesar*, the point past which there's no return. Brent, who's into the Hamlet-Claudius cat-and-mouse game, enjoying these *mighty opposites* stalking each other, gets this: "When Claudius knows that Hamlet knows." "When is that?" "When Claudius sees the play and freaks out." "Right, *The Murder of Gonzago*, 'the mousetrap,' Hamlet names it to Claudius. Claudius sees the Player Villain poison the Player King exactly the way he'd poisoned Hamlet's father, and knows that Hamlet knows. And Hamlet knows beyond a shadow of a doubt that

Claudius is guilty, and knows besides that Claudius knows he knows—and knows he's in danger. But then when he comes across Claudius praying—*now might I do it pat*—he does nothing."

"He couldn't kill him while he's praying," protests Lydia; "he'd send him to heaven."

"That's what he says. Do you buy it?"

"Not really," says Cynthia. "But I mean, why doesn't he just get on with it—I mean, what *is* his problem?"

"I felt that way when I read the play in high school," counters Lizzie. "I saw him as this spoiled brat. But then when I read the play last week, I felt like . . . I think he's tragically prevented from being who he wants to be. I mean, all he wants is to go back to school to study. What if somebody stopped me from doing that? I think it totally depends on where you're coming from, how you read this play. I mean, I wonder if I was even reading the same play before. Sometimes I wonder if we're all reading the same play in this class."

Her heartfelt words make her blush, which makes a hush. Finally Allison speaks up: "I think it's like he says, he doesn't know . . ."

"Say more."

"I mean, he's not like Fortinbras, Mr. Macho Man. He's just not that into it."

"Fortinbras. The name means 'strong arm.' Let's talk about Hamlet. What do you like about him?" They're quick with responses: he's so much smarter than everyone else, he runs rings around everyone, he's wicked funny.

"Look at those lines we've been quoting, *what a piece of work is man*—somebody read them." Can that be Lydia whose hand just shot up? She reads:

. . . how noble in reason,
how infinite in faculties, in form and moving how

express and admirable, in action how like an angel,
in apprehension how like a god! The beauty of the
world, the paragon of animals!

She reads well; knowing the Bible gives her a feel for the language. "Okay, *like an angel, like a god, noble in reason*—how would you characterize that worldview?" "Naive," says Brent. "Any other words come to mind?" Idealistic. Optimistic. Spiritual. "*Humanist,*" I add. "This is the spirit of Renaissance humanism, the belief in the dignity, the potential of human beings . . ." "Naive," Brent repeats, "unrealistic—and 'reason' isn't getting him anywhere either. I mean, he can't reason his way to do what he needs to do."

"You have a point. But are you really saying that it's 'naive' to be idealistic, to believe in the worthiness of man? And you're okay with that?" That comes out more sharply than he expected.

Ashley steps in, "But he's not very nice." "I was hoping someone would pick up on that. Not nice to whom?" "To Ophelia. *Get thee to a nunnery.* He seems to hate women." "He's devastated by his mother," says Lizzie, "betrayed by her, and now Ophelia." "What does he blame Ophelia for?" We coax this out: she gave back his gifts, rebuffed his advances; she was, he believes, in cahoots with Polonius, spying on him—"Was she really?" "Not really. Polonius set her up." "Right. She was just obeying her father, a good woman, obedient," and discussion wanders off to Kenneth Branagh locked in torrid embrace with Kate Winslet—"Do you think they really got it on?" asks Cynthia. "Nah, Branagh just wanted an excuse to make out with her," says Trevor, who has taken to sitting by Cynthia; unlikely duo, but good for them. We bat this around awhile. I turn them back to the question.

"To one who has such a lofty a conception of humankind, who sees reason as making us like a god, the falling off of those closest to him is a big blow. Hamlet is having a hard time wrapping his mind around the fact that those he loved and trusted betrayed him. Even his school-chums, Rosencrantz and Guildenstern betray him. . . . And to him now comes this momentous command to *set it right—O cursed spite / That ever I was born to set it right.* 'Set it right'—by killing? Can you think of a simple reason Hamlet might not want to kill the king, I mean something that might be true of you or anybody?"

"He's depressed," ventures Barbara. Depression is an explanation I've been hearing a lot lately, probably because so many students have experienced it themselves. "*Melancholia* was the word for it in Shakespeare's day. Many have read him this way. But do you have to be depressed to not want to . . . kill? Would you be able to . . . kill?" Nobody wants to go first on this one. "How many of you think you could kill in self-defense? Life in danger, heat of the moment?" Most hands go up, mine included. Lydia's does not. Barbara's is at half-mast. "In defense of a loved one? Of an innocent victim? In revenge?" Silence.

Sweet Revenge?

"What does the Bible say about revenge?"

"Vengeance is mine, saith the lord," Lydia quotes. "Why is revenge . . . problematic?" "You get Israel and Palestine," says Allison, "and there's no end." "Right. This is why we have laws and courts. But might there be situations when revenge is justified?" "When the law's not working," "when you have to take the law into your own hands," responses drift in. "When there's a Hitler," says Allison. "Or a Claudius?" says Danny with the Dylan hair.

"How did 'they' see revenge in Shakespeare's day?" I fill in. Revenge plays were wildly popular. Thomas Kyd's *The Spanish Tragedy* was probably the most popular play on the Elizabethan stage. Shakespeare may have had a hand in writing it, almost certainly acted in it. One of his first plays, *Titus Andronicus*, was in that mode, full of blood and overwrought rhetoric; later he parodies this bombast in *Pyramus and Thisbe* and *The Murder of Gonzago*, and in the melodramatic rant Hamlet works himself up with, *the croaking raven doth bellow for revenge*."

"Do we still thrill to revenge?" "I sure did," says Cynthia, "when Lisbeth got revenge on her rapist in *The Girl with the Dragon Tattoo*." Nods of agreement. "Name some other revenge kills in films?" *Game of Thrones, The Sopranos*. "Google 'rape and revenge films,' Wikipedia." "Tons of them!" says Samantha. "Read some." She reads: *Death Wish, An Eye for an Eye, Kill Bill, Inglorious Bastards, The Brave One, House of Cards*. They haven't heard of most of these; nor have I heard of the TV and films they tell me of. Popular culture dates fast.

"Remember that scene in *The Godfather*, in the church?" says Danny.

"That was so cool," enthuses Brent. "And in *Gladiator* . . ."

"Yes, well, revenge is alive and well. But can you see how someone of noble nature, with high humanist ideals, might not leap at it? That word *noble* recurs, mainly spoken by or about Hamlet . . ." "19 times," says Danny, ever-ready with the Mit.edu online text.

"I think he's just not that . . . into it," repeats Allison.

"I think you're right. Unlike . . . ?" Fortinbras, who's hot to revenge his father's losses, and Laertes, who swears he'd revenge his father's murder in the church. "Let's talk more about Hamlet. Look at the scene where he greets the players. Polonius orders a servant to take in the players *and treat them according to their own desert*, according to their worth or value. Hamlet protests—Alice, read the lines." She hates being called on, but she's been so quiet. She reads: *God's bodkins, man, treat them better. Use every man after his desert and who should scape whipping? Use them after your own honor and dignity. The less they deserve, the more merit is in your bounty.*

"What does he mean?"

"Like, do unto others what you would have them do to you?" she says. Good. Sometimes once they hear their own voice, they can use it again.

"Yes. The golden rule. But how do Hamlet's lines do it one better?" Silence. Finally, Alice again: "You mean, like he's saying, give back to others the *best* you have; the less they deserve it, the better it shows in you." "Good. *Bounty*—what does the word mean?" "Toilet tissue?" "Thanks, Brent." Sometimes I could do with a little less casualness in this class. "Remember Juliet said, *my bounty is a boundless as the sea*. Generosity of spirit. It's the opposite of eye for an eye, or of zero-sum. Even Claudius says Hamlet is *generous—he being . . . generous and free from all contriving*, he assures Laertes, will not suspect foul play. Now Hamlet must betray his nature and render an eye for an eye. Find the lines where he tells Horatio what he admires about him." Rustle of pages, Lydia reads:

> *Give me that man*
> *That is not passion's slave and I will wear him*
> *In my heart's core, ay, in my heart of heart.*

"So now Hamlet must betray these values too, become *passion's slave*, crude as Fortinbras. This is his tragedy, that the command to kill comes to a character woefully unsuited to it. Faced with a command so at odds with himself, his gears lock. I don't know how else to describe it—he freezes into inaction. To be a man, as his culture defines it, as his father demands, is to be capable of killing. He thrashes around for four acts trying to figure out why he can't bring himself to do it, when maybe it's just that his humane nature recoils from killing a fellow human being. *What a piece of work is man.* What are we?"

Nothing comes back. But it's a thoughtful, not an empty, silence.

"Do we glamorize killing today? Do we equate revenge with honor, confuse aggression with strength?"

"For sure," says Cynthia. "Toxic masculinity."

"But might there be another kind of manhood?" She shakes her head. "C'mon, Cynthia, there's Macho Man, but there are more humane possibilities. You know, soldiers had to be trained to kill, it didn't come naturally. War historians write of unfired guns and wounds through the foot. . . . Human nature—there's huge variability. Neither Laertes nor Fortinbras would have trouble with the ghost's command; neither is evil, they're just . . . made of different mettle. We're a mingled yarn, variable within ourselves, too—part of us thrills to revenge, 'sweet revenge'; part of us recoils from taking a human life. Most of us are untested and don't know, *know not what we might be*, as Ophelia says. Shakespeare shoves our contradictions full in our face, turns our eyes into our very soul. Who am I quoting ?"

"Gertrude?" Lizzie of the upward lilt. "Good. But when you know it, make it sound like an answer, not a question, okay?" I say gently, aware of an upward lilt of my own.

A *Hamlet* of Your Own

We're coming to Thanksgiving. Time to give them the *Hamlet* writing assignment, so they can use the break to view the films.

"YOU have been selected to direct a new production of *Hamlet*. You have your pick of any actors, living or dead, any scenes, settings, special effects from the following films: Kenneth Branagh, Laurence Olivier, Richard Burton, David Tennant, Mel Gibson, Ethan Hawke, Campbell Scott. The library has some of these, I have several, and you can find some online. You may select and recombine elements from any *three* productions, to construct a *Hamlet* of your own." I love this assignment, probably because it's something I've always wanted to do, take bits and pieces from various performances and construct a *Hamlet* of my own.

"This is a once-in-a-lifetime opportunity—just think, YOU, of all film and stage directors, get to direct *Hamlet*! Which actor would you cast as Hamlet, and who would you choose for the supporting roles, and why? Which scenes work particularly well? Which directorial choices, cuts, transpositions work for you, and which not? Since each staging or directing of a Shakespeare play is a reading or interpretation, you'll be giving your own interpretation of *Hamlet*. As you explain your reasons for choosing the actors and elements you select, make sure *a reading of your own* comes through."

"What if we don't like any of those actors—can we make up a whole new cast?" Brent.

"Okay, but you have to say why. And you have to show familiarity with at least three of these films."

It works. When we resume class after Thanksgiving, I walk in and they're deep into discussions about whether Kate Winslet or Helena Bonham Carter was a better Ophelia, whether Olivier or Branagh did the soliloquies better. "I loved the surveillance stuff in Tennant." "I liked Ethan Hawke better." "Yuck, I hated that one. Did anybody see Campbell Scott?" A few hands go up. "When he started pushing Ophelia around, that really did not work for me, not with a Black actress." "Good point. Which ghost did you like best?" "The one on closed-circuit television." "Patrick Stewart." "Anybody notice Paul Scofield in the Gibson production?" Nobody did, but I thought Scofield's ghost was the most convincing portrayal of a dead man I've ever seen on stage or film—bloodless, toneless, chilling.

"My mom called it the Thanksgiving *Hamlet* film festival, said we should do this next year with another play." "Yeah, my mom watched, too." Sandra was immensely grateful to have the films take her mind off her first Christmas without her mother. She says this was a breakthrough for her—"I didn't realize you have to not only read the play but really get into it, like, *experience* it."

Danny wrote a story about a director dealing with a bunch of unruly actors. A few cast actors who were not in the assigned films, which was fun, except that I'd never heard of most of them.

"I thought I was going to love Richard Burton, but I got sick of his laugh." "I *loved loved loved* Olivier, I cried at the end, *good night, sweet prince* . . ." I push on this: "What big change did Olivier make, to get that *sweet prince?*" Blank looks. Finally, Sandra: "There was no Rosencrantz or Guildenstern, was there?" "Right. Olivier's Hamlet would never send his schoolchums to death. Shakespeare's Hamlet does. Olivier got the nobility of Hamlet, Burton got the nastiness, neither got the full range. Actors almost never do."

What a Falling Off

"Is Hamlet a character who knows himself?"

"Yes." "No." The words come simultaneously.

"Who said no?" Trevor: "He doesn't understand why he's not killing Claudius, just goes around making up reasons, doesn't really understand." "That's true. But are there ways he's savvy about himself and others?" Of course they know when I phrase a question like that, the answer is yes.

"Look at the scene where he greets Rosencrantz and Guildenstern—how long does it take him to figure out what they're up to?" About 50 lines into the scene, he says, *Were you not sent for? . . . Come, deal justly with me.* "And look at this later scene with them, where he shoves a recorder at Guildenstern—*Would you play upon this pipe?* Guildenstern demurs, says he doesn't know how. Hamlet: *It's easy as lying,* then, *look you now, how unworthy a thing you make of me! You would play upon me; you would seem to know my stops; you would pluck out the heart of my mystery; you would sound me from my lowest note to the top of my compass. . . . You cannot play upon me."*

"What do these lines say about him?" "That's what I really like about him," says Lizzie; "he's nobody's fool." "Think back to Brutus—was he 'played upon'"? "Big time. By Cassius, by Antony," says Lizzie, who can be counted on to remember. "Remember, we talked about how Brutus doesn't know himself and that makes him vulnerable to manipulation; he gets lured into a killing he's not ruthless enough to follow through on. Hamlet doesn't let himself get jerked around like that. Find his line, *To know a man well were to know himself*—where does he say that?" Danny, who has Mit.edu open, finds it: "He says it to Osric." "Remind us who Osric is." "Robin Williams!" says Danny. "Right. Once you've seen Williams in the role, you'll never forget him, though he's easy to miss, reading. Hamlet understands that to know another, you must know yourself—he understands the principle, anyway."

"Does he ever figure out why he's not acting?" "Well, I guess it's like you said," says Allison, "it's not in his nature." "Actually, it's what *you* said, Allison—he's just not that into it. It was well said. But does he ever actually come out and say it? Can you find a soliloquy where he says, 'I can't kill my uncle because it goes against my better nature,' something like that?" Silence. "That would take the mystery out of it," ventures Lizzie. "Yes, that mystery that has us endlessly interpreting. But no, his final words about himself are, *I do not know*. Here's what I think: his human nature simply recoils from killing. That's the way I see it. I warned you, you'd be getting Shakespeare according to Gayle Greene. But no, he no more comes out and says this than he says he's jealous of Claudius for marrying his mother—but I do think my reading takes into account more of what he's been thinking about than Freud's, because he asks, and asks again, what are we, what am I, *what a piece of work is man*, and my reading speaks to that. Remember the opening line?" "*Who's there?*" quotes Lizzie.

"I sort of liked that Oedipus thing," says Samantha. "Olivier had her on the bed . . ." "I know." I'd like to let this discussion develop, but I have one eye on the clock and pull them back to act 5.

"How does he finally pull it off? He's returned from a journey—journeys are symbolic, right? We don't go with him . . ." "We do in the films," interrupts Samantha, and we're back into the films again, talking about flashbacks and when they work and when they get in the way. I pull them back. "What happens on that journey?" Claudius has sent him off to England. Hamlet puts up no resistance, though he knows he's in danger; but when pirates attack, he uses his father's ring, the royal seal of Denmark, to send Rosencrantz and Guildenstern to their deaths. *Not shriving time allowed*—what does that mean?" "No time to confess," says Lydia; "but he couldn't kill Claudius that way." "Right. Sounds a bit ruthless. Has he changed?" Silence. "Tell me how you'd stage Horatio's response, when he hears Hamlet's done this—*So Guildenstern and Rosencrantz go to't*—how does Horatio say that line? Might he be registering surprise? Horror? Because, look, Hamlet spends the next six lines justifying himself—*they are not near my conscience*. Might he be picking up on something in Horatio's look or tone? They were schoolchums, remember." A few nod, a few look unconvinced.

"Let's look at the scene where he comes back. Where does it take place?" *Alas, poor Yorick*, quotes Danny. "That one. We're in a graveyard, he's talking about *a special providence in the fall of a sparrow*." "That's Matthew," says Lydia. "Not a sparrow falls without the will of God." "Yes. And how about these lines: *if it be not now, it will come. The readiness is all*." "He sounds so resigned," says Barbara; "I really think he's depressed."

"Resigned, certainly, and grim, like he's expecting the worst. He seems to have given up trying to understand himself, resigned himself to the limits of a world he has not made and will not live to inherit. But look at his lines, *the readiness is all . . . the interim is mine.* He sounds in control. Knowing he can kill in the heat of the moment—*And praised be rashness for it*—he has faith that if he lets things take their course, *it will come.* He'll be able to kill. And sure enough, Claudius backs him into a corner, and the moment comes. The situation that lets him kill."

"And that's a good thing, because . . . ?" Cynthia.

"Because it's what he has to do," says Trevor, as much to her as to the class, "to live up to his father's command." "*Down* to it, more like it," she retorts. "How do the rest of you see it—does Hamlet grow up or down?" Thumbs down. This, they get, this story of a young man of qualities in a world that does not want his better self, a world so poisoned by the older generation that no buds bloom. "Yes, I agree, *down*, down to his culture's idea of a man. Remember the ghost's command, *taint not thy mind*, remember what he said of Gertrude, *what a falling off was there*—even as he lays on his son a command that requires that he fall off from his better nature, *taint* his mind. I mean, can you become a killer and not . . . 'fall off'? Yet in a way Hamlet seizes control of his story. It's not the story he'd have chosen, and it's a grim sort of control. But he doesn't have a lot of choices." I pause. No one says anything. But they're tuned in.

"At the end, he makes a big deal of Horatio staying alive to set the story straight; otherwise, nobody will have any idea what this blood-bath's about. What kind of story does Horatio tell?" Rustle of pages, as they flip to the end, where Horatio promises a tale

> Of carnal, bloody, and unnatural acts,
> Of accidental judgments, casual slaughters,
> Of deaths put on by cunning and forced cause.

"Is this the play we've seen?" "It sounds . . . wrong," says Lizzie. I seize on that: "Why wrong?" "Well, it's too . . ." She gropes for a word.

"Melodramatic," Allison supplies. "Yes, it sounds like the overblown rhetoric of the Player King and Queen, like Hamlet's ranting as he tries to psych himself up, *the croaking raven doth bellow for revenge*. It sounds like it's dropped into *Hamlet* from *The Spanish Tragedy*, the kind of bombast that Shakespeare has not written since *Titus Andronicus*, except to parody. The lines throw us back to an earlier, more primitive moral framework, as Hamlet sinks to 'an eye for an eye.' Shakespeare's *Hamlet* has nudged us up a notch, toward a more humane dispensation; Horatio jerks us back down, as the ghost's command does Hamlet, bellowing for revenge. It's disappointing, because Horatio is the only character who's been present throughout. But he seems not to have . . . got it."

"So is anybody left to get it, left as *audience to this act*? To interpret, tell it right?" Silence, long silence, broken finally by Trevor, who looks like he's had a Eureka moment.

"You mean, *we* are?"

"Yes. Hamlet doesn't get to live out his potential, but maybe we can take something from this waste, something to set against our . . . *falling off*. Maybe the growing up is left to us."

"Like it sort of . . . tosses the ball into our court," says Sandra, silent this last half hour, but not missing a beat.

Too Old to Learn?

"*I am too old to learn*, says Kent, who is—how old? Anyone?" Danny, quick with the mit.edu text, gets it: 48. That sounds ancient, until I ask, "How old is Lear?" Silence. "Good quiz question, see if you've read through act 4." With that hint, Lizzie pages through act 4 and reads, *Fourscore and upwards*. "What's a score?" comes the question. Oh, no, I hold my breath, please . . . somebody. Finally, a voice, timid, Lydia's. "20 years?"

"You mean Lear's over 80? Wow," says Danny. Eye rolls, amazement, like *really* old. Geezerville.

"Can you name other literary works with protagonists this old?"

The Old Man and the Sea. That comes easily; then, silence. I let the question hang there. A few film titles drift in (mainly from me): *Harold and Maude, Harry and Tonto, Cocoon, Driving Miss Daisy, The Dresser.* "Not a big theme, is it? Why not?" "I guess we don't usually think of anything interesting happening to a person past a certain age," says Sandra. "Why not?" "Well, it's kind of . . . over." "Is Lear's story over?" I try to keep my face expressionless; we all know I'm closer to Lear's age than to theirs. "Is Lear too old to learn?"

"I don't think we like to think about old age," says Samantha. "Because?" "I don't like to think I'll ever be that old." "Right. So we make the subject disappear, like we make old people disappear, don't want to think about it, right?" Exposing ageist attitudes in undergraduates is like shooting fish in a barrel, I try not to take cheap shots, but I do want these attitudes on the table for all to see. "What are some stereotypes we have of old people?" Weak. Foolish. Doddering. *A very foolish fond old man. Old fools are babes again.* We've talked about stereotyping in *Merchant*, in *Othello*, how othering lets us define ourselves as "not that." "When we make the aged other, we're saying, we'll never get like that. We don't want to imagine old age. But might it be good to try?"

"You mean because we'll be old someday?" Barbara, bless her.

"Yes. If you're lucky." That comment comes from a future beyond their ken, I should probably not say things like that. But why not? The old are the lucky ones, the ones who've lived long enough to get old; not everyone's so lucky. Let them chew on that.

"That word *old*—how often does it occur in the play?" "Wow," says Danny—"49 times." "How do the characters view age?" Depends on the character. The bad guys see it as weakness to exploit:

O, sir, you are old.

. . . you should be ruled and led

By some discretion, that discerns your state

Better than you yourself.

So says Regan, the daughter who takes pleasure gouging out old Gloucester's eyes. But Cordelia, Edgar, Kent? By their attitudes toward age, we know them.

"But isn't Lear really sort of senile? Name one reason I should care about this man!" huffs Ashley. Alicia seconds her: "Yeah, I mean, how would you like to have *him* for a father?" Alicia has taken to sitting next to Ashley, supporting whatever she says; I think she's a bit smitten.

"What makes you say that?" "Well, he's . . ." The words drift in— "horrible to Cordelia," "doesn't listen," "tyrannical," "my way or the highway." "Yes, but look at the characters who love him—name them." The names come slowly. Cordelia, the Fool, Kent, Gloucester, Edgar, Albany. "What do these characters have in common?" "They're the . . . good guys?" "Right, and how do they behave toward him?" This is pulling teeth. "They defend him, follow him, risk their lives for him— Why do they?" I'm answering too many of my own questions, this should be coming from them. No, I wouldn't want him for a father, yes, I did have him for a father, in a milder form; so did many women of my generation have fathers who were not always gentle with their authority. I have feminist friends who can't stand this play. I think the terms we make with this play have to do with the terms we've made with our fathers.

And I do know about *Lear*: it either sweeps you along or leaves you on shore, wondering what all the fuss is about. Its devotees see it as "Shakespeare's greatest achievement, the sublimest invention of the artistic imagination," as Maynard Mack summarizes. Tolstoy called it a work of childish absurdity worthy of "aversion and weariness."[3]

"Give it some effort," I urge. Ashley snorts, indignant. But a few are intrigued, sensing there's something here—these are the ones I can reach. I sigh, struck, for the millionth time, how I can only teach students who are ready to learn. Some have settled the big questions, young as they are, and seek no more. Lear has not settled them. Stripped of his fine robes and flatterers, he's just setting out. Old men should be explorers. We shall not cease from exploration.

Anyhow, it's impossible, in the four or five classes we have on *Lear*, to get this play off the ground. It is so huge, so monumental, so much going on. "Too huge for the stage," A. C. Bradley said it was.[4] Too huge for the classroom. There's a film about a tattered old Shakespearean actor at the end of his career, Albert Finney in *The Dresser*, moaning—"I can't do Lear again."

But I can't not do *Lear*. I would never not do *Lear*.

See Better, Lear

Begin at the beginning, get a toehold in the text. Lear does so many things wrong in the opening scene that it takes a whole class to unpack them. He turns a deaf ear to Cordelia, soaks up the flattery of his lying daughters, then acts immediately on his errors, banishing the good daughter for speaking truth, rewarding the evil sisters for lying. Kent tries to stop him—*check this hideous rashness; see better, Lear*—for which he too is banished. His tragic flaw? Pride, the classic flaw, dangerous because it makes you stupid. Regan says, *'Tis the infirmity of his age: yet he hath ever but slenderly known himself.* He certainly seems to fit the stereotype: no fool like an old fool. But as Goneril points out, he's always been like this: *The best and soundest of his time hath been but rash.* Everyone sees Lear's mistakes but Lear.

Look how the scene moves. At the start, the world's intact, the king is on his throne, the bonds of family and society are secure. By the end of the scene, Lear has fractured family, state, society.

"I don't get why it's such a big deal," Trevor protests; "I mean, all he wants is a little buttering up." Cynthia is having none of this: "Flattery, you mean?" "At his age, why not?" "That's patronizing, that's ageist—would you want your kids to tell you lies?" These two make an interesting couple; I'm beginning to suspect they are one. I try to get them to talk about Lear's question, How much do you love me? "Have you ever been asked that question? How does it make you feel?" "It puts you on the spot," says Danny; "I mean, what can you say? 'Okay, so I love you a lot, a really lot.' You can't put love in words." "You could if you were Shakespeare," says Brent. "Even Shakespeare," I say. "What is the problem, assuming love is in words?" Lizzie's hand is waving. "It's like Juliet says, *swear not by the moon, do not swear at all*—it's deeds that count." "You could say," continues Danny, "'if you don't know I can't tell you.' I mean, if you don't already know, there's nothing I can say." "That's what Cordelia says," says Sandra—"*Nothing.*"

"Exactly," I say. "But there's something worse about Lear's game: he says, give me words and I'll give you land, as though love were . . ." I trail off, hoping someone will supply the word. Finally, Cynthia: "For sale. Like it has a price."

"Right. What does the word *values* mean?" The word makes a silence so uncomfortable, I have to ask, "What just happened?" Finally, Cynthia says, "You mean, like 'family values'?" making scare quotes in the air. Ah, that's it. This is one of those words that's been hijacked by the right wing: "family values," an excuse for cutting social programs; "religious values," "national values," covers for bigotry, chauvinism. These kids have a nose for hypocrisy; they've seen enough of it.

"No. Strip the word of its baggage—values in a basic sense, like, what do you *value*, consider *valuable*, essential. You know, like what makes life worth living? As in—well, you tell me, what are some things people live for?" Money. Love. Status. Honor. Family. "Service," I say, "as in, serving others, as in a religious calling, as in the caring professions . . ." "You mean, like a nurse or a social worker?" "Right. Anybody here going into teaching?" Two hands, Barbara's and Lydia's, both at half-mast. "I'd like to make the world a better place," says Danny, "but I'd like to make money, too." "Right. But what if you had to make a choice between doing well for yourself and doing good for others, could you decide which matters most? *Values*, as in, what do you value above all else, as in, what do you most *need*? *Need*, a big theme in this play—what do humans need?"

"How does Lear's game show a confusion of values?" Nobody says anything, so I start to hum, to their embarrassment; finally a few catch the tune and sing along, "Money can't buy me love." The Beatles, the one sliver of popular culture I still share with my students. "It is Lear's error to imagine you can trade land for love. Look what he says to the King of France, trying to talk him out of marrying Cordelia: *Her price has fallen*. The bad guys have no problem with this; as they see it, everyone has a price, land is a prize and love is a word and words are cheap. But Cordelia cannot heave her heart into her mouth, refuses to commodify her words or her love to humor her father when he's acting like a fool."

And so Lear gives his kingdom to the calculators for whom value is price.

The Uses of Nothing

"At what point do things start coming apart for Lear?"

"You mean, when Goneril gets mad about his knights?" says Lizzie. "Right, the 100 men he's retained, a vestige of royal command. Goneril and Regan begin tasting their power and start stripping him of his.

Why does he need 100 followers in a household that has servants, they say, what need 50, 25—*What need one?*" We look closely at these lines, where Lear begins to get it, that need is more than utilitarian. "*Thou art a lady,* he says to Regan, you wear a gown. A sack is all you need. Stripped to the basics of survival, *man's life is cheap as beast's.* But we have needs beyond those that can be measured, qualitative as well as quantifiable, and *for true need* . . . Here he breaks off, unable to follow through, to articulate what *true need* is. The rest of the play will do that for us."

I'm talking too much. I got too philosophical too early, I always do with *Lear.* I don't know how not to.

"Why does he dash out into the storm? What is he obsessing about?" I step them through these scenes. He's calling for revenge, enraged at the wrongs he's endured—*tremble thou wretch unwhipped of justice*—but then, *My wits begin to turn,* and as they turn, something else turns too: *How does, my boy?* he says to the Fool; *Art cold? I have one part in my heart / That's sorry yet for thee.* "How is this a change?" I ask. "He's thinking about someone besides himself." At last a voice that's not my own; Lizzie, who remembers—"like Kate." "Yes, like Kate. A different side of him is coming out. When they come to a shelter, he insists that the Fool go in before him. But first, he says, *I'll pray.* Find the lines." Rustle of pages.

"Who is he addressing, in this prayer—*poor naked wretches, wheresoever ye are* . . . —who are these?" "You mean, like the homeless?" says Danny. "Right. Having felt what it feels like to be out *in such a night as this,* exposed to the elements, he says, *O, I have taken too little care of this.* Now look—"

Take physic, pomp;
Expose thyself to feel what wretches feel,
That thou mayst shake the superflux to them
And show the heavens more just.

"Who's he talking to here? Still the homeless?" Silence. "Could you maybe tell us what the lines . . . mean?" says Samantha. We work it out: Take some of your own medicine, you pompous ones, expose yourselves to feel what wretches feel, that you may shake the super-flux to them. "The *what*?" says Danny. "Surplus, superfluity, excess—wonderful word, too bad it didn't catch on. Think skyscraper pent-houses, private jets, yachts with helipads—that's *superflux*. Glut. He's addressing the uncaring uberrich whose excess makes others poor, among whom he includes himself: *O, I have ta'en / Too little care of this*. Then when he calls for justice, again—*show the heavens more just*—this is not the vengeful, punitive justice he was calling for a few scenes before." "He means, like, fairness?" says Samantha. "Right. You know the difference between retributive justice and distributive jus-tice?" They do now. "And he's acknowledged his responsibility for the suffering of his subjects. Quite a leap for an angry old man who's been flattered so long, he assumed he could do no wrong."

"But he has to be reduced to *nothing* to feel what justice is. Look at that word *nothing*—how many times does it occur?" Thirty-four! The word tolls through the play: *nothing will come of nothing*; *Can you make no use of nothing?* What is the *use of nothing?* As long as Lear is "something," "someone," swathed in fine robes, surrounded by flat-terers who pump up his ego, he's blind. But stripped of status and power, he comes to *see better*—remember Kent's *see better, Lear*. The whole huge tragedy comes of Cordelia's *nothing*, but so does salvation come that way. *Nothing almost sees miracles / But misery*.

"That's in the Bible," says Lydia. "Whoever finds his life will lose it."

"Yes, Christianity is full of paradoxes: lose the world to gain the world. So is this play full of paradoxes: *This unprized precious maid*, the King of France calls Cordelia, *most rich, being poor*, as he takes the hand of Lear's discarded daughter, *Most choice, forsaken*."

"But we haven't talked about the subplot."

I Stumbled When I Saw

"Why did Shakespeare graft these two plots together? What kind of a guy is Gloucester?" Old, yes, old as Lear. Anything else? Insensitive. He puns about Edmund's "conception" with Edmund standing right there, *brazed* to his bastardry, as he says. Anything else? Gullible. Tricked by the bad son, then saved by . . . "You know, the good one . . ." "Edgar," I supply. "I know, it's hard to keep the names straight, but see one of the films, you won't confuse them again." Both aged protagonists take the word of the bad child over the good, both endure afflictions that are punishment and correction, both are met and tended by the good child. Cordelia and Edgar forgive their fathers, love them, care for them. The subplot just sort of repeats the main plot. (I'm fast-forwarding here.)

But there are differences: Lear initiates his own tragedy, whereas Gloucester gets tricked by Edmund into believing Edgar is plotting against him. When we first meet him, he's muttering ominously about disorder: *friendship falls off, brothers divide . . . and the bond cracked 'twixt son and father. . . . We have seen the best of our times.* How does he account for this? *These late eclipses in the sun and moon.* Did people believe in astrology back then? Do the other characters believe in it? Edmund makes fun of it; Edgar seems dubious. You've seen act I— do you think it's the stars that make this havoc? Gloucester is a passive kind of guy; he blames the stars. His reading tells us more about himself than the events he's reading.

Let's follow Gloucester through the play. When Lear and his daughters fall out, he tries to patch things up, to temporize; but when Lear is cast out into the storm, he follows; for which he too is cast out and blinded. And—a further parallel with Lear's story—he "prays." "Find the lines. What's the context?" He's asked Edgar, who he still doesn't know is Edgar, to lead him to Dover so he can hurl himself off a cliff. "Edgar fools him into believing he stands upon a high cliff, so when he survives his fall—this is not easy to stage, the actor has to really fall—well, you tell me, why this outrageous trick?" "So he'll believe he's been saved," says Lydia. "Right, and before he leaps, he addresses the *heavens*":

> *Let the superfluous and lust-dieted man,*
> *. . . that will not see*
> *Because he doth not feel, feel your power quickly.*

"Who's he talking about?" Silence. Gads, this is as hard to get them talking about as it is to stage. "*Lust-dieted*, as in self-indulgent? Have we met anyone in the play like that?" "Himself?" Samantha. "I think so . . . *that will not see / Because he does not feel, feel your power*. Look at the way he repeats that verb *feel*. Look back at Lear's 'prayer,' find the word *feel*—Lear also says it twice. It's as though a new sensation has been born in these old men; affliction has awakened feeling. Gloucester sees better when he loses his eyes; Lear understands better when he loses his mind. And Gloucester, like Lear, prays for distributive justice: *So distribution should undo excess / And each man have enough*."

"Which would you rather be, mad or blind?" "Mad," says Ashley; "because I wouldn't know what was going on." Heads shake. "No, if you lost your mind, you'd be really lost," says Sandra, "lost to yourself." "Right, madness is the more radical affliction; Lear's was the more radical error. Besides, is he blissfully oblivious of what's going on? *Let me have surgeons, / I am cut to the brains*. Doesn't sound blissfully out of it to me."

"When they meet again, late in the play—open to act 4, scene 6—Lear is mad and Gloucester is blind, still being led by Edgar in disguise. Tell me what Lear looks like." "He's got on a sort of wreath of . . . flowers," says Samantha. "You saw the Olivier film?" She nods. "Right, that's how he's usually shown. But find Cordelia's description . . . anyone?" Barbara reads: hemlock, nettles, weeds that sting. "Thorns?" exclaims Lydia. "Right. He's given up an earthly crown for a crown of thorns. He's not in his right mind, but his ramblings sort of put back together the world he's torn apart. *Plate sin with gold, / And the strong lance of justice hurtless breaks . . . a dog's obeyed in office.* Who might that dog be? Himself, father to those *dog-hearted daughters.* Recognizing his own complicity in sin and error, he issues a . . . kind of pardon—*none does offend*—and a plea for patience":

> *Thou must be patient; we came crying hither:*
> *Thou know'st, the first time that we smell the air,*
> *We wawl and cry . . .*

"Think how revolutionary, a king owning up to his part in injustice, issuing a universal pardon, even if he is a bit bonkers. Lear, who *hath ever but slenderly known himself,* knows himself to be, when he wakes and sees Cordelia, *a very foolish fond old man . . . not in my perfect mind.* Where he was proud, he is humbled; where he was rash and wrathful, he pleads for pardon, for patience in a world defined as pain: *When we are born, we cry that we are come / To this great stage of fools.*"

"Did the king see this play? I mean, the real king?" asks Allison. Good for her, she remembers. I'd told them, the first week, how Shakespeare's players became "the King's Men" when James became king, 1603, and many of his plays had their first appearance at court. "Why do you ask?" "I mean, if this play was performed at court . . ." "It was." "It's not very flattering." "Not at all. A mighty king who's presumed too much on his power, who realizes he's taken too little care of his subjects. James had strong ideas about the divine right and absolute power of the monarch. *Lear* seems to have had only one court performance. Other plays were performed again and again, but *Lear* seems not to have been asked back."

"So you think the play might have rubbed the king the wrong way?"

"I think Shakespeare was sailing close to the wind."

A Poor Bare, Forked Animal

"Depressing," sighs Ashley. I'm caught off guard, though why, I don't know—so many people have found this play depressing that it wasn't performed on the stage with Shakespeare's ending for 200 years; the preferred ending had Cordelia married to Edgar and Lear restored to the throne. Still, I am speechless, and a good thing, too, since my silence leaves a space for others to fill.

"Well, yeah, it's a tragedy, of course it's depressing," says Allison.

"Yeah, but it's depressing to read so many plays that are so . . . depressing."

"I don't think it's depressing," says Barbara.

"Why not?"

"Because it means . . . a lot. I don't know, it's just so . . ." "Grand," I want to say, but hold my tongue, knowing better than to finish students' sentences.

"I think it's . . . beautiful," a voice shy and tentative, Lydia.

"How so?"

"I don't know. It's very spiritual."

"Yes. Lose the world to find the world. Christian, even. Lear with his crown of thorns, dispensing Christ-like pardon." She nods vigorously, turning red. (Later we'll come back to this question, widely disputed—was Shakespeare a Christian? Do Christian values make one Christian?) "Anybody here read *Waiting for Godot*?" No hands go up. "'They give birth astride of a grave,'" I quote; "'the light gleams an instant, then it's night again.' *That*'s depressing, nothing redemptive about it, man really is . . . a worm."

"Can we come back to whether the play's depressing after we've got more pieces in place? We haven't talked about Edmund. Or Edgar." (Uh-oh, more to come. That's how it is with *Lear*, always more to come.)

"Start with Edmund, the bastard son. Look at his opening soliloquy, *Thou, nature, art my goddess, to thy law / My services are bound*. Edmund makes a big deal of being a bastard, outside the social and moral order, owing nothing to anyone. *Fine word, legitimate*. Why should Edgar inherit his father's fortune just because he's legitimate? Honor, love, loyalty, all just words. Edmund vows he'll *have land by wit*."

"What does he mean by *nature*?" Survival of the fittest, law of the jungle, dog eat dog, come the responses. "Any dogs in the play?" "Seventeen," says Danny, "plus a *mongrel bitch*." "Three *mongrels*." "Name all the animals you can find." The class starts slowly—*cat, fox, worm, horse, cow*—then they get into it, as in a game of "Where's Waldo"—*hog, sheep, mice*. The woods are teeming: *bear, serpent, adder, deer, sloth, toad, lion, wolf, tigers*; the air is swarming—*vulture, kite, pelican, hedge-sparrow, cuckoo, flies*—the palaces, too: *men are become like monsters of the deep, preying on one another, dragon, gorgon, centaur*. "What's a centaur? A creature with the body of an animal and the head of a human, a beast, only worse, because it has a human brain to carry out its baseness. *But to the girdle do the gods inherit, beneath is all the fiend's*."

"What is the point of so many animals?" "A Big Theme," says Brent, making quotation marks with his fingers. "Say more." He doesn't, but Samantha does: "To say, that's what we are, animals?" "Remember what Lear said, when he saw mad Tom: *unaccommodated man is no more but such a poor bare, forked animal as thou art; thou art the thing itself*. Stripped of our fine robes and fancy gowns, we're *no more than this*. Well, are we? No better than *a poor bare, forked animal*?"

"In the play, you mean?"

"Yes, stick to the play for now."

Responses dribble in. "Some are, some aren't." "Animals aren't bad as Regan." Discussion wanders off onto the cruelty of humans, the kindness of animals. "A centaur, then, a creature with the body of a beast and the brain of a human—is this what we are, this monstrous hybrid?" Scowls, headshakes. "Why not? What's . . . left out? Do humans have something a centaur lacks?" "Soul?" the word drifts in from my left, nearly inaudible. "Speak up, Lydia." "*Soul*," she says, louder. "Good. *A soul in bliss*, Lear calls Cordelia. Does the word re-cur?" Mit.edu turns up only a few occurrences, but there is a word closely related that does recur, a word often paired with *soul*. I start to hum but nobody catches the tune, "Heart and Soul." I'm about to say the word, when I hear it. "Heart," from Trevor, who I'm begin-ning to suspect has one himself, there's a quirky sensitivity there that belies his buttoned-down looks. "Good—how many times?" "Wow, like 59." *Let them anatomize Regan, see what breeds about her heart; Is there any cause in nature that makes these hard hearts?* And Cordelia's name is related to heart, *cordis*, "of the heart." Heart, soul, spirit, what-ever you call it, some have it, some don't. *The difference of man and man.*

"There is another sort of *nature* in the play—can you find the other way the word is used?" No takers. "Look at what Edmund says about Edgar, *whose nature is so far from doing harms / That he suspects none.* What kind of nature is this?" "*Humane*," says Cynthia, "like we're supposed to be." "That's right. Humane nature. You know, in the Folio, the word *human* was spelled *humane*. The words had not di-verged. Edmund sees this as a weakness he can exploit."

"So, what are we? Back to Hamlet's question, *what a piece of work is man*? The word *nature* occurs—how many times?" Twenty. "A Big Theme," I say, heading Brent off. "Which is our *nature*, to be like Ed-mund or Edgar?" My students know by now, the answer to a question like this is both-and. "Are there more good guys or bad guys in the play?" We count; the characters are equally divided between those who sacrifice others for their own good and those who sacrifice themselves for the good of others.

"But wait," says Lizzie, "we left out Lear and Gloucester." "Right, the ones *too old to learn*. They learn the most. Lear starts out as a rash and vain old fool, but when his mettle is tested, it's gold, and Gloucester seems to have no character at first, but when faced with a choice between saving his skin or loyalty to the king, he shines. Pushed to the wall, they're true."

"So that makes more good than evil," summarizes Barbara.

"More kind that cruel, I'd say. Look at that word *kind*—how many times does it occur?" Thirteen. "What does it mean?" Good-hearted. Generous. Benevolent. Sympathetic. "Natural," I add. "Natural?" "Yes, through the fifteenth century, *kynde* meant nature or natural, native, innate, inherent. Chaucer uses it this way. It's a cognate of *kin, kinship*—remember Hamlet's pun, *a little more than kin and less than kind*? The word had associations of natural affection arising from kinship. By 1606, the year of *Lear*, the word had come to mean *kind-hearted*, having a benevolent nature, naturally well-disposed to fellowship or fellow feeling, caring, compassionate, gentle, as it means today. Built into our language is the suggestion that *kindness* is inherent to our *kind, mankind*, the family of man."

"Some family," snorts Cynthia.

"Yes, but we really *are* genetically kin, far more similar than we're different. We also share more DNA with other species than we'd imagined. We're more deeply embedded in a web of life, a network of natural systems than we in the West, with our lust for mastery, dominion, domination, have appreciated. So, what *are* we? Can we say which is our nature, to be kind or cruel? What are we, really?"

"You mean . . . *really*?" says Allison. "Not just in the play?"

"Really really."

Responses come slowly, from several quarters. "It depends." "Like in the play, some are animals, or worse." "Like in the Holocaust," says Allison, "some slaughtered Jews, some risked their lives to save them." "But I think people are basically out for themselves," says Ashley; "I wouldn't throw my friend under the bus, but my main responsibility is to myself." "You bet," says Brent. "Nobody else is going to have your back."

"*But*," says Trevor, emphatically, "if we looked out for each other, somebody *would* have our back."

"Might there be an evolutionary point to kindness? Might there be a reason it's built into our nature?" "Sure," says Allison, "we had to look out for each other to survive. We had to cooperate." "Right. Those who learned to work in groups, caring for the young, acquiring food, cooperating against predators and other groups, had the best chance of survival. Some say that's why the Neanderthals didn't survive—they didn't learn this. Humans are vulnerable for a long time, longer than other species. We think 'survival of the fittest' means the most ruthless. But what if the 'fittest' were the kindest, the caring? Evolutionarily, kindness and cooperation are as crucial to our survival as competition. A pretechnological society would have had more sense of this than we do."

Homo economicus, I write on the board. Brent is ready with the definition. "It means we're basically motivated by money and self-interest is rational."

"Right. 'Rational.' So it's 'rational' to maximize self-interest?"

"Of course it is," says Brent.

"Is it sustainable?" I ask. I get puzzled looks. "Is a war of all against all . . . sustainable? What about in the play? What happens to the bad guys?" We work this out: The sisters do themselves in. Cornwall is so outrageously cruel, blinding Gloucester, that a servant rises up and stabs him. Evil starts out strong, but undoes itself. *"Humanity must perforce prey on itself, / Like monsters of the deep*—who says this?" Danny, ever ready with the Mit.edu online text, finds the lines: "Albany." "Yes, another character who learns. Even Edmund— remember what he says when Edgar, who has just dealt him a fatal blow, reveals his identity . . . *the wheel is come full circle.* What *wheel* is he talking about?" "Like, what goes around comes around?" Samantha.

"So, what are we?" (And why—you may ask—am I spending this kind of time on this question? Because it matters, the stories we tell about ourselves, because we live up or down to our stories, and the stories we're telling ourselves now do not serve us well. If we believe humans are driven solely by greed and a lust for power, we build institutions, codes, systems around that ideology; we normalize it. We deprive kindness, generosity, compassion, idealism, of cultural authority; they come to seem "naive." It's important to see what our assumptions are, so we can decide if we want to keep them.) "I realize," I go on, "Edmund's cynicism is the way we see ourselves today, out for ourselves and proud of it. I mean, when was the last time you heard the expression, *the family of man?*"

"About two minutes ago," says Brent. "But bad guys get away with it all the time."

"They do now. They didn't when I was growing up." The looks I'm getting tell me I've said something absurd. "Oh, of course they did— I'm talking about fiction, film, the way we represent ourselves. Bad guys in movies and stories used to get punished in the end. You've heard of 'poetic justice?'" A few nods. Ashley explains, "It's where people get their just deserts." "Right. Some say the origin and purpose of stories was to bind social groups together, make social cohesion, to imbue people with norms and values so they'd pull together. What would be the point in showing evil getting away with it? Life imitates art."

"Yeah, but that kind of fiction really is a lie. We know more today."
Brent has made himself the voice for "Get Real, Professor."

"We see things *differently* today," I correct. "Now we tell stories
where bad guys get away with it. Name some films." We start a list.
(Again, I'm the one who names most of these.) *No Country for Old
Men. Match Point. Crimes and Misdemeanors. Silence of the Lambs. Primal Fear. Arbitrage.* "And not only do they get away with it, we're root-
ing for them. *House of Cards, Sopranos, The Amazing Mr. Ripley, Gone
Girl, Breaking Bad.* "When did films like this start being made? Somewhere along the line, they changed the rules. Anybody here read Ayn
Rand?"

"*The Fountainhead*—couldn't put it down," says Brent.

"What's her Big Idea?" Not trusting Brent, I fill in: "Rand's heroes
are 'self-made men' who owe nothing to anyone. Self-interest is the
highest moral good. It's a philosophy, if you can call it that, of social
irresponsibility. Her heroes are out for themselves, beholden to no one.
Rather like the villains in Shakespeare's plays. Whereas the characters we like and admire in Shakespeare are defined by their relationships to others, love, loyalty, kindness. *Fellowship.* That word *fellow*—
how many times does it occur in this play? Thirty-three. *Fellowship*
is a cardinal virtue in Shakespeare's plays. What has happened, historically, to make this change? How have Shakespeare's villains become our heroes?"

"You mean, like, capitalism?" says Allison.

"Yeah, actually," I say, a little chagrined to have my punch line so
quickly stolen.

Present at the Creation

"As a matter of fact, it seems to have been born around this time. Karl
Marx places the birth of capitalism in the late sixteenth and early sev-

enteenth centuries. Not the full-blown Industrial Revolution of the nineteenth century, but the beginnings of a moneyed economy. Commerce and trade supplanted barter and allowed for the accumulation of capital; merchants and landlords got rich. *Merchant capitalism.*" I write it on the board.

I feel some shifting in seats, uh-oh, history lesson coming up, but I go on. "In earlier agrarian arrangements, like feudalism, farming was collective; peasants could cultivate land, graze livestock, draw wood, water, peat, in common. They didn't own the land, but they could live on it, work it, make a living from it. But the growth of the wool trade made land more valuable if it was used for grazing sheep. Peasants were turned off the land, many took to the road as beggars. 'Mad Tom' was a familiar figure. 'Time of transition,' we've said this was, but that doesn't begin to describe the upheaval, the armies of beggars, outbreaks of civil strife. But change brought opportunity as well: the accumulation of capital broke down social hierarchies. Medieval society had been static; you were born into a social rank and had no thought to rise above it. But now a craftsman could become a merchant, a merchant could buy a title—why, even an "upstart" playwright could buy a coat of arms and purchase the most lavish houses in town. Shakespeare had *lands by wit.*"

"You don't have to be a Marxist to see how this reshapes older notions of value, merit, honor. *King Lear* is about the breakup of the hierarchal, feudal order. What Marx calls 'the cold cash nexus' takes the place of nonmercantile bonds, kinship, fealty, cooperation, that knit medieval communities together.[5] Not that the old order was so wonderful—the play exposes its abuses of power. But it also shows the ruthlessness that gets unleashed when everything's up for grabs."

I stop, realizing the class has gone silent. For how long they've been quiet, I'm not sure, since I've been rattling away. Tanya draws out a long black strand of hair, her eyes nearly crossed, inspecting for split ends. Brittany glances surreptitiously at her lap, Samantha's gaze drifts out the window, somebody's laptop clicks away, typing . . . what?

Ashley breaks the silence. "This play has nothing to do with me," she says, with a toss of her golden mane.

"Are you sure? Actually, this play is like being present at the creation, having a ringside seat to when our world was born."

"I just don't relate to anyone in it."

"I get that *King Lear* is not a warm fuzzy. I do get that. And when you've grown up in Edmund land, every man for himself, it's a stretch to feel we're all in this together. But to see that our ideas of ourselves and human nature are not set in stone, that they were different once and may be so again—might that not be . . . hopeful? Gives us cultural perspective . . ."

A few tentative nods. Is what I'm saying so obvious, or is it so unfamiliar that they need time to take it in? Or is it just . . . boring? How can they not find this fascinating?

"How did J. K. Rowling come to write *Harry Potter*?" This snaps them to. "Huh, you mean, where did she get her ideas?" "Well, that's interesting too—she majored in classics. But I mean, how did she live, what did she live on? She was living on the dole, what they call 'state benefits,' what this country would call 'handouts.' An enlightened social policy kept her from slipping through the cracks, which is why we have those novels. Just think, if state funding hadn't provided that safety net, she might have landed on the streets, no Harry Potter. How many books never got written because those who might have written them landed on the streets?"

Silence. Back off, Gayle. I forge on. "Human nature is made of malleable stuff. We saw in *Taming of the Shrew* how different circumstances bring out different sides of us. We know that families and environments can brutalize kids or bring out their better selves; we see on a daily basis what a difference a family, a neighborhood, a school can make. Might there be ways of organizing society, of educating ourselves . . . might we make institutions and incentives that call forth our . . . better natures? Because it looks to me like if you tried to organize a society to bring out the worst in human nature, if you set out deliberately to devise ways of stifling our capacities for caring and cooperation, you could not design a better system than we have."

A few heads nod energetically, Lizzie's, Barbara's. Lydia's eyes look moist. A few keep gazes firmly fixed on the page. Trevor is attentive, Cynthia is squinting, Brent looks quizzical, open or closed quizzical, I cannot tell. Lizzie later told me this conversation continued over dinner and into the night.

A Learning Play

"What do the characters learn?" Such an old-fashioned question, so very not cutting edge. I ask it of the characters in this play, of characters in all the plays, because always Shakespeare is interested in change.

"Turn to the last scene, look at Lear's lines over the body of Cordelia—*why should a dog, a horse a rat have life /And thou no breath at all?* How do these lines provide a gloss on Lear's question—not exactly an answer, but a response to his vision of man as *a poor bare, forked animal?* How does Lear's cry provide a refutation of his cynicism? *Is human life cheap as beast's?*" "You mean," ventures Sandra, "the grief he feels?" (She gets it, having felt it; the others, not yet.) "Right. The value of a human life, the whole huge, immeasurable difference between Cordelia and a rat, a dog—it's so obvious, when you lose someone you love— here at the end of *Lear* is this unqualified affirmation of human value beyond those beasts and birds cawing and clawing their way through the play, *tigers, not daughters*, preying on one another."

"Depressing? I don't know. I find *Death of a Salesman* or *Glengarry Glen Ross* depressing. I find the snatch and grab for power and status depressing. *King Lear* of all Shakespeare's plays pushes us to think qualitatively about human need and value. What humans *need* is one another, the love and loyalty Lear so carelessly tosses away, relationship, fellow feeling—these are necessities of life. Things don't end well for him and Cordelia. Just as he's reunited with her and realizes the inestimable value of what he's tossed away, the tragedy starts up again. Depressing? No. Wrenching, yes. Excruciating. But to be human is to feel pain—*the first time we smell the air we wawl and cry.* The carnage at the end doesn't leave us—well, me, anyway—with a sense of worthlessness, but the preciousness of what's been lost. What comes through this play is a glimpse of human value more hopeful than we . . . have today."

It's hard to get these kids to see this geezer play as a learning play, a growing-up play. But Lear keeps banging his head against the ultimate questions, interrogating, indicting, calling on the gods, though the heavens remain silent, and what insight he gains is too little and too late. Too late for him, that is, maybe not for us.

We have Edgar to help us. We haven't talked about Edgar. So many of his lines are gibberish, readers skim, directors cut, we sort of forget he's there. Yet only Lear has more lines than he has. You don't realize how important he is till you see a great actor in the role, which you almost never do. I had the luck to see Ian McKellen play him when I was a student in New York, and I saw what a key character he is, how much on stage he is, present, attentive, full of hope, urging Gloucester, *thy life's a miracle*, urging Lear, *look up*. (I read that line again, *thy life's a miracle*. Lydia hears it. Barbara, too. I'm not sure about anyone else. I'd have been deaf to it at their age, too. But I can plant a seed.) McKellen made me see how Edgar evolves from a simple dupe to a powerful agent who's present throughout and who understands what he has seen. He is a reliable narrator, unlike Horatio, who caricatures *Hamlet* as a crude story of revenge, and unlike Malcolm, in the next play we'll read, who sees only a *dead butcher and his fiendlike queen*.

Edgar pronounces an epitaph that's true to the play, my sense of it, anyway: *The oldest hath borne most: we that are young / Shall never see so much, nor live so long*. And his final adjuration, *speak what we feel, not what we ought to say*, is a message for all time.[6] This, students hear, or some do; it comes back on their papers. Sounds so simple, yet think how difficult. First you have to know what you feel. Then you have to find the words to say it. *Speak what we feel*, not what the rulebook tells us to say.

"You'll be relieved to know," I say, "next week we'll be turning from one of Shakespeare's longest plays to one of his shortest."

"The Scottish play," intones Ashley ominously.

"Right. Where we'll see how unsustainable evil really is." But that is too long a story to go into here.[7]

NINE

Ask a Graduate

I will not say that our lives have been easy, that we do not feel stress in our present, or uncertainty about our futures. But I will say that many of us feel up to the challenge. That we are seeking lives that fulfill more than aspirations of social status or income. The value of a liberal arts education is that it taught us to trust and to value ourselves.

—EMILY KUGLER, '02

Because out of all this work of self-building might emerge an individual capable of humility in the face of complexity; an individual formed through questioning and therefore unlikely to cede that right; an individual resistant to coercion, to manipulation and demagoguery in all their forms.

—MARK SLOUKA, "Dehumanized"

So I did get through the last class. *My* last class. I'd been dreading that class, wondering how I could read those lines of Prospero, *Our revels now are ended.* I did not get through them, I choked up—*These our actors . . . were all spirits and are melted into air, thin air*—and had to stop. But it wasn't horrible, a catch in the voice, a few tears, a short silence, not so bad; it even lent a kind of drama. *We that are young / Shall never live so long, nor see so much.* I got that on a course evaluation. Amazingly, from Brittany, who I'd thought was nowhere in the room.

My decision was sudden. My friends thought I'd be one of those who'd teach till I dropped, and so did I. But I woke up one morning, knowing it was time. Time to stop doing it and start writing about it. It announced itself with a kind of urgency.

It was not easy, signing away tenure. First, I lost the form and had to go back to the dean's office for another. Then the form got mixed in with a batch of papers I handed back to class, so it drifted under students' eyes before I'd told anyone of my decision. My dread focused on the moments after the last class, how I'd feel after the students filed out, leaving me alone in Humanities 120. How desolate a classroom, emptied of students, that palpable void of a room recently inhabited, still a trace of human presence, all that humanity, all that baggage, backpacks, books, egos, clamoring, compelling, suddenly not there. Bare stage, no actors, no audience, *not one spirit to command.*

I could see myself doing what I'd done so many times, walking around the table, picking up remnants of the day, an empty cup, a half-eaten bagel. I'd glance at the board—Plato *Republic* → Montaigne "Cannibals" → *Tempest* → Huxley *Brave New World*—and decide to leave it for the amusement of whoever comes in next. I'd pack up, glance back, switch off the light, and leave this room forever.

But that's not how it happened.

The way it happened, the last day, was Danny, Lizzie, Cynthia, Barbara, Samantha, Trevor, and Brent (yes, Brent) hung around, talking about summer plans, films, saying we'll see each other again. "Call if you ever come to Seattle," "Are you on Facebook?" I kept expecting them to leave, but they stayed, that good comfortable feeling when people just want to hang out. Several said they'd be at my party the next day (Scripps gave a party), asked me what I'd be doing, thanked me for the course. Then Lizzie, who has worked up to nerve to tell her parents she's majoring in English, followed me back to my office, asking me what classes she should take, telling me her parents are in town, would I like to meet them; and they came up to my office and we chatted, about them, about me, about Lizzie, about things she can do with an English major . . . and it was jolly, not awful.

Something's Happened

I can usually tell when something's happened in a class. I can tell, reading their last papers, that they're seeing connections, meaning what they say, not just parroting back what they think I've said. The prose is less clunky, thoughts have a better chance of getting expressed. Not always, of course; there are still papers I'd like to toss on the P pile, perfunctory, pointless, purposeless. But as a class becomes more engaged, there are fewer of these.

The good classes end on a high. Some say "thank you" as they file out, and I can tell from their eyes, they mean it. Some say they'll miss our class, it was their favorite, and even when accolades don't pour in, there's a general sense that we have come through something to-gether, scaled a mountain, had a brush with greatness, that they're leaving with more than they came in with. Not all, of course—some scoot out with no eye contact and no words.

I can't always tell what the course has meant to them, and they may not either, may not know for years. Student evaluations tell next to nothing. How can a student know, in the 10 minutes at the end of the last class, when she's anxious about the final, perhaps resentful that I'm giving one, since her roommate's prof is not—how can she possibly know what a course will come to mean? I had a student write, years later, apologizing for the way she'd evaluated the course, saying she now understood why I made them watch all those *Hamlet* films, what I was trying to get across.

This semester, these are some things I notice.

Brent, from being the self-designated wise guy, prickly when discussion veered toward anything political, has basked in our appreciation of his one-liners. "This class gave me a lot to think about," he says; "I didn't always agree with you, but it's been an eye-opener." "A lot to think about" is no bad thing to take to the world of corporate law, where he's headed. Samantha says she won't be transferring, she'll stay at Scripps and major in English, which she feels her writing is up to, thanks to this class. Barbara has cast off some of her shyness, emboldened by the sound of her own voice. "Thank you for Shakespeare," she says. (I have given her Shakespeare? An outcome I'm proud to own.) Danny, who has landed a job in Silicon Valley, pats his book on his way out, "This comes with me. No resale for Shakespeare."

"At first I wanted there to be more definitive answers to the things we talked about, now I see how complicated these questions are," says Trevor, whose hair is definitely longer. And yes, he and Cynthia are a couple. "I didn't always love the plays," she says, "but I loved the discussions"; I could see, she appreciated being taken seriously, she's less prickly now. She and Trevor plan to design a video game. "Yeah, I always loved art, I guess I'll get geeky and check out digital art. I'll definitely take more literature—we got good ideas from these plays." She's the kind of student the self-designed interdisciplinary major was made for.

Lydia has come out of her shell, at first correcting my biblical misquotations, then risking that comment about Desdemona as a battered woman that blew us all away, then actually speaking up. She came into office hours a few weeks ago, told me how terrified she'd been when she got here, the first in her family to go to college; everyone in her classes seemed to know so much more than she. She feels more confident now, only the last time she went home, the Central Valley didn't feel like home. She hopes to be a teacher in the kind of public school she went to, plans to major in English—"that's where you see, like you said, everyone has a story." But she's "not sure where home is."

Brittany, who I thought unreachable, at least by me, astounded me by her evaluation, *we that are young shall never see so much . . .* Tanya of the long, black hair said not a word, nor missed one either, judging by her final paper; she caught my eye as she scooted out, flashed me a grin, saying nothing, as mysterious at the end as at the beginning. Where she goes from here, where any of them goes, what they seek or what they find, is beyond my power to predict.

Be free and fare thee well. Plato said teaching was a kind of midwifery, a bringing forth.[1] Yes, a birthing of new life, a much more appealing and accurate metaphor than Obama's "bang for the buck."

And if a class works, the curiosity, the interest, keep on perking, the yeast keeps on rising. Some write years later about plays they've gone to see, that they've taken their kids to see. One writes that she went back to India to see her grandparents and could better understand their arranged marriage from our discussions of *Taming of the Shrew*. Another tells me our class gave her a perspective on her father that enabled her to forgive him. One posts a review on my Facebook page that relates *Measure for Measure* to MeToo. And a pre-med student who took a few literature courses from me wrote and said, "I can *read*! I always wondered how people got those things out of books—now I *see*!"

When I posted an obituary of Norman Rabkin, my Shakespeare professor, on Facebook (*New York Times*, June 2012), with a few words about how much he'd meant to me, this came back: "I'm sorry to hear this, Gayle. Through you, he taught so many more than he ever saw." That was from Kara Amundson, '87, who's been a teacher a long while now. I love it when they become teachers. And even when they don't go into teaching, they can be teachers, as mothers, partners, colleagues, whatever.

Ask a Graduate

Anna Petkovich, '14, now a literary agent in New York, said, "It's kind of hard to describe that Scripps thing that happens. I heard about it when I got here but I didn't really understand. I guess I'd say, I know who I am. It's not easy to put in words. It's a qualitative thing." She realized when she was abroad, "that whole confident courageous, hopeful thing is real. There I was in another country, feeling equipped to take it all on. I realized Scripps had done that for me. I knew nothing when I applied to this college, had no idea what a liberal arts college was, let alone a women's college. Now I see the point of it. I have friends graduating from Berkeley who've gone the pre-professional route. Now they're looking at jobs in Silicon Valley and not sure they want them."

Liz, '14, came to Scripps because she was captivated by the campus tour: "It was breathtakingly beautiful and all of the students who talked to us were kind and different . . . a punk chic, a hipster and a hippie and they were all friends. I liked that." When she spent a semester abroad at the University of Edinburgh, "those kinds of conversations we have in our classes didn't seem to naturally occur, didn't have the frankness and passion as discussions in Scripps classes. I've come into my own as a feminist, I feel more confident in myself as a woman. It's made me a better sister, friend, and person in general."

Nicole Carr, '84, speaks of Scripps as a catalyst for her transformation from "a shy, intelligent girl with uneven grades" who had "an impoverished childhood," to a "confident woman who would go on to lead a public service organization," director of human resources at the California Department of Social Services (*Scripps Magazine*, Winter 2019). There are those words again, *transformational, transformative, life-changing, eye-opening.* "This college really turned me around . . ."

"I don't know what I'd have been if I hadn't come to Claremont. Certainly nothing like what I am today."

"A school can transform a life," says David Brooks, who was changed by the University of Chicago precisely because it made him read things that made him uncomfortable: "I don't know about you, but I felt more formed by my college education twenty-five years out than I did on the day I graduated."[2] Joseph Epstein writes that his years at Chicago made him "a strikingly different person," "allowed me to consider other possibilities than the one destiny would appear to have set in grooves for me . . . less locked into the social categories—Jewish, middle-class, Midwestern—in which I had grown up."[3] Ken Burns says of Hampshire College, "It completely rearranged all my molecules . . . it was transformational. . . . I don't recognize the person who entered Hampshire in 1971, and the person who emerged in the spring of 1975." Burns, who can probably be credited with teaching more history to more people than many high school and college courses combined, is leading the fundraising to keep this scrappy little college from going under.[4] I could quote many more people to this effect—Diane Ravitch, Wellesley "changed my life"[5]—but you get the point.

Then there are the surprises.

A woman wearing a power suit stood in my office door, all angles and style, striking amidst us schlumpy academics on the third floor. "Hi, I'm Dana. You won't remember me." (I did not.) She told me she did marketing for some organization she assumed I'd heard of. (I had not.) "You know, I never forgot when you said about Claudius, 'that guy sure knew how to run a meeting.'" "Whoa, you remember *that?*" I laughed. It had been a throwaway line, a joke. I'd said it to illustrate Claudius's skill, in the scene where we first meet him, dispatching Fortinbras—*so much for him*—then Laertes—*and now, Laertes*—and finally, Hamlet, pawns in his game of thrones. Dana, in a career in corporate board rooms, remembered the moves.

Then there was Katie, back a decade after she'd graduated, telling me, "I'll never forget the time you said . . ." and quoted me saying something I could never imagine myself saying (and can't recall now). And I thought, okay, if that's what you heard, that's fine; it lodged, a grain of sand you made into a pearl.

And Elaine, stopping by my office several years after she'd graduated, tells me, "I learned so much in your classes," and I am preening for a compliment, and she says: "Yeah, I learned I was nothing like Sophie." "Oh." Instant deflation. Sophie, hand always waving, always showing she was the smartest in the class, she tired us all out, that Sophie—Elaine realized she had no desire to be like that, which nudged her to think about what she *did* want to be; she became a teacher of special needs children. But then I thought, okay, these sorting-out moments are important, moments you realize, no, I am not like that, or, yes, I am like that, or, I would like to be like that, steps toward figuring out who you are. "Studying literature, you learn about yourself. It all comes down to what kind of a life you see yourself leading, you know, what do you want for yourself," said Julia, '14: "On account of those novels we read, I know how to go about my life."

Once when Andrew Delbanco was holding forth on the virtues of Columbia's core curriculum of classics and the arts, an elderly alum spoke up: "You've missed the main point. Columbia taught me how to enjoy life."[6] "You want the inside of your head to be an interesting place to spend the rest of your life," said Judith Shapiro, former president of Barnard College;[7] and who has not felt the truth of this during months of lockdown, when our inner resources have been sorely taxed? Alums have told me how the literature we read "got me through my mother's death," ". . . my son's death," "cancer, when it returned": "I remembered those lines from *Julius Caesar, cowards die many times before their deaths, / The valiant never taste of death but once.*" So did

Nelson Mandela cherish those lines when he was in prison. *The Complete Works of Shakespeare* was smuggled into Robben Island as a Bible, and the well-thumbed volume brought courage to the anti-apartheid activists, as "Shakespeare behind Bars" programs provide inspiration to many incarcerated today.

In the old days, they'd write letters, which I prized but never answered and lost most of in my many moves. These days, e-mail and Facebook make it easier to stay in touch. You never know what turns up. Summer of 2018, Claire Hermann, '02, posted a photo on Facebook of a restroom wall papered with cards from a defunct card catalogue, Linda's Bar and Grill, Chapel Hill; and there, above the light switch, was my name on a card for a volume of feminist criticism of Shakespeare. You really never know. The writing on the restroom wall.

When you talk to alums, when you read what they post on Facebook, Yelp, College Confidential, Cappex.com/colleges, when you compare their enthusiasm to the withering contempt of "disrupters" and detractors who claim higher education is broken, who do you trust? Do you listen to the graduates who describe how much their education has meant to them or the snake oil salesmen who have just the thing to "fix" it?

"Personalized" Learning

Nothing else matters so much to a graduate's sense of well-being in life, says Adam Falk, former president of Williams College, "not the details of the curriculum, not the choice of major, not the student's GPA," nothing correlates so closely with the gains students report "nearly as well as how much time a student spent with professors." "What we do is expensive—and worth it," he concludes from his study of Williams students.[8] Daniel Chambliss found, on the basis of a 10-year study of students and alums of Hamilton College, "Students who had a single dinner at a professor's house were significantly more likely to say they would choose the college again."[9] Human contact "has leverage, producing positive results far beyond the efforts you put into it," he and Christopher Takacs write in *How College Works*: "Specific human beings matter."[10] The odds are nearly twice as high that a student will find college worth the cost if "my professors . . . cared about me as a person," summarizes a 2015 Gallup-Purdue Index Report. This report surveyed more than 30,000 alums from across the country to determine which factors had contributed to the quality of their lives, their engagement with work and sense of well-being, and found that interaction with professors or mentors was what mattered most to them, years later. The type of school, private, public, selective or not, was less important than having "supportive relationships with professors and mentors," "with those who could help them carve out a vision for their future." If "they had at least one professor who made them excited about learning and they had a mentor who encouraged them to pursue their goals and dreams, their odds of being engaged at work nearly doubled."[11]

When Richard Detweiler surveyed 1,000 graduates of various ages from different kinds of colleges, asking whether they were generally satisfied with their lives and viewed their professional and family lives as meaningful, he found that personal interaction with professors, meaningful discussions in and out of class, were what had the greatest impact. "Studying a variety of fields outside the major, and having classroom talks that go into issues of ethics and life"—these also mattered, as did classes that "encouraged [students] to examine the strengths and weaknesses of their views and those of others," and regularly talking about "issues for which there was no single correct answer." Happiness was 25 to 35% more likely for those who'd "had conversations with those who disagreed with them and had in-class discussions of different philosophical, literary and ethical perspectives."[12]

What an extraordinary finding, that peoples' satisfaction in their lives and work may be traced to these few college experiences: having a professor or a mentor who took an interest in them, had them to dinner or into their office to chat or go over their writing or offer them advice; having open-ended discussions in a class where they were exposed to different perspectives on questions with "no single correct answer"; doing an extended project that involved developing their own arguments and analyzing what others say. "Could it be that all this time, we have been asking the wrong questions," suggests Aaron Basko, enrollment manager at the University of Lynchburg; perhaps now, "after a decade of algorithms and spreadsheets," we should get back to "old-fashioned advising" and helping students "understand who they are and what they could become."[13] New athletic facilities or posh dorms may bump up a college in the rankings, but for long-term value, the conditions that promote learning and the quality of graduates' lives are what count most: small classes with well-resourced educators whose primary commitment is teaching.

In her study for the Council of Independent Colleges, Georgia Nugent summarizes a survey of 3,000 alums that found that "60 percent of liberal arts college graduates indicated they felt 'better prepared for life after college,'" as opposed to 34% of public university alumni. The survey also found that "87 percent of students at liberal arts colleges graduated within four years; at the flagship publics, only 51 percent did so."[14] In their scathing critique, *Higher Education?*, Andrew Hacker and Claudia Dreifus excoriate higher education for doing a terrible job educating—except at small liberal arts colleges.[15]

Cultures of Disengagement, Cultures of Engagement

Disengagement seems to be the default state of undergraduates most places. In *My Freshman Year: What a Professor Learned by Becoming a*

Student, an anthropology professor at Northern Arizona University disguised herself to experience life as a student and was struck by "how little intellectual life seemed to matter"; students do the minimum to get the degree.[16] However, "young people of college age have a capacity for intellectual curiosity, and will respond when their minds are aroused," says Hacker, which he sees "happening at many independent liberal arts colleges, where their professors' first commitment is to teaching undergraduates."[17] He and Dreifus tell of a group of students at a research university who complained to a department chair about the poor teaching they were getting and were told, "if you want that sort of thing you should have gone to a liberal arts school. That's not what we do here."[18] When students complained to Lawrence Summers, then president of Harvard, that a renowned teacher was let go, he replied, "If you wanted somewhere that focused on undergraduate teaching, you should go to a place like Amherst or Swarthmore."[19] Susan Blum, in her depressing account of teaching at Notre Dame, *I Love Learning, I Hate School*, remarks, "Some lucky students attend liberal arts colleges that are not factories churning out masses of credentialed widgets."[20] She says this in passing, as though it's too obvious for comment—but I thought, whoa, if everybody knows what works, teaching undergraduates, why doesn't everybody organize undergraduate teaching so it works that way?

"Built to engage"—that's how an educational expert described small liberal arts colleges.[21] Since we live in a society that has little respect for education, colleges must build a culture that makes it "cool" to be engaged. "I feel like in really small classes that we have, everyone's forced to be on top of their subject matter and it just helps in terms of, like, everyone participating and feeding off . . . what other people are saying, so that new ideas are being put into your head, not just what the teacher's saying," said a sophomore at Hamilton College.[22] "Do not think you can come to this college and cut classes," a

Scripps alum warned prospective applicants. "You absolutely could not hide," said another; "You should expect to participate." An alum posted this, February 2020, on Facebook: "I couldn't fade into the background; the administration, my professors, and my friends simply wouldn't let me. It was the most inspiring, nurturing, and challenging environment for me to grow."[23]

Jennifer Hardy, '82, wrote me that her Scripps professors pushed her to take herself seriously: "I pretty much felt invisible and misunderstood as I moved through grammar and high school. But when I came to Scripps, someone took note. Actually, more than one person. I was pushed, queried, and praised. And the more I produced, the more was expected of me. It was exhilarating to get feedback (and respect!) from professors who took an interest in what I had to say, who mirrored my intellect back to me and encouraged me to speak up and speak out." "In high school, I didn't care about school," said Julia, '14; "Then I came to Scripps, and—oh, I get it. The profs invest in you, they know you, they care, so you do too. . . . When Malala Yousatzai was shot by the Taliban for trying to get an education, I even stopped griping about studying for finals."

Crucial to a culture of engagement is a faculty that's engaged. In a Princeton Review survey of undergraduates at 357 big-name schools (cited by Hacker in 2005), students were asked to rate their professors according to the statement, "My professors bring material to life." The responses were generally dismal, but they were "highest in colleges that keep their enrollments small, don't have graduate programs, and are not necessarily nationally known."[24] In a survey of 3,000 alums of private and public schools summarized by Georgia Nugent, 79% of small liberal arts colleges alums said, yes, they had benefited from "high-quality, teaching-oriented faculty," compared with 40% from flagship public institutions. The report found that "83% of liberal arts alumni agreed that their professors 'challenged me academically and also personally helped me meet those challenges,' compared with 46% of public university graduates."[25] A 2015 survey of faculty workplace engagement by Gallup found that faculty at smaller, private under-graduate institutions are "the most engaged group," "the most emo-tionally and intellectually connected to what they do." The level of engagement varied with job security (no surprise) and was 39% at small liberal arts colleges as opposed to 32% at institutions with 5,000 to 10,000 students and 29% at institutions with an enrollment of 10,000 or greater.[26] That sounds appallingly low to me. I'd guess the level of faculty engagement at Scripps is more like 80–85%.

Faculty at these colleges are able to "bring material to life" because small classes let us connect with our students and see the results of our teaching, because we have a say in what we teach and some sem-blance of self-governance, and because tenure has survived better at small liberal arts colleges than elsewhere. Tenure is a great morale booster; it turns us into stakeholders, gives us a long-term investment in the institution.

Kids who are losing the ability to concentrate, converse, and inter-act, are not well served by huge classes where they can sleep or do on-line shopping in the back rows, or by a campus culture where parties and football are the main event. I have given guest lectures in amphi-theaters where students sat staring into space or focused on digital devices. I taught for one incredibly dispiriting quarter at a flagship university where, in a Shakespeare class of 50, maybe 15 were tuned in. I could have done something with those 15, and occasionally did, but the rest sat like zombies and pulled us all down. Not that all 50 were often in the room; attendance was much spottier than at Scripps. I was so glad to get back to Scripps, where classes are likelier to have a critical mass of students who are engaged.

Several large state universities have been making efforts to give un-dergraduates a small-college experience, by creating colleges within the university: University of Washington, UCLA, University of Michigan, University of Texas at Austin, University of Mississippi, Arizona State University, City University of New York, to name a few. These are highly successful, from what I've heard: "It was an island of engagement amidst an impersonal sea, an experience of intimacy," said a Michigan alum. They are also, as McWilliams and Seery suggest, "a tacit acknowledgment of the superiority of the small liberal arts college way of doing things."[27] We're told that teaching to human scale costs too much, but look: Notre Dame, where disengagement prevails, has about four times the endowment wealth per undergraduate as Scripps. (Its endowment is $13.3 billion to Scripps's $375 million; it has about 8,700 undergraduates to Scripps's 936.) So it's not a matter of wealth: it's the way wealth is allocated.

Okay, downsizing might not be the way most universities want to go, but there are things they could do: provide a small-college experience within the university, thin out the ranks of overpaid managerial administrators, junk the assessment office and the "consultants" barnacled to it, reduce spending on athletics, create conditions optimal to learning. Hire some unemployed liberal arts PhD's, give them job security and a living wage. Direct more of the university's resources to providing small discussion classes where students get personal attention and learn to read something longer than a tweet, learn to express and support their ideas, to realize they *have* ideas and can make their education their own.

I've said that community colleges show that this kind of education does not have to cost the earth. (Interestingly, in community colleges, humanities enrollments have been robust, even through the pandemic.)[28] In a *Washington Post* article, "Community College Saved My Life," Jen Balderama describes how, when she was 18 and at a loss, City College, San Francisco provided her "a safe, stable haven," as it has for others who are "trying to get back on track," who need "the counseling, career guidance and additional support services . . . the structure and inspiration an educational environment can provide."[29] (This is the community college described in *Free City!* that had to fight for its life against an accreditation board trying to shut it down.) Balderama, who went on to become an editor at the *Washington Post*, reminds us, as Matt Reed suggests, "not to cut down the future to the size of the present. Education . . . by definition . . . puts faith in what has not yet been seen."[30]

"A Connected Kind of Thing"

"As long as you can read and write, synthesize information, communicate—all those things we did in our courses—you'll find someone who wants to hire you," said Sarah, '98. *Communicate* and *connect* are words I hear again and again. "The thing that consistently keeps me grounded is my ability to communicate and connect with others. I can say unequivocally that was a gift nurtured . . . at Scripps," says Jennifer, '82. When I asked Loralyn Cropper, '84, about her most memorable moments at Scripps, she replied, "when I was asked to connect the readings to my life and perspective." Working as a fundraiser, "I turned out to be as good as anyone who majored in business or econ because I can communicate": "Doing a marketing report is like those papers we did—you collect the evidence to make an argument. You have to connect with your audience, get them to believe your story. When it comes to being able to pitch an idea, communicate to peers and supervisors, write a compelling letter or proposal, I'm the one."

And this from Emily Kugler, '02, an assistant professor at Howard University: "I always had options. My education taught me to look for connections, patterns, and outliers. . . . The ability to connect and formulate new ideas and put information together and synthesize data, to have conversations and take in different opinions—all this came from my Scripps classes and led me to my job." "I'm the designated grant writer," said an alum I met at a Reunion Weekend who'd majored in Humanities, gone on to get a PhD in chemistry and a job in biotech. "The problems that come up in research—you get contradictory findings, go back and listen to the data, try to figure out what's relevant, find a common thread, a working hypothesis—they're not so different from problems writing a paper on history or literature, balancing different inputs, coming up with a thesis statement."[31]

"While my education at Scripps prepared me to dissect, analyze, and reflect on the world around me, it also prepared me to do something else: *to care*," says Jessica Heaton, '01; "having learned this at Scripps, I know I must teach this to my own students" (*Scripps Magazine*, Fall 2008). "I truly appreciated my liberal arts education at Scripps when I went to Hastings for law school—impersonal, disgustingly competitive, and just plain cold," wrote an alum on Facebook: "Hastings brought out the worst in people, and if it weren't for my experience at Scripps, it would have brought out the worst in me. Scripps was competitive, but never in a way that forced you to become ugly to your classmates. I've never met to so many genuine people in my life, profs and students alike . . . so many smart, funny and lively women who really take pride in their community. I have come to believe all college life should be like ours."

"I don't know, I just sort of see the world in less competitive terms," said another alum; "it's a connected kind of thing." Liberal arts colleges are not just about "individual advancement," reports Victor Ferrall, but about "assuming the mantle of social responsibility, of making constructive contributions to the community and larger society of which one is a part."[32] Emily Allen, '00, an attorney who does legal aid and work on housing for the homeless, describes how Scripps awakened social awareness in her: "I can't remember being socially engaged before I came to Scripps, but when I was there, I got involved." "Students at Scripps want to change the world, make the world a better place," wrote a student in College Confidential. "Scripps really does give you this amazing feeling that it's possible to change the world," wrote Annie Lyn Freitas, '11 (*Scripps Magazine*, Fall 2018), who, after participating in a writing workshop at a state women's prison organized by Scripps philosophy professor Sue Castagnetto, has made it her life's work to create educational opportunities for women in prisons. Alison Omens, '06, says there were many moments at this college she could describe as "beautiful, engaging, inspiring, poetic, meaningful," but the legacy she really appreciates is "anger": Scripps was "where I got—dare I say it?—angry? . . . I currently work for America's labor movement because I believe that through economic empowerment and a voice at work comes power over one's life. . . . In my job, I tell people's stories because I believe we need to understand what's happening to people—what each other is going through" (*Scripps Magazine*, Fall 2012).

Graduates of liberal arts colleges tend to be more civically engaged, have a stronger sense of social responsibility, than graduates of other types of colleges.[33] They are 26 to 66% more likely to contribute to society and "30 to 100% more likely to show leadership," Detweiler found.[34] A high proportion pursue careers in social work, political and environmental advocacy, environmental law, immigration law, voting rights legislation, work for charitable organizations, nonprofits, homeless shelters, community organizing. It's a simple principle: when students are treated as human beings and see others treated as human, they get the message—go and do likewise. It doesn't guarantee that they will, but it increases the chances. Nathalie Cannon, '13, posted a picture of herself on Facebook holding a picture of a man sliding into home plate, with the caption: "I went to a better college than you did, because Scripps College actually taught me how to care and support my fellow human beings."

A senior, Sean McCoy, '16, looks back on his years at Pomona and describes what the college community meant to him. "We learn together, challenge one another's assumptions, and exercise ownership over our environment: we invite speakers, hold meetings, create clubs, set up conferences, revise our laws, protest, engage in community service and local outreach, and fight for what we believe in." He describes how the "ivory tower" can be preparation for life: "I now realize the value of spending four years with the same people . . . in a world largely apart from the rest of society. I cherish . . . the meetings and social functions, the blurring of work and study and play, the tension between students and administrators over divestment, or alcohol policy, or curriculum changes, or the unionization of our dining-hall employees—because we learn . . . how to debate, assess and understand opposing views, empathize with people, respect their ideas, and, ultimately, we strengthen our civic life." He concludes, "The civic experience of attending a small liberal arts college cannot be understated." To anyone who complains there's no room for conservatives in academia, note that this piece was published in the *Imaginative Conservative*.[35]

Ellen Browning Scripps founded Scripps in a spirit of social responsibility. She gave her generous endowment with no strings attached, didn't even want her name on the college. She gave away billions in today's dollars, quietly, surreptitiously, to schools, hospitals, parks. More than one alum I've talked to mentioned her, often in relation to the beauty of the campus, which was a part of her plan. "I came here for the landscape," an alum told me. Asked about what Scripps gave her as a writer, Tanya Quaife, '94, replied, "Oddly enough, the first thing that comes to mind is neither the thesis experience nor the heavy emphasis on writing . . . [but] the campus itself, and how it gave me such an appreciation for beauty, form, balance, and place."

Education is an accretion of experiences, many of which take place outside the classroom in campus clubs and teams, late-night bull sessions in the dorm, work on a student newspaper or literary magazine or at the student-run coffee shop, volunteering at a women's shelter, a homeless shelter, a prison. Detweiler finds an "engaging learning community" to be as important, even more important, than the content of an education, in terms of producing positive life outcomes.[36] Yet "disrupters" would eliminate this educational ecosystem, do away with the campus, and "unbundle" degree programs into online learning and workplace-directed programs. This leaves something more like training than education. Education is a building of the connections and experiences that unbundling undoes.

Education May Save Us. Really.

When I sent out questions to alums, asking what was the most important thing they'd got from Scripps, several said they felt that their education had been the very antithesis and antidote to what they saw happening in the world and was more relevant today than ever. Rebecca Dutta, '15, said she'd been "horrified at the dogmatic views she'd encountered in people who don't have a liberal arts background. When I talk to people who have never taken a class in the humanities, I am stunned by how one-dimensionally they sometimes see the world. I am surprised at how quickly they jump to conclusions and how dangerous their seemingly innocuous assumptions can be."

Cultivating an intelligence that can deal with complexity, uncertainty, ambiguity may be one of the most valuable contributions a liberal arts education can make. Alice Laskin, '10, describes a major takeaway from Scripps as a "spirit of rejecting either/or's in favor of yes/and's—of learning broadly in order to be able to choose different aspects in favor of synthesizing anything and everything that works—this attitude has taken me far personally and professionally." I see how it's taken her far, since the capacity to leave questions open and weigh alternatives, to consider that both X and "not X" may have claims, is something we seek in anyone we trust, a doctor, a lawyer, a president, a friend. Premature closure shuts off possibilities, leads to disaster.

"This may sound nuts," wrote Lisa Shahriari, '98, "but I see the kind of education I got at Scripps as an antidote to bomb-throwing extremism. Recent events have made me think that one overlooked and significant value of a liberal arts education is countering extremism. An education that includes . . . critical analysis of texts makes it harder to fall under the sway of the rhetoric of extremism." Far from "nuts," Lisa's observation is corroborated by Arie Kruglanski's studies of terrorism, which found an association of extremism with the need for certainty and closure. Fundamentalist ideologies satisfy "cravings for coherence and closure" by presenting a world of "sharp dichotomies and clear choices, good versus evil, saints versus sinners, order versus chaos; a pure universe in black and white admitting no shades of gray."[37] Seeing the world in terms of "us-versus-them" encourages easy solidarity with "us" and relieves us of the effort it takes to keep questions open and consider complexities, to allow for the possibility of a middle ground. The demonization of the other has special appeal to confused youth bewildered by the insecurities of a world in flux, as politicians well know. "Either they win or we win," said presidential hopeful Marco Rubio.[38] It doesn't matter who "they" are, as long as there's a "they": McCarthy's Red Scare, Reagan's Evil Empire, G. W. Bush's Axis of Evil.

The past few decades have seen a flare-up of fundamentalism, tribalism, religious and ethnic violence throughout the world. As the future becomes less certain, people become willing to trade civil liberties for the promises of demagogues, and democracies are threatened. The study I referred to in chapter 3, "The Role of Education in Taming Authoritarian Attitudes," found that Americans "show moderate inclinations" toward authoritarianism, ranking 16th of 51 countries surveyed, on a par with Chile and Uruguay.[39] But the study also found that "authoritarian preferences and attitudes are weaker among people with higher levels of educational attainment" and weakest among those with a background the liberal arts. In all the countries surveyed, higher education correlated with resistance to authoritarianism, but it made the greatest difference in the United States—on account of our unique system of general education based in the liberal arts. The liberal arts can help us to a sense of social solidarity based not on tribal ties, not "us versus them," but us along with them, all in this together, living with differences. The liberal arts as counterterrorism, un-doer of dogma, of tribalism, a bringer-down of walls. Which is why it's a heartbreak to see "wokeness" making divisions and building new walls.

The liberal arts are about connections, and that includes connections among disciplines. They are inherently interdisciplinary, in that they include the arts (more than one), the humanities, and some of the sciences and social sciences. The Claremont Colleges offer (last I counted) 25 interdisciplinary majors. About half of Scripps students do double or dual majors. The Princeton Review attributes this to the interdisciplinary emphasis of the Scripps humanities program, the idea that "no academic field exists in a vacuum." "This is *huge*," said an alum, "when you're applying your education to the real world, trying to imagine where it might take you, knowing that ideas and areas are related." Alums often mention the interdisciplinary humanities program as formative in their education. A graduate wrote me from UC Davis medical school that "The Poetry and Science of Sleep," a humanities course she took from me, made her truly understand "there were connections between the humanities and science," which was "transformative" for her. Cindy Cruz, '86, urban ethnographer and associate professor in the education department at UC Santa Cruz: "My Scripps education allowed me to break away from disciplinarity—in my research, I have never felt bound by any 'rules' about method or epistemology. It has also given me ways to make connections with the narratives that youth offer me. . . . [It] gave me the freedom to refuse to be 'disciplined,' and that has made all the difference" (*Scripps Magazine*, Winter 2016).

"Graduates in all walks of life (from corporate leadership to crime prevention, from diplomacy to dentistry, from medicine to media) speak passionately of the value of having been introduced to art, anthropology, philosophy, history, world religions, literature, languages," summarizes Nugent in *The Liberal Arts in Action*. Thus a digital marketer can say that studying Marxist and post-Marxist theory "has ironically made me really good at digital marketing. That is not a joke."[40] And an oncologist can say that "his undergraduate study of philosophy was one of the most significant factors contributing to his success in cancer research."[41] The wider and deeper the pools of knowledge a person probes, the greater the likelihood of new discovery. Entrepreneur Damon Horowitz got a doctorate in philosophy because "becoming a humanist" gave him a perspective that enabled him to overcome the limitations of a purely technical approach and take on larger questions.[42] Steve Jobs describes a calligraphy course he audited: "It was beautiful, historical, artistically subtle in a way that science can't capture, and I found it fascinating. None of this had even a hope of practical application in my life. But . . . we designed it all into the Mac."[43] Nobel laureates in science are 22 times likelier than those who've not won Nobels to have artistic pursuits outside their field, according to David Epstein, in *Range*.[44]

The challenges our graduates face will not be solved by "one traditionally defined profession working alone," write James Engell and Anthony Dangerfield; they'll take "the combined insights of science, history, religion, business, medicine, and ethical traditions."[45] They'll require minds "large enough for paradox," in Maxine Hong Kingston's memorable phrase.[46]

"Student Learning Outcomes"

I realize it can sound facile, tossing the word *freedom* around in an economy as bad and worsening as this is. But these are the things I hear: "If you know how to bring ideas together in clear communication, you won't get trapped in the first situation that comes along. A lot of paths open to you, though you might not know at first what they are." Alums tell me of circuitous routes that led nowhere, and through nowhere, somewhere: "I did not like the classroom, but I loved one-on-one contact with students, so I became a high school counselor." They tell me of work that started as an internship, a part-time job, a gig designing websites, working with nonprofits, teaching English in Japan, teaching dance—that turned into a full-blown career. "I never thought I'd end up working in film, but I got an internship, then a job editing, now I'm part owner of a film company." Liberal arts graduates may be slower out of the gate than those with preprofessional degrees, their career paths not as smooth, but the savvy they develop in their courses may give them the freedom to try things out, to find the work that works for them. And since they're not likely to make salary their highest priority, "90% of humanities graduates are happy with their lives, about the same as graduates of other fields."[47] But there may also be payback in terms of salary. Detweiler, who's calculated how specific elements of a liberal arts education produce specific outcomes, found that, of the 1,000 graduates he interviewed, "those who studied more broadly, by taking more than half their courses outside their major, were 24% more likely to report higher income as adults."[48]

Occasionally I find myself gazing at a photo in the *New York Times* or *Ms. Magazine*, thinking, vaguely, that looks like someone I had in class; then I snap to and realize, that really *is* someone I had in class. They're out there in the world, doing good works. There's Gabby Giffords, Arizona's first Jewish female representative, the youngest woman to be elected to the Arizona State Senate, and the third woman from Arizona to be elected to the US Congress. She's been a tireless advocate of gun control, since she was nearly fatally shot; her husband Mark Kelly was elected to the US Senate. Hannah-Beth Jackson, '71, elected to the California State Senate in 2012, was responsible for the equal pay bill signed into law in October 2015, "one of the toughest pay equity laws in the nation," and for legislation requiring corporations headquartered in California to have at least one woman on their board of directors (2020), a law that "set off ripples across the country."[49] Natalie Naylor, '02, elected to lead her labor union in 2013, is the youngest labor leader in San Francisco and in the history of her Office and Professional Employees International Union. She began her work for union rights while at Scripps, when the new food service vendor would not honor the existing union contract. One of our alums, Ellen Rosenblum, made headlines in July 2020, as the Oregon attorney general who was suing the Department of Homeland Security over the federal intrusion into the Portland demonstrations.[50]

Our graduates have worked in the Department of Energy, in the office of Chief of Staff, the Foreign Service, and the Treasury Department. We've had an Academy Award winner, a software tester and subsystem engineer at the Jet Propulsion Laboratory (NASA's longest-serving woman, since 1958), a college president, a MacArthur Genius Award winner, a fashion magazine editor, a landscape and urban designer, a public health worker, nutritionist, the president of the Central Park Conservancy. Browsing through alum magazines, I read about a country folksinger, a judge, a film editor, a librarian, a park ranger, a wilderness therapy counselor, an environmental scientist, a human rights activist. I read about writers, lawyers, doctors, actors, artists, entrepreneurs, video game designers, social workers, psychologists and psychotherapists (lots of these), teachers (lots). When you're talking to parents who are opposed to a liberal arts major for their kid, advises Lynn Pasquerella, president of the Association of American Colleges and Universities and former president of Mount Holyoke College, bring in alums to tell their stories.

Most colleges can make lists of stand-out graduates like this, but most of our graduates—most graduates anywhere—go on to do what George Eliot calls "unhistoric acts": "The growing good of the world is partly dependent on unhistoric acts."[51] ("Unhistoric," as in parenting the next generation.) Maybe that should go on my syllabus: acts that make the growing good of the world. What could be more *useful*, long-term *useful* to you and me and everyone we know, than to graduate human beings who are happy and productive in ways that call on the best in them so they can give their best back to the world? Michelle Dowd, '90, who came to Pitzer from an unpromising background, a cult, to become a tenured professor and author, said I'd helped her "craft a life." This is a part of the story I hope has come through my account: we don't just teach rich kids at colleges like this.

So here I am, in my 40th year at this liberal arts college, required by law to put "student learning outcomes" (SLOs) on my syllabi. Only that "O" should stand for "objectives," not "outcomes." The objectives are mine; the outcomes are theirs.

Objectives, then? In a way, this entire book has been an attempt to describe my "student learning objectives." The objective of a liberal arts education is to produce . . . an educated human being. *Bildung,* the German word for "education," means the formation of a self, development of an individual, the shaping of a person of qualities. What qualities? *Judgment, wisdom, vision, generosity. Judgment,* as in dealing with complexities, tolerating uncertainty, sorting out information from disinformation, seeing what's there. *Wisdom,* as in thinking things through, knowing enough about yourself to make choices that don't lop off essential parts of yourself. *Vision,* as in seeing things whole, understanding your relation to other living things, drawing on the past to interpret the present and extrapolate into the future, gaining a critical perspective on your life and times that enables you to envision new possibilities. *Generosity,* as in *trust, hope, caring.* We in the liberal arts place a higher value on human beings, hold out higher hopes, than those who would reduce them to tools for production.

SLO, then, human development, human(e) development. Humanization, to make humane, to imbue with human kindness. People are born with vastly different capacities for entering into the experience of others, but empathy can be cultivated. It's not that the humanities necessarily make a person kinder, but that a liberal arts education and ecosystem can provide a culture that promotes access our inner human, helps us "rise to the occasion of our own humanity," as Douglas Rushkoff writes in *Team Human*.[52] If my students come out of my classes with an iota more fellow feeling than they came in with, with the slightest more understanding that others are not there to be used or exploited, and neither are they, with a smidgen more kindness, curiosity, or sympathy, I will have done the world some service.

"Every debate about the ideals of education is trivial and inconsequential compared to this single ideal: never again Auschwitz," wrote Theodor Adorno in 1967.[53] Whatever shape post-pandemic education assumes, it must not lose sight of this: *never again Auschwitz.* Whatever the "new normal" turns out to be—whenever we can safely resume

the kind of small class, person-to-person teaching I've described—
it must not lose sight of the human or the humanities, the subjects
that teach us what we are and what we may become. To give up on
the humanities is to give up on humanity.

I'll let one of our alums have the last words. Rebecca Dutta, '15,
was in second grade when No Child Left Behind was set in place. Her
high school was in a high-powered competitive Silicon Valley school
system that left her "hollowed out . . . disconnected. It was a school
where we were all ranked and our scores posted on the classroom door,
for all to see—just our ID numbers, but everyone had memorized
those. It's funny, I loved elementary school but grew to hate the rest,
so when I graduated high school, I felt sucked dry." She was left feeling "jaded by countless multiple-choice tests," feeling that she'd "done
well but had not actually learned anything in four years."

Something about her campus visit to Scripps made her think "there
might be something different here." Her decision was "an unexpected
choice for a student at a high school where UC Berkeley seemed like
the only fit for potential STEM majors." She arrived at Scripps in a
"burnt-out" state, viewing college as "the next thing to be got on with,"
"a stepping stone" to becoming a doctor.

> I had wanted to become a doctor for many years, but it was not until
> I graduated Scripps that I felt like I was ready to make the commit-
> ment to serve people. Before Scripps, being a doctor was an academic
> fascination. But somewhere among my liberal arts classes, friends,
> discussions, and internships, I finally learned what it meant to genu-
> inely care and feel through the lens of another human being. I learned,
> and am still learning, how to challenge the status quo in an effort to
> make society a more inclusive place for those around me. Over the
> course of four years and countless classes that seemed to have little to

do with my major, I shed the ugly side of being a pre-med, the unhealthy competition, the mad fight for GPA, the interview rhetoric, and the tunnel vision—in favor of immersing myself in patient care.

Of course, those "countless classes that seemed to have nothing to do with [her] major" turned out to have everything to do with it:

A liberal arts education challenges its students to remove the masks that we wear in public and to see each person as a vulnerable, complicated, and multifaceted individual. I began to see each patient as more than a body on a hospital bed. They became people with pasts and futures, with families and pets, with stories to tell that I still keep close to me as I continue my pursuit of a medical degree. I attribute a lot of this transformation to the discussions I have had with my peers and professors.

I truly believe that Scripps taught me how to be an empathetic person. I'll be honest, I am not 100% comfortable saying this. . . . In a work setting where people expect you to have a high-profile and extremely technical education, it sometimes feels uncomfortable to tell someone that the most important thing you learned in college was to become a human being. A lot of people just don't understand what that means.

ACKNOWLEDGMENTS

The liberal arts have been defended every which way, except this: where are the voices of the students, the scenes from the classroom that convey the life and urgency of what goes on, the energy, the synergy, that make the magic? So I began searching my office and home for notes, e-mails, letters from former students. I did informal interviews with graduating seniors, attended reunion weekends, combed through the *Scripps Magazine* and Scripps Alumnae Association sites, Yelp, CollegeConfidential, and Facebook postings. I sent out 150 questionnaires to Facebook friends who'd taken classes with me.

My deepest thanks to the many students who helped me remember: Emily Allen, Kara Amundson, Dottie Ashley, Margaret Bostrom, Nathalie Cannon, Bella Carter, Julie Lydon-Cornell and Keara Cornell, Loralyn Cropper, Leanne Day, Cindy Dellinger, Shiyuan Deng, Michelle Dowd, Rebecca Dutta, Winslow Eliot, Claire Ellen, Fatima Elkbati, Alison Gee, Julia Gillam, Linda Hance, Jennifer Hardy, Julia Hughes, Abbey Hye, Ruthie Jones, Irene Keliher, Emily Kugler, Alice Laskin, Lauren Shannon Meersseman, Emmiline Miles, Caroline Novit, Sharon O'Dair, George Pappy, Jasmine Payne, Anna Petkovitch, Victoria Podesta, Catherine Pyke, Ellen Rissman-Wong, Jill Russell, Lindsey Senway, Lisa Shahriari, Dorothy Shapiro, Sharon Snyder, Aish Subramanian, Liz Tyson, June Konoya Wachi, Molly Waste, Tess Williams, Jaime Willis, Jennifer Yoo-Brannon, Anita Zachary. Thanks also to Merrilee Gae Howard for bringing me up to speed on recent doings of alums, to Jacqueline Legazcu for her splendid photography, and, as always, to Becky Rodriguez, whose title, "faculty administrative assistant," doesn't begin to describe how much she's meant to Scripps faculty through the years. Apologies to anyone I've left out, and regrets for the many stories I had no room to tell.

As I reread e-mails and interviews, writing these acknowledgments, I was struck by how many students stressed the importance of Scripps being a women's college, how our classes made them feel "comfortable talking," "better prepared for grad school than my peers," "used to seeing women in positions of authority." I did not emphasize this in my book—I've written about women's issues elsewhere—so I'll say it here: women's colleges *work*.

Heartfelt gratitude to friends who made time to read this book in its original 600+ pages, when it included more about K–12 "reform": Roberta Johnson, Hank Reichman, John Seery, Kay Trimberger. Special appreciation to Jean Hegland, who brought hours of careful reading and the imagination of a novelist to the project, and to Vicki Ratner, whose friendship has been a pleasure and sustenance through the years. Thanks also to those who read and commented on parts: Abbe Blum, Anthony Cody, Julia Epstein, Rena Fraden, Jeanne Maracek, Randy Milden, Elizabeth Minnich, Carol Neely, Elizabeth Sandel. And to friends—besides those just mentioned—who helped me process, through conversations and e-mails, my ideas and experiences about teaching, and shared their own: Elizabeth Abel, Martha Andresen, Audrey Bilger, Carol Christ, Toni Clark, David Claus, Anne Coffey, William Deresiewicz, Barbara Epstein, Sandra Gilbert, Myra Goldberg, Ann Jones, Coppélia Kahn, Georgina Kleege, Suzanne Lacke, Wendy Martin, Kathy Moore, Marianne Novy, Ilene Philpson, Michael Roth, Madelon Sprengnether, Peter Stallybrass, Cheryl Walker, Jean Wyatt, Mike Zeller. Special thanks to Garret Keizer and Vicki Nelson for some last-minute rescue operations.

I felt it important to contextualize my discussion of the liberal arts in relation to K–12 because connections between the crisis of the humanities and so-called reform have not been recognized. Since 2002, when G. W. Bush's No Child Left Behind turned public schools into test-taking factories, through Race to the Top and the Common Core State Standards, public funding has been routed to private profits. Teachers have been fired for students' test scores and schools have been closed by the hundreds, especially in disadvantaged neighborhoods, where kids tend not to test well, to be replaced by charters; far from "leveling the playing field," as "reform" promised to do, it has tilted it all the more. Curricula have been stripped of "extraneous" subjects like literature, history, the arts, and languages, to make room for testing. It's no wonder students arrive in college with little interest in the liberal arts.

It astounds me now that someone teaching as long as I had so little awareness about the educational system most of my students come from (94% of US schoolchildren still go to public schools). I had not given it a thought. Unless we have kids or grandkids in the public schools, unless there's a teacher in the family, K–12 is something that happens to someone else. It took a lot of reading to convince me that a society could be so craven as to sacrifice its children like this. But when I thought about other socially suicidal policies—the planet is incinerating, the seas are rising, and we elect politicians who deny it's happening and push for more burning of fossil fuels—it became less unthinkable. A painting by Francisco Goya, *Saturn Devouring His Son*, says it all: a white-haired, hoary-headed patriarch holds the blood-drenched body of a boy, and, with bulging eyes and gaping mouth, prepares to take another bite.

Major thanks to Diane Ravitch, whose books *The Death and Life of the Great American School System, Reign of Error*, and *Slaying Goliath* blew the whistle on the privatization of public education, and whose tireless advocacy on behalf of public schools and teachers has been a guiding light. And to the many teachers whose impassioned and informed blogging has filled in the picture: Nancy Bailey, Jennifer Berkshire and Jack Schneider (Have You Heard?), Chicago Public Fools, Anthony Cody (Living in Dialogue), Jeannette Deutermann (Long Island Opt Out), Susan DuFresne, David Greene (Doing the Right Thing), Peter Greene (Curmudgucation), Leonie Haimson (Class Size Matters), Denisha Jones (Denisha's Blog), Diane Ravitch.com, Jan Resseger, Peggy Robertson (Peg with Pen), Gary Rubenstein, Mercedes Schneider, Steven Singer (gadflyonthewallblog), Emily Talmage (Save Maine Schools), Teacher in a Strange Land, Thomas Ultican (Tultican), The War Report on Public Education. Other writers include Joanne Barkan, Marion Brady, Jeff Bryant, Larry Ferlazzo, Michael Flanagan, Jesse Hagopian, Alfie Kohn, Mark Naison (cofounder, with Priscilla Sanstead, of BadAss Teachers), Susan Ohanian, Robert Shepherd, Ira Shor, Christine Vaccaro. Appreciation to Valerie Strauss at the *Washington Post* for giving teachers a voice in mainstream media.

Thanks also to my intrepid agent Andy Ross, to my editor Greg Britton, and to my sharp-eyed and patient copy editor, Beth Gianfagna. And as always and ever, to my best reader, best critic, best all-round everything Robert Jourdain, who talked me through, cajoled me through, and cheered me on through the many stages of this project.

https://www.gaylegreene.org

NOTES

Epigraphs

Anthony Grafton and James Grossman, "The Humanities in Dubious Battle: What a New Harvard Report Doesn't Tell Us," *Chronicle of Higher Education*, July 1, 2013.

Christopher Newfield, *Unmaking the Public University: The Forty-Year Assault on the Middle Class* (Harvard University Press, 2008), 274.

Introduction

Epigraphs: Tillerson quoted in Valerie Strauss, "Why Education Activists Are Furious at Exxon Mobil CEO," *Washington Post*, December 29, 2015, my emphasis; and Anthony Kronman, *The Assault on American Excellence* (Free Press, 2019), 28.

1. As, for example, Paul Krugman, "We Don't Need No Education," *New York Times*, April 23, 2018.

2. Of the world's top 20 universities, 15 to 17 are in the United States, according to recent rankings, and in the history of the Nobel Prizes, 40% have been awarded to Americans. David Labaree, *A Perfect Mess: The Unlikely Ascendency of American Higher Education* (University of Chicago Press, 2017), 3.

3. Reagan quoted in Dan Berrett, "The Day the Purpose of Higher Education Changed," *Chronicle of Higher Education*, January 26, 2015.

4. The term *return on investment* appears throughout the Gates Foundation report, "Equitable Value: Promoting Economic Mobility and Social Justice through Postsecondary Education," May 2021, https://www.postsecondaryvalue .org/wp-content/uploads/2021/05/PVC-Final-Report-FINAL.pdf.

5. Gates quoted in Richard Waters, "An Exclusive Interview with Bill Gates," *Financial Times*, November 1, 2013. See also Stephanie Simon, "Bill Gates Plugs Common Core, Arne Duncan," *Politico*, September 29, 2014: "He said he thought of the Common Core as 'a technocratic issue,' akin to making sure all states use the same type of electrical outlet."

6. "Return on investment" is the major purpose of college, according to a Gates Foundation report that is, as I write, making its way around Congress: Postsecondary Value Commission, *Equitable Value: Promoting Economic Mobility and Social Justice through Postsecondary Education*, May 2021, https://www.postsecondaryvalue.org/wp-content/uploads/2021/05/PVC-Final-Report-FINAL.pdf. This report is part of the foundation's effort to "educate" Congress about the "value" of postsecondary education so they'll know how to vote when the Higher Education Act comes up for renewal (as we'll see in chapter 7).

7. Barack Obama, "State of the Union Address," 2016, The White House, https://obamawhitehouse.archives.gov/the-press-office/2016/01/12/remarks-president-barack-obama-%E2%80%93-prepared-delivery-state-union-address.

8. Joanne Barkan, "Got Dough? How Billionaires Rule Our Schools," *Dissent* (Winter 2011): https://www.dissentmagazine.org/article/got-dough-how-billionaires-rule-our-schools.

9. On product-market fit, see Ryan Craig, "America Needs Faster and Cheaper Pathways to Good Jobs," Big Think, sponsored by the Charles Koch Foundation, April 15, 2020, https://bigthink.com/Charles-Koch-Foundation/education-pathways?rebelltitem=1#rebelltitem1.

10. "U.S. higher education routinely awards more degrees in science and engineering than can be employed in science and engineering occupations." Michael Teitelbaum, *Falling Behind* (Princeton University Press, 2014), 22; quoted by Andrew Hacker, "The Frenzy about High-Tech Talent," *New York Review*, July 9, 2015. Hacker notes in his own book, "In the summer of 2014, mighty Microsoft laid off 18,000 of its employees." *The Math Myth and Other STEM Delusions* (New Press, 2016), 31.

11. Karl Voss, "Embracing the Uncertain, Scary Future—with a Liberal Arts Degree," *Hechinger Report*, August 14, 2018, https://hechingerreport.org/opinion-embracing-the-uncertain-scary-future-with-a-liberal-arts-degree. A spate of books written between 2015 and 2017 documents the employability of liberal arts graduates: George Anders, *You Can Do Anything: The Surprising Power of a "Useless" Liberal Arts Education* (Little, Brown, 2017); Scott Hartley, *The Fuzzy and the Techie: Why the Liberal Arts Will Rule the Digital World* (Houghton Mifflin Harcourt, 2017); Christian Madsbjerg, *Sensemaking: The Power of the Humanities in the Age of the Algorithm* (Hachette, 2017); Geoff Colvin, *Humans Are Underrated: What High Achievers Know That Brilliant Machines Never Will* (Penguin, 2015); Gary Saul Morson and Morton Schapiro, *Cents and Sensibility: What Economics Can Learn from the Humanities* (Princeton University Press, 2017); Randall Stross, *A Practical Education: Why Liberal Arts Majors Make Great Employees* (Redwood Press, 2017).

12. Benjamin Schmidt, "The Humanities Are in Crisis," *Atlantic*, August 23, 2018.

13. Bill Gates, "Lakeside School," September 23, 2005, Bill & Melinda Gates Foundation, https://www.gatesfoundation.org/Media-Center/Speeches/2005/09 /Bill-Gates-Lakeside-School.

14. Joshua Kim, "How Would You Answer These 9 Reimagine Education Questions?," *Inside Higher Ed*, December 8, 2015; and Kim, "The 3 Things I'll Say about EdTech in 2016," *Inside Higher Ed*, January 3, 2016.

15. Daniel Chambliss and Christopher Takacs, *How College Works* (Harvard University Press, 2014).

16. Adam Falk, "In Defense of the Living, Breathing Professor," *Wall Street Journal*, August 28, 2012. More on this in chapter 9.

17. Student-faculty interactions "enhance learning, completion, motivation, critical thinking, career aspirations, belonging, and self-confidence," as Peter Felten and Leo Lambert document in *Relationship-Rich Education: How Human Connections Drive Success in College* (Johns Hopkins University Press, 2020). They also happen to be "the single most significant factor in positive educational outcomes for students of color, and are also especially significant for first-generation students" (83; studies referred to, 174).

18. Richard Detweiler, *The Evidence Liberal Arts Needs: Lives of Consequence, Inquiry, and Accomplishment* (MIT Press, 2021), 224–28.

19. Hardwick Day, *The Value and Impact of the College Experience: A Comparative Study*, commissioned by the Annapolis Group, November 2011, https://mroche.nd .edu/assets/204648/the_value_and_impact_of_the_college_experience.pdf. The Annapolis Group is a group of 130 small liberal arts colleges whose alums gave their colleges higher rankings than alums at flagship universities, sometimes twice as high, in terms of professors who challenged them and helped them personally, conversations with professors outside class, small classes taught by professors rather than adjuncts, and a college experience that left them feeling prepared for life.

20. Detweiler, *The Evidence Liberal Arts Needs*, 191–92. Detweiler stresses that breadth and meaning are part of a liberal arts education, the "study of the full span of human knowledge" and the "exploration of different perspectives on issues of significance to humanity" (225, 229). He points out that the liberal arts include some of the social sciences and sciences (83). The *liberal arts* is a more inclusive term than the *humanities*, but since the distinction isn't important to my discussion, I use the terms more or less interchangeably.

21. Steven Mintz, "Can These Colleges Be Saved?" *Inside Higher Ed*, November 5, 2020. Small liberal arts colleges boast "a higher proportion of first-generation and low-income students [that] graduate with no student loan debt." Georgia Nugent, *The Liberal Arts in Action, Past, Present, and Future* (Council of Independent Colleges, 2015), http://webmedia.jcu.edu/institutionaleffectiveness/files/2016 /09/Liberal-Arts-in-Action-Symposium-Essay.pdf.

22. *What Matters in College after College: A Comparative Alumnae Research Study*, prepared for the Women's College Coalition, February 24 and March 7,

2012, https://www.womenscolleges.org/sites/default/files/report/files/main/2012har dwickdaycomparativealumnaesurveymarch2012_0.pdf. Graduates of women's colleges constitute more than 20% of women in the US Congress and 30% of rising women in corporate America. Best Value Schools, "What Are the Benefits of Attending a Women's College?," March 24, 2021, https://www.bestvalueschools .com/faq/benefits-attending-womens-college.

23. Hammond quoted in Jasmine Garsd, "Are Women's Colleges Doomed? What Sweet Briar's Demise Tells Us," NPREd, March 26, 2015, https://www.npr .org/sections/ed/2015/03/26/395120853/are-womens-colleges-doomed-what-sweet -briars-demise-tells-us.

24. Rachel Toor, "What I Know about My Students," *Chronicle of Higher Education*, December 23, 2017.

25. Cathy Davidson, *The New Education: How to Revolutionize the University to Prepare Students for a World in Flux* (Basic Books, 2017), 49–51.

26. Dick Startz, "When It Comes to Student Success, HBCUs Do More with Less," Brookings, January 18, 2021, https://www.brookings.edu/blog/brown-center -chalkboard/2021/01/18/when-it-comes-to-student-success-hbcus-do-more-with-less.

27. Nathan Greenfield, "HBCUs Lead at Propelling Graduates into Middle Class," *University World News*, December 2, 2021.

28. Peter Felten and Leo Lambert, *Relationship-Rich Education: How Human Connections Drive Success in College* (Johns Hopkins University Press, 2020). Detweiler corroborates this in *The Evidence Liberal Arts Needs*, 216–19.

29. Katherine Long, "As STEM Majors Soar at University of Washington, Interest in Humanities Shrinks—a Potentially Costly Loss," *Seattle Times*, January 20, 2019.

30. Scott Jaschik, "Disappearing Liberal Arts Colleges," *Inside Higher Ed*, October 11, 2012.

31. Christopher Newfield, "Bleeding Meritocracy: Responding to the Admissions Scandal as Outrage Fades," *Academe*, March 25, 2019, https://academeblog.org/2019 /03/25/bleeding-meritocracy-responding-to-the-admissions-scandal-as-outrage-fades.

32. Joseph Traester, "Liberal Arts, a Lost Cause?," *New York Times*, July 31, 2015. Carol Christ, personal communication. Interestingly, however, there has been a significant uptick in applications to HBCUs and to women's colleges since 2016. Scott Jaschik, "Women's Colleges See Boost in Yield in Wake of 2016 Election," *Inside Higher Ed*, August 13, 2018; Alejandra Marchevsky and Jeanne Theoharis, "Restoring the People's Universities," AAUP.org, Spring 2021, https://www.aaup.org/article/restoring-people%E2%80%99s-universities# .YRtI65NKgbw.

33. Robinson quoted in Corrie Goldman, "Novelist Marilynne Robinson Warns Stanford Audience against Utilitarian Trends in Higher Education," *Stanford News*, November 3, 2015.

34. Andrew Delbanco, *College: What It Was, Is, and Should Be* (Princeton University Press, 2012), 171. So many writers have emphasized our need to explain ourselves that it's almost a trope. As, for example, Anthony Grafton, James Grossman, and Christopher Newfield, in the epigraphs to this book; and Elaine Tuttle Hansen, who speaks of "our failure to translate the intangible, perhaps even ineffable aims of our educational model into terms that touch directly on the concrete and pressing needs of both individuals and society today," to communicate our "lived knowledge" and "deep conviction." "Liberated Consumers and the Liberal Arts College," in *What Is College For? The Public Purpose of Higher Education*, ed. Ellen Condliffe Lagemann and Harry Lewis (Teachers College Press, 2012), 66–67.

35. Roosevelt Montás concurs: "The value of . . . [a liberal arts education] cannot be extracted and delivered apart from the experience of the thing," but what does work is "*doing* liberal education," experiencing it. Montás communicates the experience by telling his story. I communicate it by bringing you into my class. *Rescuing Socrates: How the Great Books Changed My Life and Why They Matter for a New Generation* (Princeton University Press, 2021), 6, 128.

36. Jerry Muller, *The Tyranny of Metrics* (Princeton University Press, 2018); see also Muller, "The Tyranny of Metrics: The Quest to Quantify Everything Undermines Higher Education," *Chronicle of Higher Education*, January 21, 2018. *Computationalism* is what Jaron Lanier calls this quantifying mentality that sees everything as reducible to what can be computed. Lanier is a Silicon Valley pioneer who turned whistleblower, appalled by this reductiveness, as he explains in *You Are Not a Gadget: A Manifesto* (Vintage, 2010).

37. Gayle Greene, *The Woman Who Knew Too Much: Alice Stewart and the Secrets of Radiation* (University of Michigan Press, 1999); Greene, "Alice Stewart and Richard Doll: Reputation and the Shaping of Scientific 'Truth,'" *Perspectives in Biology and Medicine* (Autumn 2011): 504–31.

ONE: First Day

Epigraph: Geoffrey Harpham, "Finding Ourselves: The Humanities as a Discipline," *American Literary History* 25, no. 3 (Fall 2013): 509–34.

1. McCrory quoted in Mark Blinker and Julia Sims, "McCrory: Fund Higher Education Based on Results," wral.com, January 29, 2013, https://www.wral.com/mccrory-fund-higher-education-based-on-results/12037347.

2. Gates quoted in Lyndsey Layton, "Bill Gates Calls on Teachers to Defend the Common Core," *Washington Post*, March 14, 2014.

3. Stephen Beard, "Shakespeare Brand Still Strong after 400 Years," *Marketplace*, Minnesota Public Radio, April 21, 2016, https://www.marketplace.org/2016/04/21/400-years-shakespeare-remains-money-spinner.

4. Andrew Delbanco, *College: What It Was, Is, and Should Be* (Princeton University Press, 2012), 153.

5. McCrory quoted in Kevin Kiley, "Another Liberal Arts Critic," *Inside Higher Ed*, January 30, 2013.

6. Rubio quoted in Jon Marcus, "The Unexpected Schools Fighting to Save the Liberal Arts," *Atlantic*, October 15, 2015.

7. Adaptability, flexibility, versatility are qualities employers are looking for. David Finegold and Alexis Spencer Notabartolo, "21st-Century Competencies and Their Impact: An Interdisciplinary Literature Review," William + Flora Hewlett Foundation, November 23, 2016, https://hewlett.org/wp-content/uploads/2016/11/21st _Century_Competencies_Impact.pdf; Kevin Riley et al., "Do Humans Still Need to Study the Humanities?," *New Republic*, March 19, 2015. See also the spate of books cited in the introduction.

8. David Deming, "In the Salary Race, Engineers Sprint but English Majors Endure," *New York Times*, September 20, 2019.

9. Michael Anft, "The STEM Crisis: Reality or Myth?," *Chronicle of Higher Education*, November 11, 2013.

10. George Carlin, "The American Dream," YouTube, https://www.youtube .com/watch?v=acLWIvFO-2Q&ab_channel=wutdaflek.

11. Paulo Freire, *We Make the Road by Walking: Conversations on Education and Social Change*, ed. Brenda Bell, John Gaventa, and John Peters (Temple University Press, 1990), 181.

12. This account of corporate reform of K–12 follows Diane Ravitch, *Reign of Error: The Hoax of the Privatization Movement and the Danger to America's Public Schools* (Knopf Doubleday, 2013). I'm also indebted to the many teacher bloggers mentioned in the acknowledgments.

13. Sheryl Stolberg and William Yardly, "For Giffords, Tucson Roots Shaped Views," *New York Times*, January 14, 2011.

14. Susan McWilliams and John Seery, *The Best Kind of College: An Insiders' Guide to America's Small Liberal Arts Colleges* (SUNY Press, 2015), 6.

15. Victor Ferrall, *Liberal Arts at the Brink* (Harvard University Press, 2011), 21.

16. Georgia Nugent, *The Liberal Arts in Action, Past, Present, and Future* (Council of Independent Colleges, 2015), http://webmedia.jcu.edu /institutionaleffectiveness/files/2016/09/Liberal-Arts-in-Action-Symposium-Essay .pdf, is drawing on another study by the Council of Independent Colleges, *Expanding Access and Opportunity: How Small and Mid-sized Independent Colleges Serve First-Generation and Low-Income Students*, March 2015, https://www.cic.edu /r/r/Documents/ExpandingAccessReport-2015.pdf

17. Brandon Busteed, "Hey, Higher Education: You're on Mute," *Forbes*, January 12, 2021.

18. William Cronan, "Only Connect: The Goals of a Liberal Education," *Liberal Education*, 85, no. 1 (Winter 1999): 6–12.

19. Johann Hari, "Is Neoliberalism Making Our Depression and Anxiety Crisis Worse?," *In These Times*, February 21, 2018, http://inthesetimes.com/article /20930/depressed-anxious-blame-neoliberalism.

20. Audrey Bilger quoted in Chris Lydgate, "Scholar. Writer. Teacher. President," *Reed Magazine*, August 30, 2019, https://www.reed.edu/reed-magazine /articles/2019/audrey-bilger-new-president.html.

21. Frank Bruni, "The End of College as We Knew It," *New York Times*, June 4, 2020.

22. Robin Headlam Wells, *Shakespeare's Humanism* (Cambridge University Press, 2005).

23. Reagan was "an admirer" of Ayn Rand. So are Trump, Rex Tillerson, Mike Pompeo, Ron Paul, Clarence Thomas, and entrepreneurs Peter Theil and Mark Cuban. Alan Greenspan was one of the "inner circle" of admirers she gathered around her. Paul Ryan made his entire staff read her: "I grew up reading Ayn Rand, and it taught me quite a bit about who I am and what my value systems are, and what my beliefs are." (She died, incidentally, alone and collecting Social Security.) Kurt Andersen, "How America Lost Its Mind," *Atlantic*, September 15, 2017; Jonathan Freedland, "The New Age of Ayn Rand: How She Won Over Trump and Silicon Valley," *Guardian*, April 10, 2017; Thom Hartmann, "The Right-Wing American Love Affair with One of the Most Disturbing Serial Killers," *Salon*, August 20, 2019.

24. Martin Luther King Jr., "Letter from a Birmingham Jail," April 16, 1963, Center for Africana Studies, University of Pennsylvania, https://www.africa .upenn.edu/Articles_Gen/Letter_Birmingham.html.

TWO: Once upon a Time in the Twentieth Century

Epigraphs: George Eliot, *Daniel Deronda* (1876; rpt., Penguin, 1995), 227; and Jane Jacobs, *Dark Age Ahead* (2004; rpt., Vintage, 2005), 63.

1. "Education shall be directed to the full development of the human personality and to the strengthening of respect for human rights and fundamental freedoms." Universal Declaration of Human Rights, UN, December 10, 1948, article 26, https://www.un.org/en/about-us/universal-declaration-of-human-rights.

2. Gordon Lafer, *The One Percent Solution: How Corporations Are Remaking America One State at a Time* (ILR Press, 2017), 4.

3. Chris Hedges, *Empire of Illusion: The End of Literacy and the Triumph of Spectacle* (Nation Books, 2009), 141.

4. John Thelin, *Going to College in the Sixties* (Johns Hopkins University Press, 2018), 20.

5. Diana Hembree, "CEO Pay Skyrockets to 361," *Forbes*, May 22, 2018.

6. Talbot Brewer, "The Coup That Failed: How the Near-Sacking of a University President Exposed the Fault Lines of American Higher Education,"

reprinted from *Hedgehog Review* 16, no. 2 (Summer 2014), California Conference of the American Association of University Professors, http://www.caaaup.org /blog/philosopher-talbot-brewer-on-the-corporate-managerial-take-over-of-the -university.

7. Robin Chapman, "Family Papers Reveal Jim Crow Restrictions in Early Los Altos," *Los Altos Town Crier*, April 2, 2019. Thanks to Lynne Pfeiffer for the yearbook information.

8. Neil Gaiman, "Why Our Future Depends on Libraries, Reading and Daydreaming," *View from the Cheap Seats: Selected Nonfiction* (Morrow, 2016), 7.

9. David Brooks, *The Second Mountain: The Quest for a Moral Life* (Random House, 2019), 95–96.

10. Lindsey Layton, "Common Core Standards in English Spark War over Words," *Washington Post*, December 2, 2012.

11. Christopher Newfield, *Unmaking the Public University* (Harvard University Press, 2008), 28, 4.

12. Wendy Brown, *Undoing the Demos: Neoliberalism's Stealth Revolution* (Zone Books, 2015), 180.

13. Brown, *Undoing the Demos*, 187; Newfield, *Unmaking of the Public University*, 7; Jeffrey Williams, "The Need for Critical University Studies," in *A New Deal for the Humanities: Liberal Arts and the Future of Public Higher Education*, ed. Gordon Hutner and Fiesal Mohamed (Rutgers University Press, 2016), 145–59; 145, 147.

14. Brown, *Undoing the Demos*, 185.

15. "By 1956, roughly 8.8 million veterans had used the GI Bill education benefits. . . . Historians and economists judge the GI Bill a major political and economic success . . . and a major contribution to America's stock of human capital that encouraged long-term economic growth." Kathleen Frydl, *The GI Bill* (Cambridge University Press, 2009).

16. Paul Tough, *The Years That Matter Most: How College Makes or Breaks Us* (Houghton Mifflin Harcourt, 2019), 315.

17. Tough, *The Years That Matter Most*, 316, quoting Suzanne Mettler, *Soldiers to Citizens: The G.I. Bill and the Making of the Greatest Generation* (Oxford University Press, 2005).

18. Brown quoted in Newfield, *Unmaking of the Public University*, 7, reference on 293.

19. Jeffrey Williams, *How to Be an Intellectual: Essays on Criticism, Culture, and the University* (Fordham University Press, 2014), 127.

20. "Best States for Business, 2019," *Forbes*, https://www.forbes.com/places/ca /?sh=6355d9163fef.

21. John F. Kennedy, address at the University of California at Berkeley, March 23, 1962, John F. Kennedy Presidential Library and Museum, https://www .jfklibrary.org/archives/other-resources/john-f-kennedy-speeches/university-of -california-berkeley-19620323.

22. Miriam Pawel, "Can Californians Still Find a Path to Mobility in the State's Universities?," *New York Times*, May 30, 2019.

23. Christian Kreznar, "America's Top Colleges 2021: For the First Time a Public School Is Number One," *Forbes*, September 8, 2021.

24. Madison Fernandez, "Why Berkeley Is Number One," *Forbes*, September 8, 2021.

25. "Stanford's endowment per student dwarfs Berkeley's." Compare its $28 billion for 16,000 students to Berkeley's less than $5 billion for 42,000 students. David Labaree, "How Not to Defend Elite Universities," *Chronicle of Higher Education*, August 10, 2020.

26. In California, "The undergraduate universities consistently rank as the most effective schools in the country as drivers of upward economic mobility." Pawel, "Can Californians Still Find a Path to Mobility in the State's Universities?"

27. Colleen Flaherty, "A Non-Tenure-Track Profession," *Inside Higher Ed*, October 12, 2018.

28. Karen Arensen, "Study Details CUNY Successes from Open Admissions Policy," *New York Times*, May 7, 1996.

29. David Lavin and David Hyllegard, *Changing the Odds: Open Admissions and the Life Chances of the Disadvantaged* (Yale University Press, 1996).

30. Paul Attewell and David Lavin, *Passing the Torch: Does Higher Education for the Disadvantaged Pay Off across the Generations?* (Russell Sage Foundation, 2007); cited in Steven Brint, *Two Cheers for Higher Education: Why American Universities Are Stronger Than Ever—and How to Meet the Challenges They Face* (Princeton University Press, 2018), 139.

31. David Leonhardt, "America's Great Working Class Colleges," *New York Times*, January 18, 2017.

32. Newfield, *Unmaking of the Public University*, 28, 30, 25, 269.

33. Lewis Powell, "Attack on the American Free Enterprise System," memo to Eugene B. Sydnor Jr., chairman, Education Committee, US Chamber of Commerce, August 23, 1971, Greenpeace, https://www.greenpeace.org/usa/democracy/the-lewis-powell-memo-a-corporate-blueprint-to-dominate-democracy.

34. Jane Mayer, *Dark Money: The Hidden History of the Billionaires behind the Rise of the Radical Right* (Anchor, 2017), 88.

35. "ALEC Corporations," SourceWatch, https://www.sourcewatch.org/index.php/ALEC_Corporations.

36. Mayer, *Dark Money*, 108.

37. Reagan railed against student radicalism at Berkeley in KRON-TV news footage from May 12, 1966, at the Cow Palace in San Francisco. "Ronald Reagan's 'Morality Gap' Speech," Diva, San Francisco State University, https://diva.sfsu.edu/collections/sfbatv/bundles/229317.

38. Aaron Bady and Mike Konczal, "From Master Plan to No Plan: The Slow Death of Public Higher Education," *Dissent*, Fall 2012.

39. Margaret Thatcher, interview in *Women's Own* magazine, October 31, 1987, reprinted at Brian Deer: Award-Winning Investigations, https://briandeer.com /social/thatcher-society.htm.

40. Newfield, *Unmaking of the Public University*, 240.

41. Paul Krugman, "Nasty, Brutish, and Trump," *New York Times*, February 22, 2018.

42. Kim Parker, "The Growing Partisan Divide in Views of Higher Education," August 19, 2019, Pew Research Center, https://www.pewsocialtrends.org /essay/the-growing-partisan-divide-in-views-of-higher-education.

43. Rebecca Ora, quoted by Kim Christensen, "Is UC Spending Too Little on Teaching, Too Much on Administration?," *Los Angeles Times*, October 17, 2015.

44. Tom Mortenson, "The Race to the Bottom: State Fiscal Support for Higher Education," quoted by F. King Alexander, "The Reality of State Disinvestment in Public Higher Education," *Inside Higher Ed*, November 26, 2019.

45. Valerie Strauss, "What Ohio Governor John Kasich Is Doing to Public Education in His State," *Washington Post*, July 20, 2015.

46. Chuck Rybak, *University of Wisconsin Struggle: When a State Attacks Its University* (University of Minnesota Press, 2017), 4.

47. Cas Mudde, "Alaska's Governor Is Trying to Destroy Its Universities: The State May Never Recover," *Guardian*, July 6, 2019.

48. Sam Davenport, "Dunleavy, Funded by the Koch Brothers and the Oil Industry, Just Made Unprecedented Cuts to Health, Education and Climate Change Initiatives," *Vice*, July 9, 2019.

49. Dan Reed, quoted in Jon Marcus, "The Looming Decline of the Public Research University," *Hechinger Report*, October 10, 2017, https://hechingerreport .org/the-looming-decline-of-the-public-research-university.

50. Katie Billotte, "Conservatives Killed the Liberal Arts," *Salon*, September 14, 2012.

51. National Commission on Excellence in Education, *A Nation at Risk: The Imperative for Educational Reform*, April 1983, https://www2.ed.gov/pubs /NatAtRisk/risk.html.

52. Spellings report, *A Test of Leadership: Charting the Future of U.S. Higher Education*, https://www.learningoutcomesassessment.org/wp-content/uploads /2019/08/SpellingsReport.pdf.

53. Brint, *Two Cheers*, 310. More on this in chapter 7.

54. Kelly Field, "Obama Puts Federal Weight behind Calls for College Affordability," *Chronicle of Higher Education*, February 12, 2013.

55. Doug Lederman and Paul Fain, "The Higher Education President," *Inside Higher Ed*, January 19, 2017. The Scorecard also offered colleges "regulatory flexibility to innovate," which higher education blogger Aaron Bady found worrying, concerned that this might motivate "colleges to defund tried and tested programs in favor of flavor-of-the-month Silicon Valley start-up partnerships." Bady

added that "the idea that ranking universities according to new metrics will do anything to lower costs seems delusional." Quoted in Coleen Flaherty, "Faculty Advocates React to Obama's Plan for Higher Ed," *Inside Higher Ed*, August 23, 2013.

56. On Obama's 2013 State of the Union message, see Field, "Obama Puts Federal Weight behind Calls for College Affordability."

57. Larry Gordon, "Occidental Recalls 'Barry' Obama," *Los Angeles Times*, January 29, 2007.

58. David Maraniss, *Barack Obama: The Story* (Simon and Schuster, 2012), 335–36, 387.

59. "Remarks by the President on Opportunity for All and Skills for America's Workers," Office of the Press Secretary, White House, January 30, 2014, https://obamawhitehouse.archives.gov/the-press-office/2014/01/30/remarks-president-opportunity-all-and-skills-americas-workers; Scott Jaschik, "Obama vs. Art History," *Inside Higher Ed*, January 31, 2014.

60. Daniels quoted in Paul Fain, "It's the Results, Stupid," *Inside Higher Ed*, June 7, 2013.

61. Williams, "The Need for Critical University Studies," 149.

62. Brown quoted in Daniel Denvir, "Is American Higher Education Screwed? Conservatives Try to Privatize College as Tuition Soars," *Alternet*, January 22, 2011.

63. Brown in an interview with Timothy Shenk, "What Exactly Is Neoliberalism?" *Dissent*, April 2, 2014.

64. Sorton quoted in Brown, *Undoing the Demos*, 175.

65. Wendy Brown quotes Yudof at a teach-in, "Save the University," September 2009, "Why Privatization Is about More Than Who Pays," YouTube, https://www.youtube.com/watch?v=aR4xYBGdQgw.

66. "College President Resigns after 'Drown the Bunnies' Comment," CBS News / Associated Press, March 1, 2016, https://www.cbsnews.com/news/mount-st-marys-university-president-simon-newman-resigns.

67. "U.S. Income Inequality at Highest Level in 50 Years," NBC News / Associated Press, September 26, 2019, https://www.nbcnews.com/news/us-news/u-s-income-inequality-highest-level-50-years-economic-gap-n1058956.

68. Sara Goldrick-Rab, "It's Hard to Study if You're Hungry," *New York Times*, January 14, 2018.

69. Katie Jones, "Ranked: The Social Mobility of 82 Countries." Social mobility, which this report measured in terms of health care, education, tech access, work opportunities, social protection, "dictates whether children are in the path to having a better life than their parents, or if they will remain tethered to their socio-economic status." Visual Capitalist, February 7, 2020, https://www.visualcapitalist.com/ranked-the-social-mobility-of-82-countries.

70. Sean McElwee, "Six Ways America Is like a Third World Country," *Rolling Stone*, March 5, 2014.

71. George Carlin, "The American Dream," YouTube, https://www.youtube .com/watch?v=acLW1vFO-2Q&ab_channel=wutdaflek.

72. Douglas Rushkoff, *Team Human* (Norton, 2019), 3.

73. Molly McClain, *Ellen Browning Scripps: New Money and American Philanthropy* (University of Nebraska Press, 2017), 209.

THREE: What's Trust Got to Do with It?

Epigraph: Student quoted by Peter Herman, "Online Learning Is Not the Future," *Inside Higher Ed*, June 10, 2020.

1. Caitlan Flanagan, "That's Not Funny," *Atlantic*, September 2015.

2. Will Shelton, quoted by Michael Winerup, "In Tennessee, Following the Rules for Evaluations off a Cliff," *New York Times*, November 2, 2011.

3. Conti quoted in Valerie Strauss, "Teacher's Resignation Letter: 'My Profession . . . No Longer Exists," *Washington Post*, April 6, 2013.

4. Rob Jenkins, "Carrot versus Stick Teaching," *Chronicle of Higher Education*, January 3, 2018. "We can't make children learn, but we can let them learn," says Alison Gopnik, *The Gardener and the Carpenter* (Picador, 2016), 20.

5. Garret Keizer, *Getting Schooled* (Metropolitan Books, 2014), 51–52.

6. Mano Singham, "Death to the Syllabus!," *Liberal Education* 93, no. 4 (Fall 2007).

7. Joseph Berger, "Jewish Prayers Are Modernized in New Book," *New York Times*, September 17, 2010.

8. Pasteur quoted in Kay Redfield Jamison, *Exuberance: The Passion for Life* (Vintage, 2005), 5.

9. Albert Einstein, "The World as I See It," in *Ideas and Opinions*, ed. Carl Seelig (Bonanza Books, 1954), 8–11, https://history.aip.org/history/exhibits /einstein/essay.htm.

10. Jill Barshay, "Evidence Increases for Reading with Paper instead of Screens," *Hechinger Report*, August 12, 2019, https://hechingerreport.org/evidence -increases-for-reading-on-paper-instead-of-screens.

11. Paula Cohen, "What I've Learned in the Classroom," *Chronicle of Higher Education*, July 22, 2013. Several other comments quoted in this chapter are to Cohen's article. Comments have been removed from most *Chronicle of Higher Education* and *Inside Higher Ed* articles, so some are untraceable.

12. Paula Wasley, "The Syllabus Becomes a Repository of Legalese," *Chronicle of Higher Education*, March 14, 2008.

13. John Warner, "A Syllabus Is Not a Contract," *Inside Higher Ed*, November 25, 2018.

14. Michael Stein, Christopher Scribner, and David Brown, "Market Forces and the College Classroom: Losing Sovereignty," *AAUP Journal of Academic Freedom* 4 (2013).

15. Singham, "Death to the Syllabus!"

16. Garavalia quoted by Wasley, "The Syllabus Becomes a Repository of Legalese."

17. ACHA report cited by Brad Wolverton, "As Students Struggle with Stress and Depression Colleges Act as Counselors," *New York Times*, February 21, 2019.

18. Wendy Lecker, Sarah Littman, and Jonathan Pelton, "Take It from Parents: Teenagers Are People, Not Data Points," *Parents across America* (blog), May 9, 2013, http://parentsacrossamerica.org/parents-teenagers-people-data-points.

19. Hanna Rosin, "The Silicon Valley Suicides," *Atlantic*, December 2015; Yanan Wang, "CDC Investigates Why So Many Students in Wealthy Palo Alto, California, Commit Suicide," *Washington Post*, February 16, 2016.

20. Jackson quoted in Chris Quintana, "After Seven Suicides, a Professor Unearths Stories of Where People Find Resilience," *Chronicle of Higher Education*, January 21, 2018.

21. Samantha Raphelson, "Many Large Public Universities Don't Collect Data on Suicides, Report Finds," NPR.org, January 4, 2018, https://www.npr.org/2018/01/04/575418561/most-large-public-universities-dont-collect-data-on-suicides-report-finds.

22. Lythcott-Haims quoted in Emma Brown, "Former Stanford Dean Explains Why Helicopter Parenting Is Ruining a Generation of Children," *Washington Post*, October 16, 2015.

23. James Steele and Lance Williams, "Who Got Rich off the Student Debt Crisis," revealnews.org, June 28, 2016, https://www.revealnews.org/article/who-got-rich-off-the-student-debt-crisis. They also note, "The federal government holds roughly 90 percent of the $1.3 trillion in outstanding student loans. That makes the Department of Education effectively one of the world's largest banks, but one that rarely deals with its customers. That job has been turned over to private contractors that are paid commissions and sometimes bonuses to collect on student loans." The national average student indebtedness is $37,750. Averages for Scripps graduates seem to be around $20,000. Scripps was ranked number 22 in "Which Colleges Give the Best Return on Investment," April 27, 2021, in Lend.edu's "risk-reward indicator," which shows students' ability to pay off student loan debt, https://lendedu.com/blog/college-risk-reward-indicator.

24. Paul Tough, *The Years That Matter Most: How College Makes or Breaks Us* (Houghton Mifflin Harcourt, 2019), 326–27.

25. Singham, "Death to the Syllabus!"

26. Harry Lewis, *Excellence without a Soul: Does Liberal Education Have a Future?* (Public Affairs, 2007), 83, citing Nalini Ambady and Robert Rosenthal, "Half a Minute: Predicting Teacher Evaluations from Thin Slices of Nonverbal Behavior and Physical Attractiveness," *Journal of Personality and Social Psychology* (1993), http://citeseerx.ist.psu.edu/viewdoc/summary?doi=10.1.1.233.2216.

27. Colleen Flaherty, "Bias against Female Instructors," *Inside Higher Ed*, January 11, 2016; and Flaherty, "The Skinny on Teaching Evaluations and Bias," *Inside Higher Ed*, February 17, 2021.

28. Frank McCourt calls it "teacher-student solidarity. They might complain in class but when a principal or any other outsider appeared there was immediate unity, a solid front." *Teacher Man* (Scribner, 2005), 17.

29. Teller quoted in Jessica Lahey, "Teaching: Just Like Performing Magic," *Atlantic*, January 21, 2016.

30. DeVos quoted in Marybeth Gasman, "No, Betsy DeVos, Faculty Aren't Telling Students What to Think, Ivy League Professor Says," *Washington Post*, March 7, 2017.

31. DeVos quoted in Benjamin Wermund, "Trump's Education Pick Says Reform Can 'Advance God's Kingdom,'" *Politico*, December 12, 2016.

32. Angela Fritz, "A Political Organization That Doubts Climate Science Is Sending This Book to 200,000 Teachers," *Washington Post*, March 29, 2017.

33. Scott Jaschik, "Liberal Indoctrination? Not So Much," *Inside Higher Ed*, February 5, 2018.

34. Anthony Carnevale, "The Role of Education in Taming Authoritarian Attitudes," Georgetown Center on Higher Education and the Workforce, October 2020 (in collaboration with Lenka Druzanova, author of *Education and Tolerance*, 2017), https://cew.georgetown.edu/cew-reports/authoritarianism.

35. David Foster Wallace, "This Is Water," 2005 talk to the graduating class of Kenyon College, Farnan Street, https://fs.blog/2012/04/david-foster-wallace-this-is-water.

36. Neil Gross, "The Indoctrination Myth," *New York Times*, March 4, 2012. He notes that "the tendency of college graduates to be more liberal reflects to a large extent the fact that more liberal students are more likely to go to college in the first place" and finds that attending college tends to make students more moderate, not more extreme. See also Aaron Hanlon, "Lies about the Humanities—and the Lying Liars Who Tell Them," *Chronicle of Higher Education*, December 7, 2018. Naomi Oreskes and Charlie Tyson quote Ashley Montague, "reality has a well-known liberal bias," rephrasing it to "conservatives have become biased against reality. Until the right faces reality it will have trouble winning over anyone who pays attention to evidence—as of course all good professors do." Oreskes and Tyson, "Reactionary Propaganda Rides Again: Is Academe Biased against Conservatives? No: Reality Is," *Chronicle of Higher Education*, October 12, 2020.

37. The 2007 study by Matthew Woessner and April Kelly-Woessner, "Left Pipeline: Why Conservatives Don't Get Doctorates," is summarized by Scott Jaschik, "Professors and Politics: What the Research Says," *Inside Higher Ed*, February 27, 2017. Norman Bradburn and Robert Townsend, "Use Data to Make a Strong Case for the Humanities," *Chronicle of Higher Education*, November 27, 2016, note, "Those whose

goal in life is to make a lot of money turn away from the humanities. Data from the Department of Education's most recent Baccalaureate and Beyond Longitudinal Study show that humanities majors tend to be less materialistic than their peers. . . . Humanities majors are much more likely to end up in jobs that are essential to society—such as teaching—but which are traditionally undercompensated." Yet "90% reported satisfaction with their jobs after 10 years."

38. Paulo Freire, *We Make the Road by Walking: Conversations on Education and Social Change*, ed. Brenda Bell, John Gaventa, and John Peters (Temple University Press, 1990), 181.

FOUR: "The Reading Thing"

Epigraph: George Saunders, *A Swim in a Pond in the Rain* (Random House, 2021), 8.

1. Neil Gaiman, "Why Our Future Depends on Libraries, Reading and Daydreaming," *View from the Cheap Seats: Selected Nonfiction* (Morrow, 2016), 13.

2. Oskar Eustis, "What Joseph Papp Got Right," *American Theater*, January 1, 2007.

3. Sheila Heti quoted in Nicole Lamy, "Contemporary Womanhood in Fact and Fiction," *New York Times*, November 28, 2017.

4. Richard Picardi, *Skills of Workplace Communication: A Handbook for T&D Specialists and Their Organizations* (Praeger, 2001). Doreen Carvajal, "Forsooth, Check This Consultant," *New York Times*, December 22, 1999.

5. Thinking back to what he retained from reading online, David Denby recalls "a sliding, unstable mass. I couldn't remember a lot of it. I read it too quickly and jumped ahead." Reading online "dissolves deep concentration." *Lit Up: One Reporter. Three Schools. Twenty-Four Books That Can Change Lives* (Picador, 2017), 57.

6. William Hazlitt, "On the Ignorance of the Learned," *Table-Talk: Essays on Men and Manners*, 1821–22, Project Gutenberg EBook of Table-Talk, https://www.gutenberg.org/files/3020/3020-h/3020-h.htm#link2H_4_0009. The actual quote is: "If we wish to know the force of human genius we should read Shakespeare. If we wish to see the insignificance of human learning we may study his commentators."

7. Walter Kirn describes how, at Princeton, literary theory made reading seem not worth the while. "Thanks to an impression I've gained from certain professors that the Great Books are not as great as advertised (and may indeed be pernicious instruments of social manipulation and oppression), I've done much less reading here than I expected." *Lost in the Meritocracy* (Anchor, 2010), 5. His experience is not untypical.

8. *To Read or Not to Read* (National Endowment for the Arts, 2007), https://www.arts.gov/sites/default/files/ToRead.pdf.

9. Gates to the National Council of State Legislatures, July 2009, Gates Foundation, https://www.gatesfoundation.org/media-center/speeches/2009/07/bill-gates-national-conference-of-state-legislatures-ncsl.

10. Marion Brady, "What Do Standardized Tests Actually Test?," *Washington Post*, August 1, 2014.

11. "Without the Gates money," said the education commissioner of Kentucky, the first state to adopt the standards, "we wouldn't have been able to do this." Lindsey Layton, "How Bill Gates Pulled Off the Common Core Revolution," *Washington Post*, June 7, 2014.

12. David Coleman, "Close Reading of Text: Letter from Birmingham Jail, Martin Luther King, Jr.," Vimeo, https://vimeo.com/27056255.

13. "Analyze Thomas Jefferson's Declaration of Independence," R.I.11-12.9 in Marilee Sprenger, *Teaching the Critical Vocabulary of the Common Core* (ASCD [Association for Supervision and Curriculum Development].org, 2013), 163–64.

14. Simcoe quoted by Alia Wong, "What if America's Teachers Made More Money?," *Atlantic*, February 18, 2016.

15. Maryanne Wolf, *Reader, Come Home: The Reading Brain in a Digital World* (HarperCollins, 2018), 163.

16. Peter Greene, "Outside the Four Corners (or How the Common Core Almost Broke Reading)," *Forbes*, September 23, 2019.

17. "English Language Arts Standards," Common Core State Standards Initiative, http://www.corestandards.org/ELA-Literacy/introduction/key-design-consideration.

18. Michael Godsey, "The Wisdom Deficit in Schools," *Atlantic*, January 22, 2015.

19. Highfill quoted in Lindsey Layton, "Common Core State Standards in English Spark War," *Washington Post*, December 2, 2012.

20. Nora de la Cour, "Abolish High-Stakes Testing," On One, https://onone.substack.com/p/abolish-high-stakes-testing.

21. Teacher quoted by Perry Chiaramonte, "Teachers Complain Common Core-Linked Lessons Little More Than Scripts to Read," Fox News Channel, December 8, 2018.

22. "I don't want to be a teacher anymore," said a teacher, anonymous, quoted in Valerie Strauss, "Teacher Slams Scripted Common Core Lessons That Must Be Taught 'Word for Word,'" *Washington Post*, November 30, 2013.

23. Dana Goldstein, "'It Just Isn't Working': PISA Test Scores Cast Doubt on U.S. Education Efforts," *New York Times*, December 3, 2019.

24. Sara H. Konrath, Edward H. O'Brien, and Courtney Hsing, "Changes in Dispositional Empathy in American College Students over Time: A Meta-Analysis," *Personality and Social Psychology Review* 15, no. 2 (2011): 180–98.

25. John Keats, letter to his brothers, December 22, 1817, Project Gutenberg EBook, *Letters of John Keats to His Family and Friends*, ed. Sidney Colvin, https://www.gutenberg.org/files/35698/35698-h/35698-h.htm.

26. Sandeep Jauhar, "Empathy Gadgets," *New York Times*, July 30, 2017.

27. Rita Charon quoted by Scott Jaschik, "To See the Suffering," *Inside Higher Ed*, October 16, 2018.

28. "Teaching narrative medicine and clinical empathy has improved outcomes and reduced the risk of malpractice suits." Traci Carlson, "Humanities and Business Go Hand in Hand," *Boston Globe*, April 25, 2016.

29. "Active listening" is "our most underutilized tool in solving complex social problems," said an international kidnapping negotiator in the FBI. Christian Madsbjerg, *Sensemaking: The Power of the Humanities in the Age of the Algorithm* (Hachette Books, 2017), 175.

30. In *The Better Angels of Our Nature: Why Violence Has Declined* (Viking, 2011), 586–87, Pinker describes a study by C. D. Batson et al., "Empathy and Attitudes: Can Feeling for a Member of a Stigmatized Group Improve Feelings toward the Group?," *Journal of Personality & Social Psychology* 72 (1997): 105–18.

31. Nicholson Baker, *Substitute: Going to School with a Thousand Kids* (Penguin, 2017), 472–73.

32. Henry Giroux, "The Politics of Disimagination and the Pathologies of Power," *Truthout*, February 27, 2013. Giroux attributes the term to Georges Didi-Huberman, *Images in Spite of All: Four Photographs from Auschwitz*, trans. Shane B. Lillis (University of Chicago Press, 2008), 1–2.

33. Walter quoted in "Up Front," by the Editors, *New York Times*, February 24, 2013.

34. Maryanne Wolf suggests that "critical analysis, empathy, and other deep reading processes could become the unintended "collateral damage" of our digital culture. "Skim Reading Is the New Normal," *Guardian*, August 25, 2018.

FIVE: The Play's the Thing

Epigraphs: "Let my playing be my learning" is widely attributed to Johan Huizinga, *Homo Ludens: A Study of the Play-Element in Culture* (1938; rpt., Beacon, 1971), though I can't find it and neither can anyone else. I've also seen it attributed to Friedrich Schiller, *On the Aesthetic Education of Man*, though I can't find it there either. Nancy Carlsson-Paige, "How 'Twisted' Early Childhood Education Has Become—from a Child Development Expert," *Washington Post*, November 24, 2015.

1. George Bernard Shaw quoted in Dana Aspinall, "The Play and the Critics," in *The Taming of the Shrew: Critical Essays*, ed. Dana Aspinall (Garland, 2001), 3–40.

2. Stuart Brown with Christopher Vaughan, *Play: How It Shapes the Brain, Opens the Imagination, and Invigorates the Soul* (Avery, 2010), 21–24. In a TED talk, Brown shows slides of the polar bear and the husky and comments that they're "in an altered state, they are in a state of play, and it's this state that allows these two creatures to explore the possible," illustrating "how a differential in

power can be overridden by a process of nature that's in all of us" (https://www .ted.com/talks/stuart_brown_play_is_more_than_just_fun?language=en).

3. Andrew Kay, "Jokes Over, Academics Are Too Scared to Laugh," *Chronicle of Higher Education*, March 14, 2018.

4. Samuel Taylor Coleridge, *Biographia Literaria*, chap. 15, Project Gutenberg, https://www.gutenberg.org/files/6081/6081-h/6081-h.htm.

5. Marianne Novy, "Patriarchy and Play in *The Taming of the Shrew*," *English Literary Renaissance* 9 (1979): 264–80.

6. John Keats, letter to his brothers, December 22, 1817, Project Gutenberg EBook, *Letters of John Keats to His Family and Friends*, ed. Sidney Colvin, https://www.gutenberg.org/files/35698/35698-h/35698-h.htm.

7. F. Scott Fitzgerald, "The Crack-Up," *Esquire,* February, March, and April 1936, https://www.esquire.com/lifestyle/a4310/the-crack-up.

8. Norman Rabkin, *Shakespeare and the Common Understanding* (Free Press, 1967).

9. Stanley Fish, *Surprised by Sin: The Reader in "Paradise Lost"* (Harvard University Press, 1967).

10. Brian Boyd, *On the Origin of Stories: Evolution, Cognition, Fiction* (Belknap Press, 2010). All animals that have been studied "grow more neural tissue" in environments where they've had "more friends, toys, ladders, and wheels to play with" (92–93).

11. Joan Almon, former chair of the Waldorf Early Childhood Association of North America, "The Vital Role of Play in Early Childhood Education," Research Institute for Waldorf Education, https://www.waldorfresearchinstitute.org/pdf /BAPlayAlmon.pdf.

12. Peter Gray, *Free to Learn* (Basic Books, 2012), 18, 40.

13. Martha Nussbaum, *Not for Profit: Why Democracy Needs the Humanities* (Princeton University Press, 2010), 101, 109.

14. Huizinga, *Homo Ludens*, 8.

15. Alison Gopnik, *The Gardener and the Carpenter* (Picador, 2016), 169.

16. Carlsson-Paige, "How 'Twisted' Early Childhood Education Has Become."

17. Susan Sluyter, "My Job Is Now about Tests and Data—Not Children. I Quit," *Washington Post*, March 23, 2014.

18. Noam Chomsky, "On Democracy and Education in the 21st Century and Beyond," interview by Daniel Falcone, *Truthout*, June 1, 2013.

19. Steven Horwitz, "Cooperation over Coercion: The Importance of Childhood Play for Democracy and Liberalism," Cosmos + Taxis, November 2015, https:// cosmosandtaxis.files.wordpress.com/2015/11/horwitz.pdf.

20. Nussbaum, *Not for Profit*, 101, draws on Donald Winnicott, *Playing and Reality* (Routledge, 2005), originally published 1971.

21. Boyd, *On the Origin of Stories*, 85–86, 49–50.

22. Peter Gray, *Free to Learn*, 136–37.

23. Coleridge, *Biographia Literaria*, chap. 14, https://www.gutenberg.org/files /6081/6081-h/6081-h.htm.

24. Ben Kingsley, "The Architecture of Ideas," in *Living with Shakespeare: Essays by Writers, Actors, and Directors,* ed. Susannah Carson (Vintage, 2013), 54–55, 53.

25. Marilynne Robinson, "What Are We Doing Here?" *New York Review of Books*, November 9, 2017.

26. Ayad Akhtar, "An Antidote to Digital Dehumanization? Live Theater," *New York Times*, December 29, 2017.

27. Kingsley, "Architecture of Ideas," 55.

28. "Kate in Hartford," comment on Gary Gutting, "The Real Crisis of the Humanities," *New York Times*, December 1, 2013.

29. Dacher Keltner, *Born to Be Good: The Science of a Meaningful Life* (Norton, 2019), 259–60.

30. Boyd, *On the Origin of Stories*, 124.

31. Zoe Tidman, "Gavin Williamson Criticised for 'Galling' Comment on 'Dead-End' University Courses," *Independent*, May 17, 2021.

32. Sarah Cassidy, "School's Results Go from Bottom to Top, Thanks to Shakespeare," *Guardian*, June 21, 2016; and Annie Holmquist, "Studying Shakespeare Brings School 40% Jump in Test Scores," *Intellectual Takeout*, June 21, 2016.

33. *The Hobart Shakespeareans* (film), Wikipedia, https://en.wikipedia.org/wiki /The_Hobart_Shakespeareans.

34. Michael Roth, "A Place in the Classroom for Faith," *Wall Street Journal*, February 20, 2015.

35. Andrew Delbanco, *College: What It Was, Is, and Should Be* (Princeton University Press, 2012), 60.

36. Noam Chomsky, "Interview with Noam Chomsky on Education," by Arianne Robichaud, March 26, 2013, Chomsky.info, https://chomsky.info/20130326.

six: Teaching Is an Art, Not an Algorithm

Epigraphs: Joseph Epstein, "Who Killed the Liberal Arts?," *Washington Examiner*, from the archives of the *Weekly Standard*, September 17, 2012, https://www .washingtonexaminer.com/weekly-standard/who-killed-the-liberal-arts; David Labaree, "Targeting Teachers," in *Public Education under Siege*, ed. Michael Katz and Mike Rose (University of Pennsylvania Press, 2003), 34–35; and Parker Palmer, *The Courage to Teach: Exploring the Inner Landscape of a Teacher's Life* (John Wiley & Sons, 1998), 17.

1. Mike Rose, *Possible Lives: The Promise of Public Education in America* (Penguin, 1995), 419.

2. Palmer, *The Courage to Teach*, 137–38.

3. Noam Chomsky, "Interview with Noam Chomsky on Education," by Arianne Robichaud, March 26, 2013, Chomsky.info, https://chomsky.info/20130326.

4. Vanessa Rodriguez with Michelle Fitzpatrick, *The Teaching Brain: An Evolutionary Trait at the Heart of Education* (New Press, 2014), 72.

5. Jerry Muller, "The Costs of Accountability," *American Interest* 11, no. 1 (August 3, 2015).

6. Glass quoted in Rebecca Mead, "The Scourge of 'Relatability,'" *New Yorker*, August 1, 2014.

7. Toni Morrison, *Sula* (Knopf, 1973), 52.

8. David Brooks, "Students Learn from People They Love," *New York Times*, January 18, 2018.

9. Maxine Hong Kingston, *The Woman Warrior: Memoirs of a Girlhood among Ghosts* (Knopf, 1976), 19.

10. David Brooks, *The Second Mountain: The Quest for a Moral Life* (Random House, 2019), 194–95.

11. Doug Lemov, paraphrased by David Brooks, "Changing Skill Sets for a Changing World," Straitstimes.com, March 19, 2015, https://www.straitstimes .com/opinion/changing-skill-sets-for-a-changing-world.

12. Bill Gates, "Teachers Need Real Feedback," TED Talks Education, May 2013, https://www.ted.com/talks/bill_gates_teachers_need_real_feedback ?language=en.

13. Ryan Fuller, "Teaching Isn't Rocket Science. It's Harder," *Slate*, December 18, 2013.

14. Bob Shepherd, "The Hard Work of Teaching," Diane Ravitch's blog, July 5, 2015, http://dianeravitch.net/2015/07/05/bob-shepherd-the-hard-work-of-teaching.

15. Frank McCourt, *Teacher Man* (Scribner, 2005), 10.

16. Rita Pierson, "Every Kid Needs a Champion," TED Talks, May 3, 2013, https://www.youtube.com/watch?v=SFnMTHhKdkw&ab_channel=TED.

17. Andrew Delbanco, *College: What It Was, Is, and Should Be* (Princeton University Press, 2012), 48.

18. Edward Said, personal communication.

19. Mark Edmundson, *Why Read?* (Bloomsbury, 2004), 90–91.

20. Palmer, *The Courage to Teach*, 122.

21. Rylance quoted in Ben Brantley, "How Mark Rylance Became Olivia Onstage," *New York Times*, August 15, 2016.

22. McCourt, *Teacher Man*, 11, 19, 73, 190, 207.

23. Bill Ayers, *To Teach: The Journey of a Teacher* (Teachers College Press, 2010), 136–37.

24. Sarah Blaine, "You Think You Know What Teachers Do. Right? Wrong," *Washington Post*, February 2, 2014.

25. Douglas Rushkoff, *Team Human* (Norton, 2019), 48.

26. Frank McCourt, interviewed in *"Only" a Teacher*, PBS, http://www.pbs.org /onlyateacher/today8.html.

27. Rose, *Possible Lives*, 418–19.

28. Diane Ravitch, *Reign of Error: The Hoax of the Privatization Movement and the Danger to America's Public Schools* (Knopf Doubleday, 2013), 143, 132.

29. Richard Culatta quoted in Jeffrey Young, "Buzzwords May Be Stifling Teaching Innovation at Colleges," *Chronicle of Higher Education*, August 26, 2015.

30. Vanessa Rodriguez with Michelle Fitzpatrick, *The Teaching Brain: An Evolutionary Trait at the Heart of Education* (New Press, 2014), 69–71.

SEVEN: De-grading the Professors

Epigraphs: Reader's comment on Erik Gilbert, "Does Assessment Make Colleges Better? Who Knows?," *Chronicle of Higher Education*, August 14, 2014; and Laurie Fendrich, "A Pedagogical Straitjacket," *Chronicle of Higher Education*, June 8, 2007.

1. Caroline Fredrickson, "There Is No Excuse for How Universities Treat Adjuncts," *Atlantic,* September 15, 2019. She notes, "Administrative salaries rose at public institutions 75% between 1978 and 2013 and 170% at private institutions." Also, Matt Saccaro, "Professors on Food Stamps: The Shocking True Story of Academia in 2014," *Salon*, September 21, 2014.

2. Reader comment on Erik Gilbert, "Why Assessment Is a Waste of Time," *Inside Higher Ed*, November 11, 2016.

3. Reader comment on Gilbert, "Does Assessment Make Colleges Better?"

4. Steven Brint, *Two Cheers for Higher Education* (Princeton University Press, 2018), 310–12, gives a detailed account of how higher education got saddled with outcomes assessment.

5. Diane Ravitch, "Common Core Standards: Past, Present, Future," MLA Profession, January 11, 2014, https://profession.mla.org/common-core-standards -past-present-future. This was followed by a warning from Catharine Stimpson, "Beware, Be Wary," MLA Profession, January 2014, https://profession.mla.org /beware-be-wary.

6. Paul Horton, "Common Core Standards Are the Tip of a Corporate Iceberg," *Chronicle of Higher Education*, June 30, 2014.

7. Michael Stratford, "Challenges of an Accreditor Crack-Down," *Inside Higher Ed*, November 17, 2015.

8. Clifford Adelman, *To Imagine a Verb: The Language and Syntax of Learning Outcomes Statements*, Occasional Paper No. 24 (University of Illinois and Indiana University, National Institute for Learning Outcomes Assessment, 2015), https://files.eric.ed.gov/fulltext/ED555528.pdf.

9. Frank Furedi, "The Unhappiness Principle," *Times Higher Education*, November 29, 2012.

10. Garret Keizer, *Getting Schooled: The Reeducation of an American Teacher* (Metropolitan Books, 2014), 3. Keizer gives a vivid sense of his school's "almost insatiable thirst for 'data,'" citing a "productivity rubric," a "two page spread-sheet" designed by a faculty committee "that defines the meaning for each

criterion of 'productivity'—what distinguishes a 3 for behavior from a 2, for instance—and also attempts to reduce the vexing overlap between categories like 'initiative' and 'responsibility.'" Keizer criticizes this as "trying to mask the ambiguities of evaluating student performance by a pretense of rigorous objectivity" (87–88) and feels like he's "increasingly devoting more time to the generation and recording of data and less time to the educational substance of what the data is supposed to measure," like a man who spends more time "counting his money" than earning it (52).

11. Eubanks quoted in Erik Gilbert, "An Insider's Take on Assessment: It May Be Worse Than You Thought," *Chronicle of Higher Education*, January 12, 2018.

12. Stefan Collini, *What Are Universities For?* (Penguin, 2012), 108.

13. Christopher Nelson, "Assessing Assessment," *Inside Higher Ed*, November 24, 2014.

14. Natasha Jankowski et al., *Assessment That Matters: Trending toward Practices That Document Authentic Student Learning*, report by the National Institute for Learning Outcomes Assessment, January 2018, https://files.eric.ed .gov/fulltext/ED590514.pdf.

15. S. Robert Shireman, "SLO Madness," *Inside Higher Ed*, April 7, 2016.

16. The first two comments are to Gilbert, "Does Assessment Make Colleges Better?" The third is to Scott Hippensteel, "Be Hard to Get Along With," *Chronicle of Higher Education*, October 12, 2013.

17. Comments have been removed from most *Chronicle of Higher Education* and *Inside Higher Ed* articles, so some are untraceable.

18. Robert Shireman, "The Real Value of What Students Do in College," Century Foundation, February 21, 2016, https://tcf.org/content/report/the-real -value-of-what-students-do-in-college.

19. Gordon Hutner and Feisal Mohamed, eds., *A New Deal for the Humanities: Liberal Arts and the Future of Public Higher Education* (Rutgers University Press, 2016), 1–17; 7.

20. Lamott quoted in Bruce Feiler, "The United States of Metrics," *New York Times*, May 18.

21. Frank Furedi, "Learning Outcomes Are Corrosive," *CAUT/ACPPU Bulletin Online—Canada's Voice for Academics* 60, no. 1 (January 2013), https://chalkdot.files.wordpress.com/2013/01/furedi_learning_objectives _corrosive.pdf.

22. John Powell, "Outcomes Assessment: Conceptual and Other Problems," *AAUP Journal of Academic Freedom* 2 (2011), https://www.aaup.org/sites/default /files/Powell.pdf.

23. Laurie Fendrich, "You Will Be Held Accountable," *Chronicle of Higher Education*, February 10, 2009.

24. Jankowski quoted by Doug Lederman, "Harsh Take on Assessment . . . from Assessment Pros," *Inside Higher Ed*, April 17, 2019.

25. Gilbert, "An Insider's Take on Assessment."

26. Jerry Muller, "The Tyranny of Metrics," *Chronicle of Higher Education*, January 21, 2018; my emphasis.

27. Joe Palermo, "Reclaiming the Master Plan for Higher Education in California," *HuffPost*, September 26, 2015.

28. Mark Hulsether, "Assessment: Turning the Precious Public Resource of a University into a Second-Rate High School," *Academe*, March 7, 2018.

29. Collini, *What Are Universities For?*, 151–53.

30. Furedi, "Learning Outcomes Are Corrosive."

31. Alka Cuthbert, "What Happened to the Caring Professions?," *Independent*, October 29, 2012.

32. David Labaree interviewed by Scott Jaschik, "A Perfect Mess," *Inside Higher Ed*, May 3, 2017.

33. John Warner, "An Education Necessity: Mind Blowing Experiences," *Inside Higher Ed*, July 26, 2015.

34. Richard Feynman, "The Value of Science," in *The Pleasure of Finding Things Out: The Best Short Works of Richard P. Feynman*, ed. Jeffrey Robbins (Perseus, 1999), 146, 149, 112.

35. Powell, "Outcomes Assessment."

36. Richard Eldridge, "What Was Liberal Education?," *Los Angeles Review of Books*, January 21, 2018.

37. Jerry Muller, "A Cure for Our Fixation on Metrics," *Wall Street Journal*, January 12, 2018.

38. Fredrik deBoer, "Why We Should Fear University, Inc.," *New York Times*, September 13, 2015.

39. David Graeber, *Bullshit Jobs: A Theory* (Simon and Schuster, 2018), 55.

40. Andrew Hacker, "The Frenzy about High-Tech Talent," *New York Review*, July 9, 2015.

41. John McCumber, "How Humanities Can Help Fix the World," *Chronicle of Higher Education*, October 2, 2016.

42. Tarak Barkawi, "The Neoliberal Assault on Academia," *Al Jazeera*, April 24, 2013.

43. Simon Head, "The Grim Threat to British Universities," *New York Review*, January 13, 2011.

44. Collini, *What Are Universities For?*, 19.

45. Christopher Newfield, *Unmaking the Public University* (Harvard University Press, 2008), 258, 356; my emphasis.

46. Karin Fischer, "A Grand Plan for Public Higher Education Is Aging: Can It Be Reinvented?," *Chronicle of Higher Education*, April 4, 2018.

47. John Thompson, review of *Who's Afraid of the Big Bad Dragon?*, by Yong Zhao, Living in Dialogue, February 8, 2015, http://www.livingindialogue.com /yong-zhaos-whos-afraid-big-bad-dragon-wake-us.

48. Christian Smith, "Higher Ed Is Drowning in BS," *Chronicle of Higher Education*, January 9, 2018; my emphasis.

49. Stefan Collini, *Speaking of Universities* (Verso, 2017), 41.

50. Nicholas Tampio, "Gates Launches Lobbying Arm—Higher Education on Agenda," *Conversation*, June 26, 2019, https://theconversation.com/gates-launches-lobbying-arm-higher-education-on-agenda-119077. "By launching a 501(c)(4) nonprofit, also known as a social welfare group, the Gateses can now talk directly with legislators about laws."

51. Gates Foundation, *Equitable Value: Promoting Economic Mobility and Social Justice through Postsecondary Education*, May 2021, https://www.postsecondaryvalue.org/wp-content/uploads/2021/05/PVC-Final-Report-FINAL.pdf.

52. Nicholas Tampio, "New Gates-Funded Commission Aims to Put a Value on a College Education," *Conversation*, May 16, 2019, https://theconversation.com/new-gates-funded-commission-aims-to-put-a-value-on-a-college-education-116930.

53. So says the Gates Foundation website, along with lots more verbiage: "strengthening the metrics available to gauge equitable student outcomes and institutional performance; the systems for gathering and reporting those metrics; and policies and practices around using these metrics to take action." "U.S. Program: Data and Information," https://usprogram.gatesfoundation.org/what-we-do/postsecondary-success/data-and-information.

54. The phrase "visually engaging slide decks and graphics" is in the report's own description. The Gates Foundation has made a huge investment in this effort, including a series of slick YouTube videos on the foundation's website, as well as webinars and podcasts and cheerleading articles in respected journals. Postsecondary Value Commission, "Defining Value" and "Measuring Value," YouTube, https://www.youtube.com/watch?v=CwUIcI2H7nY&ab_channel=GatesFoundation.

55. Anthony Carnevale, "The Revolution Is upon Us," *Inside Higher Ed*, March 26, 2019.

56. Itzkowitz quoted by Andrew Kreighbaum, "Beefing Up the College Scorecard," *Inside Higher Ed*, May 22, 2019.

57. In *Free City! The Fight for San Francisco's City College and Education for All* (PM Press, 2021), Marcy Rein, Mickey Ellinger, and Vicki Legion recount the five-year struggle of City College to remain open against an accreditation board's attempt to close it, on the basis of SLOs, no less. This account "connects the dots between the neoliberal assault on K–12 schools and the downsizing and corporate makeover of community colleges," writes Pauline Lipman in the foreword; it traces the assault to "the same cabal of billionaire venture philanthropists and corporate foundations . . . that's engineering the remake of K–12 public education" (xi–xii). The "restructuring" of City College was an attempt to curb the community mission

of this vast complex that served more than 90,000 students, to focus on career and technical training. Activists and students won an inspiring battle to keep it open, against losses of a third of its full-time faculty and 23,000 students; and the war goes on.

58. Richard Drury, "Community Colleges in America: A Historical Perspective," *Inquiry* 8, no. 1 (Spring 2003).

59. For the liveliest accounts of the erosion of democracy in the past half-century, see Kurt Andersen's *Evil Geniuses: The Unmaking of America* (Random House, 2020); and Robert Reich's *The System: Who Rigged It, How We Fix It* (Knopf, 2020).

60. Eric Kelderman, "MacKenzie Scott Donates Millions More to 30 'Overlooked' Colleges," *Chronicle of Higher Education*, June 15, 2021. "Higher education is a proven pathway to opportunity," she wrote in a blog post announcing the gifts, "so we looked for two- and four-year institutions successfully educating students who come from communities that have been chronically underserved."

61. John Warner, "Bill Gates, Please Stay away from Higher Education," *Inside Higher Ed*, June 28, 2019.

62. Loveless quoted by Nick Anderson, "Bill and Melinda Gates Foundation Help Hillsborough Schools More Than Any," *Washington Post*, July 15, 2011.

EIGHT: Growing Up Human

1. My readings of these plays have been indelibly stamped by humanist critics I read when I was young, old chestnuts like Robert Heilman's *This Great Stage: Image and Structure in "King Lear"* (University of Washington Press, 1963); Maynard Mack, "The World of *Hamlet*," *Yale Review* 41 (1951–52): 502–23; and Mack, *King Lear in Our Time* (University of California Press, 1972). I had run-ins with both Heilman and Mack, neither of whom had any use for feminist criticism—that's another story—but their writings opened up the plays for me. Also, *Shakespeare in a Changing World*, ed. Arnold Kettle (Lawrence & Wishart, 1964), particularly essays by Robert Weimann, "The Soul of the Age," 17–42; Victor Kiernan, "Human Relationships in Shakespeare," 43–64; and Kettle, "From *Hamlet* to *Lear*," 146–71. Also, Margot Heinemann, "Demystifying the Mystery of State: *King Lear* and the World Upside Down," *Shakespeare Survey* 44 (1992): 75–83; reprinted in *King Lear, Norton Critical Edition*, ed. Grace Ioppolo (Norton, 2008), 227–40; Robert Weimann, *Shakespeare and the Popular Tradition in the Theater: Studies in the Social Dimension of Dramatic Form and Function* (Johns Hopkins University Press, 1978); and Norman Rabkin, *Shakespeare and the Common Understanding* (Free Press, 1967).

2. Ernest Jones, "The Oedipus-Complex as an Explanation of Hamlet's Mystery: A Study in Motive," *American Journal of Psychology* 21 (January 1910), expanded into *Hamlet and Oedipus* (1949).

3. Mack, *King Lear in Our Time*, 7. Mack cites Leo Tolstoy, "On Shakespeare and the Drama (II)," trans. V. Tchertkoff and E. A., *Fortnightly Review* 87, no. 1 (January 1907): 62–67.

4. A. C. Bradley, *Shakespearean Tragedy* (Meridian, 1963), 200.

5. Karl Marx, *Das Capital: A Critique of Political Economy* (1867), vol. 1, trans. Ben Fowkes (Vintage, 1977), 876, quoted in *Rewriting the Renaissance: The Discourses of Sexual Difference in Early Modern Europe*, ed. Margaret Ferguson, Maureen Quilligan, and Nancy Vickers (University of Chicago Press, 1987). See introduction xvii, n.8, and 318, for the beginnings of capitalism and further references.

6. There's another way of looking at Edgar, and at the play itself (there always is with Shakespeare), a view suggested by Stephen Booth, *King Lear, Macbeth, Indefinition, and Tragedy* (Yale University Press, 1983; reissued by Cybereditions, 2001). I've charted a route through *Lear* that works (sort of) in the classroom, but the play doesn't always seem so manageable: there are times it wants to reach up and pull me back down into it, another fathom deep, and I get the vertiginous feeling I had when I first started teaching Shakespeare, there's no bottom here. This is a feeling I try to avoid in the classroom because it makes me incoherent. Booth charges through that barbed wire, demonstrating how "the play pushes inexorably beyond its own identity, rolling across and crushing the very frame-work that enables its audience to endure the otherwise terrifying explosion of all manner of ordinarily indispensable mental contrivances for isolating, limiting, and comprehending" (23). (I stumble on that sentence, but I think that's part of the point.) He faults Edgar for the "hollow but summary-sounding moral" he pronounces on Gloucester's death: *The gods are just, and of our pleasant vices / Make instruments to plague us.* I agree, those lines are pat and inadequate, but so are all the other characters' attempts at summing up: Kent's, *The stars above us, govern our conditions*; Gloucester's, *As flies to wanton boys are we to the gods. They kill us for their sport.* As Booth says, "no system for comprehending" the actions and characters of the play "can hold them" (56). But he hears nothing special in Edgar's final lines, *speak what we feel, not what we ought to say*—and I do. They may not "hold" or sum up the play, but they have a meaning for all time.

7. A story I've told in "Shakespeare's Faust: A Parable of Our Time," in *Thought Work: Thinking, Action, and the Fate of the World*, ed. Elizabeth Minnich and Michael Patton (Rowman and Littlefield, 2019), 109–26.

NINE: Ask a Graduate

Epigraph: Mark Slouka, "Dehumanized: When Math and Science Rule the School," *Atlantic*, September 2009.

1. Plato, *Theaetetus* 148e–151d, Illinois State University, https://www.phy.ilstu.edu/pte/209content/theaetetus.html.

2. David Brooks, *The Second Mountain* (Random House, 2019), 192, 195.

3. Joseph Epstein, "Who Killed the Liberal Arts?"

4. Nick Anderson, "Ken Burns Is Pushing to Save Hampshire College," *Washington Post*, May 3, 2019.

5. Valerie Strauss, "Diane Ravitch to Obama: I Will Never Understand Why You Decided to Align Your Educational Policy with That of George W. Bush," *Washington Post*, June 12, 2016.

6. Andrew Delbanco, *College: What It Was, Is, and Should Be* (Princeton University Press, 2012), 32.

7. Shapiro quoted in David DeVries, "The Consolations of an Occupied Mind," *Chronicle of Higher Education*, June 5, 2016.

8. Adam Falk, "In Defense of the Living, Breathing Professor," *Wall Street Journal*, August 28, 2012.

9. Tamar Lewin, interview with Chambliss, "What Makes a Positive College Experience?," *New York Times*, April 11, 2014. Chambliss adds, "It makes a lasting difference to a student's learning to write if she had at least one experience of sitting down with a professor to go over her work, paragraph by paragraph; it was someone serious saying their writing was important."

10. Daniel Chambliss and Christopher Takacs, *How College Works* (Harvard University Press, 2014), 344, 155.

11. Frank Bruni, "How to Measure a College's Value," *New York Times*, September 12, 2015, cites the Gallup-Purdue Index 2015 Report, "Great Jobs, Great Lives: The Relationship between Student Debt, Experiences, and Perceptions of College Worth."

12. Detweiler quoted in Scott Jaschik, "The Proof Liberal Arts Colleges Need?," *Inside Higher Ed*, January 22, 2016.

13. Aaron Basko, "Have We Gotten Student Success Completely Backward?," *Chronicle of Higher Education*, November 29, 2021.

14. Georgia Nugent, *The Liberal Arts in Action, Past, Present, and Future* (Council of Independent Colleges, 2015), http://webmedia.jcu.edu /institutionaleffectiveness/files/2016/09/Liberal-Arts-in-Action-Symposium-Essay .pdf. Nugent also summarizes a study by the National Survey of Student Engagement that found "a more supportive environment for learning" at small, private colleges than at large public institutions, as well as a "greater exposure to academically challenging experiences, especially with coursework emphasizing higher-order learning and reflection . . . [and] more effort dedicated to studying, writing, and reading, more frequent and high-quality interactions with faculty and exposure to effective teaching practices."

15. Andrew Hacker and Claudia Dreifus, *Higher Education? How Colleges Are Wasting Our Money and Failing Our Kids—and What We Can Do about It* (St. Martin's, 2010), 79.

16. Rebekah Nathan [Cathy Small], *My Freshman Year: What a Professor Learned by Becoming a Student* (Penguin, 2005), 100, 119.

17. Andrew Hacker, "The Truth about the Colleges," *New York Review*, November 3, 2005.

18. Hacker and Dreifus, *Higher Education?*, 79.

19. Summers quoted in Jonathan Zimmerman, *The Amateur Hour: A History of College Teaching in America* (Johns Hopkins University Press, 2020), 232.

20. Susan Blum, *I Love Learning, I Hate School: An Anthropology of College* (Cornell University Press, 2016), 256.

21. George Kuh, director of the National Institute for Learning Outcomes Assessment at Indiana University at Bloomington as well as the founder of the National Survey of Student Engagement, quoted by Jason Jones, "The Endangered Liberal Arts College," *Inside Higher Ed*, April 6, 2015.

22. Sophomore at Hamilton College quoted in Chambliss and Takacs, *How College Works*, 69.

23. "Gavin," alum on Facebook group *Incipit Opus Nova*, February 19, 2020.

24. Hacker, "The Truth about the Colleges."

25. The same study, by the consulting firm Hardwick Day, 2011, found that 87% of students at small liberal arts colleges graduate within four years, as compared with 51% at the flagships.

26. This survey of faculty workplace engagement was conducted by Gallup for *Inside Higher Education*. Colleen Flaherty, "Going through the Motions? The 2015 Survey of Faculty Workplace Engagement," *Inside Higher Ed*, October 23, 2015.

27. Susan McWilliams and John Seery, *The Best Kind of College: An Insider's Guide to America's Small Liberal Arts Colleges* (SUNY Press, 2015), 8.

28. Scott Jaschik, "Study Finds Community Colleges Are the Only Colleges in the World with Growing Humanities," *Inside Higher Ed*, June 14, 2021.

29. Jen Balderama, "Community College Saved My Life. Thank You, Joe Biden, for Trying to Make It Free," *Washington Post*, May 2, 2021. Marcy Rein, Mickey Ellinger, and Vicki Legion give a harrowing account of how City College of San Francisco had to fight for its life against an accreditation board funded by the Gates Foundation. *Free City! The Fight for San Francisco's City College and Education for All* (PM Press, 2021).

30. Matt Reed, "We All Know This Story, and Yet . . ." *Inside Higher Ed*, May 4, 2021.

31. Liberal arts colleges punch way above their weight in the production of PhDs in the sciences, generating twice as many as most institutions. Their graduates compare well to graduates of Ivy League schools and research universities in terms of publications and distinctions. "The classroom and laboratory sessions are more personal, while the broad distribution of nonscience courses promotes the development of critical thinking skills and facility with written and oral communication," writes Thomas Cech, a Nobel Laureate in chemistry with a

BA from Grinnell College. "Science at Liberal Arts Colleges: A Better Education?," *Daedalus* 128, no. 1 (1999): 128–216.

   32. Victor Ferrall, *Liberal Arts at the Brink* (Harvard University Press, 2011), 22.

   33. "Liberal arts graduates disproportionally pursue careers in social service sectors," says Goldie Blumenstyk, *American Higher Education in Crisis? What Everyone Needs to Know* (Oxford University Press, 2014), 144.

   34. Detweiler interviewed in Scott Jaschik, "Author Discusses His Book on Evidence of Value of Liberal Arts," *Inside Higher Ed*, November 18, 2021.

   35. Sean McCoy, "Community, Democracy, and the Liberal Arts," *Imaginative Conservative*, March 2016, http://www.theimaginativeconservative.org/2016/03/community-democracy-liberal-arts.html.

   36. Richard Detweiler, *The Evidence the Liberal Arts Needs: Lives of Consequence, Inquiry, and Accomplishment* (MIT Press, 2021), 76, 74, 19.

   37. Arie Kruglanski, "Psychology Not Theology: Overcoming Isis' Secret Appeal," October 28, 2014, E-International Relations, http://www.e-ir.info/2014/10/28/psychology-not-theology-overcoming-isis-secret-appeal.

   38. Marco Rubio, "This Is a Clash of Civilizations: Either They Win or We Win," YouTube, November 14, 2015, https://www.youtube.com/watch?v=q8qa2ZRaOmc&ab_channel=MarcoRubio.

   39. Anthony Carnevale, in collaboration with Lenka Druzanova, "The Role of Education in Taming Authoritarian Attitudes," Georgetown Center on Higher Education and the Workforce, October 2020, https://cew.georgetown.edu/cew-reports/authoritarianism.

   40. Beckie Supiano, "This College Asks Alumni to Choose Their Own Way to Define Its Value," *Chronicle of Higher Education*, February 24, 2014.

   41. Oncologist quoted in Nugent, *The Liberal Arts in Action, Past, Present, and Future*.

   42. Damon Horowitz, "From Technologist to Philosopher," *Chronicle of Higher Education*, July 17, 2011.

   43. Steve Jobs, Commencement address, Stanford University, June 12, 2005, *Stanford News*, https://news.stanford.edu/2005/06/14/jobs-061505.

   44. David Epstein, *Range: Why Generalists Triumph in a Specialized World* (Riverhead, 2019), 38.

   45. James Engell and Anthony Dangerfield, "Humanities in the Age of Money," *Harvard Magazine*, June 12, 2019.

   46. Maxine Hong Kingston, *The Woman Warrior: Memoirs of a Girlhood among Ghosts* (Knopf, 1976), 19.

   47. Scott Jaschik, "Humanities Graduates Are Happy with Their Lives, Survey Says," *Inside Higher Ed*, November 8, 2021. The survey is *State of the Humanities 2021: Workforce and Beyond* (American Academy of Arts and Sciences, November 2021), https://www.amacad.org/publication/humanities-workforce-beyond.

48. Detweiler, *The Evidence the Liberal Arts Needs*, 161–62. One can hope the statistical evidence he's gleaned from interviews will provide what the title of his book promises; it may help, since "data" is the language policymakers hear. But a liberal arts education (as he well knows) can't be reduced to the simple push-pull system—"push this lever and get this result"—that admissions offices might like. The experience of a liberal arts education, the stories our graduates tell, are as important a measure as Delbanco and Montás suggest and as I hope I've shown.

49. Patrick McGreevy and Chris Megerian, "California Now Has One of the Toughest Equal Pay Laws in the Country," *Los Angeles Times*, October 6, 2016; Alisha Gupta, "Meet the State Senator Shifting California's Workplace Culture," *New York Times*, September 23, 2020.

50. Emily Gillespie and Rachel Siegel, "Oregon Attorney General Sues Federal Agencies for Allegedly Violating Protestors' Civil Rights," *Washington Post*, July 19, 2020.

51. George Eliot, *Middlemarch* (1871–72) (reprint, Riverside, 1958), 613.

52. Douglas Rushkoff, *Team Human* (Norton, 2019), 216.

53. Theodor Adorno, "Education after Auschwitz" (1967), Semantic Scholar, https://www.semanticscholar.org/paper/Education-After-Auschwitz-Adorno/66fea ed4d856efdef4249a23d79c45e74ed61348.

SELECT BIBLIOGRAPHY

Higher Education

Alexander, Bryan. *Academia Next: The Futures of Higher Education*. Johns Hopkins University Press, 2020.

Anders, George. *You Can Do Anything: The Surprising Power of a "Useless" Liberal Arts Education*. Little Brown, 2017.

Arum, Richard, and Jospia Roksa. *Academically Adrift: Limited Learning on College Campuses*. University of Chicago Press, 2011.

Berg, Maggie, and Barbara Seeber. *The Slow Professor: Challenging the Culture of Speed in the Academy*. University of Toronto Press, 2016.

Berlinerblau, Jacques. *Campus Confidential: How College Works, or Doesn't, for Professors, Parents, and Students*. Melville House, 2017.

Berube, Michael. *What's Liberal about the Liberal Arts: Classroom Politics and "Bias" in Higher Education*, Norton, 2006.

Berube, Michael, and Jennifer Ruth. *The Humanities, Higher Education, and Academic Freedom: Three Necessary Arguments*. Palgrave Macmillan, 2015.

Blum, Susan. *I Love Learning, I Hate School: An Anthropology of College*. Cornell University Press, 2016.

Blumenstyk, Goldie. *American Higher Education in Crisis? What Everyone Needs to Know*. Oxford University Press, 2014.

Bok, Derek. *Higher Education in America*. Princeton University Press, 2013.

Brint, Steven. *Two Cheers for Higher Education: Why American Universities Are Stronger Than Ever—and How to Meet the Challenges They Face*. Princeton University Press, 2018.

Brooks, Peter, with Hilary Jewett, eds. *The Humanities and Public Life*. Fordham University Press, 2014.

Chambliss, Daniel, and Christopher Takacs. *How College Works*. Harvard University Press, 2014.

Cole, Jonathan. *The Great American University: Its Rise to Preeminence, Its Indispensable National Role, Why It Must be Protected*. Public Affairs, 2009.

Collini, Stefan. *What Are Universities For?* Penguin, 2012.

———. *Speaking of Universities*. Verso, 2017.

Davidson, Cathy. *The New Education: How to Revolutionize the University to Prepare Students for a World in Flux*. Basic Books, 2017.

Delbanco, Andrew. *College: What It Was, Is, and Should Be*. Princeton University Press, 2012.

Deresiewicz, William. *Excellent Sheep: The Miseducation of the American Elite and the Way to a Meaningful Life*. Simon and Schuster, 2014.

Detweiler, Richard. *The Evidence the Liberal Arts Needs: Lives of Consequence, Inquiry, and Accomplishment*. MIT Press, 2021.

Donoghue, Frank. *The Last Professors: The Corporate University and the Fate of the Humanities*. Fordham University Press, 2008.

Ferrall, Victor, Jr. *Liberal Arts at the Brink*. Harvard University Press, 2011.

Felten Peter, and Leo Lambert. *Relationship-Rich Education: How Human Connections Drive Success in College*. Johns Hopkins University Press, 2020.

Gallagher, Chris. *College Made Whole: Integrative Learning for a Divided World*. Johns Hopkins University Press, 2019.

Ginsberg, Benjamin. *The Fall of the Faculty, the Rise of the All-Administrative University and Why It Matters*. Oxford University Press, 2011.

Gould, Eric. *The University in a Corporate Culture*. Yale University Press, 2003.

Guinier, Lani. *The Tyranny of the Meritocracy: Democratizing Higher Education in America*. Beacon, 2015.

Hacker, Andrew, and Claudia Dreifus. *Higher Education? How Colleges Are Wasting Our Money and Failing Our Kids—and What We Can Do about It*. St. Martin's, 2010.

Harpham, Geoffrey Galt. *What Do You Think, Mr. Ramirez? The American Revolution in Education*. University of Chicago Press, 2017.

Hartley, Scott. *The Fuzzy and the Techie: Why the Liberal Arts Will Rule the Digital World*. Houghton Mifflin Harcourt, 2017.

Hutner, Gordon, and Fiesal Mohamed, eds. *A New Deal for the Humanities: Liberal Arts and the Future of Public Higher Education*. Rutgers University Press, 2015.

Kirp, David L. *Shakespeare, Einstein, and the Bottom Line: The Marketing of Higher Education*. Harvard University Press, 2003.

Kronman, Anthony. *Education's End: Why Our Colleges and Universities Have Given Up on the Meaning of Life*. Yale University Press, 2007.

———. *The Assault on American Excellence*. Free Press, 2019.

Labaree, David. *A Perfect Mess: The Unlikely Ascendency of American Higher Education*. University of Chicago Press, 2017.

Lagemann, Helen, and Harry Lewis. *What Is College For? The Public Purpose of Higher Education*. Teachers College Press, 2011.

Lewis, Harry. *Excellence without a Soul: Does Liberal Education Have a Future?* Public Affairs, 2007.

Madsbjerg, Christian. *Sensemaking: The Power of the Humanities in the Age of the Algorithm.* Hachette Books, 2017.

McWilliams, Susan, and John Seery. *The Best Kind of College: An Insider's Guide to America's Small Liberal Arts Colleges.* SUNY Press, 2015.

Montás, Roosevelt. *How the Great Books Changed My Life and Why They Matter for a New Generation.* Princeton University Press, 2021.

Nathan, Rebekah [Cathy Small]. *My Freshman Year: What a Professor Learned by Becoming a Student.* Penguin, 2005.

Neem, Johann. *What's the Point of College? Seeking Purpose in an Age of Reform.* Johns Hopkins University Press, 2019.

Newfield, Christopher. *Unmaking the Public University: The Forty-Year Assault on the Middle Class.* Harvard University Press, 2008.

———. *The Great Mistake: How We Wrecked Public Universities and How We Can Fix Them.* Johns Hopkins University Press, 2018.

Nussbaum, Martha. *Cultivating Humanity: A Classical Defense of Reform in Liberal Education.* Harvard University Press, 1997.

———. *Not for Profit: Why Democracy Needs the Humanities.* Princeton University Press, 2010.

Readings, Bill. *The University in Ruins.* Harvard University Press, 1996.

Reichman, Henry. *Academic Freedom.* Johns Hopkins University Press, 2019.

Rein, Marcy, Mickey Ellinger, and Vicki Legion. *Free City! The Fight for San Francisco's City College and Education for All.* PM Press, 2021.

Rojstaczer, Stuart. *Gone for Good: Tales of the University Life after the Golden Age.* Oxford University Press, 1999.

Roth, Michael. *Beyond the University: Why Liberal Education Matters.* Yale University Press, 2014.

Rybak, Chuck. *University of Wisconsin Struggle: When a State Attacks Its University.* University of Minnesota Press, 2017.

Schapiro, Morton. *Cents and Sensibility: What Economics Can Learn from the Humanities.* Princeton University Press, 2017.

Schrecker, Ellen. *The Lost Soul of Higher Education: Corporatization, the Assault on Academic Freedom, and the End of the American University.* New Press, 2010.

Scott, Joan. *Knowledge, Power, and Academic Freedom.* Columbia University Press, 2019.

Stross, Randall. *A Practical Education: Why Liberal Arts Majors Make Great Employees.* Redwood Press, 2017.

Tough, Paul. *The Years That Matter Most: How College Makes or Breaks Us.* Houghton Mifflin Harcourt, 2019.

Tuchman, Gaye. *Wannabe U: Inside the Corporate University.* University of Chicago Press, 2009.

Warner, John. *Why They Can't Write: Killing the Five-Paragraph Essay and Other Necessities.* Johns Hopkins University Press, 2018.

———. *Sustainable. Resilient. Free: The Future of Public Higher Education.* Belt Publishing, 2020.

Washburn, Jennifer. *University Inc.: The Corporate Corruption of Higher Education.* Basic Books, 2005.

Williams, Jeffrey. *How to Be an Intellectual: Essays on Criticism, Culture, and the University.* Fordham University Press, 2014.

Zakaria, Fareed. *In Defense of a Liberal Education.* Norton, 2015.

Zimmerman, Jonathan. *The Amateur Hour: A History of College Teaching in America.* Johns Hopkins University Press, 2020.

K–12

Abeles, Vicki, with Grace Rubenstein. *Beyond Measure: Rescuing an Overscheduled, Overtested, Underestimated Generation.* Simon and Schuster, 2015.

Ayers, William. *To Teach: The Journey of a Teacher.* Teachers College Press, 2010.

Blanc, Eric. *Red State Revolt: The Teachers' Strikes and Working-Class Politics.* Verso, 2019.

Burch, Patricia, and Annalee Good. *Equal Scrutiny: Privatization and Accountability in Digital Education.* Harvard Education Press, 2014.

Clement, Joe, and Matt Miles. *Screen Schooled: Two Veteran Teachers Expose How Technology Overuse Is Making Our Kids Dumber.* Chicago Review Press, 2018.

Cody, Antony. *The Educator and the Oligarch: A Teacher Challenges the Gates Foundation.* Garn Press, 2014.

Emery, Kathy, and Susan Ohanian. *Why Is Corporate America Bashing Our Public Schools?* Heinemann, 2004.

Gallagher, Kelly. *Readicide: How Schools Are Killing Reading and What You Can Do about It.* Stenhouse, 2009.

Goyal, Nikhil. *Schools on Trial: How Freedom and Creativity Can Fix Our Educational Malpractice.* Doubleday, 2016.

Greene, Peter. *What Fresh Hell.* CreateSpace Publishing, 2015.

Hagopian, Jesse, ed. *More Than a Score: The New Uprising against High-Stakes Testing.* Haymarket, 2015.

Katz, Michael, and Mike Rose. *Public Education under Siege.* University of Pennsylvania Press, 2003.

Kozol, Jonathan. *Letters to a Young Teacher.* Three Rivers Press, 2007.

———. *On Being a Teacher.* Oneworld Publications, 2009.

———. *Savage Inequalities.* Broadway Books, 2012.

Moulthrop, Daniel, Ninive Clements Calegari, and David Eggars. *Teachers Have It Easy: The Big Sacrifices and Small Salaries of America's Teachers.* New Press, 2005.

Ohanian, Susan. *One Size Fits Few: The Folly of Educational Standards.* Heinemann, 1999.

Olson, Kirsten. *Wounded by School: Recapturing the Joy in Learning and Standing Up to Old School Culture.* Teachers College Press, 2009.

Ravitch, Diane. *Reign of Error: The Hoax of the Privatization Movement and the Danger to America's Public Schools.* Knopf Doubleday, 2013.

———. *The Death and Life of the Great American School System: How Testing and Choice Are Undermining Education.* Basic Books, 2016.

———. *Slaying Goliath: The Passionate Resistance to Privatization and the Fight to Save America's Public Schools.* Knopf, 2020.

Ravitch, Diane, and Nancy Bailey. *EdSpeak and Doubletalk: A Glossary to Decipher Hypocrisy and Save Public Schooling.* Teachers College Press, 2020.

Rodriguez, Vanessa, with Michelle Fitzpatrick. *The Teaching Brain: An Evolutionary Trait at the Heart of Education.* New Press, 2014.

Rose, Mike. *Possible Lives: The Promise of Public Education in America.* Penguin, 1995.

Schneider, Jack, and Jennifer Berkshire. *A Wolf at the Schoolhouse Door: The Dismantling of Public Education and the Future of School.* New Press, 2020.

Schneider, Mercedes. *A Chronicle of Echoes: Who's Who in the Implosion of American Public Education.* Information Age Publishing, 2014.

Tampio, Nicholas. *Common Core: National Education Standards and the Threat to Democracy.* Johns Hopkins University Press, 2018.

Cultural and Political Backgrounds

Andersen, Kurt. *Fantasyland: How America Went Haywire.* Random House, 2017.

———. *Evil Geniuses: The Unmaking of America.* Random House, 2020.

Ball, James. *Post-Truth: How Bullshit Conquered the World.* Biteback Publishing, 2017.

Bauerlein, Mark. *The Dumbest Generation: How the Digital Age Stupefies Young Americans and Jeopardizes Our Future (Or, Don't Trust Anyone under 30).* Jeremy P. Tarcher / Penguin, 2008.

Brown, Wendy. *Undoing the Demos: Neoliberalism's Stealth Revolution.* Zone Books, 2015.

Callahan, David. *The Givers: Wealth, Power, and Philanthropy in a New Gilded Age.* Vintage, 2018.

Carr, Nicholas. *The Shallows: What the Internet Is Doing to Our Brains.* Norton, 2010.

———. *The Glass Cage: Automation and Us.* Norton, 2014.

Coles, Gerald. *Miseducating for the Global Economy: How Corporate Power Damages Education and Subverts Students' Futures.* Monthly Review Press, 2018.

Colvin, Geoff. *Humans Are Underrated: What High Achievers Know That Brilliant Machines Never Will*. Penguin, 2015.

Edwards, Michael. *Small Change: Why Business Won't Save the World*. Demos, 2008.

Egginton, William. *The Splintering of the American Mind: Identity Politics, Inequality, and Community on Today's College Campuses*. Bloomsbury, 2018.

Fraser, Steve. *The Age of Acquiescence: The Life and Death of American Resistance to Organized Wealth and Power*. Basic Books, 2015.

Giridharadas, Anand. *Winners Take All: The Elite Charade of Changing the World*. Random House, 2018.

Giroux, Henry. *Zombie Politics and Culture in the Age of Casino Capitalism*. Peter Lang, 2011.

———. *America's Educational Deficit and the War on Youth*. Monthly Review Press, 2013.

———. *Neoliberalism's War on Higher Education*. Haymarket, 2014.

Graeber, David. *Bullshit Jobs: A Theory*. Simon and Schuster, 2018.

Hacker, Andrew. *The Math Myth and Other STEM Delusions*. New Press, 2016.

Hari, Jonathan. *The Lost Connections: Uncovering the Real Causes of Depression and the Unexpected Solutions*. Bloomsbury, 2018.

Hayes, Chris. *The Twilight of the Elites: America after Meritocracy*. Penguin, 2012.

Head, Simon. *Mindless: Why Smarter Machines Are Making Dumber Humans*. Basic Books, 2014.

Hedges, Chris. *Empire of Illusion: The End of Literacy and the Triumph of Spectacle*. Nation Books, 2009.

———. *Death of the Liberal Class*. Nation Books, 2010.

Herbert, Bob. *Losing Our Way: An Intimate Portrait of a Troubled America*. Penguin, 2014.

Hess, Frederick, ed. *With the Best of Intentions: How Philanthropy Is Reshaping K-12 Education*. Harvard Education Press, 2005.

Jacoby, Susan. *The Age of American Unreason*. Pantheon, 2008.

Kakutani, Michiko. *The Death of Truth: Notes on Falsehood in the Age of Trump*. Tim Duggan Books, 2018.

Keltner, Dacher. *Born to Be Good: The Science of a Meaningful Life*. Norton, 2019.

Klein, Naomi. *Shock Doctrine: The Rise of Disaster Capitalism*. Picador, 2007.

Lafer, Gordon. *The One Percent Solution: How Corporations Are Remaking America One State at a Time*. Cornell University Press, 2017.

Lanier, Jaron. *You Are Not a Gadget*. Vintage, 2010.

Lukianoff, Greg, and Jonathan Haidt. *The Coddling of the American Mind: How Good Intentions and Bad Ideas Are Setting Up a Generation for Failure*. Penguin, 2018.

Lynch, Michael Patrick. *The Internet of Us: Knowing More and Understanding Less in the Age of Big Data*. Norton, 2016.

Mayer, Jane. *Dark Money: The Hidden History of the Billionaires behind the Rise of the Radical Right.* Anchor Books, 2016.

McGoey, Linsey. *No Such Thing as a Free Gift: The Gates Foundation and the Price of Philanthropy.* Verso, 2016.

Monbiot, George. *How Did We Get into This Mess? Politics, Equality, Nature.* Verso, 2016.

Neiman, Susan. *Why Grow Up? Subversive Thoughts for an Infantile Age.* Farrar, Strauss, Giroux, 2014.

Pink, Daniel. *Drive: The Surprising Truth about What Motivates Us.* Riverhead, 2009.

Postman, Neil. *Amusing Ourselves to Death.* Penguin, 1986.

———. *The End of Education.* Vintage, 1996.

Rushkoff, Douglas. *Team Human,* Norton, 2019.

Stiglitz, Joseph. *The Price of Inequality: How Today's Divided Society Endangers Our Future.* Norton, 2012.

Turkle, Sherry. *Alone Together: Why We Expect More from Technology and Less from Each Other.* Basic Books, 2011.

———. *Reclaiming Conversation.* Penguin, 2015.

Shakespeare

Bloom, Harold. *Shakespeare and the Invention of the Human.* Riverhead, 1999.

Booth, Stephen. *King Lear, Macbeth, Indefinition, and Tragedy.* Cybereditions, 2001.

Carson, Susannah, ed. *Living with Shakespeare: Essays by Writers, Actors, and Directors.* Vintage, 2012.

Garber, Marjorie. *Shakespeare After All.* Pantheon, 2004.

Heilman, Robert. *This Great Stage: Image and Structure in "King Lear."* University of Washington Press, 1963.

Kettle, Arnold, ed. *Shakespeare in a Changing World.* Lawrence & Wishart, 1964.

Mack, Maynard. *King Lear in Our Time.* University of California Press, 1972.

McGinn, Colin. *Shakespeare's Philosophy: Discovering the Meaning Behind the Plays.* HarperPerennial, 2006.

Montrose, Louis. *The Purpose of Playing: Shakespeare and the Cultural Politics of the Elizabethan Theater.* University of Chicago Press, 1996.

Newstok, Scott. *How to Think like Shakespeare: Lessons from a Renaissance Education.* Princeton University Press, 2020.

Palfrey, Simon, and Tiffany Stern. *Shakespeare in Parts.* Oxford University Pres, 2007.

Rabkin, Norman, *Shakespeare and the Common Understanding.* Free Press, 1967.

Shapiro, James. *1599: A Year in the Life of Shakespeare.* Harper Collins, 2006.

———. *1606: The Year of Lear.* Simon and Schuster, 2015.

Smith, Emma. *This Is Shakespeare*. Pantheon, 2019.

Southworth, John. *Shakespeare the Player: A Life in the Theater*. Sutton, 2000.

Weimann, Robert. *Shakespeare and the Popular Tradition in the Theater: Studies in the Social Dimension of Dramatic Form and Function*. Johns Hopkins University Press, 1978.

Wells, Robin Headlam. *Shakespeare's Humanism*. Cambridge University Press, 2005.

Stories, Reading

Alter, Robert. *The Pleasures of Reading in an Ideological Age*. Norton, 1989, 1996.

De Botton, Alain. *How Proust Can Change Your Life*. Vintage, 1997.

Denby, David. *Lit Up: One Reporter. Three Schools. Twenty-Four Books That Can Change Lives*. Picador, 2017.

Edmundson, Mark. *Why Read?* Bloomsbury, 2004.

Gottschall, Jonathan. *The Storytelling Animal: How Stories Make Us Human*. Mariner, 2012.

Quindlen, Anna. *How Reading Changed My Life*. Ballantine, 1998.

Saunders, George. *A Swim in a Pond in the Rain*. Random House, 2021.

Wolf, Maryanne. *Proust and the Squid: The Story and Science of the Reading Brain*. Harper Perennial, 2007.

———. *Reader, Come Home: The Reading Brain in a Digital World*. HarperCollins, 2018.

Play

Boyd, Brian, *On the Origin of Stories: Evolution, Cognition, and Fiction*. Belknap Press of Harvard University Press, 2009.

Brown, Stuart. *Play: How It Shapes the Brain, Opens the Imagination, and Invigorates the Soul*. Avery, 2006.

Gray, Peter. *Free to Learn*. Basic Books, 2012.

Sutton-Smith, Brian. *The Ambiguity of Play*. Harvard University Press, 1997.

Memoirs, Miscellaneous

Allen, Paul. *Idea Man: A Memoir by the Cofounder of Microsoft*. Penguin, 2011.

Brooks, David. *The Second Mountain: The Quest for a Moral Life*. Random House, 2019.

Edmundson, Mark. *Teacher: The One Who Made the Difference*. Vintage, 2002.

Gopnik, Alison. *The Gardener and the Carpenter*. Picador, 2016.

Keizer, Garret. *Getting Schooled: The Reeducation of an American Teacher*. Metropolitan Books, 2014.

Kirn, Walter. *Lost in the Meritrocracy.* Doubleday, 2009.

Palmer, Parker. *The Courage to Teach: Exploring the Inner Landscape of a Teacher's Life.* John Wiley & Sons, 1998.

Professor X. *In the Basement of the Ivory Tower.* Viking, 2011.

Robinson, Ken. *The Element: How Finding Your Passion Changes Everything.* Penguin, 2009.

Thelin, John. *Going to College in the Sixties.* Johns Hopkins University Press, 2018.

INDEX

academia. *See* higher education; higher
education, future; higher education,
UK; higher education, value of; liberal
education
accountability: accountability regime,
204–11; from G. W. Bush, 29–30;
demand for, 18; from Gates Foundation, 213; narrows teaching to easily
measurable outcomes, 226, 231; reduces
responsibility, 88, 225, 227; responsibility, 20, 30, 178; as return on investment, 66–67, 232; Spellings Report,
65, 212; as test scores, 29–30;
unaccountability, 62, 233. *See also* No
Child Left Behind (NCLB); outcomes
assessment; student learning outcomes;
teaching; value-added metrics
accreditation. *See* reaccreditation
adaptive learning. *See* competency-based
learning; personalized learning
ADD, ADHD (Attention Deficit
Disorder, Attention Deficit Hyperac-
tivity Disorder), 46
Adelman, Clifford, *To Imagine a Verb,*
215
adjunct faculty, outnumber tenure-track
faculty, 57
Adorno, Theodor, "Education After
Auschwitz," 304
advertising, 41–42
ageism, 95–96, 256
Age of Elizabeth, 140
Akhtar, Ayad, 167

Aleppo, 64
algorithm, 4, 5, 17, 193; asks wrong
questions, 288; steals aliveness, 222;
student learning outcomes, 208.
See also competency-based learning;
personalized learning
American Association of University
Professors (AAUP), 212
American dream, 68
American Enterprise Institute, 59
American Legislative Exchange Council
(ALEC), 60, 100, 101
Americans for Prosperity, 59
analogy, 140, 141
Anders, George, *You Can Do Anything,*
312n11
Andersen, Kurt, 233; *Evil Geniuses,* 335n59
Annapolis Group, 313n19
Antony and Cleopatra, 190–94; "bounty,"
191; Cleopatra, 109, 118, 123; Octavius
Caesar, 191, 193
assessment, 219. *See also* outcomes
assessment; student learning outcomes
Association of American Colleges and
Universities, 303
As You Like It, 154, 194
Auschwitz, 132, 304
authoritarianism, 129, 158, 161; rising tide
of, 232; tempered by liberal arts
education, 299
awe, 82–83; evolutionary purpose, 168;
Dacher Keltner, *Born to be Good,* 168
Ayers, Bill, 197

Feynman, Richard, *The Pleasure of Finding Things Out,* 227
fiction: *vs.* nonfiction, 111–12. *See also* imaginative literature; reading
Fischer, Karin, 231
Fish, Stanley, 52, 158; *Surprised by Sin,* 328n9
Fitzgerald, Scott, 157
Fitzpatrick, Michelle, *The Teaching Brain,* 202
Flaherty, Colleen, 319n27, 321n55, 324n27, 338n26
freedom: finding the right role, 154–55; and liberal arts, 35, 82, 301; responsibility, 35; Sartre, 152. *See also* comedy; liberal arts; play
Free Speech Movement, 38
Freire, Paulo, 29, 102
Freitas, Annie Lyn, 295
Freud, Sigmund, Oedipus and *Hamlet,* 242, 243, 252, 253
Friedan, Betty, 43
Frydl, Kathleen, *The GI Bill,* 318n15
Fuller, Ryan, 185
fundamentalism: free-market fundamentalism, 60; liberal arts as antidote to, 297, 298, 299; on rise, 64; us *vs.* them, 298–99
Furedi, Frank, 216, 222, 225

Gaimon, Neil, 46, 111
Gallup-Purdue Index Report, 2015, 287, 291; cited by Frank Bruni, 337n11
Garavalia, Linda, 89
Gates, Bill: "accountability," 213; causes social inequities he purports to address, 237; coding for K-12, 10; computerized learning, 130; disrupter, 2; "feedback system" for teachers, 184; financed Common Core, 15, 30, 128–30, 326n11; Lakeside School, 4; "personalized learning," 4–5; technocrat, sees education as "technocratic issue," 2, 15, 311n5; test scores measure learning, 128; "value" is return on investment, 236. *See also* Coleman, David; Common Core; Gates Foundation

Gates Foundation: destructive, 238; influence on academia, 212; lobbying group, Postsecondary Value, 213, 233–38; on media, 212; packed Obama's Education Department, 3, 65; shaped Obama's "Scorecard," 66. *See also* Postsecondary Value Commission
gender, as performative art, 154;
Gettysburg Address, 128
GI Bill: promoted social equity, 29, 237; success, 51, 318n15, n17
Giffords, Gabby, 32, 302
Gilbert, Erik, 216, 224
Giroux, Henry, 233; disimagination machine, 133; Georges Didi-Huberman, 327n32
Glass, Ira, 180
Globe Theater, 16, 136, 154, 166
Godsey, Michael, 130
Goffman, Erving, *Presentation of Self in Everyday Life,* 154
Goldstein, Dana, 326n23
Goldwater, Barry, 37, 60
Gopnik, Alison, *The Gardner and the Carpenter,* 160, 322n4
Graeber, David, 228
Grafton, Anthony, v, 311, 315n34
Gray, Peter, *Free to Learn,* 160
Greene, Gayle: "Shakespeare's Faust," 336n7; *The Woman Who Knew Too Much,* 315n37
Greene, Peter, 129
Greig, Kate, 169
Grossman, James, v, 311, 315n34

Hacker, Andrew: *Higher Education?* with Claudia Dreifus, 289–90; *The Math Myth and Other Delusions,* 312n10; metrics narrow us, 229
Hamilton College, 5, 286
Hamlet, 240–55; Claudius, 109, 241–43, 252, 284; films, 85, 249–52; Fortinbras, 243–44, 247–49, 284, 286; Gertrude, 118, 175, 249; ghost, 174–75, 242, 249, 250, 254; Horatio, 119, 248, 253, 254–55; Laertes, 24–29, 240, 284; *Murder of Gonzago,* 243, 247; "mystery of," 240; opening of, 174–75; Ophelia, 178, 245,